Praise for Property Management For Dummies

"Robert Griswold is the guru of smart property management. You won't find a better written, more practical book on the subject."

— Kenneth Harney, nationally-syndicated real estate columnist, *Washington Post* Writers Group

"Anyone who is contemplating becoming a landlord — or for that matter anyone who already is — would do well to read Robert Griswold's book, *Property Management For Dummies.* Griswold offers some solid ideas for those property owners who don't necessarily want to 'manage' their real estate investments themselves. This handbook for property management successes comes complete with tips on preparing and keeping your property in top condition, finding, handling, selecting and keeping good tenants, showing techniques, maintenance ideas, dealing with contractors, rent collection ideas, financial management and record keeping, and much more. Mr. Griswold covers all the bases of property management. *Property Management For Dummies* probably should have been titled "Property Management For Ex-Dummies." Whether you have one rental or hundreds, this is a book to keep close by."

— Dave Liniger, Chairman of the Board, RE/MAX International, Inc.

"Not just theory — great advice in plain English for all rental property owners and managers."

— Arthur B. Laffer, Laffer Associates, San Diego, CA

"Robert Griswold is a national leader in the property management field. This is an outstanding reference guide authored by an experienced and outstanding property management professional."

— Dr. Rocky Tarantello, Tarantello & Associates, Newport Beach, CA

"If you're a first-time landlord, this is the only book you'll need. Robert Griswold is a real pro and simplifies every step of the process."

— Dick Barnes, Inman News Features

Praise for Home Buying For Dummies

"If you are considering buying a home, don't fail to read this excellent new book. The book is full of profitable 'insider tips,' which most real estate writers either don't know or are afraid to reveal. The advice is so good I wish I had written it. . . . On my scale of 1 to 10, this outstanding book rates a 12."

— Robert J. Bruss, Tribune Media Services

". . . takes you step by step through the process . . . humorous insights that keep the pages turning. This is a reference you'll turn to time after time."

— Judy Stark, St. Petersburg Times

". . . *Home Buying For Dummies* immediately earned a prominent spot on my reference bookshelf . . . takes a holistic approach to home buying."

—Broderick Perkins, San Jose Mercury News

". . . *Home Buying For Dummies* provides a much-needed emotional stabilizer."

— Judy Rose, Knight-Ridder News Service

"The humorous *Home Buying For Dummies* by Ray Brown and Eric Tyson is a favorite . . . because the editorial is so good. They check their facts very well. They set out to make you understand this subject and make it fun reading and informative."

— Michelle Wong, Star Tribune, Minneapolis, Minnesota

"The book *[Home Buying For Dummies]* is a primer on all things to do and not to do when buying a home."

— Brian Banmiller, FOX-TV

"A survival guide to buying . . . fun to read and very clearly written. . . . Whether taking over a foreclosure, determining not how much you can borrow but how much you can actually afford to spend, how to find a good broker, landing a lender . . . Tyson and Brown definitely help ease the trauma of the transaction. . . ."

— Paula Lee Aldridge, Homes and Real Estate Magazine

Property Management FOR DUMMIES®

About the Author

Robert Griswold earned a Bachelors degree and two Masters degrees in real estate and related fields from the University of Southern California's School of Business.

Robert is a hands-on property manager with more than 20 years of practical experience, having managed over 600 properties representing over 35,000 rental units. He owns and runs Griswold Real Estate Management, a property management firm with offices in southern California and southern Nevada.

For the last ten years, Robert has hosted a live, weekly, call-in, real estate news and information talk show called *Real Estate Today! with Robert Griswold,* heard in southern California on Clear Channel's AM 1130 KSDO radio and around the world on the Internet at the radio show's Web site at www.retodayradio.com. Since 1995, Robert has been the Real Estate Expert for NBC San Diego, a network-owned and number-one-rated station where he provides impromptu answers to viewers' real estate questions live on the air.

He has been twice named the #1 Radio or Television Real Estate Journalist in the Country by the National Association of Real Estate Editors in their 48th and 49th Annual National Journalism competition. The first award was for *Real Estate Today! with Robert Griswold* and the second for his work for NBC News.

Robert is the lead columnist for the syndicated *Rental Roundtable* tenant/ landlord question-and-answer column at www.rentalroundtable.com and featured in the *Los Angeles Times, San Diego Union-Tribune,* and *San Francisco Chronicle.* He also writes a nationally syndicated column, *Rental Forum,* at www.inman.com.

He has earned the distinguished Counselor of Real Estate designation, held by only 1,100 real estate practitioners in the world and received by invitation only. Robert is also a Certified Property Manager (CPM), the most recognized professional designation in the property management industry, awarded by the Institute of Real Estate Management (IREM). He has earned IREM's Accredited Residential Manager designation and is a nationally recognized real estate litigation expert, having been retained on nearly 400 real estate legal matters — as well as serving over 150 times as a court-appointed receiver, referee, or bankruptcy custodian.

Robert is a member of the National Faculty of IREM, and a National Apartment Association (NAA) and California Department of Real Estate Certified Instructor. He is a licensed California Broker, a Realtor, and an active member of NAA and his local apartment association, the San Diego County Apartment Association.

In his spare time (?!), he enjoys travel, coaching youth sports, and family activities with his wife, Carol, and their four children, Sheri, Stephen, Kim, and Michael. Above all, he still has a sense of humor and truly enjoys what he's doing!

Dedication

I dedicate this book to my best friend and wife, Carol, for her nearly 20 years of love, support, patience, and persistent attempts to bring the proper balance to my life. Of course, life is always exciting and has real meaning thanks to my four great kids — Sheri, Stephen, Kimberly, and Michael. I also want to express my appreciation to my dad, Wes, and my mom, Carol, for their unconditional love and infinite encouragement. Most of all, I want to praise and thank God for the wonderful gifts and incredible opportunities He has given me.

Property Management FOR DUMMIES®

by Robert Griswold

Wiley Publishing, Inc.

Property Management For Dummies®
Published by
Wiley Publishing, Inc.
111 River St.
Hoboken, NJ 07030
www.wiley.com

For general information on our other products and services or to obtain technical support, please contact our Customer Care Department within the U.S. at 800-762-2974, outside the U.S. at 317-572-3993, or fax 317-572-4002.

Wiley also publishes its books in a variety of electronic formats. Some content that appears in print may not be available in electronic books.

Library of Congress Control Number: 00-110942

ISBN: 0-7645-5330-5

Manufactured in the United States of America

15 14 13 12 11 10

1B/TQ/RS/QU/IN

Chapter 6: FOR RENT: Generating Interest in Your Rental 67

Developing a Marketing Plan 67
Determining your target market 68
Knowing what your renters stand to gain from your property 69
Understanding the Importance of Good Advertising 70
Looking at the different advertising approaches: Rifle versus shotgun 71
Knowing which advertising approach is best for your rental property 72
Getting your property to rent itself 73
Being Aware of Fair-Housing Laws in Advertising 74
Looking at Your Advertising Options 76
Word of mouth 76
Property signs 78
Newspapers 81
Flyers 88
Rental publications 91
Internet 92
Community bulletin boards 93
Local employers 94
Direct mailings 94
Leasing agencies 95
Broker referrals 95
Property brochure 96
Television and radio 97

Chapter 7: Handling Prospects and Showing the Rental 99

Making the Most of Technology 99
Using your telephone's special features to your advantage 100
Knowing which additional technological devices you need 102
Preparing for Phone Calls 103
Having the basic tools ready 104
Answering the phone 108
Providing and obtaining the basic information 110
Selling the prospect on your rental property 111
Pre-qualifying the rental prospect over the phone 112
Handling phone objections 114
Converting phone calls to rental showings 115
Planning Ahead for Open Houses and Walk-Throughs 117
Holding an open house 117
Scheduling individual appointments 118
Providing directions to the property 119
Showing Your Rental Unit 119
Showing a vacant rental 120
Showing an occupied rental 121
Pre-qualifying your prospects during the rental showing 122
Resolving objections 122
Convincing your prospect 123

Inviting your prospects to lease 124
Having the prospect complete a rental application 124
Holding a deposit 125
Developing priority waiting lists 127
Handling Mandatory Disclosures and Environmental Issues 129
Lead-based paint disclosures 130
Asbestos 133
Radon 135
Sexual offenders 136

Chapter 8: Eenie, Meenie, Miney, Mo: Selecting Your Tenants 139

Understanding the Importance of Screening 140
Establishing Tenant Selection Criteria 140
Verifying Rental Applications 144
Verifying the identity of all adults 145
Reviewing occupancy guidelines 145
Checking rental history 148
Verifying employment and income 149
Reviewing the applicant's credit history 150
Checking the applicant's criminal history 153
Talking with all personal references 154
Dealing with guarantors 154
Notifying the Applicant of Your Decision 155
Avoiding Housing Discrimination Complaints 159
Discrimination 161
Steering 162
Children 162
Reasonable accommodations 163
Reasonable modifications 164
Americans with Disabilities Act 165
Companion or service animals 165
Sexual harassment 166

Part III: The Brass Tacks of Managing Rentals 167

Chapter 9: Moving In the Tenants 169

Establishing the Move-In Date 169
Meeting with Your Tenant Prior to Move-In 171
Going over the rules with your new tenant 171
Reviewing and signing documents 175
Collecting the money 177
Inspecting the property with your tenant before the move-in 180
Giving your tenant an informational letter prior to move-in 188
Distributing the keys 190
Setting Up the Tenant File 191
Preparing a Welcome Package for Your New Tenant 192

Refinance Your Rental Property 335
Give Your Tenants a Lease Option 335
Upgrade Your Rental Property 336
Pre-Lease to Minimize Downtime between Tenants 336
Use the Tax Advantages of Depreciation 336

Appendix: Resources 337

Media 337
Professional and Trade Organizations 338
Computer and Manual Accounting Systems 339
Legal Information 339
Rental Housing Suppliers 340
Credit Reporting Agencies 340

Index....................341

Chapter 10: Collecting and Increasing Rent 195
Creating a Written Rent Collection Policy 196
When rent is due 196
Where rent is paid 198
How rent is paid 199
Dealing with Rent Collection Problems 201
Collecting late rent 202
Charging late fees 203
Handling returned checks 204
Dealing with partial rental payments 205
Serving legal notices 206
Offering incentives for paying on time 207
Increasing the Rent 207

Chapter 11: Keeping the Good Tenants — and Your Sanity 211
What Tenants Want 212
Timely and effective communication 212
Quick responses to maintenance requests 212
Respect for their privacy 213
Enforcement of house rules 214
Fair rental rates and increases 214
Renewing Leases 215

Chapter 12: Dealing with Problem Tenants 217
Recognizing and Responding to Common Tenant Problems 217
Late payment of rent 218
Additional occupants 218
Inappropriate noise level 220
Unsupervised children 220
Exploring Alternatives to Eviction 221
Negotiating a voluntary move-out 221
Using mediation or arbitration services 221
Taking your tenant to court 222
Evicting a Tenant 222
Serving legal notices 222
Collecting judgments 225
Knowing What to Do in Unusual Tenant Situations 225
Bankruptcy 226
Illegal holdovers 226
Broken leases 226
Assignments or subleases 227
Departing roommates 227
Domestic problems 228
Death of a tenant 228

Chapter 13: Moving Out Tenants 231
Requiring Written Notice of Your Tenant's Move-Out Plans 232
Providing Your Tenants with a Move-Out Information Letter 233
Walking through the Unit to Check Its Condition at Move-Out 236
Defining "ordinary wear and tear" 237
Using a Security Deposit Itemization form 239
Handling Special Move-Out Situations 241
When damage and unpaid rent exceed the security deposit 241
When disputes arise over the deposit 242
When the rental is abandoned 242

Part IV: Techniques and Tools for Managing 245

Chapter 14: Working with Employees and Contractors 247
Hiring Employees 247
Establishing job duties, work schedule, and compensation 248
Screening employees 249
Knowing your responsibilities 250
Working with your manager 252
Firing an employee 253
Building Your Contractor and Vendor Dream Team 254

Chapter 15: Maintenance 257
Recognizing the Importance of a Maintenance Plan 258
Being Prepared for the Different Types of Maintenance Issues 259
Emergency maintenance 259
Preventive maintenance 260
Corrective maintenance 261
Custodial maintenance 261
Cosmetic maintenance 262
Handling Rental Property Maintenance 262
Responding to a tenant's request for maintenance 262
Keeping tenants from fixing things themselves 266
Purchasing maintenance parts and supplies 267

Chapter 16: Safety and Security 269
Tackling Crime in and around Your Rental Property 269
Participating in the Crime-Free Multi-Housing Program 270
Paying attention to tenant questions and complaints about safety-related issues 270
Responding to crimes when they occur 273
Taking Security Precautions 273
Keys and access control systems 274
Lighting 275
Security firms 276

Addressing Environmental Issues 277
Fire safety 277
Carbon monoxide 278
Electromagnetic fields 279
Natural disasters 279

Part V: Money, Money, Money! 281

Chapter 17: Two Necessities of Property Management: Insurance and Taxes 283

Cover Me, I'm Going In!: Making Sure You Have the Insurance You Need 283
Knowing the difference between the different types of insurance coverage you can get 284
Determining the right deductible 287
Letting your tenants know about renter's insurance 288
Handling potential claims 288
The Tax Man Cometh: Knowing Which Taxes You're Responsible for Paying 289
Income taxes 289
Property taxes 293

Chapter 18: Financial Management and Recordkeeping 295

Organizing Your Files 295
Maintaining Property Records 297
Taking Care of Business: Rental Property Accounting 298
Creating a budget and managing your cash flow 298
Doing your accounting manually 299
Using computers for financial management 300

Part VI: Only for the Daring 303

Chapter 19: Non-Rent Revenue and Lease Options 305

Finding New Ways to Increase Your Cash Flow with Non-Rent Revenue 305
Laundry machines 306
Storage 306
Parking 307
Internet access 307
Furnished rentals 308
Putting Lease Options to Work for You 308

Chapter 20: Government Programs 311
Rental Subsidy Programs 312
Section 8 312
Rehabilitation Loans 315

Chapter 21: Working in Niche Markets: Students, Seniors, and More 317
Taking Another Look at Your Pet Policy 317
Renting to Students: It Doesn't Have to Be Animal House 319
Catering to Senior Citizens 319
Designating Your Rental Units Smoke-Free 320

Part VII: The Part of Tens 323

Chapter 22: Ten Reasons to Become a Rental Property Owner 325
You Can Diversify Your Investments 325
You Don't Need Much Money to Start 325
It Can Be a Second Income 326
You Gain Tax Advantages 326
Real Estate Holds Its Value 327
You Get Leverage 327
It Beats Inflation 327
You Can Shelter Your Income 328
You Get a Positive Cash Flow 328
It Can Help You Retire 328

Chapter 23: Ten Ways to Rent Your Vacancy 329
Maintain Curb Appeal 329
Keep the Unit in Rent-Ready Condition 329
Establish a Competitive Rent 330
Offer Prospects a Rental Rate Guarantee 330
Stay Ahead of the Technology Curve 330
Offer Referral Fees 331
Accept Pets 331
Offer Move-In Gifts or Upgrades 331
Contact Corporate Relocation Services 332
Accept Section 8 332

Chapter 24: Ten Ways to Increase Cash Flow 333
Raise the Rent 333
Decrease Your Operating Expenses 333
Make Your Tenant Pay for Utility Costs 334
Appeal Your Property Taxes 334
Reduce Your Turnover 335

Introduction

Welcome to *Property Management For Dummies*. You can discover many of life's lessons by doing some on-the-job trial and error. But property management shouldn't be one of them — the mistakes are too costly and the legal ramifications too severe. In this book, you'll find proven strategies to make rental property ownership and management not only profitable but pleasant as well.

About This Book

Although these pages are overflowing with useful advice and information, I present it in a light, easy-to-access format. This book explains how to wear many hats in this business: advertiser/promoter (in seeking tenants), host (in showing the property), handyman (in keeping up with and arranging repairs), bookkeeper (in maintaining records), and even counselor (in dealing with tenants and their problems). Just as important, this book will help you maintain your sense of humor — as well as your sanity — as you deal with these challenges and more.

Foolish Assumptions

In this book, I make some general assumptions about who you are. You may be an unintentional property owner — someone who, through a series of circumstances, suddenly and unexpectedly came upon an opportunity to own property. If you're a part of this group, you may have inherited a house from a relative and, not wanting it to sit idle, you've decided to rent it out. Or you may have transferred to a job in another city and, because you've been unable to sell your home, you've been forced to rent the property to help cover the mortgage and operating expenses. Maybe you were looking to own your own place and found a great duplex, so you decided to live in one unit and rent out the other. Whatever the circumstances, the bottom line is the same: You hope to generate sufficient income from the property to cover the debt service, cover all operating expenses, and possibly even provide some cash flow along with appreciation and equity buildup. The key to your success is management. And this book has plenty to offer you on that front.

On the other hand, you may have entered the world of property ownership intentionally, because you see real estate investing as a cornerstone to your long-term personal financial plan and you've noticed that many of the most successful people own income-producing real estate. In a world in which people seem to have more and more demands on their time, many aspects of rental property ownership are very appealing. Many people want to supplement their current retirement plans with additional sources of cash flow — and real estate has a proven track record of being one of the greatest wealth-builders of all time. If you fall into this group, the key to success is finding a way to make money while still retaining control over your life. Real estate offers one of the best opportunities to develop a steady stream of residual income that is being earned whether you are sleeping, participating in your favorite leisure activity, enjoying your retirement, or even relaxing on vacation. And in this book, I show you how you can do exactly that.

How This Book Is Organized

Property Management For Dummies is organized into seven parts. The chapters within each part cover specific topic areas in more detail. So you can easily and quickly scan a topic that interests you, or you can troubleshoot the source of your latest major headache!

Part I: So You Want to Be a Landlord?

Managing rental property is not everyone's cup of tea. The chapters in this part assist you in evaluating your skills and personality to see whether you have what it takes to manage rental units. You'll also figure out whether you should call in the property management cavalry. If a management company is the answer to your prayers, you'll discover how to select one, what you can expect, and how much it will cost. Finally, the day of your escrow closing has arrived and the ink is dry, so you find out what your immediate priorities are as you take over your new rental property.

Part II: Renting Your Property

The most important aspect of rental housing is keeping the units occupied with paying tenants who don't destroy the property and terrorize the neighbors. In this part, you figure out how to prepare the property for rent, set the rents and security deposits, develop a comprehensive yet cost-effective advertising campaign, and show your rental unit to prospective tenants. Because all tenants look great on paper, I fill you in on some tricks and techniques for establishing tenant selection criteria.

Publisher's Acknowledgments

We're proud of this book; please send us your comments through our Dummies online registration form located at www.dummies.com/register/.

Some of the people who helped bring this book to market include the following:

Acquisitions, Editorial, and Media Development

Project Editor: Elizabeth Netedu Kuball

Acquisitions Editor: Jonathan Malysiak

Acquisitions Coordinator: Lauren Cundiff

Technical Editor: Joe DeCarlo

Senior Permissions Editor: Carmen Krikorian

Editorial Manager: Pamela Mourouzis

Media Development Manager: Laura Carpenter

Editorial Administrator: Michelle Hacker

Cover Photos: © Alan Hochman/ International Stock

Composition

Project Coordinator: Jennifer Bingham

Layout and Graphics: Amy Adrian, LeAndra Johnson, Jacque Schneider, Rashell Smith, Julie Trippetti, Jeremey Unger

Proofreaders: Andy Hollandbeck, Susan Moritz, Angel Perez, Sossity R. Smith, York Production Services, Inc.

Indexer: York Production Services, Inc.

Publishing and Editorial for Consumer Dummies

Diane Graves Steele, Vice President and Publisher, Consumer Dummies

Joyce Pepple, Acquisitions Director, Consumer Dummies

Kristin A. Cocks, Product Development Director, Consumer Dummies

Michael Spring, Vice President and Publisher, Travel

Brice Gosnell, Associate Publisher, Travel

Suzanne Jannetta, Editorial Director, Travel

Publishing for Technology Dummies

Andy Cummings, Vice President and Publisher, Dummies Technology/General User

Composition Services

Gerry Fahey, Vice President of Production Services

Debbie Stailey, Director of Composition Services

Author's Acknowledgments

This book was made possible through the efforts of some very fine people at Hungry Minds. Mark Butler initially believed in my concept, and Jon Malysiak stepped in and really made my dream a reality. I am also grateful to Kathy Welton, Kevin Thornton, and Lauren Cundiff, for their support and assistance.

My Project Editor, Elizabeth Kuball, was a true delight to work with, and her sage advice has made this book better in ways that may not ever be fully appreciated. I would also like to thank Pam Sourelis, for her wisdom and valuable feedback, and my Technical Editor, Joe DeCarlo, who helped make sure that my information was accurate and my advice hit the mark.

My interest in real estate can be traced back to my father and mentor, attorney Wes Griswold, who advised me to excel in real estate, not law; and my friend and first real estate professor at USC, Dr. Rocky Tarantello. Thank you!

I was blessed to formally begin my real estate management career working with two of the most savvy, knowledgeable, and ethical men in real estate — thank you Rod Stone and George Fermanian for starting me on the right track. In my property management days, I have met many fine people, and two of the best are my friends Ted Smith and Steve Kellman, both attorneys in San Diego.

I will always be thankful to Carl Larsen, Homes Editor of the *San Diego Union-Tribune,* who gave me a shot with the first *Rental Roundtable* column while his lovely wife, Sharon Larsen, assisted in creating my original book proposal. Kris and Brad Inman and especially Editor Dick Barnes of Inman News Features have allowed me to expand to a national real estate audience with *Rental Forum.*

My heartfelt appreciation also to syndicated columnist and newsletter author Bob Bruss, who offered encouragement and invaluable advice for this book.

Finally, I would like to thank all of my radio listeners, *Rental Roundtable* readers, and NBC news viewers who have educated me weekly with their interesting and thought-provoking questions on literally every aspect of real estate management.

Cartoons at a Glance

By Rich Tennant

page 5

page 323

page 303

page 33

page 245

page 167

page 281

Cartoon Information:
Fax: 978-546-7747
E-Mail: richtennant@the5thwave.com
World Wide Web: www.the5thwave.com

Table of Contents

Introduction 1

About This Book 1
Foolish Assumptions 1
How This Book Is Organized 2
Part I: So You Want to Be a Landlord? 2
Part II: Renting Your Property 2
Part III: The Brass Tacks of Managing Rentals 3
Part IV: Techniques and Tools for Managing 3
Part V: Money, Money, Money! 3
Part VI: Only for the Daring 3
Part VII: The Part of Tens 4
Icons Used in This Book 4

Part I: So You Want to Be a Landlord? 5

Chapter 1: Do You Have What It Takes to Manage Your Own Rental Property? 7

Recognizing the Advantages of Owning Rental Property 8
Being Honest with Yourself about Your Skills and Experience 9
People who need people: Putting your interpersonal skills to the test 9
Making sure you have good management skills 11

Chapter 2: Deciding Whether to Manage Your Property Yourself or Hire a Pro 13

Bring It On!: Managing Your Rental Yourself 14
Recognizing the advantages of self-management 14
Paying attention to the drawbacks 14
Managing your property from a distance 15
Exploring Professional Management 16
Knowing what to look for in a management company 17
Telling the good from the bad 18
Compensating your property manager 21
Making sense of management agreements 23
Knowing the tax consequences of using a management company 24

Chapter 3: Taking Over Property 25

Knowing What to Get Up Front 25
- A list of all personal property included in the sale 26
- Copies of the tenant files 26
- A seller-verified rent roll and a list of all tenant security deposits on hand 26
- Copies of all required governmental licenses and permits 27
- Copies of the latest utility billing 27
- Copies of every service agreement or contract 28
- A copy of the seller's current insurance policy 28

Working with the Current Tenants during the Transition 29
- Meeting with the tenants in person 29
- Inspecting the rental unit 30
- Using a new lease or rental agreement 30
- Raising rents 31

Part II: Renting Your Property 33

Chapter 4: Preparing Your Rental Property for Prospective Tenants 35

Coming Up with a Plan to Handle Vacancies 36
- Considering renovations and upgrades 36
- Paying attention to the exterior or common areas 37
- Making sure the interior of the unit is up to snuff 38

Preparing Your Rental Unit the Right Way 40
- General cleaning 41
- Maintenance 41
- Painting 42
- Final cleaning 43
- Carpet or floor covering cleaning 44

Inspecting Safety Items 45

Using Outside Contractors 46

Chapter 5: Rent, Security Deposits, and Leases: The Big Three of Property Management 47

Setting the Rent 48
- Examining the return on your investment 49
- Conducting a market analysis of rents in your area 50

Coming Up with a Fair Security Deposit 51
- Keeping security deposits separate from your other funds 52
- Setting the amount of the security deposit within legal limits 52
- Avoiding nonrefundable deposits 53
- Paying interest on security deposits 53
- Increasing deposits 54

Deciding Whether to Use a Fixed-Term Lease or a Month-to-Month Rental Agreement 54

Part VII: The Part of Tens 323
Chapter 22: Ten Reasons to Become a Rental Property Owner 325
Chapter 23: Ten Ways to Rent Your Vacancy 329
Chapter 24: Ten Ways to Increase Cash Flow 333
Appendix: Resources 337
Index 341

Contents at a Glance

Introduction 1

Part I: So You Want to Be a Landlord? 5

Chapter 1: Do You Have What It Takes to Manage Your Own Rental Property? 7

Chapter 2: Deciding Whether to Manage Your Property Yourself or Hire a Pro 13

Chapter 3: Taking Over Property 25

Part II: Renting Your Property 33

Chapter 4: Preparing Your Rental Property for Prospective Tenants 35

Chapter 5: Rent, Security Deposits, and Leases: The Big Three of Property Management 47

Chapter 6: FOR RENT: Generating Interest in Your Rental 67

Chapter 7: Handling Prospects and Showing the Rental 99

Chapter 8: Eenie, Meenie, Miney, Mo: Selecting Your Tenants 139

Part III: The Brass Tacks of Managing Rentals 167

Chapter 9: Moving In the Tenants 169

Chapter 10: Collecting and Increasing Rent 195

Chapter 11: Keeping the Good Tenants — and Your Sanity 211

Chapter 12: Dealing with Problem Tenants 217

Chapter 13: Moving Out Tenants 231

Part IV: Techniques and Tools for Managing 245

Chapter 14: Working with Employees and Contractors 247

Chapter 15: Maintenance 257

Chapter 16: Safety and Security 269

Part V: Money, Money, Money! 281

Chapter 17: Two Necessities of Property Management: Insurance and Taxes 283

Chapter 18: Financial Management and Recordkeeping 295

Part VI: Only for the Daring 303

Chapter 19: Non-Rent Revenue and Lease Options 305

Chapter 20: Government Programs 311

Chapter 21: Working in Niche Markets: Students, Seniors, and More 317

Part III: The Brass Tacks of Managing Rentals

This part takes you from moving in your new tenants to moving them out — and everything in between. You'll get some strategies for collecting and increasing rent, retaining tenants, and dealing with those few tenants who give you a headache whenever your paths cross. Minimizing vacancies and retaining tenants is the key to success as a rental owner. But when your tenant complains incessantly, decides to repaint in nontraditional colors, or stops paying the rent, the real challenge of managing rental housing begins. In this part, you discover techniques for dealing with these issues and more.

Part IV: Techniques and Tools for Managing

One of the most important keys to your success as a landlord is assembling the right team of professionals to help you — from employees to contractors. Maintenance can be one of the largest controllable expenses most rental owners face. In this part, I also discuss the requirements to meet the warranty of habitability and the pros and cons of different alternatives for handling maintenance. Finally, because landlords and property managers are sued more than any other business entity, reviewing the issues of crime, fire protection, environmental hazards, and the safety and security of your rentals is important — and I do that in this part.

Part V: Money, Money, Money!

Insurance carriers are quick to tell you how often rental owners are sued, so in this part I guide you through the ins and outs of insurance. Even more certain than a lawsuit is taxes. So in this part you'll find some of the advantages of rental property ownership along with a review of property taxes as well. Finally, you'll want to know just how much cash flow your rental empire is generating, so I provide you with some basics on rental accounting and record keeping.

Part VI: Only for the Daring

Every owner should look for additional sources of income beyond rent, including the opportunities and pitfalls of lease options, which I cover in this part. The effect of government-subsidized housing programs continues to play an important role in many communities. Here you'll find information on the advantages and disadvantages of working with public rental assistance programs like Section 8. Niche rental markets — like those catering to students and seniors — are also worthy of your consideration, and I let you know how you can use them to your advantage in this part.

Part VII: The Part of Tens

Here, in a concise and lively set of condensed chapters are the tips to make the difference between success and foreclosure. In these chapters, I address the benefits of owning rental properties, tips to rent your vacancy today, and techniques to increase your cash flow.

Icons Used in This Book

Scattered throughout the book are icons to guide you along your way and highlight some of the suggestions, solutions, and cautions of property management.

Keep your sights on the bull's-eye for important advice and critical insight into the best practices in property management.

Remember these important points of information and you will have great success as a rental property owner.

This icon highlights the landmines that both novice and experienced rental property owners need to avoid.

This icon covers the boring stuff that only contestants on *Jeopardy!* would ever know (and only because they are told the answers in advance!). You can skip paragraphs marked by this icon without missing the point — or you can read it and impress your friends with what you know.

This icon highlights the real-life anecdotes from my many years of experience and mistakes. I've managed over 35,000 rental units in 20 years, so I've seen some interesting situations — and I share them with you here.

Part I
So You Want to Be a Landlord?

"I'm well aware that I ask a lot from my rental applicants, Mr. Harvey. However, sarcasm is rarely required."

In this part . . .

Managing rental property isn't for the faint of heart, but it can be very rewarding for the right person. The chapters in this part guide you through the process of figuring out whether you have what it takes to manage rental property or whether you're better off leaving it to a pro — someone you hire to do the dirty work for you. I also fill you in on what you need to know if you're taking over ownership of a rental property, including how to deal with the current tenants and inform them of your policies and procedures. This is the part for you if you're just starting to think about purchasing a rental property, but you're not quite sure what it entails.

Chapter 1

Do You Have What It Takes to Manage Your Own Rental Property?

In This Chapter

- Being aware of the advantages of owning rental property
- Identifying the differences between owning property and managing it
- Assessing your own management skills

Congratulations! Either you already own rental property or you've made the decision to buy. Real estate is great whether you're looking for a steady, supplemental retirement income or a secure financial future. Most residential rental property owners want to become financially independent, and real estate is a proven investment strategy for achieving that goal.

But after you sign your name on the dotted line and officially enter the world of owning rental property, you face some tough decisions. One of the very first concerns is who will handle the day-to-day management of your rental property. You have units to lease, rents to collect, tenant complaints to respond to, and a whole host of property management issues to deal with. So you need to determine whether you have what it takes to manage your own rental property or whether you should hire and oversee a professional property management firm. In this chapter, I start by giving you the lowdown on some of the advantages of owning rental property. Then I help you assess whether you have what it takes to manage your own property.

Recognizing the Advantages of Owning Rental Property

A great advantage to building wealth through real estate is the ability to use other people's money — both for the initial purchase of the rental property and for the ongoing expenses.

The wide availability and low cost of real estate financing makes real estate investing a viable and realistic option for virtually everyone. Most people buy real estate using leverage by borrowing from the seller or a lender. *Leverage* is when real estate is purchased with financing, and it usually consists of a small cash down payment from the buyer along with a loan or other people's money.

Although you can actually purchase some rental properties without a down payment, remember that you get what you pay for. The rental properties that will be the best performers in the long run will generally not be available with creative financing.

The ability to control significant real estate assets with only a small cash investment is one of the best reasons to invest in real estate. For example, you may have purchased a $100,000 rental home with $20,000 in cash and a bank loan for $80,000. If the home value doubles in the next decade and you sell this home for $200,000 you will have turned your $20,000 cash investment into a $100,000 profit. This is an example of *positive leverage,* where you are able to earn a return not only on your cash investment but also on the entire value of the real estate.

Rental real estate also offers you the opportunity to pay off your mortgage using your tenant's money. If you've been prudent in purchasing a well-located rental property in a stable area, you'll have enough income to pay all the expenses, utilities, maintenance, taxes, insurance, and your debt service. Each month your property is becoming more valuable while your tenant is essentially paying all your expenses, including principal and interest payments on your loan.

Your lender and tenant aren't the only ones who can help you with the purchase of your rental investment property. Even the government is willing to offer its money to help your cash flow and encourage more investment in real estate. In calculating your income tax obligations each year, the government allows rental property owners to take a deduction or offset to income for depreciation. *Depreciation* is not an actual out-of-pocket cash expense but an accounting concept that provides you with an allowance for expected wear and tear. Depreciation deductions basically reduce the taxable income from rental properties and give you more cash flow during your ownership.

Over time, you will generally find that your rental income collections increase faster than your operating expenses for increased monthly cash flow. And after your tenants have finished paying your mortgage for you, you'll suddenly find that you have a *positive* cash flow — in other words, you're making a profit.

Being Honest with Yourself about Your Skills and Experience

One of the first steps in determining whether to completely self-manage your rental property or delegate some or all of the duties to other people is to analyze your own skills and experience. Many very successful property owners find that they're better suited to deal-making, so they leave the day-to-day management for someone else. This decision is a personal one, but you can make it more easily by thinking about some of the specifics of managing property.

Property management requires basic skills, including marketing management, accounting, and people skills. You don't need a college degree or a lot of experience to get started, and you're sure to pick up all kinds of ideas of ways to do things better along the way.

Examine your own personality. Are you a people person? Serving as a landlord is a labor of love; you must love people, you must love working with your hands, you must love solving problems. Most of all, you must be able to do all this without getting much in the way of appreciation.

If you're impatient or easily manipulated, you aren't suited to being a property manager. Conveying a professional demeanor to your tenants is important. You want them to see you as someone who will take responsibility for the condition of the unit. You must also insist that tenants live up to their part of the deal, pay their rent regularly, and refrain from causing unreasonable damage to your property.

People who need people: Putting your interpersonal skills to the test

Whether you're confident you have what it takes to be a good rental property manager or you're still not sure, take stock of yourself and your abilities by answering these questions. Interview yourself as though you were a job applicant. Ask the tough questions. And more important, answer honestly.

- Are you a people person who enjoys working with others?
- Are you able to keep your emotions in check and out of your business decisions?
- Are you a patient and reasonably tolerant person?

- Do you have the temperament to handle problems, respond to complaints, and service requests in a positive and rational manner?
- Are you well organized in your daily routine?
- Do you have strong time-management skills?
- Are you meticulous with your paperwork?
- Do you have basic accounting skills?
- Do you have maintenance and repair abilities?
- Are you willing to work and take phone calls on evenings and weekends?
- Do you have sales skills?
- Are you a good negotiator?
- Are you willing to commit the time and effort required to determine the right rent for your rental unit?
- Are you familiar with or willing to find out about the laws affecting property management in your area?
- Are you willing to consistently and fairly enforce all property rules and rental policies?
- Are you interested in finding out more about property management?
- Are you willing to make the commitment to being your own property manager?

Ideally, you answered yes to each of these questions. This assessment is not scientific, of course, but it does raise some important issues, particularly the level of commitment that you need to succeed as a rental property manager.

You need to be fair, firm, and friendly to all rental prospects and tenants. Treat everyone impartially and remain patient and calm under stress. Be determined and unemotional in enforcing rent collection and your policies and rules. And maintain a positive attitude through it all. Not as simple as it looks, is it?

Even if you didn't answer with an enthusiastic "yes" to all the questions in this section, you may still make a good rental property manager if you're prepared to be flexible. Learn from your property management experiences. The really good property managers graduated from the school of hard knocks. The following sections give an overview of the key skills you need to manage your property effectively.

If your assessment revealed that your skills may be better served doing something other than managing your own property, turn to Chapter 2 for some alternatives. Owning rental property can still be a great investment, even if you don't manage it yourself.

Making sure you have good management skills

Good management leads to good financial results. Having tenants who pay on time, stay for several years, and treat the property and their neighbors with respect is the key to profitable property management. But, like most things, it's easier said than done. One of the greatest deterrents to financial independence through real estate investments is the fear of management and dealing with tenants.

If you choose the wrong tenant or fail to address certain maintenance issues, your real estate investment may turn into a costly nightmare. By doing your homework in advance, you can reduce those beginners' mistakes. Experience is a great teacher — if you can afford the lessons.

Contact your local chapter of The Institute of Real Estate Management (IREM) and your local affiliate of the National Apartment Association (NAA). They routinely present educational offerings for rental property owners and managers. Look in your local Yellow Pages for the information on the chapter nearest you, or visit them online at `www.irem.org` or `www.naahq.com`.

If you already own your *own* home, then you already have some basic knowledge about the ins and outs of owning and maintaining real estate. The question then becomes how to translate that knowledge into managing *rental* property.

Delegating management activities

As a landlord, you may choose to handle many responsibilities while delegating some of them to others. Look at your own set of skills in order to determine which items you should delegate. A contractor may be able to handle the maintenance of your rental property and grounds more efficiently and effectively than you can. Or maybe you'd benefit from the services of a rental locator service to provide prescreened rental applicants.

The skills you need to successfully manage your own rental properties are different from the skills you need to handle your own property maintenance. Most rental property owners find that using trusted and reasonably priced contractors can be a valuable option in the long run.

Ultimately, you can delegate all the management activities to a professional property manager. But having a property manager doesn't mean you're off the hook. Depending on the arrangement you have with your property manager, you may still oversee the big picture. Even the best property managers need and seek the input of the property owner so that they can develop a property management plan that will meet the owner's investment goals.

Keep in mind that no one will ever manage your rental property like you will. After all, you're more motivated than anyone else to watch out for your real estate investment interests. Only *you* will work through the night painting your rental unit for the new tenant moving in the next day. And who else would spend her vacation in Hawaii looking through the local newspaper classifieds for creative ad ideas?

Start by being honest with yourself. Know your strengths and your weaknesses as a property manager. You may find that you're *able* to do the job but wind up with frazzled nerves when you do. If you're not truly excited and challenged by handling your own property management tasks, then you're not likely to have success in the long run.

You may find that a professional property management specialist can run the property more competently than you can. Many rental property owners possess the necessary skills and personality to efficiently and effectively manage their rental properties, but they have other skills or interests that are more financially rewarding or enjoyable. Hiring professionals and supervising them is often the best possible option.

Recognizing how well you manage your time

If you're like most rental property owners, managing your rental units is a part-time job. You can handle tenant calls, collect the rent, show the rental units, and even perform most maintenance in the early evenings or on weekends. The challenge is finding the time required to do this. The good news is that the time required to be a landlord is in your control.

If you develop the proper skills of marketing, tenant screening, and tenant selection, you can greatly reduce the amount of time you spend managing rental property. You also have to work smart or you may find that your time is better spent in other areas than management.

You can save a lot of time by having your tenants mail their rent checks to you each month. To increase your rent collections, provide your tenants in advance with prepaid, self-addressed envelopes so they just have to put the payment in the mail.

Many of your contractors and suppliers will want to be paid immediately. But you can be more efficient and save time if you have a policy of paying all your invoices at the end of each month.

Time management is really about evaluating how much time you have and then looking for ways to streamline your tasks so that you make the best use of your time.

Chapter 2

Deciding Whether to Manage Your Property Yourself or Hire a Pro

In This Chapter

- Deciding whether to manage your own property
- Assessing the benefits of working with a pro
- Knowing what to look for in a property management firm

The late-night TV real estate gurus can make real estate investing sound so simple. But just as important as buying the right property for the right price, the key to success in real estate is a well-managed property. So in this chapter, I guide you through the pros and cons of managing your own property (as opposed to hiring a pro to do it for you).

When you first start out, try to manage your rental property yourself, particularly if you have a single-family rental home or duplex. If you're like most owners, though, at some point you'll consider hiring a professional property management firm. So in this chapter, I give you some tools for evaluating property management companies, from the services they offer to the fees they charge. I discuss the importance of experience, qualifications, and credentials. Also, I reveal some of the common tricks that management companies use to generate additional income that are not in your best interest.

Even if you ultimately decide that *you* are the best manager for your rental property, the more you learn about how the professionals manage property, the better you will be at management yourself.

Bring It On!: Managing Your Rental Yourself

When you first start out, you'll probably do all the work yourself — painting, cleaning, making repairs, collecting the rent, paying the bills, and showing the rental units. In this section, I let you know some of the advantages and disadvantages to doing it yourself. Use this information as a way to help you decide whether you want to go it alone or whether hiring a pro is for you. If you decide the latter, check out the information later in this chapter about working with a professional management company. This is one of the most important decisions you'll make as a rental property owner, so take the time to look at all your options.

Recognizing the advantages of self-management

If you have the right traits for managing property, and if you have the time and live close to your property, you should definitely do it yourself. Managing your own rental property has some definite advantages. For example, by managing your own property, you don't have to pay a monthly management fee.

If you purchase a single-family rental home or condo as an investment property, you most likely won't be able to generate enough money to pay for a professional property manager and make a profit — at least not right away.

By keeping direct control of the management of your rental property, you also may save on maintenance costs, because *you* decide who does the repair work or mows the lawn. Doing your own maintenance or yard work is usually a good idea; if you hire someone else to do it for you, the cost can devour your monthly cash flow in a hurry.

Develop a list of reliable fix-it and landscape personnel who do good work and charge low rates. Even if you hire someone to manage your property for you, you're better off choosing the maintenance contractors yourself, rather than turning over the decision — and your money — to a professional property management firm.

Paying attention to the drawbacks

If you're just starting in the world of property management, you may be thinking of it as a part-time venture — something you'll do in addition to your day job. And if you want, you can keep it that way by keeping the number of properties you own to a minimum. But you may find yourself spending far more time on managing your rentals than you anticipated — either because you've bought more rentals, or because you just didn't anticipate the time requirements.

If you earn your living regularly from something other than managing your rental property, managing that property may not be worth your valuable time. If you're a higher-income, full-time professional, rushing off on weekdays to handle some minor crisis at your rental unit is not only impractical, it could be downright damaging to your career. Most employers have little tolerance for a second job, particularly one that often has unpredictable and unscheduled demands.

As a jobholder, look at your annual income and figure out approximately what you earn per hour. Do the same for the cash you're saving by managing your own property. Unless your management efforts produce significant cash savings compared to your job, you may be better off hiring a property manager for your rental units. The same guideline holds true even if you are an independent business owner or are self-employed. Your schedule may be more flexible than the fixed workday of a 9-to-5 employee. But if you're earning $50 an hour as a consultant, devoting hours of your productive work time to managing rental units, which may only amount to savings of $25 an hour, may not make sense.

Managing your property from a distance

If you own rental property in another city or state, you may initially consider managing your unit from afar. As long as your tenants mail their rent checks and make only a few maintenance demands, this arrangement can work — but it's a fragile one. One major problem can turn the job of managing the rental property into a nightmare.

I once had a client who hired me after having a very bad experience trying to manage his single-family home from another state. He had been transferred over 1,000 miles away by his company but wanted to rent his home as an investment. He found a nice family to rent to, and everything was fine for the first six months. Then one day he got an urgent call from his tenants, complaining that torrential rains caused the roof to leak, making the house uninhabitable. The owner, still out of state, asked his tenants to assist him in hiring someone to repair the roof. The work was botched, and he wound up flying back and forth twice to straighten out the mess and finally get the roof fixed properly. This negative experience ended up costing thousands, easily wiping out whatever small profit he could have made.

Think twice about handling your own rental property maintenance from hundreds of miles away. You need to be in the immediate area to routinely inspect and maintain a rental property, especially when a roof leak or broken pipe demands immediate attention.

Exploring Professional Management

Many rental property owners who are just starting out frequently drift blindly into self-management by default, because they assume they can't afford to use a management company. "Why pay someone to manage my rental property when I can keep the money myself?" is a common refrain.

Other owners would really prefer to hire a professional management company, but they've heard so many horror stories that they don't know whom to trust. Many of their concerns are real — some property managers mismanage properties and have a total lack of ethics. Luckily, there is a detectable pattern that can help you avoid hiring the wrong management company.

If you think that hiring a professional management company may be the right choice for you, take the time to study this option. Here are some pros to using a management firm:

- They have the expertise and experience to manage rental property, plus knowledge about current laws affecting rental housing.
- They're able to remain fair, firm, and friendly with tenants.
- They have screening procedures and can typically screen tenants more objectively than you can yourself.
- They handle property management issues throughout the day and have staffing for after-hour emergencies.
- They have contacts and preferential pricing with many suppliers and vendors who can quickly and efficiently get work done.
- They handle all bookkeeping, including rent collection.
- They have well-established rent collection policies and procedures to follow when tenants' rental payments are late.
- They can be excellent sources for purchasing additional properties, because they are often the first to know when their current clients want to sell.

Of course there are some disadvantages to using a management company as well:

- Using a management company for small rental properties that you've recently acquired may not be cost-effective.
- Some management companies may have in-house maintenance that charges markups or surcharges on supplies and materials as well as increased labor costs.
- They often won't have the same care, consideration, and concern you have for the rental property.
- They often charge extra to fill vacancies or they may take longer to fill if the property management firm has several other vacancies they're dealing with at the same time.
- Some management companies require the tenants to drive to their office to pay rent, which can be a disadvantage if the management company is not located close to the rental property.
- Management companies may not be as diligent in collecting delinquent rent, particularly if the management contract provides that they keep all late fees and other administrative charges.
- Some management companies may try to falsely impress you by not spending enough on repairs and maintenance needed to properly maintain the property.

Be sure to consider the pros and cons to determine whether working with a management company is right for you.

Knowing what to look for in a management company

Size isn't the determining factor in whether a professional property manager can deliver quality service. Some management companies specialize in large rental projects, whereas small operations may focus on managing individual home rentals and apartment complexes with only a few units. Don't assume that a big company managing mega-complexes will do the best job for your duplex or that the small company has the credentials, experience, and knowledge that you need. Try to find property managers familiar with your kind of rental unit. With a little research, you can find the right fit for your property.

Professional property managers normally handle a wide range of duties. If you hire a full-service management company, you'll typically get the following services:

- Preparing, advertising, and showing the rental unit
- Screening and selecting the tenants
- Collecting the rent

- Handling repairs
- Providing regular accounting reports
- Inspecting the property
- Enforcing the property's rules and regulations
- Dealing with complaints from the tenants

More limited management services are also available from some management companies. Maybe you just need help with the rental of your property and are willing to pay a leasing fee. Or you may want a property manager that only charges a small fee to cover the basic service and not much more.

A good management company may be able to operate your rental properties better and more efficiently than you can on your own. Their superior knowledge and experience can result in lower costs, higher rents, better residents, and a property that is well maintained. These companies will more than pay for the costs, and you will have more time to pursue additional properties or other pursuits. Of course, a poor management company will cut into your profits, not only with their fees, but also with improper maintenance and poor quality tenants who will run your property into the ground. A bad property manager can leave you in worse shape than if you'd never hired one in the first place.

Telling the good from the bad

Management companies accept the responsibility for all operations of the property, including marketing, tenant selection, rent collection, maintenance, and accounting. The right property manager can make a big difference in the cash flow your rental unit generates, because he finds good replacement tenants quickly or makes sure that maintenance is done in a timely manner without breaking your budget. You need a property manager who is committed to helping you get the optimum results from your rentals.

Be sure to visit the office of the management company and spend time interviewing the specific property manager who will have control of the hands-on management of your property. Make a few extra phone calls to check references, and don't sign a management contract until you feel confident that the company you hire has a sound track record. Checking with the property management company's chosen referrals is not enough. Ask for a list of all their clients and contact the ones with rental properties similar in size and type to your own. Make sure the rental owners you contact have been with the property management company long enough to have a meaningful opinion on the quality of the service.

Make sure that the firm you hire manages property exclusively. This is particularly important when selecting a management company for a single-family home, condo, or very small rental property. Many traditional real estate sales offices (as opposed to property management firms) offer property management services; however, property management is often a *loss leader* (meaning that it costs more for the real estate sales office to manage your property than they're charging you for that service, because they're hoping to get your business later on when you're ready to sell the property). Many property managers in real estate sales offices do not have the same credentials, experience, and expertise that an employee of a property management firm would have. The skills required to represent clients in *selling* property are entirely different than the skills required to *manage* property.

Most states require property managers to have either a real estate license or a property manager's license. Call or use the Internet to verify that the property manager and the management company have a current license that is in good standing. Simply holding a license does not ensure exceptional services, but it does show the property manager is motivated enough to comply with state law.

Examine the property manager's credentials. The Institute of Real Estate Management (IREM), an organization of professional property managers, provides professional designations, including the Certified Property Manager (CPM) and Accredited Residential Manager (ARM). A very select group of management firms have earned the Accredited Management Organization (AMO) designation. These designations signify excellence and dedication.

Verify that the property management company is properly insured. The company should carry insurance for general liability, automobile liability, worker's compensation, and professional liability. The management company is your agent and will be collecting your rents and security deposits, so they should also have a fidelity bond to protect you in case an employee embezzles or mishandles your money. Look for a management company that has a separate accounting for each property managed. Many property managers use a single master trust bank account for all properties. Although this is legal in most states, avoid this practice because, typically, the number one violation encountered during audits of property managers by state oversight agencies is related to shortages and other misuse of the master trust bank account.

In most management contracts, property management companies have the ability and right to perform emergency repairs without advance approval from the owner. Of course, this allows the property management company to take care of problems that occur unexpectedly. Most management contracts contain clauses that allow property managers to undertake repairs up to a specified dollar amount without the owner's advance approval. When you're in the early stages of working with a new management company, make sure you closely monitor their expenses. Even though they may have the legal right to use funds up to a certain amount, they should always keep you informed as the owner.

Repairs serve as a profit center for many management companies. They may offer very low property management fees knowing that they will make it up through markups on repairs — and often the repairs aren't even necessary. Look for a property management firm that doesn't mark up materials, supplies, or maintenance labor.

The quality of your property management company will directly affect the success of your real estate investments and your peace of mind. Here are some important questions to ask as you interview management firms:

- Can you provide a list of exactly what management services are provided, including dates I will receive reports, and a breakdown of management costs?
- Can I contact several of your current and former client references with rental properties that are similar in size and location to mine?
- Is your firm an Accredited Management Organization (AMO) recognized by the Institute of Real Estate Management (IREM)?
- Do your staff members hold IREM's distinguished Certified Property Manager (CPM) designation or Accredited Residential Manager (ARM) designation?
- Is your firm an active member in good standing with a local affiliate of the National Apartment Association (NAA), and does it hold any NAA designations?
- Who will actually manage the day-to-day activities at my property? What are his qualifications and does he exclusively manage real estate?
- Do you provide 24-hour on-call maintenance services with e-mail capability?
- If maintenance is provided in-house or by an affiliated firm, do you only charge the actual cost of labor and materials without any surcharges, markups, administrative fees or other such add-ons?
- Do you pass along any volume purchasing discounts fully and directly to clients for appliances, carpeting, and other items without any markups?
- Do all funds collected for applicant screening fees, tenant late charges, and other administrative charges go directly to the owner and not the manager?
- If allowed by law, are all employees given pre-employment screenings that include thorough background checking by an independent security consultant, plus drug and alcohol testing by a certified lab?

- Do you carry Errors and Omissions coverage of at least $500,000, plus general liability coverage of at least $2,000,000?
- Do you have a $1,000,000 fidelity bond for all employees?
- Are your legally required state licenses current and without any history of violations?
- Do you have separate bank trust accounts for each client rather than a single master trust bank account containing multiple owners' funds?

When you hire outside property managers, treat them as valued members of your management team — but be sure they know that you're the team manager. They should ask before spending significant amounts of your money, and they should keep you informed on a regular basis.

Compensating your property manager

Management companies are compensated in a variety of ways, and the type of fees and typical compensation vary widely throughout the country. Make sure that you understand the compensation of your property manager, but never evaluate the management company based on the management fee alone.

Property management companies essentially charge for services based on the amount of time that is required of different staff members to manage your property. An experienced property management company owner will know the average number of hours that the property manager, the accounting staff, and other support personnel will spend each month on managing your property. She will then calculate a management fee schedule that should generate the fees necessary to provide the proper management company resources to effectively manage your rental units.

Typically, management companies receive a percentage of the collected income for managing a rental property; however, some management fees also charge a flat fee per month or a dollar amount per unit per month. Try to find a company that has a management fee that is a percentage of the collected income; this kind of fee is a strong motivator to the management company to ensure that the rents are kept at market rate and actually collected on time. Never pay a management fee based on the potential income of a rental unit.

Management fees are typically tied to the size and the expected rental collections of the property. However, for certain properties that may be more difficult to manage, the management company may have higher management fees or additional charges for certain types of services or for a certain period of time. Management companies may also propose charging a minimum monthly management fee or a percentage fee (opting for whichever of the two is greater). For example, a property that is in very poor physical condition and requires extensive repairs and renovations will require a significant increase in the time spent by the property manager in bidding and supervising the improvements. This additional time is worthy of separate compensation to the property manager.

Distressed rental properties typically have very low occupancy and require extensive marketing and leasing activities. The lease-up of this type of property will usually be an extra cost item, because the property manager will spend much more time managing this property. As an owner, structuring the compensation so that the management company has an incentive to get the property leased-up as soon as possible is best. For example, have a finite period of time so the property manager is motivated to quickly fill vacancies.

The typical professional management fees for single-family homes or individual rental condominiums are 10 percent of the actual collected income with an additional fee earned each time the unit is rented. The rental fee can range from a flat fee of $250 to $500 or a percentage of the monthly rental rate, such as 50 percent. If the rental home or condo has a high rental value then the management fee will often be lower, in the 8 to 10 percent range.

Additional fees for the leasing of rental units is often justified, because the most time-intensive portion of property management is tenant turnover. When one tenant leaves, the rental unit must be made rent-ready; then the property manager must show the property and screen the tenants. Charges for rentals can vary, but they are often either a flat fee of a few hundred dollars or a percentage of the rent, such as half of the monthly rental rate.

Generally, the larger the rental property, the lower the management fee as a percentage of collected income. Fees also vary by geographic area and by the income potential of the rental unit with a higher end rental property commanding a lower percentage management fee.

A friend of mine was relocating to another state and wanted to retain his beautiful suburban home in case he was ever transferred back into the area. He inquired into the cost of hiring a professional management firm and was shocked by the wide variation in management fees quoted. So he began asking more questions of one prospective management company and learned that this particular property manager was already overseeing over 170 other rental units and homes and would be glad to add another management account. My friend quickly calculated that this property manager would only be able to spend an average of one hour a month on the management of his rental home, including rent collection, accounting, tenant calls, property inspections, and all the other property management duties — for a management fee that was quoted at 10 percent, or over $150 per month. Be sure that you know how many other rental properties will have a claim on your property manager's time before you sign up!

Making sense of management agreements

The management agreement is a pivotal document; it spells out the obligations of the property management company to you, their client. Be sure to study the fine print — it's tedious but necessary in order to avoid unpleasant surprises. Even the management agreements available through state and national real estate organizations can contain clauses that are clearly one-sided in the favor of the management company. For example, many management agreements call for the property manager to collect and keep all the income from applicant screening fees, late charges, or returned check charges. Of course, property managers justify this policy on the basis that they incur additional time and costs. But these fees should belong to you, because you want to give the property manager a financial incentive to fill your unit with a tenant who pays rent on time and cares for the property. A management fee based on actual rents collected is a better arrangement.

Some property management agreements indicate that there is no management fee charged when the unit is vacant between tenants. Although this seems like an arrangement that saves you money, especially when rental revenues are not coming in, the property manager could rush to fill the vacancy without properly screening tenants — and a destructive tenant can be worse than no tenant in the long run.

Watch for management agreements that have a broad "hold harmless" clause protecting the property manager from liability for his own errors in judgment or the mistakes of the workers the firm sends to your rental unit. One solution is to include a "reasonable care" provision so the property manager is motivated to be diligent in his management and avoid workers he knows have had problems in the past. Your agreement should also mention such obvious requirements as informing you of what is happening with your rental property.

Some property management companies request long-term management contracts that cannot be cancelled or can only be cancelled for cause. Avoid signing any property management contract that cannot be cancelled by either party with or without cause upon a 30-day written notice. A property management company that knows they are only as good as their most recent month's performance will stay motivated to treat your property with the time and attention needed to get top results.

Make sure all your concerns are addressed in the management agreement. You need to know exactly what weekly or monthly reporting they provide, when your property expenses will be paid, and who is responsible for payment of critical items like mortgages, insurance, and property taxes. Leave nothing to chance.

If the property manager won't agree to reasonable clarifications of the contract language or a complete list of the services provided for his fee, he may not go out of his way to help you later. Consider it a warning sign, and find a property management company willing to accept your reasonable terms.

Many property managers use their own proprietary agreements written strictly in the best interests of the property management company. So be sure to have your attorney review this agreement very early in the discussions with your potential property manager.

Knowing the tax consequences of using a management company

As a rental property owner, you're running a business and must file Schedule E with your federal tax return. The tax laws allow your rental housing business to deduct all operating expenses, including the cost of advertising, maintenance, payroll, insurance, property taxes, and management fees whether paid to yourself or a property management firm.

But although your expenses are deductible, they erode your net income from your property. If your annual expenses are greater than the rent revenues, you may find that you can use those losses to help ease the tax burden from your full-time job or other sources of income unrelated to your rental property. But a loss is a loss, and trying to keep your rental property in the black is still a good idea, even if you have to pay some taxes on the income.

Although federal real estate taxation laws consider most real estate activities passive rather than active investments, there are definite tax advantages to those individuals that are "actively involved" in the management of their rental properties. The definition of "actively involved" allows you to hire a property management firm and still take advantage of the tax write-offs available for rental income property, as long as you're involved in setting the rents and policies for the property.

Federal and state tax codes change from year to year, so discuss your personal tax situation with your accountant or tax preparer in advance.

Chapter 3

Taking Over Property

In This Chapter

- Knowing what to look for before the deal is final
- Helping existing tenants through the transition process

Somewhere during the process of thinking about investing in rental property, you may have thought about acquiring a rental property that is already occupied with tenants. On the surface, in fact, this kind of deal looks like a positive, because you don't have to advertise and select tenants yourself — at least right off the bat. But just how positive an experience taking over a rental property is depends on the quality of your tenants. Taking over an existing rental property may be a great idea, but don't set foot into these often-murky waters without at least knowing what you're getting into.

In this chapter, I focus on some of the important issues involved in taking over a rental property. Here you find out how to begin the all-important task of implementing your own policies and procedures with the existing tenants, who may be living under an entirely different set of rules. The proper procedures for taking over a rental property actually begin even before you are legally the new owner. Ensuring that you'll have a smooth transition requires some know-how, and in this chapter I give you exactly that.

Knowing What to Get Up Front

If you're thinking about buying a rental property, you need to start by investigating all aspects of the property. After all, no one is going to represent your interests as well as you will. During the *due diligence period,* in which the escrow and purchase are pending, put on your Sherlock Holmes cap and ask lots of questions. Don't be shy. Talk to the tenants, the neighbors, and the contractors or suppliers to the property, and be sure that you know what you're getting. Communicate regularly and work closely with the seller and his representatives, but only rely upon information provided in writing. This time period may be your best or only opportunity to seek adjustments, if important issues have been misrepresented. When you've signed your name on the dotted line and the deal is done, you can't go back and ask them to fix the leaky roof.

In the following sections, I cover some things to make sure you have on hand *before* the deal if final.

A list of all personal property included in the sale

This may include appliances, equipment, and supplies owned by the current property owner. One of the most significant disputes can arise if there is a misunderstanding about who owns the appliances in the rental unit. For example, if the seller says that all the refrigerators are owned by the rental property (as opposed to the tenants), you want to verify that in writing with each tenant. Otherwise, you run the risk of a serious dispute or loss in future years as tenants take appliances when they leave, claiming the appliances belong to them. ***Remember:*** Don't assume anything is included in the sale unless you have it in writing.

Copies of the tenant files

Make sure you have the rental application, current and past leases or rental agreements, all legal notices, maintenance work orders, and correspondence for each and every tenant.

A seller-verified rent roll and a list of all tenant security deposits on hand

A *rent roll* is a listing of all rental units with information on the tenant's name, move-in date, current and market rent, and the security deposit. Be sure you get a seller statement that no undisclosed verbal agreements, concessions, or side agreements have been made with any tenant regarding the rent or security deposits.

When acquiring a new rental property, be sure that you follow state or local laws in properly handling the tenant's security deposit. Many state laws require the seller and/or purchaser of a rental property to advise the tenants in writing of the status of their security deposit. The law usually gives the seller the right to either return the security deposit to the tenant or transfer the deposit to the new owner. If the seller refunds the security deposits, you will have the challenge of collecting deposits from tenants already in possession of the rental unit, which is never easy. For this reason, you should strongly urge the seller to provide you a credit for the full amount of the security deposits on hand in escrow and have each tenant agree in writing to the amount of the security deposit transferred during the sale. To avoid problems at the time of move-out, send your tenant a letter confirming the security deposit amount.

In the sale of *commercial* rental properties, each tenant usually signs a legal document known as an *estoppel agreement,* which confirms and verifies the terms of their lease or rental agreement. Although not as commonly used in the sale or transfer of *residential* rental properties, you get the same potential benefits by having each tenant sign such an agreement. This type of verification protects both you as the new owner and the tenant — and it can go a long way toward preventing any misunderstandings in the future.

Without written proof to the contrary, some crafty or desperate tenants may later claim that they had a verbal agreement with the former owner or manager for a monthly rent credit or discount for maintaining the grounds, or that they were promised new carpeting or another significant unit upgrade. If this happens to you, offer to get the former owner or manager on the phone to verify the tenant's story. In my experience, when you offer to verify the story, the tenant typically begins to back-pedal, and the truth comes out. But to avoid any surprises, obtain a written statement from each tenant indicating that no verbal agreements exist and that no promises have been made by the former owner.

Copies of all required governmental licenses and permits

Rental property owners in many areas are now required to have business licenses or permits. Contact the appropriate governmental office in writing and make sure that they are properly notified of the change in ownership and/or billing address. Often these governmental entities have stiff penalties if you fail to notify them of a change in ownership in a timely manner. They will eventually learn of the change in ownership, because they usually monitor the local recording of deeds as well as receiving notification of changes in billing responsibility from local utility companies, so don't try to get away with delaying the inevitable. Make sure that you have current copies of all state and local rental laws and ordinances that affect your rental property.

Copies of the latest utility billing

Get copies of all account and payment information for every utility that provides services to the rental property. These may include electricity, natural gas, water/sewer, trash collection, telephone, cable, and Internet access.

Prior to the close of escrow, contact each of the utility companies and arrange for the transfer of utilities or change in the billing responsibility as of the estimated escrow closing date. If provided with sufficient advance notice, many utility companies are able to have the meters read and/or the billing cutoff coincide with the close of escrow, which prevents the need to prorate any of the utility billings between the owners.

Copies of every service agreement or contract

These agreements or contracts may include ones made with maintenance landscapers, pest control services, boiler maintenance services, and other providers. Review all current contractors and service providers the current owner uses. If you plan to terminate the services of a particular contractor or service provider, the seller may be willing to voluntarily send a written conditional notice of termination indicating that, should the property sell as planned, their services will no longer be needed as of the close of escrow. You are then free to make your own plans for services and can even renegotiate with the current company under better terms. Of course, if you find that the seller already had favorable pricing from the contractors or service providers, you may be able to negotiate the same terms.

A copy of the seller's current insurance policy

One of the most important steps that you will handle in the takeover of your new rental property is securing insurance coverage. You need to make sure that you have the proper insurance policy in place at the time that you legally become the new owner. Although the seller's policy will not protect you in any way, you should request a copy of the seller's policy or declaration of coverage, because this information can be very helpful to your insurance broker or agent when analyzing the property to determine the proper coverage that you may need. ***Remember:*** Always seek the advice of a professional insurance broker or agent when obtaining insurance coverage.

Although you may trust your insurance broker or agent implicitly, do not allow your escrow to close until you have written documentation confirming that your insurance coverage is in force. Even though it may seem improbable, there are many instances in which a property suffered a catastrophic loss or liability claim in a matter of hours after the property changed hands and the new owner's insurance coverage was not yet in place.

When you receive this information, take steps to verify the accuracy of all records. Most sellers are honest and don't intentionally withhold information or fail to disclose important facts; however, the old adage "buyer beware" rings particularly true in the purchase of rental real estate. Questions and issues that can be resolved at this time will eliminate some very unpleasant and possibly contentious disagreements with your tenants in the future. Although the takeover of your new rental property can be chaotic, don't fall into the trap of just verbally verifying the facts. Be sure to verify all information in writing and begin to set up a detailed filing system for your new property.

Working with the Current Tenants during the Transition

If you're like most rental property owners, and you're acquiring property that's already occupied, the tenants are probably well aware of the pending change of ownership. Tenants are typically full of apprehension when their rental unit is changing ownership, not because they think you'll be an unreasonable landlord, but because of the uncertainty of change. So be sure to begin your relationship with your tenants on a positive note. In the following sections, I guide you through the process step by step.

Meeting with the tenants in person

When you first acquire your new rental property, contact your tenants personally and reassure them that you intend to treat them with respect and have a cordial yet business-like relationship. Deal with your tenants' questions honestly and directly. The most common concerns are usually the potential for a rent increase, the status of their security deposit, the proper maintenance or condition of their rental unit, and the continuation of certain policies, such as allowing pets. If you're not honest with the tenants, you'll lose credibility if you later decide to implement changes that you didn't acknowledge upfront.

Provide your tenants with a letter of introduction during this brief in-person meeting. This letter provides your tenant with your contact information, plus explains your rent collection policies, the status of their security deposit, and the proper procedures for requesting maintenance.

Be sure to request an opportunity to perform a property walkthrough with each tenant. Let the tenant know if you will be implementing your own standard lease or rental agreement form as well.

Inspecting the rental unit

Although you most likely had a brief chance to view the interior of the rental unit during the due diligence period before escrow closed, walking through again with the tenant now that you are the owner can be helpful.

Don't just knock on the door and expect to walk through your tenant's rental unit. But if you're at the rental property delivering the letter of introduction, you can schedule a mutually convenient time to meet. Some tenants will be glad to meet with you right then, but don't necessarily count on that. Giving your tenants time to think about any issues they would like to discuss is beneficial for both of you.

In most states, tenants do not have to let you enter their rental unit unless you have a legal reason and have given proper advance notice. If you set a voluntary appointment, the tenant will know that you're coming and will be prepared.

The former owner of the rental property may have had a policy of documenting the condition of the rental unit at the time the tenant took possession of the unit. If so, you may want to compare the noted condition on the Move-In/Move-Out Inspection Checklist (see Chapter 9) when you actually walk through the rental unit. If proper documentation of the move-in condition was not made, consider preparing such information during your walkthrough. This information will allow you to establish some sort of baseline for the condition of the unit to use upon the tenant's move-out, which will help you determine the proper amount of the security deposit to be returned to the tenant.

Using a new lease or rental agreement

Another one of the first steps that you should take as the new owner of a rental property is to begin converting your existing tenants to your own lease or rental agreement. If you have a single-family rental or a small rental property, implementing your own rental agreement as soon as legally allowed is relatively easy. However, with larger rental properties, you may want to gradually transition to a new agreement upon tenant turnover.

Your tenant will have one of the following:

- A valid written lease
- An expired written lease that has become a month-to-month rental agreement
- A written month-to-month rental agreement

- A written rental agreement for some period of time less than a month
- A verbal agreement

Although you may want to make some changes in the terms or policies, when you acquire an occupied rental property your legal and business relationship is already established by whatever agreement the tenants had with the former owner. Wait until the expiration of the lease to change the terms — or provide the tenant with proper legal notice of any proposed changes.

Consider the potential impact of making significant changes in the rental rates or policies immediately after you acquire the rental property. For example, although you may have strong feelings against allowing pets on your rental property, your new tenants may have pets already. Although you legally have the right to implement your no-pet policy upon lease renewal or upon giving proper legal notice, you are almost guaranteed a vacant rental unit if you do so. Impose your policies over a reasonable timeframe, but be sure you're aware of the potential financial consequences in the short run.

The sooner you begin to convert your new property to your leases and rental agreements, the better. Establish uniform policies at all your rental units so the terms and policies are consistent for all your tenants.

The tenant information the seller provided you with during escrow may be outdated. One quick way to update your records is to have the tenants voluntarily complete your rental application form. In many states, you may not have a strong legal argument for requiring existing tenants to provide this information; however, many tenants will understand your reasoning and not mind. Other tenants may be reluctant to complete an entirely new rental application. Even if you receive initial resistance, seek this updated information prior to renewing any lease. You need to be able to properly determine the financial qualifications of your tenants, particularly if you anticipate future rent increases.

Raising rents

When you acquire a rental property, part of your research is to establish the fair market rental value of your new property. If the tenant's current rent is below market value, one of your toughest decisions as the new owner of a rental property is how to handle rent increases.

As the new owner, you often will have much higher mortgage payments and typically higher expenses to make necessary repairs and upgrades to the property than the last owner did. Some tenants will be very upset and antagonistic about any rent increase, however, and there is nothing you will be able to do to appease them.

Buying unoccupied rental property

The takeover procedure for a rental property that is unoccupied or has vacant rental units is not much different than that for an occupied property. Quickly implement a plan to get the rental ready for renting as soon as possible. ***Remember:*** Every day that the rental unit sits vacant after the close of escrow is lost income, so you want to work diligently during the escrow timeframe to make as much progress as possible.

Begin your marketing and advertising of the rental property to coincide with the close of escrow and completion of the rental unit renovation. Time is of the essence, and you want to minimize any lost rent.

The majority of tenants just expect to be treated fairly and honestly. They understand that you may have higher expenses and will reluctantly accept a rent increase as long as two basic conditions are met:

- **The rent is not raised beyond the current market rent for a comparable rental unit in the area.** Providing the tenants with documented information on comparable rentals in your area is all you need to do to show them that you're not asking for an unreasonable rent.
- **You're willing to make basic repairs to the rental unit.**

Seek cost-effective improvements or upgrades that will enhance the rental unit. Most tenants just want to be sure that they're receiving some of the benefit of paying higher rent. And if you're asking for more rent, be willing to reinvest a portion of the rent increase into improving the rental property. Clean the carpet, repaint the interior of the rental unit, or send in a maintenance person for a few hours to repair the miscellaneous items that need attention. Of course, if you have a very good and stable tenant, you may want to consider more significant upgrades to the rental unit. Replacing the carpet, installing a new appliance, or adding a ceiling fan and microwave oven may be an incentive for your tenant to sign a new lease at a higher rental rate.

Although tempting, be wary of making significant renovation or repairs to the rental property before the close of escrow. If the sale of the property does not go through as planned, you may have spent considerable sums to upgrade the seller's property without any recourse. Of course, you can obtain all your bids and proposals so that you're ready to begin as soon as the escrow closes. Do all your homework in advance, but only begin the actual renovation when you legally have ownership of the property.

Part II
Renting Your Property

The 5th Wave
By Rich Tennant
©RICHTENNANT
Before we go in, let me ask you- do you like to bowl?
FOR SALE

In this part . . .

The chapters in this part guide you through the process of actually renting your property — everything from getting your rental unit ready, to setting the rent, to advertising. I also give you some great tips for showing your property to prospective tenants and fill you in on the importance of good tenant-screening policies. So if you have a vacancy on your hands — or you will soon — read on.

Chapter 4

Preparing Your Rental Property for Prospective Tenants

In This Chapter

- Knowing what to upgrade and what to repair
- Renovating your rental unit to get more out of your property
- Paying attention to the exterior of the unit
- Getting everything done on time in an order that makes sense
- Working with a professional to get your unit ready to rent

You may think of preparing your rental property as one of the most basic skills, but it is critical to your overall success. Because vacant rental units don't generate rental income, you need to fill your vacancies with good, stable, rent-paying tenants as quickly as possible. And one of the best ways to do this is to make sure that your vacant rental units are clean and in rent-ready condition when you show them to prospective tenants.

A poor first impression of your rental unit's exterior is hard to reverse — regardless of how great the inside may look.

You may think you're saving time and money by allowing a new tenant to lease a rental unit that hasn't been properly prepared. After all, if they don't mind that the unit isn't rent-ready, why should you? Unfortunately, this strategy isn't as problem-free as it seems on the surface. In fact, it's a big mistake. Why? Because the kind of tenants you will attract with a rental unit that hasn't been properly prepared is someone who has lower standards and may even be desperate. New tenants who will accept a dirty and poorly maintained rental unit will surely not make any effort to leave the property in good condition when they leave.

In this chapter, I help you figure out whether you need to upgrade your rental unit before a new tenant moves in. And I fill you in on the proper methods of preparing the rental unit so that you can get the kind of tenant you want in as little time as possible.

Coming Up with a Plan to Handle Vacancies

The first step in getting good tenants is to develop a plan to get each vacant unit in top condition. Ideally, your vacating tenant will be cooperative and allow you access to the rental unit so that you can determine what items need to be cleaned, repaired, replaced, or even upgraded. As you walk through the unit, take lots of notes on the condition of the unit and what needs attention in order to get the unit ready to rent again. These notes will serve as the foundation for a detailed plan for getting the unit ready to rent. That plan will in turn help you attract several qualified rental prospects who will want to lease the rental unit at the rental rate you're seeking.

Not everyone appreciates or values the same features in a rental unit as you do. For example, although you may prefer draperies in your own home, you may soon find that vertical blinds can tolerate the heavier wear and tear of rental units much better. Although cleanliness has universal appeal, some features such as ceiling fans and microwave ovens will appeal more to some prospects than others.

Considering renovations and upgrades

Almost every rental unit has potential for renovation or upgrades. Often this is where the real value can be created in rental units: When you have a rental unit that is dated, you can renovate it and increase the rent.

If you have an older rental property, renovating may be more difficult due to some of the hazardous materials used in your unit's original construction. Asbestos and lead-based paint were commonly used in construction of many older rental properties, and these materials can be quite costly to remove. Often, you're better off just leaving them in place as long as they haven't been disturbed. Consult with experts in these issues before determining the extent of the renovation. Also, be sure that you check with your local building, code enforcement, or health department for its requirements in the proper handling and disposal of hazardous materials.

Be sure to evaluate the cost of the renovation or upgrade versus the rent increase that you'll be able to get out of a particular improvement before you start renovating. You need to be sure you'll get your money back from your investment.

There is no way you can come up with an exact answer to what amount of increased rent a particular upgrade will generate; some tenants value certain improvements more than others. A ceiling fan or new light bar in the bathroom will have a different impact on each prospective tenant; some will be willing to pay more for those amenities, and others won't.

Keep in mind what features and strengths your prospective renters will find in competitive rental units. Look for outmoded or outdated features in your own unit. For example, if most of your competition offers dishwashers but your unit doesn't have one, you may want to install a dishwasher so that you remain competitive. Your unit may have a very old dining room lighting fixture that you can easily replace with a modern light fixture or ceiling fan with a light kit. Another simple upgrade is to replace your old electrical switches and outlets for a more modern look. Pay particular attention to those items that would be quick, easy, and inexpensive to replace but that can really improve the overall look of your rental unit.

When upgrading or replacing your current appliances, try to standardize the brand and model wherever possible. Often appliance vendors will have certain models on closeout or special pricing. Although this may save you money upfront, it can cost you much more in the long run when you're unable to find replacement parts. Many stove parts are modular and easily replaceable to give the stove new life, but this fact will be worthless if you've bought an obscure brand that doesn't have replacement parts available either from the manufacturer or from a third party.

When you are considering renovations or upgrades to your rental units, make sure that you obtain the appropriate building permits or licenses as required in your area. Evaluate your property and ensure that the planned work will meet current building codes. Every state and many local municipalities have building codes that dictate the minimum standards to which all buildings must comply. Often, there are also housing, fire, and safety codes as well. If inspectors find that your rental property is not in compliance with the proper codes, then violation notices and potentially expensive fines may be sent your way. These codes are regularly updated and changed, and typically properties are not required to meet the new code requirements unless the property is renovated and building permits obtained. Be sure that you or your contractors are aware of the code requirements, and incorporate the required code-compliance measures in your renovation to ensure the safety of your tenants and to protect yourself from violations and fines.

Paying attention to the exterior or common areas

You want to make sure that your rental prospects' first impression of your rental property is a positive one. If the property exterior and grounds don't look nice, your prospect won't even bother to see the interior — where you may have just installed new appliances and high-quality carpeting. Start at the street and carefully critique your property as if you were entering a contest for the best-looking property in your area.

If you own a rental unit in a community-interest development or homeowners' association, the responsibility for the maintenance and repair of the common areas will typically fall to the association. Contact the association or its property manager to advise them of any common area concerns that you have. The association has a vested interest in ensuring the proper maintenance of the premises as well as maintaining a sense of desirability for owners and tenants.

To attract tenants who will treat your property properly and stay for a long time, be sure that your grounds and exterior areas are sparkling clean and the landscaping well maintained. Renovating the grounds by making sure that there is no trash, junk, or weeds is often a very inexpensive task. A nice green lawn, healthy shrubs, and shade trees will enhance any rental property.

Make sure that the building structure is presentable and inviting. Although major architectural changes are often cost-prohibitive, you can do a lot with a little paint, landscaping, and cleanup. The good news is that these items generally don't cost much compared to the positive benefits you gain. Some specific exterior improvements to consider are ground level or hanging planters, brass house numbers, awnings, or freshly painted fence or house trim.

First impressions are critical, and one of the key areas seen by all prospective tenants is the front entry. Make sure the entryway is clean, well kept, and well lighted. The front door should be cleaned or freshly painted or stained. Buy a new welcome mat. Remove or replace a broken screen door.

Making sure the interior of the unit is up to snuff

The most qualified, stable renters will always have choices, no matter how good or bad the rental market is. You are in competition for these excellent tenants, and you need to make sure that your rental unit stands out from the rest. The positive first impression of the exterior of your rental property will soon disappear if the interior of the rental unit is not just as sharp and well maintained.

Don't show your rental unit until it is completely rent-ready. Rental prospects understandably have little imagination, and if you show them a dirty rental unit, *that* is the way they will always think of it. Although you may lose a couple of potential showing days by taking the time to get the unit ready to rent, you will benefit in the long run with a more conscientious tenant.

There are no do-overs when it comes to showing a rental

Early in my property management career I learned a valuable lesson about the importance of cleanliness and first impressions. I had just arrived at a rental property for a management inspection and was speaking to the onsite manager when a rental prospect entered the rental office and asked to see a vacant unit. The rental prospect was a local college student who was looking for an apartment with her mother. I told my manager to go ahead and show the rental unit, and I would just follow along if they didn't mind.

They left the rental office and toured the property grounds, and I followed along and observed the prospective tenant and her mother as they were given the rental tour. The property grounds were very well maintained and the onsite manager was doing a great job getting to know the prospect's needs and determining the right rental unit to show.

They decided on an upstairs unit away from the street. Everything was going great, and it seemed almost certain that the prospect would become our newest tenant. When we got to the rental unit, things immediately went south. The entryway had cobwebs and dirt, the interior of the unit had been cleaned but had not been touched up for at least one week, and a large tree branch was hanging precariously over the balcony rail. I could immediately sense a 180-degree shift in the interest of this young lady and her mother. Up to that point, they had been very positive and had been talking about how soon she could be approved and move in. Suddenly, they stopped asking questions, barely answered any, and became very noncommittal.

The lesson I learned? That the cleanliness of the rental unit is paramount, and that you should never show a rental unit without having gone through it yourself just prior to the showing.

When preparing a rental unit for a new tenant, make sure that you don't overlook or forget a single item. I recommend using an inspection checklist to guide you through the process and as a final inspection tool. Here's a list of things to check:

- **When you have legal possession, remove all of the prior tenants' personal possessions and trash.**
- **Check all plumbing (toilets, faucets, and pipes) for proper operation.** Make sure that there are no leaks, that the plumbing has the proper pressure, and that there is adequate drainage.
- **Check all appliances for proper operation.** Run the dishwasher through a full cycle. Be sure that the oven's drip pan, broiler pan, and racks are there.
- **Check all hardware.** Be sure the locks have been changed and are operational. Pay attention to all latches and catches, doorknobs and pulls, doorstops, and sliding doors.

- **Check all windows, screens, and window coverings.** They should be clean, unbroken, secure, and operate properly. All window locks should work as well.
- **Check all walls, ceilings, and baseboards.** The paint and/or wall coverings should provide proper coverage, without holes, cuts, scratches, nails, or bad seams.
- **Check all floor coverings.** They should be clean and in good condition. The flooring should be properly installed, with no bad seams.
- **Check bathrooms.** Thoroughly clean the toilet, tub, shower, sink, mirrors, and cabinets. Check the toilet paper holder and towel bars to be sure they're clean. Put a paper sanitary ring around each toilet seat and a new roll of toilet paper in each bathroom.
- **Check all closets and storage areas.** Rods, closet dowels, hooks, shelves, lights, floors, and walls should be clean.
- **Check all counters, cabinets, doors, molding, thresholds, and metal strips.** They should be clean and fully operational, presenting no hazards.
- **Check smoke detectors and all lighting and electrical outlets, including GFI and circuit breakers, for proper operation.**
- **Check all patios, balconies, and entryways.** They should be clean and the railings should be secure.
- **Check the heating and air conditioning for proper operation.** Be sure the thermostat, filters, vents, and registers are all in working order.
- **Check the rental unit's curb appeal, including the exterior landscaping, driveways, and walkways.** Keep them as neat and tidy as possible.
- **Perform a final walkthrough of the entire rental unit for appearance and cleanliness.** Be sure to recheck the unit every few days that the unit is vacant.

You can also find this handy list on the Cheat Sheet in the front of this book. Tear it out and take it with you when you do your inspections.

Preparing Your Rental Unit the Right Way

One of the best ways to maximize your rental income is to develop a system to improve your efficiency by completing your rent-ready processing in minimum time. But you may be so overwhelmed by the amount of work you need to get done in the amount of time you have that you don't stop to consider which order you should do it in. Here's the order I recommend in order to maximize your time and be as efficient as possible:

1. **General cleaning**
2. **Maintenance, including repairs and upgrades**
3. **Painting**
4. **Final cleaning**
5. **Carpet or floor covering cleaning**

General cleaning

As soon the old tenants move out, clean the vacant rental unit. This initial cleaning should include the following:

- **Remove all trash left behind by the former tenant.** Remember to check drawers, cabinets, and closets.
- **Wipe down countertops.**
- **Sweep or vacuum the floors.**
- **Wash the windows and doors.**
- **Clean out the storage areas or garage as well.**

If you were unable to gain access before the tenant vacated, this is when you should walk through the rental and come up with your plan for getting the unit ready to rent again.

Maintenance

The majority of the items requiring maintenance in your vacancy will be minor items such as closet doors that are off their track, door knobs and towel bars that are loose, and burned out light bulbs. But be sure to carefully evaluate the current condition of all systems and equipment, including plumbing, electrical, appliances, and heating, ventilating, and air conditioning (HVAC).

Carefully inspect all plumbing fixtures. Look for leaky faucets, clogged aerators, or toilets that run. Test the angle stops or shutoff valves under each sink and look for signs of leaks.

Inspect and test the electrical components of the rental unit. Make sure that the circuit breakers or fuses are all in place and operating properly. Replace burned out light bulbs and check light switches and outlets. If possible, verify that the cable television and telephone lines are working, too.

Inspect each of the appliances and make sure that they are operating properly. Stoves and ovens contain modular parts, and you can replace the burner drip pans and control knobs very easily, because replacement parts for most major appliances are readily available. Run the dishwasher through a cycle and look carefully for any signs of leaks around the gasket or underneath near the pump housing.

Conserve energy by turning off the water heater, furnace, and air conditioning units at the breaker and setting the refrigerator to low. Your turnover work should also include cleaning or replacement of all filters. This simple, low-cost item will greatly improve the energy-efficiency and lower the wear on the equipment.

Tenants are becoming increasingly aware of the importance of conservation and energy-efficiency when selecting their homes. If you install water-saving fixtures, pilot-less ignition gas stoves and water heaters, weatherproofing, insulated windows and doors, and energy-efficient appliances, you'll have a competitive advantage in the rental marketplace.

Window treatments can really make your rental property look great. Not only will your prospective tenant want attractive and functional window coverings, but you also will want to control the appearance of your rental property from the street. The appropriate window coverings will vary; some tenants prefer drapes, whereas others may appreciate mini-blinds, vertical blinds, or shutters. You want window coverings that will appeal to you prospective tenants and are easy to maintain. I recommend vertical blinds or drapes, because they are much easier to maintain and clean than mini-blinds.

During your turnover work, be sure to perform maintenance that will minimize the likelihood of pests — by caulking all cracks around the windows, foundations, drains, and pipes that might afford entry into the rental unit. Almost every rental property will have the need for pest control at some point in time. An occasional cockroach or ants in search of water or food are commonplace, and there are consumer products available to handle these limited situations. However, use professional exterminators to treat more significant problems, and talk to your exterminator about establishing a regular schedule of follow-up treatments to be sure your rental unit is free of pests.

If your rental unit has a fireplace, be sure to clean out the ashes and debris as well as have the chimney flue inspected periodically based on the amount of usage. If your property has a pool or spa, have a professional company evaluate the condition and provide a written report documenting its condition, including the equipment and water quality. This will establish a baseline and often can head off any tenant complaints later on.

Painting

The next step in getting your vacant rental unit ready is painting. And the key to success in painting is preparation and having the proper tools. Make sure that all nails, screws, picture anchors, and other similar items are removed and that the wall is properly patched. Remove all door hardware and electrical cover plates before you start. Make sure the walls have been cleaned of any dirt. Treat grease, crayons, water stains, and other blemishes with special products designed for this purpose. You may also need to do some scraping and sanding to ensure that the new coat of paint will adhere properly.

One coat of a high-quality flat white latex paint is usually sufficient, unless you're changing the paint color to a much lighter shade than what it is currently. Use a semi-gloss paint in kitchens and baths for easy cleanup and resistance to moisture. Unless you have recently painted the rental unit in its entirety and only need to touch up one or two walls, you should paint the entire rental unit, including the walls, doors, door and window frames, baseboards, and closets. Don't forget to paint the closet dowels as well.

Unless you have an acoustic ceiling, be sure to paint it. Acoustic ceilings present special problems, particularly if they contain asbestos. Always consult with a professional painter or licensed acoustic contactor before attempting to patch or paint an acoustic ceiling. Spray paint instead of using a roller.

Reinstall all the switch plates and outlet covers, replacing any that are damaged or covered with paint. Remove any paint that has strayed or splattered onto the floor, windows, countertops, cabinets, appliances, and woodwork, and be sure to clean out sinks or bathtubs if they were used for paint clean up.

Final cleaning

Cleanliness sells. And the only people you want as renters are ones who will only accept dirt in their home as a temporary condition.

Pay particular attention to the kitchens and baths. A dirty or grimy kitchen and bath can be a real turnoff to a potential tenant. Be sure that you clean and regrout the tile, completely caulk around all countertops and bathroom fixtures, and clean the single dirtiest spot in most rental properties — the shower door track. Another final touch is to install a new toilet seat and place a paper sanitary ring around the toilet indicating that it has been professionally sanitized.

For many rental property owners, the thought of cleaning up after someone else is too much to bear. Luckily, many local cleaning services will do a great job for a very reasonable price. ***Remember:*** You don't have to do everything yourself.

If a rental unit doesn't smell clean, it won't matter how diligently you've cleaned it. Use a pine oil or lemon disinfectant and cleanser to neutralize any bad odors from the prior tenants. Baking soda in the refrigerator and drains, plus a lemon in the garbage disposal can suppress any bad odors. Some great air freshener products are available, but you need to be careful because certain fragrances may be offensive to your prospective tenant. I recommend placing a cinnamon stick in a shallow pan of water and placing it in the oven on low heat. In a short time, the rental unit will be filled with a smell that will remind your prospective tenant of Mom and apple pie.

Carpet or floor covering cleaning

The cleaning of the carpet or floor covering is the last step in preparing your rental unit for new tenants. Most floor coverings such as linoleum or sheet vinyl can be cleaned during the final cleaning stage; however, carpet cleaning should be handled only by outside contractors with professional truck-mounted steam cleaning equipment. The cost of cleaning the carpet is very competitive, and you cannot achieve the same results with the hand-held equipment that is available for rent.

If the carpets are too dated, severely worn, or badly stained and damaged, you should replace it. Carpeting is a decorator item, and care should be taken to select colors and styles of carpet that are designed for use in rental property. I recommend selecting a standard carpet for all your rental properties. Although sculptured carpet works well for some rental properties, a non-sculptured carpet with short nap, and in one or two neutral colors will have the broadest appeal. If you own a lot of rental units and have proper storage space available, purchasing your standard carpet by the roll can offer significant savings. The extra carpeting can be used to patch or even replace a full room if needed; however, be aware that each roll of even the same carpet style and color can be different, because the manufacturer's dye lot may vary slightly each time the carpet is produced.

Many rental property owners will make the mistake of purchasing a higher-grade of carpeting and try to save money on the carpet pad. But the carpet pad can make all the difference in the world. Consider using a higher-grade of rebond padding with a medium-grade carpet for competitively priced, yet excellent results.

Unless they're damaged, thoroughly clean your floor coverings before deciding to make replacements. Linoleum or sheet vinyl is very competitively priced, and the range of materials available is impressive. The most common problem with sheet vinyl is that any damage will require complete replacement. Some rental owners prefer individual floor tiles that can be replaced as needed; however, these tiles quickly trap dirt at the seams and can look unsightly. The best choice in floor covering material will be determined by your tenant profile and the expectations of your prospective tenant and your competition in the area. Be sure to select neutral colors and basic patterns.

Inspecting Safety Items

Although tenants need to take an active role in and have the ultimate responsibility for their own safety, you need to check all safety items upon unit turnover. The most basic items found in virtually every rental unit include door locks, window locks, and smoke detectors. Be sure that these items are in place and working before the new tenant takes occupancy.

Providing each tenant with a small fire extinguisher may also be a good idea. Although there is always the potential liability that the tenant will not use the fire extinguisher properly, most life-safety professionals advise that quickly using a fire extinguisher can keep a fire from spreading. (Of course, the tenant should first ensure that someone is immediately contacting 911 or the appropriate agency before attempting to put out the fire himself.)

Every door should have adequate locking mechanisms. Many local and state building codes have specific requirements concerning the type and specifications of door locksets. Recent changes in legislation are requiring that all windows that open and are accessible from the ground have proper window locks. Window screens should be in place and in good condition. The primary purpose of window screens is to keep the elements and insects out; however, screens can also serve as a crime deterrent and a safety feature.

Smoke detectors are very inexpensive and extremely important to the safety of the tenants. Be sure to check with your local fire department for its code requirements, because some areas require smoke detectors to be electrically hard-wired and others allow the typical battery-operated units. You need to be aware of the latest information; fire and safety codes have changed in recent years in many areas, particularly regarding the number and locations of required smoke detectors. Make sure that your records clearly indicate that you tested the smoke detectors and they were operating properly before your new tenant moved in. Then the tenant needs to take an active role in regularly testing the smoke detector and must not disconnect or disable the smoke detector in any way.

Your rental unit preparation work should also include testing of the ground-fault interrupter (GFI) circuits in kitchens and baths, plus any other safety items, such as carbon monoxide detectors and radon detectors.

At some rental properties, your tenants may be tempted to use portions of the roof area for their personal use, such as for sunbathing, hanging clothes, or even watching fireworks or hosting parties. This is never a good idea, because roofs are only designed to shelter the rental unit from the natural elements, not to handle foot traffic. In addition to potential premature damage to your roof, you will be exposed to significant liability if there is an injury.

Be sure that the house number or address is clearly marked on the exterior of your rental unit so that it is easy to locate the property from the street. This simple measure can be a huge help to life-saving personnel in an emergency.

Using Outside Contractors

Determining how to handle the required turnover work in vacant rental units is one of the toughest decisions that rental property owners have to make. Owners of large apartment buildings have maintenance personnel on staff and many contractors ready to assist them as needed. They routinely handle vacant units and just need to schedule the work. But owners of small rental properties are typically on their own to either handle the work personally or locate contractors to quickly prepare the vacant units.

Even if you're inclined to do your own turnover preparation work, certain maintenance functions are best handled by outside contractors. Use outside contractors for those trades that require specialized licensing or training. For example, it would be unwise for you to act as an exterminator or a contractor dealing with environmental hazards, or to attempt to recharge the coolant in an air-conditioning unit. Specific regulations are in place and unique knowledge is required in these areas.

Your skill level, time constraints, and opportunity cost may help determine whether you do some chores yourself or hire a pro. For example, cleaning, painting, and light maintenance may be items that you feel qualified to handle, can complete promptly, and will not cause you to forgo significant income in other areas. The ultimate answer is to let others do what they do best while you focus on what *you* do best.

Every day your rental unit sits vacant is costing you rental income that you can never recover. If you decide to paint your own rental unit, it may take you six days working in the evenings and weekends to completely paint a single-family rental home. If the rental market is strong and the daily rental rate is $50 per day, you're actually losing money if you could have had the rental home professionally painted in one day for $200.

Regardless of how much work you choose to handle yourself, you need to have on hand a list of competent and competitively priced service companies and suppliers for those times when you need a quick response. Your local affiliate of the National Apartment Association (NAA) can often provide names of service companies. Make sure that you carefully check the references and the status of any bonds or license with the appropriate governmental agency, and ensure that they have the proper insurance in place prior to allowing them to commence any work on your property. If services exceed $600 in a calendar year and the vendor is not a corporation or LLC, you may need to file Form 1099 with the IRS.

Chapter 5

Rent, Security Deposits, and Leases: The Big Three of Property Management

In This Chapter

- Determining the appropriate rent for your rental unit
- Using security deposits wisely
- Deciding on whether to use a lease or a month-to-month rental agreement

Before you can begin to advertise and show your rental unit, you need to set your asking rent, determine the appropriate security deposit, and have a lease or rental agreement ready to go.

You can determine the amount of rent to charge by calculating a desired return on your investment and setting the rent accordingly, but typically the best way to set your rent is to conduct a market survey of comparable rental properties in your area.

Setting the rent is an important decision because your net income from your rental property will be determined by the amount of rent you charge. If your rent is too high, you will have difficulty renting your vacant unit. If it's too low, you will have plenty of prospective tenants but not enough money to cover your costs and generate a return on your investment. Finding the optimum price takes time and effort.

If you purchase a rental property that already has tenants, you won't need to immediately address the issue of rent, because the tenants' rent will be set through the end of their lease or rental agreement — or until you give sufficient written notice of a rent increase (for more information on working with existing tenants, see Chapter 3). But even if you buy a property with tenants already in place, you will need to determine market rents so that you can calculate the appropriate rent when it comes time to renew a lease or consider increasing rents to market level.

In addition to setting the rent, you need to make sure that the security deposit on hand adequately protects you from tenant damage or default. Security deposits serve as the lifeline or protection you need before you turn over your significant real estate asset (your rental unit) to a tenant. The security deposit needs to be large enough to motivate the tenant to return the rental property in good condition, plus serve as an accessible resource to cover the tenant's unpaid rent or reimburse the costs to repair any damage. But if your security deposit is set too high, many qualified tenants may not be able to afford the move-in costs for your rental property, and you will have fewer rental applicants.

Another important decision you need to make before you begin to advertise and show your rental is whether you will use a lease or a month-to-month rental agreement. A lease is advantageous for tenants because it locks the rent in place for the term of the lease, and it's potentially advantageous for you because you can theoretically count on having a tenant for a set period of time. The month-to-month rental agreement, on the other hand, provides flexibility for both the tenant and you, but it can be a problem for tenants concerned about changing rental rates or policies, and it doesn't give you the peace of mind that having a tenant locked in for a certain lease term offers.

In this chapter, I give you some tips on setting the asking rent and determining the appropriate security deposit. I also guide you through the advantages and disadvantages of leases and month-to-month rental agreements and give you recommendations on how to get the benefits of each.

Setting the Rent

Setting the rent is one of the most important yet difficult tasks for most rental property owners. Although you may be tempted to pull numbers out of the air, resist that urge. If you set your rent too high, you will have a vacant rental unit. And if you set your rent too low, your profits will suffer or, worse, you won't even cover your expenses.

If you currently own a rental property, you probably already know how much rental income is necessary to cover your mortgage and other basic expenses of operating your rental property. And if you're looking to buy a rental property, you'll want to determine your minimum income needs *before* the deal is final.

You can use two common methods for determining how much rent you should charge for your rental property — return on investment and market analysis.

Knowing how much money you need to break even is important for evaluating the potential return on your real estate investment. But the reality is that the amount you need or want to collect in rent is subject to market conditions and your abilities as a rental property owner.

Examining the return on your investment

The first step in determining your rent based on the return on your investment is to calculate your costs of owning and operating your rental property. You need to estimate your costs for your mortgage, taxes, insurance, maintenance, leasing, management, and a profit on your invested funds.

For example, if your annual expenses per rental unit are $6,000 for your mortgage and tax payments and another $3,500 for other annual operating expenses, plus you want a 10 percent or $2,500 annual return on your original cash investment of $25,000 in this rental property, you need to generate a total rent of $12,000 per year or $1,000 per month. (Of course, this simple calculation does not account for increasing equity or other tax advantages of real estate, but it's a place to start.)

Although you may have calculated that you need $1,000 per month for your rental unit to achieve your estimated breakeven point (including your 10 percent profit), if the rental market has determined that comparable units are readily available for $950 you may not be able to fully achieve your financial goals at this time. With most real estate investments, the initial returns may not match your original projections; however, in the long run, rents will often increase at a greater rate than your expenses, and your return on your investment will improve.

Many new rental property owners make a major mistake by overestimating the potential income from their rental property. They develop unrealistic operating budgets or projections using above-market rents, allowing for no rental discounts, and anticipating virtually no vacancy or bad debt. When reality strikes, they are faced with negative cash flow, and ultimately they may even lose their rental property.

Setting the rent is particularly critical if you own single-family or condo rental units and other small rental properties, because the rent loss from an extended vacancy or one bad tenant can seriously jeopardize your entire investment. If you're among this group of rental property owners, be conservative in setting your rents, very cautious in tenant screening, and aggressive in maintaining your rental properties in excellent condition to attract good, long-term tenants who pay on time. To avoid surprises, use a conservative budget for your rental property that anticipates rental income at 95 percent of the market rent for a comparable rental unit plus provides for a vacancy allowance of one full month each year.

Conducting a market analysis of rents in your area

Setting your rents properly is an independent decision based on current market conditions. Unfortunately, the realities of the rental market may put limits on the rent you can reasonably charge for your rental unit, regardless of your costs of owning and maintaining the rental property.

Evaluating the rental rates being charged for similar rental units in comparable locations is a great way to gather information before setting your own rent. Make minor adjustments in your rent because of variations in the location, age, size, and features of the properties you're comparing. For example, if one of your competitors has an available rental unit that is nearly identical to yours, your rent should be slightly higher if you also have a swimming pool. Of course, be honest and make downward adjustments for aspects of your rental property that are not as competitive or as desirable as well.

The rental value of a particular property is subjective and can vary dramatically from one person to another. When estimating the proper market rent for your rental unit, be careful not to make adjustments based strictly on your own personal preferences. For example, you may prefer upstairs units and believe that these units should be priced higher than comparable downstairs units. Although this will definitely hold true for many prospective renters, there are just as many prospects who would similarly value the downstairs unit because they may not want to climb stairs.

In order to determine the market rents in your area, do your homework and locate comparable rental properties. *Comparable properties* are those properties that your tenants are most likely to have also considered when looking for a rental unit. They may be located right in the neighborhood or they may be located across town. For example, many of your rental prospects may work at the local hospital located six blocks west of your property. But these rental prospects are just as likely to choose a rental that is within six blocks of the hospital in another direction. So your comparable properties could be 12 blocks away. Don't assume that your comparable properties are only in your own neighborhood.

When you've determined which rental units are comparable, finding out the current market rent is easy. Begin by checking the For Rent signs in your area and call for the asking rent and other details. The local or regional newspaper will generally have ads listing the rental units for rent in the area along with some details and a phone number to call for more information. Although calling on ads will give you some good general information, you need to go see the properties in person to truly determine whether the rental properties are comparable to yours.

There are two schools of thought when performing a rent survey to determine the proper asking rent for your rental units:

- **You can pose as a prospective renter and ask all the typical questions that a prospect might ask.** The owner or manager will give you only the information that a prospective tenant would need about the rental property.
- **You can be honest and tell the owner that you're a rental property owner and you're doing market analysis.** This is the method I recommend, particularly if you have a small rental property. You will find that most rental owners will cooperate and share the information you need. They may even be willing to give you additional important information that you could not get otherwise, such as how long their rental unit has been vacant, the number and types of phone calls that they have received to date, and feedback from their own research into rental rates and vacancies in the local rental market.

If you are competing against a larger apartment community in your area, they probably won't provide you with any information about their current occupancy. Their actual occupancy rate is important, however, because it can provide a good indication of overall demand for rental units. Over the years, I have discovered some creative ways to determine the actual vacancy levels, such as talking with the mail carrier who delivers to the complex; the mail carrier doesn't have exact numbers, but he or she can tell you whether the complex is completely full or whether there are a good number of vacancies. Or a common vendor such as a carpet-cleaning firm or exterminator may service both your property and the large apartment complex, and that vendor will have the inside information you need. You can also drive through the property at night and see how many parking spaces are being used.

Rental rates can vary greatly from neighborhood to neighborhood and even from street to street, because many factors affect rents. Determining the proper asking rent is not scientific; views, landscaping, and traffic noise are just a few examples of the issues renters will consider. So be realistic in setting your asking rent. Starting a little too high is better than starting too low, because you can always reduce your asking rent slightly if you encounter too much resistance. But you can't very easily raise your asking rent if you get a large response to your ads.

Coming Up with a Fair Security Deposit

As an owner of rental property, you are allowed to collect a security deposit from your tenant upon move-in and hold it until the tenant leaves. The general purpose of the security deposit is to ensure that the tenant pays rent when it's due and keeps the rental unit in good condition. If you collect the first month's rent upon move-in, this is not considered part of the security deposit.

State laws typically limit the amount of the security deposit you can collect and regulate the return of the security deposit and any lawful deductions. Check with your local affiliate of the National Apartment Association for your state security deposit laws. Some states specifically allow certain small rental owners to be exempt from these rules.

Do not lower or waive the security deposit. If the required funds to move in are too high, collect a reasonable portion of the deposit prior to move in and allow the tenant to pay the balance of the security deposit in installments.

Security deposits are more than just money that you hold for protection against unpaid rent or damage caused by your tenant. Although the actual cash amount may be relatively small compared to the overall value of your rental unit, the security deposit is a psychological tool that is often your best insurance policy for getting your rental unit back in decent condition.

Keeping security deposits separate from your other funds

Security deposits are a liability, because they are funds that legally belong to the tenant. You hold these funds in trust as protection in the event that the tenant defaults in the payment of rent or damages the property.

Because the funds don't belong to you, several states have requirements that security deposits must be held in a separate trust bank account rather than mixed in with the other funds from the owner's rental properties or personal resources. Some states require that owners provide their tenants with a written notice indicating the location of this bank trust account at the beginning of the tenancy.

If you keep the security deposits separate from the rest of your funds, the security deposit will be readily available whenever the tenant moves out and is potentially entitled to the return of some or all of that money.

Setting the amount of the security deposit within legal limits

Many states limit the amount you can collect as a deposit to the equivalent of one or two months' rent. The limit varies in each state depending on certain factors, such as whether the rental is furnished, whether the tenant is on a lease or a month-to-month rental agreement, whether the tenant has pets or waterbeds, or whether the tenant is a senior citizen.

In most rental markets, the security deposits are well below the maximum allowed by law. While staying within the legal limits, I recommend that you collect as large of a security deposit as the market will bear.

Avoiding nonrefundable deposits

Approximately a dozen states have laws that permit rental property owners to have nonrefundable fees, such as cleaning or pet fees. But I recommend avoiding such nonrefundable fees and just include these charges into your rent. This way, you avoid potentially time-consuming disputes with your tenants.

If you have a specific concern, such as a pet, increase the amount of your refundable security deposit to protect yourself from any damage.

Having the security deposit fully refundable is an incentive to the tenant to return the premises in good condition. A nonrefundable deposit can actually cause the tenants to not make any effort to return the premises in good condition, because they figure that they will forfeit the deposit anyway.

Paying interest on security deposits

Several states have laws that require rental property owners to pay interest on the security deposit paid by the tenant. Check with your local affiliate of the National Apartment Association for the exact requirements, because the laws vary dramatically between the states.

Last month's rent

Until recently, many rental property owners collected the first month's rent, the last month's rent, and a security deposit from new tenants. Because there are some disadvantages to this method, I strongly recommend that you collect the first month's rent, plus a security deposit equal to or greater than one month's rent. Collecting the "last month's rent" can create unnecessary problems.

For example, if the rental rate increases during the tenancy and you have already collected a lesser amount as the "last month's rent," upon move-out, the tenant, and often the courts, will likely take the position that the "last month's rent" has already been paid in full, even though the rental rate has increased. When giving rent increases, many owners fail to also require the tenant to increase the amount held as the "last month's rent." Plus, in some states, the designation of "last month's rent" limits your use of these funds to only that specific use. Thus, even if there is extensive damage to the rental unit and the security deposit is fully exhausted, the "last month's rent" cannot be used to cover those damages.

Set your security deposit to an amount that is different than the monthly rental rate to minimize attempts by your tenant to claim that they thought the security deposit would cover their last month's rent. Ideally, you can collect a security deposit that is higher than the monthly rental rate; but even if you collect a deposit that is $25 to $50 less than the monthly rent, you will effectively eliminate any attempt by the tenants to claim that the deposit was for their last month's rent.

The method of calculating interest varies greatly, with some states providing a formula tied to the Federal Reserve board rates or flat percentage amounts. Most states require interest payments to be made at termination of the tenancy and annually.

There is no law that prevents you from voluntarily paying interest on deposits, and some owners offer to pay interest as a competitive advantage or an inducement to collect a larger security deposit. If you are able to get a much larger deposit, I recommend paying interest on that deposit. The additional peace of mind is worth the relatively small amount you will pay in interest.

Increasing deposits

If you have a long-term tenant and your rents have increased significantly over time, you may want to consider increasing your security deposit. This is legal as long as you comply with the normal requirements for any change in the terms of the agreement.

For example, if you have a fixed-term lease in effect, you must wait until the lease expires before requiring an increase in the security deposit. If you have a month-to-month rental agreement, then you can increase the security deposit the same way that you raise the rent, typically by giving the tenant a written 30-day notice in advance.

Deciding Whether to Use a Fixed-Term Lease or a Month-to-Month Rental Agreement

The lease or rental agreement is the primary document that specifies the terms and conditions of the agreement binding the property owner and the tenant. It is a contract between the owner of the rental property and the tenant for the possession and use of the rental property in exchange for the payment of rent.

Rental property owners commonly use one of two types of agreements — a lease or a periodic rental agreement. Periodic rental agreements can be for any term, but are generally month-to-month tenancies.

A month-to-month rental agreement is automatically renewed each month unless the owner or tenant gives the other proper written notice (usually 30 days) to terminate the tenancy. Month-to-month agreements give you much more flexibility than leases, because you can increase the rent or change other terms of the tenancy on 30 days' notice.

A lease is a fixed-term contract that obligates you and the tenant for a set period of time, and some owners like the commitment required from the tenant. The most common lease term is for 6 months or 12 months, and the majority are written to automatically convert to a month-to-month rental agreement after the expiration of the initial term. However, some leases are for fixed terms, and the owner and tenant must agree to sign a new lease for the tenant to stay.

With a lease, you cannot increase the rent or change other terms of the tenancy until the lease expires. Also, you cannot terminate or end the tenancy before the lease expires, unless the tenant does not pay his rent or violates another term of the lease. And in court, you will have the burden of proof, which means you're the one who has to prove that the tenant didn't live up to his part of the contract. With a month-to-month rental agreement, you may increase the rent or change other terms of the tenancy, usually on 30 days' written notice. You or the tenant may terminate or end the tenancy at any time by giving the required amount of written notice, again usually 30 days.

Some owners prefer the flexibility offered by a month-to-month rental agreement over a lease. Although the month-to-month rental agreement does allow your tenants the right to move at any time merely by giving a 30-day written notice, the reality is that most tenants do not like to move and will often stay long-term.

The majority of tenants only move because of a job transfer or another significant reason, or because the rental owner does not properly maintain the property.

Rental property owners generally charge a higher rental rate for a tenant on a month-to-month rental agreement because there is higher risk associated with the additional turnover that can accompany the short-term agreement.

Although the lease legally binds both you and the tenant, the current tenant/landlord laws in virtually every state favor the tenants. For example, for a tenant to walk away from a lease is not difficult, and in most states the owner has the duty to mitigate or minimize the potential damages. That means that you must make a reasonable effort to re-rent the premises and can only charge for the rent incurred until the new tenant begins paying rent.

Although oral rental agreements of up to one year are binding, make sure all your leases or rental agreements are in writing, because so many issues surrounding those agreements involve monetary considerations. Memories fade and disputes can arise that will usually be resolved in the favor of the tenant should legal action be required. Oral agreements also create the potential for charges of discriminatory treatment. Always put all terms and conditions in writing even if you only intend to have a short-term agreement or even if you know the tenant personally. Oral agreements are only as good as the paper they are written on, because they cannot be substantiated and are not always enforceable.

Form 5-1 shows a standard Lease Agreement. You can easily modify this form to be a month-to-month rental agreement by changing the language in the first paragraph to "Term: The term of this agreement shall be from month-to-month, beginning on the ___day of ________, 20__." Be sure to have an attorney specializing in tenant/landlord law review these documents and all other forms in this book before using them in your area. In some states, special language must be included in the leases and rental agreements. For example, Florida has required language about radon, and many states have required information that must be given to the tenants concerning access to a Megan's Law or sexual offender database.

LEASE AGREEMENT

This agreement, entered into this ______ day of ________________, 20 ___ between
________________________________ (hereinafter called Tenant) and
________________________________ (hereinafter called Owner).

Leased Premises: The Leased premises are located in the City of ________________, County of ________________, State of ________________, and commonly described as ________________________________, Unit number _____ (if any), together with the inventory of furniture, if any, and appliances attached hereto (Premises) for use as a private residence only. If anyone else has guaranteed performance of this Lease Agreement, a separate Guaranty of Lease is attached.

1. **Term**: The term of this agreement shall be for a term of ___________, beginning on the _____day of __________, 20 ____, and ending at midnight the ______ day of ________________, 20 ____. This Lease Agreement will automatically renew month-to-month unless either party gives at least thirty (30) days written notice of termination or intent to vacate as required by paragraph 14.

2. **Monthly Rent**:

   Base Rent: $__________________
   Furniture: __________________
   Refrigerator: __________________
   Cable: __________________
   Washer Dryer: __________________
   Carport/Garage: __________________
   Other: __________________
   Total Monthly Rent: $__________________

   Parking Space Assignment (if any): Space No. ___________ (see paragraph 11).

   A. Payment of Rent. Tenant agrees to pay rent to Owner in advance and without demand, at the office of the Owner or their designated agent, or at such other place as may be designated by Owner, as follows:

   $_____________ for the period ________________ through ______________ (first full month).

   $_____________ for the period ________________ through (second month prorated) payable on ____________________.

   $_____________ commencing on the first day of the month of _______________ and thereafter on the first day of each succeeding month. For calculation and pro-ration of rent, each calendar month is a 30-day period.

   B. Late Payment. If the rent is not paid in full by the THIRD (3rd) day of any calendar month, a late charge of $_____ per day shall be immediately due and payable, with a maximum charge of $_______. If the THIRD (3rd) day of any calendar month falls on a Sunday or federal legal holiday, then the rent is late if not paid in full on the next business day. Further, if the rent is paid by a check or other financial instrument returned by the financial institution for any reason, in addition to the late charge set forth above, a Returned check

1

Form 5-1: Lease Agreement (Page 1 of 8).

charge shall also be due and payable in the sum of $_____. Tenant agrees that the combination of late charges and returned check charges provided for by this paragraph is a reasonable estimate of Owners bank charges, administrative fees, loss of use of the rent due and other damages which could otherwise be difficult or impractical to ascertain. All payments received after the tenth of the month must be in the form of cashier's check or money order.

C. **Method and Allocation of Payments Received**. All monies paid will be applied first to any previous balance due on Tenant's account, including rent, late charges, returned check charges, and damages; and secondly, to current rent. No cash will be accepted. All checks must be from Tenant of record named in the lease. No third party checks will be accepted unless approved by the Owner in advance. All personal checks will be run through Tenants bank one time only. If Tenant has had two returned checks, or in the event of a Three Day Notice to Pay Rent or Quit, Tenant agrees that payment must be made in the form of cashier's check or money order only.

3. **Security Deposit**.

A. Tenant agrees to deposit with Owner, prior to taking possession of Premises, the additional sum of $_________________ as security to be held by Owner for the faithful performance by Tenant of each and every provision of this Lease, which security Tenant hereby authorizes Owner to use for any one or more of the following purposes:
(1) For payment of delinquent rent;
(2) For repair of damages to the premises, including furnishings and appliances, caused by Tenant exclusive of ordinary wear and tear;
(3) For cleaning the premises, if necessary, upon termination of the tenancy;
(4) For payment of any liquidated damages resulting from late rental payment and/or returned checks;
(5) For locks and keys in the event keys are not returned upon termination of the tenancy.
(6) If Tenant vacates or abandons the premises prior to the end of the Term, for daily rent equal to 1/30th of the Total Monthly Rent for each day rent is unpaid until the end of the Term or until Owner re-rents the premises, whichever event occurs first.

B. Within ____ days after Tenant vacates the premises, Owner will furnish Tenant with an itemized statement of the amount of the security received, and the basis for and disposition of such security, and shall return any remaining portion of such security to Tenant. Owner shall bill Tenant for amounts expended which result in a deficiency in Tenant's security deposit, which deficiency Tenant agrees to pay Owner upon receipt of such deficiency statement. Interest will not be paid on the security deposit unless required by law.

C. Security deposit refund checks will be made payable jointly to all parties to the original Lease Agreement. Owner must have a written notice signed by the party vacating the apartment if he/she wishes to release their interest in the security deposit or transfer that interest to another party. Security Deposits are not refunded until all parties have vacated the apartment.

D. Tenant has conducted a walk-through inspection of the Premises and has or will execute a Move-in, Move-out Inspection Checklist. The absence of an entry shall signify that the item was in a good, clean, complete, undamaged, and working condition. Tenant agrees that it shall not enter into possession of the Premises unless it is tenantable. Tenant taking possession of the Premises shall be conclusive evidence that the Premises were tenantable. On move-out, the Premises shall be surrendered to Owner in a clean and good condition. Upon termination of this tenancy, the Move-in, Move-out Inspection Checklist will be used upon move-out and shall be executed by both parties when possible, but at the discretion of the Owner. The absence of an entry on said Move-in, Move-out Inspection Checklist upon move-out shall signify that

2

Form 5-1: Lease Agreement (Page 2 of 8).

the item was in a good, clean, complete, undamaged, and working condition.

4. **Occupants.** The Premises shall be occupied only by the following named person(s):

Name	Birth Date	Name	Birth Date (if a minor)
Name	Birth Date (if a minor)	Name	Birth Date (if a minor)
Name	Birth Date (if a minor)	Name	Birth Date (if a minor)
Name	Birth Date (if a minor)	Name	Birth Date (if a minor)

No one else may occupy the Premises. Tenant agrees that it shall be a material violation of this Lease Agreement if a guest or invitee occupies the Premises for: 1) a period of seven (7) consecutive days or more; or 2) any portion of thirty (30) days or more within any given ninety (90) day period, without obtaining the advance written consent of the Owner.

5. **Use of Premises**. The Premises shall be used solely by Tenant for residential purposes and shall be occupied only by the number of occupants provided in this Lease Agreement.

6. **Animals or Pets.** Tenant and such others for whom Tenant is responsible shall not keep or maintain any animal in or about the Premises without first obtaining Owner's written consent. If approved, an Animal Agreement shall become an integral part of this Lease when executed by Owner and Tenant.

7. **Conduct**. Tenant covenants and warrants to Owner as follows:
   A. **Quiet Conduct**: The conduct of Tenant and such others for whom Tenant is responsible shall not, in any manner, disturb the quiet enjoyment of other Tenants, invitees, or visitors, in or near where the Premises are located, including the common areas and any or all recreational facilities.
   B. **Damage**: The conduct of Tenant and such others for whom Tenant is responsible shall not result in or cause destruction or damage to the Premises, or any part thereof including, but not limited to any and all recreational facilities and recreation equipment, or the property of other Tenants, their invitees and visitors.
   C. **Nuisance, Property Damage and Waste**: Tenant and such others for whom Tenant is responsible shall not maintain, commit, or permit the maintenance or commission of a nuisance, and shall not commit or permit property damage or waste, upon the Premises or any part thereof. Further, Tenant shall not violate any criminal or civil law, ordinance or statute in the use and occupancy of the Premises.

8. **Alterations and Repairs.**
   A. **Alterations**: Except as provided by law, no repairs, decorating or alterations shall be done by Tenant without Owner's prior written consent. Tenant shall notify Owner in writing of any repairs or alterations contemplated. Decorations include but are not limited to painting, wallpapering, hanging of murals or posters. Tenant shall hold Owner harmless as to any mechanics lien recordation or proceeding caused by Tenant.

3

Form 5-1: Lease Agreement (Page 3 of 8).

B. Repairs: Tenant shall keep and maintain the Premises and every part thereof in good and sanitary condition. Tenant agrees to pay for any repairs of the Premises due to Tenant's negligence. Tenant shall immediately notify Owner, in writing, should any plumbing, electrical, mechanical, or other equipment or part of the Premises become damaged, faulty, or in disrepair. Further, Tenant shall immediately notify Owner, in writing, when Tenant becomes aware of an inoperable lock or window security. Owner is not liable for a violation of this section unless Owner fails to correct a violation within a reasonable time after Owner or agent has actual knowledge of the deficiency or receives notice of any inoperable lock or window security deficiency.

9. **Utilities.**

A. Tenant shall pay for all utilities, services, charges, fees, and related deposits, if any, made payable by or predicated upon occupancy of Tenant. Owner will only pay for ______________________________. Tenant shall comply with any Owner rules or any city, municipal, county, state, and special district rules, regulations, ordinances or statutes now in force or which may be subsequently adopted or enacted relating to the use and conservation of all utilities, including water. Owner may enter the Premises for the purpose of installing and insuring the proper use of any water conservation devices. Such devices include, but are not limited to, flow restrictions and toilet water displacement equipment required by any regulatory authority or in Owner's opinion, necessary for the conservation of water. Tenant understands that the utility or billing provider will issue the utility bills. Utility bills are issued separately from rent bills and are to be paid directly to the utility provider. Owner shall make reasonable arrangements to establish the water and sewer account with the billing provider. Thereafter, Tenant shall be solely responsible for maintaining and paying for the account with the water and sewer billing provider.

B. If any utilities are submetered for the Premises, or prorated by an allocation formula, an addendum will be attached to this Lease Agreement in compliance with state agency rules or local ordinance.

C. Notwithstanding anything to the contrary contained in the Lease, Owner shall not be required to furnish utilities and/or water to the premises unless the same shall be made regularly available to the Owner. The furnishing of utilities and/or water shall not be a condition precedent to Tenant's performance of any of its obligations. Owner shall not be liable for damages resulting from the interruption of any utility services provided to the Premises, including, but not limited to, power outages, or Owner shut-off for purpose of repair.

D. Tenant must pay all utility bills in accordance with its agreement with the utility provider. Failure to pay any utility is a material and substantial breach of this Lease, and shall entitle Owner to exercise all remedies available under the lease terms. Further, if Tenant fails to pay all utility charges assessed by utility companies in connection with the use of utility services for which Tenant has agreed to pay, and Owner is assessed by the utility company for these utility services, then Owner may, but is not required to, pay these utility assessments to such utility company and subtract any amounts from Tenant's security deposit. In the event that a penalty, premium, excess use charge, or other charge based upon or intended to mitigate against excess use is imposed in connection with the use of utilities and/or water by the project in which the Premises are located, Tenant shall pay its pro rata share thereof as additional rent. If such penalty or charge is not separately stated for the apartment occupied by Tenant, then it shall be prorated in proportion to the square footage the Premises bears to the entire square footage of all apartments in the project during the period for which it is imposed. Owner shall notify Tenant in writing of such amount, and Tenant shall pay said amount at the time the next installment of rent is due.

E. Owner has advised Tenant of the current utility company selected by Owner to provide electricity and gas service for the community and its apartments. Notwithstanding the foregoing, if permitted by law, Owner shall have the right at any time, and from time to time during the lease term, to either contract for service

4

Form 5-1: Lease Agreement (Page 4 of 8).

from a different company providing electricity or gas service, or to continue to contract with the current utility company for the community's common areas and its apartments.

F. (1) Owner shall not be liable or responsible for any loss, damage, or expense Tenant may sustain or incur by reason of any change, interference, or defect in the supply or character of the gas or electric energy furnished to the community or its apartments, or if the quantity or character of the electric energy supplied by the utility or other utility provider is no longer available or suitable for Owner's requirements.

(2) No such change, failure, defect, unavailability, or unsuitability shall constitute an actual or constructive eviction, in whole or in part, or entitle Tenant to any abatement or diminution of rent, or relieve Tenant from any obligation of the Lease.

(3) To the extent Tenant is permitted by law to select a different utility service provider other than the company selected by Owner, Tenant shall:

(a) Reimburse Owner for the cost of repairing any and all damage to the apartment and the community common areas caused directly or indirectly by Tenant's utility selection or its equipment. Owner reserves the right to deduct said costs from Tenant's security deposit.

(b) Indemnify Owner from any claims, demands, and expenses, including attorney's fees, arising out of or in any manner related to the action or inaction by Tenant's utility provider, including, but not limited to, expenses and/or fines incurred by Owner in the event Tenant's utility provider fails to provide power or provides insufficient power.

10. **Smoke Detector.** The Premises is equipped with a smoke detection device. Tenant acknowledges the smoke detection device was tested and its operation explained by Owner or agent at the time of initial occupancy, and the detector was operating at that time. Tenant shall perform the manufacturer's recommended test at least once a week to determine if the smoke detector is operating properly. If the detector is battery operated, Tenant further agrees to (a) ensure the battery is in operating condition at all times; (b) replace the battery, as needed (unless otherwise provided by law); and (c) if, after replacing the battery, the smoke detector does not work, inform Owner or agent immediately. Tenant must inform Owner or agent in writing of any defect, malfunction, or failure of any detector. In accordance with California law, Tenant shall allow Owner or agent access to the Premises for purposes of inspection and maintenance of the smoke detection device. It is an actionable offense to disconnect or otherwise impair the function of a smoke detection device.

11. **Parking**. Owner does not provide Tenant with an assigned parking space for the Leased Premises, unless otherwise provided on Page 1 of this Lease Agreement. If assigned parking is provided, Tenant is to park in designated space only. Unauthorized vehicles will be towed away immediately. If assigned parking is provided, such parking may be altered, modified, or discontinued by Owner upon five (5) days written notice to Tenant. Owner, at its sole option, may adopt a parking arrangement for the Premises that modifies any prior arrangement or deletes assignment of parking spaces. All guests will park on the street. Tenant is responsible for keeping the assigned space, carport, or garage clean. Alcoholic beverages shall not be consumed in the parking area. Working on vehicles in parking spaces or garages is prohibited. Inoperable or abandoned vehicles will be towed away at the Owner's expense. Please refer to the Parking section of the Policies and Rules for further parking rules.

12. **Entry by Owner**

A. Tenant agrees that Owner and its agents may enter the Premises in case of an emergency, to make necessary or agreed repairs or improvements, or to exhibit the premises to prospective or actual purchasers, mortgagees, tenants, workmen or contractors. Such entry, other than in case of emergency, will be made during normal business hours, unless Tenant otherwise consents at the time of entry.

5

Form 5-1: Lease Agreement (Page 5 of 8).

B. Owner must give Tenant twenty-four (24) hours notice of Owner's intent to enter the Premises during normal business hours, other than in cases of emergency or if it is impractical to do so.

13. **Assignment and Sublease.** No portion of the Premises shall be sublet nor this Agreement assigned. Any attempted subletting or assignment by Tenant shall, at the election of Owner, be an irremediable breach of this Agreement and cause for immediate termination as provided herein and by law.

14. **Notice of Termination**. Before vacating, Tenant must give Owner advance written notice as provided herein. Tenant's Notice of Intent to Vacate Rental Unit does not release Tenant from liability for the full term of the Lease Agreement or any renewal or extension. Tenant's Notice of Intent to Vacate Rental Unit must be in writing and cannot terminate the Lease Agreement sooner than the end of the original full term, any renewal or extension. Tenants verbal notice of intent to vacate will not be accepted and is not valid to terminate this Lease Agreement. If Tenant chooses to vacate upon expiration of the lease, a written 30-day notice shall be required. The lease shall automatically convert to a month-to-month tenancy unless Owner receives from Tenant 30 days advance written notice of Tenant's intention to vacate. Failure to comply with this provision shall result in Tenant's responsibility for thirty (30) day's rent from when said notice was received by Owner. In the event Tenant tenders to Owner rent for an additional month, Owner's acceptance thereof shall result in this Lease being converted to a month-to-month tenancy, all other terms of the Lease remaining in full force and effect. If this Lease is, or is converted to, a month-to-month term, the Lease may be terminated by Tenant or Owner giving a 30-day written notice of termination at any time. Owner may serve any notice or demand upon Tenant personally, or by posting a copy at the Premises and mailing a copy thereof by regular mail, postage prepaid, addressed to Tenant at the address of the Premises, or in the event Tenant has provided Owner, in writing, with a forwarding address, to such forwarding address.

Tenant may serve any notice or demand upon Owner or their agent personally or by mailing such notice to Owner or their agent for the Premises by certified mail, postage prepaid, return receipt requested.

15. **Default/Abandonment**. In event of forfeiture, Owner reserves the right to all rental and other damages as provided by the Lease or by law. A notice or judgment for unlawful detainer declaring a forfeiture of the Lease shall not relieve Tenant from liability. Owner may recover from Tenant the worth at the time of the award of the amount by which the rent then unpaid hereunder for the balance of the Lease Term exceeds the amount of such rental loss for the same period which Tenant proves could be reasonably avoided by Owner.

16. **Non-Responsibility of Owner for Damages**. Owner is not liable for bodily injury to or damage to the personal property of Tenant, members of Tenant's household, or any other Tenants, Tenant's guests, invitees, or licensees, or any other person in or about the Premises, that is caused by or results from latent or patent defects, criminal acts, fire, steam, electricity, gas, water or the weather, or from breakage, leakage, obstruction or other defects of pipes, sprinklers, wires, appliances, plumbing, air conditioning or lighting fixtures, or from any other cause. Tenant assumes all risk of, and waives all claims against Owner from any such injury or damage, except for injury or damage resulting from negligent acts of Owner.

17. **Indemnification**. Tenant shall indemnify and save harmless Owner against and from all claims arising from the following, and against all costs, attorney fees, expenses and liabilities incurred in the defense of any such claim, action or proceeding brought on such claim:

Form 5-1: Lease Agreement (Page 6 of 8).

A. Use of the Premises by Tenant, members of Tenant's household, other Tenants, or Tenant's guests, invitees or licensees,
B. Any activity done, permitted or suffered by Tenant in or about the Premises or elsewhere,
C. Any breach or default by Tenant under this Lease, or
D. Any negligence of Tenant, members of Tenant's household, any other Tenants, or any of Tenant's guests, invitees or licensees.

Tenants obligations, as set forth above, arising by reason of any occurrence taking place during the Term of this Lease, shall survive any termination of this Lease.

18. **Insurance**. Owner does not insure Tenant, the members of Tenant's household, Tenant's guests, invitees, licensees, or any other Tenants or persons in or about the Premises, from any loss occurring in or about the Premises, whether from bodily injury or property damage of any kind whatsoever.

    Owner strongly recommends that Tenant maintain, at Tenant's sole expense, a standard type of Renters insurance policy or its equivalent, which provides limits of liability adequate to protect Owner's and other Tenant's property, as well as Tenant's personal property from loss by fire, burglary, water and other perils. Without such insurance, Tenant could incur a substantial financial burden in the event of fire or other perils outside of Owner's control.

    Tenant hereby releases Owner from any and all claims for damages or loss to Tenant's personal property in, on, or about the Premises that are caused by or result from risks that are or would be insured under the insurance described above. Tenant hereby waives any and all rights of recovery and rights of subrogation against Owner in connection with any damage or claim that is or would be covered by such insurance, except for damage resulting from negligent acts of Owner.

19. **Phone jacks**. Owner shall be responsible for providing only one functioning telephone jack to the Premises. Tenant shall install no additional jacks without Owner's express written consent. Tenant shall be responsible for repair of inside wiring if damaged by Tenant and such others for whom Tenant is responsible.

20. **Waiver**. The waiver of either party of any breach shall not be construed to be a continuing waiver of any subsequent breach. The receipt by Owner of the rent with the knowledge of any violation of a covenant or condition hereto shall not be deemed a waiver of such breach. No waiver by either party of the provisions herein shall be deemed to have been made unless expressed in writing and signed by all parties to this Lease.

21. **Joint and Several Responsibility**. Each person executing this Lease as Tenant is jointly and severally liable hereunder, and is required to perform fully all obligations imposed on Tenant in this Lease.

22. **Attorney's Fees and Litigation.** If any legal action or other proceeding is brought by any party to enforce any part of this Lease, the prevailing party shall recover, in addition to all other relief, reasonable attorneys fees and costs. Notice may be served upon Owner by Tenant at the location that rent is routinely tendered.

23. **Credit Report.** As required by law, Tenant is hereby notified that a negative credit report reflecting on Tenant's credit history may be submitted to a credit reporting agency if Tenant fails to fulfill the terms of its credit obligations.

24. **Only Agreement**. This Lease, which includes all the attachments referred to below, constitutes the entire lease between the parties and cannot be modified except in writing and signed by all parties. Owner, nor any agent or employee of Owner, has not made any representation or promise other than those set forth herein.

7

Form 5-1: Lease Agreement (Page 7 of 8).

25. **Addenda**. By initialing as provided, Tenant acknowledges receipt of the following optional addenda, as indicated, copies of which are attached hereto and are incorporated as part of this Lease:

____ A. Policies and Rules
____ B. Move-in/Move-out Inspection Checklist
____ C. Lead Paint Disclosure and Lead Hazard Information, if applicable
____ D. Asbestos Disclosure, only if asbestos is present
____ E. Animal Agreement
____ F. Drug and Crime-Free Addendum
____ G. Utility Submetering or Allocation Formula Addendum
____ H. Other ____________________
____ I. Other ____________________
____ J. Other ____________________

The undersigned Tenant(s) acknowledge having read and understood the foregoing, and receipt of a copy hereof.

Dated: ____________________________ Dated: ____________________________

OWNER: TENANT(S):
Property Name:______________________

By________________________________ ________________________________
Owner or Agent for Owner

____

____

8

Form 5-1: Lease Agreement (Page 8 of 8).

Standard lease forms are great, but they don't allow you to add your own clauses. However, you can modify the terms of your lease or rental agreement fairly easily with the Addendum to Lease or Rental Agreement shown in Form 5-2. For example, maybe you want to include the requirement that the tenant will maintain the grounds in exchange for a rent credit off of the next month's rent as long as they do a good job. This can be easily incorporated into the lease by using the Addendum. ***Remember:*** Be careful about adding additional clauses or language to your lease or rental agreement unless you seek the advice of an attorney.

The number one reason for tenants to insist on a lease is that the rent is locked in for a minimum period of time. But in most instances, owners want the flexibility and latitude afforded by the month-to-month rental agreement. But there is an effective way to achieve both goals, and I strongly recommend using a month-to-month rental agreement in conjunction with a Rental Rate Guarantee Certificate (see Figure 5-1). This method allows your tenant the benefits of a stable rental rate for a minimum period of time, while not restricting your ability to change other rules or even ask the tenant to leave in 30 days if there are other problems.

Addendum to Lease or Rental Agreement

This Addendum to the lease or rental agreement entered into this _______ day of _______________, 20 ___ between _______________________________ (Tenant) and _______________________________ (Owner) for the premises located at: ____ (Rental unit).

This Addendum shall be and is incorporated into the Lease or Rental Agreement dated the ____ day of _______________, 20 ___ between Tenant and Owner.

Tenant and Owner agree to the following changes and/or additions to the Lease or Rental Agreement:

____
____
____
____
____
____
____
____
____

This Addendum to be effective as of _______________________________, 20 ___.

Dated: ___________________________ Dated: ___________________________

OWNER: TENANT(S):
Property Name: ____________________

By____________________________ ____________________________
Owner or Agent for Owner

____

____

Form 5-2: Addendum to Lease or Rental Agreement.

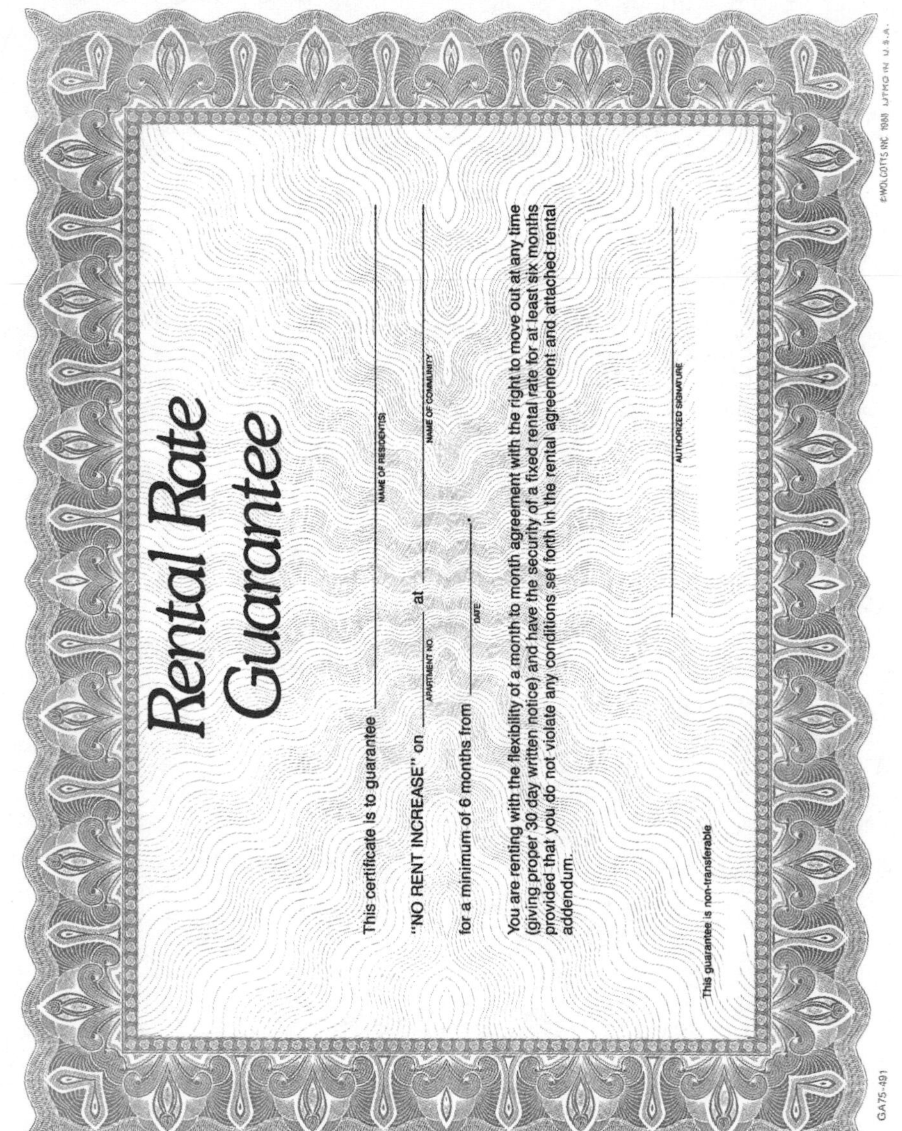

Rental Rate Guarantee

This certificate is to guarantee ______________________
NAME OF RESIDENT(S)

"NO RENT INCREASE" on ____________ at ______________________
APARTMENT NO. NAME OF COMMUNITY

for a minimum of 6 months from ____________.
DATE

You are renting with the flexibility of a month to month agreement with the right to move out at any time (giving proper 30 day written notice) and have the security of a fixed rental rate for at least six months provided that you do not violate any conditions set forth in the rental agreement and attached rental addendum.

____
AUTHORIZED SIGNATURE

This guarantee is non-transferable

GA75-491

©WOLCOTTS INC 1988 LITHO IN U.S.A.

Figure 5-1: Rental Rate Guarantee Certificate.

Chapter 6

FOR RENT: Generating Interest in Your Rental

In This Chapter

- Planning your marketing strategy
- Figuring out what role advertising plays
- Making sure you don't violate any fair-housing laws in your search for a good tenant
- Finding the methods of advertising that will work best for you

More than almost any other single item, locating and renting to good quality tenants will make your experience as a property manager enjoyable and profitable. But finding a good tenant can be a long and arduous process if you don't know how to do it well. So in this chapter, I take you through the process from beginning to end — from creating a marketing plan (which will help you narrow your focus and set goals) to writing solid ads. This is the place to start if you just found out one of your units will be vacant in a month, and it's the place to turn if you've already had a vacancy for twice that long. It's never too late to start advertising effectively, and in this chapter, I give you all the tools you need to do exactly that.

Developing a Marketing Plan

A *marketing plan* can be anything from a formal written outline of your marketing strategies to some general marketing ideas you keep in mind as you try to find renters for your property. If you only own one or two properties, or even if you own 20 or 30 rental units in multiple locations, you may not think that you need a marketing plan. Developing a marketing plan may seem like an unnecessary use of your time and energy. But the basic concepts of a marketing plan are important for *all* owners of rental property, regardless of the number of rental units they may own.

The key to success in owning and managing rental properties is to keep your rental units full with long-term paying tenants who treat your rental property and their neighbors respectfully. But first you need to determine the best way to attract and retain these highly desirable tenants. A marketing plan can help you do just that.

If you don't attract and retain tenants, you can rest assured that your competition will. And you are in competition with other owners and property managers for the best tenants, even if you only have a few rental units. In most rental markets, prospective tenants have many options, and the most responsible tenants are very selective, because the rental unit they select will be their home.

The likelihood of finding responsible renters is often a numbers game. The more prospective renters you are able to attract, the greater your opportunity to carefully evaluate their qualifications and the higher the probability that you will be able to select the most qualified applicant.

A good marketing plan consists of strategies for attracting prospective tenants as well as retaining your current tenants. The importance of retaining your current tenants is so vital to your long-term success as a rental property owner that I devote an entire chapter to it. Turn to Chapter 11 for more information.

Determining your target market

One of the first steps in developing a basic marketing plan is to determine the *target market* for your rental property. The target market consists of the most likely rental prospects who will find that your rental unit meets their needs. The target market can be relatively broad or it can be fairly narrow, depending on the location, size, and features of your rental property. If you have multiple rental properties, you may find that each property has a different target market or you may find that the target markets overlap.

Carefully evaluate your rental unit by looking at the location, size, and the specific features of the property that make it unique.

- **Location:** What are some of the benefits of your property's location? Is your rental unit located near employment, medical services, shopping, or other important neighborhood or regional facilities? Paying attention to your property's location may provide you with a target market that includes employees of certain companies or people who have a need to live in close proximity to certain local facilities.
- **Size:** Larger units tend to be more attractive to families or roommates, whereas studio units are more suitable to a single renter or a couple.

- **Amenities:** A property that allows pets and has a large yard typically appeals to pet owners and/or renters with children. If your rental property has storage space or a garage, some hobbyists may be particularly interested in what you have to offer.

When you compare the attributes of your rental property to the needs of all prospective renters in your rental market, you will probably discover that certain renters may find your rental unit meets their needs more than other renters do. You can use this knowledge to target specific audiences, but your rental efforts must never discourage, limit, or exclude *any* prospective renter from having an equal opportunity to qualify and rent from you.

Knowing what your renters stand to gain from your property

When you have established who your most likely rental prospects are, you need to shift your focus to incorporating and implementing the concept of a target market into the marketing plans for your rental property. This is when I usually think of the WIFM approach. WIFM stands for "what's in it for me," and it represents the thought process of virtually all consumers (including your potential tenants) when evaluating a purchase decision. (I discovered this important concept at the national faculty training sessions of Sander Smiles and the Institute of Real Estate Management.) The WIFM concept can be used in all business and interpersonal relationships and reminds us that, in general, people are most interested in the benefits that they personally will receive in any given relationship or business transaction.

When it comes to marketing and advertising your rental property, the important concept of WIFM can help you see the rental decision process through the eyes of your prospective tenants and makes your goal of finding long-term, stable tenants more attainable. Unfortunately, owners and managers of rental property are human and, just like most people, although they are very good at seeing the world from their own perspective, they often fail to critically evaluate the advantages and disadvantages of the product that they are selling — their rental housing unit. As a rental property owner or manager, you have a competitive advantage if you understand the opportunities and challenges presented by your particular rental property. You can also have a competitive advantage if you find ways to enhance the deficits or narrow your marketing focus to those specific types of tenants who will be attracted to your rental property.

Looking at your property through your prospective tenants' eyes

I once had a rental property located near a major university. The property had several vacancies in the 2-bedroom/1-bath units. Because I was wary of renting to large numbers of undergraduate students, my marketing plan was to attract university faculty or graduate students who I thought would have a roommate and be perfect for the 2-bedroom unit. Although many prospective tenants looked at the units, our actual rentals were very slow and our 2-bedroom vacancies remained unacceptable. Clearly, I was trying to define and force the rental market and prospective renters to adapt to my perception of their needs.

When it became obvious that my rental efforts were not having much success, I began to carefully review the comments of prospective tenants and actually listen to their needs. What I found was that there was a strong market for faculty and graduate students, but that they preferred to live alone. The WIFM from the perspective of the faculty and graduate students was the desire for a quiet place to work or study without roommates. With this new perspective on the needs of our prospective tenants, I quickly realized that I could market these very same 2-bedroom/1-bath units to this new target market.

Armed with this knowledge, I revised my marketing efforts and changed my advertising in the college newspaper to read, "1 bedroom plus den." This change led to an increased interest in the property as well as a greater occupancy percentage. Just by changing the way the units were advertised, I found that I was able to reach my original target market of faculty and graduate students who wanted to live off campus.

Remember: Look at your rental property from the perspective of the most likely tenants. Then promote and accentuate the features of your rental property that will be of greatest interest to that market.

Understanding the Importance of Good Advertising

Tenants rarely come looking for you. Your local newspaper may have a column for "Rentals Wanted" or one of your current tenants may contact you inquiring on behalf of a friend who is looking for a rental unit. But this is the exception, not the rule. The majority of your tenants will come from the efforts you make to locate qualified rental prospects for your rental unit.

Advertising is how you let people know that you have a vacant rental property available. If people don't know that you have vacant units, then they can't rent them. When it's done well, the money you spend on advertising is money extremely well spent. But when it's done poorly, advertising can be another black hole for your precious resources. Advertising is more of an art than a science at times, because what works for one particular rental property may not work for another.

Advertising rental properties is no different in many ways than all other types of advertising for which Madison Avenue spends billions on market research. The key to success in rental property advertising is determining how you can reach that very small, select group of qualified renters who will be interested in your rental property when it's available to rent.

The best way to determine the most desirable features of your rental property for your target market is to use the WIFM approach and ask your current renters what they like about where they live. You may also figure out from talking with the qualified *rental traffic* (all the people who look at your property, whether or not they agree to rent) what they found of interest in your rental property. The key is to remember that your rental property has different features that appeal to different prospective renters, but over a period of time you will be able to determine certain common factors that most prospects desire. Incorporate these selling points into your marketing and advertising efforts.

Review the information from your marketing plan about the most marketable features and attributes of your rental property and present it to rental prospects in your advertising.

Looking at the different advertising approaches: Rifle versus shotgun

Although you can creatively and effectively market and advertise your rental property in many different ways, one of the fundamental differences between the advertising methods at your disposal is the precision with which you reach your target audience and the ultimate cost involved. Advertising that is very specific and targets a narrow group of prospective renters is often described as a *rifle approach,* whereas advertising that blankets the market with information to renters and non-renters, qualified and unqualified alike, is commonly called a *shotgun approach.* In an ideal world, you would only pay for the ability to reach those limited number of qualified renters in your area who are looking for a rental property just like yours and who want it the day it is ready to rent. Of course, in the real world, this dream doesn't turn into reality, but it does give you a goal to strive for when you evaluate the different ways you can advertise.

Many methods of advertising your rental property fall into the shotgun category and very few fall into the rifle category. The major daily newspapers in most metropolitan markets can deliver very impressive numbers for their circulation. However, they can't tell you how many of those readers actually read the rental property ads or are actually looking for an apartment on the specific day your ad will run. Advertising is, for the most part, a numbers game. Reach enough readers and you are bound to find a few that will be looking for a rental property like yours on a given day.

The best rifle approaches to advertising are word-of-mouth referrals and "For Rent" signs on the property. But if you rely solely on these approaches to find tenants, you may end up with vacant properties much longer than you'd like.

Knowing which advertising approach is best for your rental property

Creating interest in your rental property used to be as simple as putting up a sign or placing an ad in the local newspaper. Although these tried-and-true methods of informing the potential renters in your area are still very successful, many other excellent options are available for you to consider. The target market for your rental property has a lot to do with which method of advertising works best for your particular rental unit.

One size rarely fits all. When it comes to advertising a rental property, you need to employ a combination of both the shotgun and the rifle approach to be successful. Clearly, both methods have advantages. Referrals and property signs often give you good exposure to renters in your local area, whereas newspaper and Internet ads have the ability to let people relocating to your area know about your rental property as well. Check out Table 6-1 for a comparison of the pros and cons of various approaches to advertising.

Table 6-1 Pros and Cons of Different Advertising Approaches

Approach	*Pros*	*Cons*
Community bulletin boards	Inexpensive	Narrow market
Direct mailings	Inexpensive	Low response rate
Flyers	Allows more details	Limited distribution
Internet	Ease of use	Uncertain effectiveness
Local employers	Qualified prospects	Narrow market
Newspaper	Widely used by prospects, broad reach	Potentially expensive
Property signs	Very effective, inexpensive	Narrow market
Rental publications	Widely used by prospects	Expensive for small properties
Word of mouth	High credibility, inexpensive	Narrow market

Getting your property to rent itself

The best advertisement for your rental unit is the curb appeal or exterior appearance of the property. The *curb appeal* is the impression created when the building is first seen from the street. The importance of a good first impression is well documented in business and clearly applies in rental housing as well. Properties that have well kept grounds with green grass, trimmed shrubs, beautiful flowers, and fresh paint are much more appealing to your rental prospects than a property that looks as though it has seen better days.

Curb appeal can be positive or negative. Positive curb appeal can be generated by having litter-free grounds, well-manicured landscaping and lawns, building surfaces that are well-maintained, a clearly identifiable address, and clean windows. All property amenities (such as the swimming pool and parking lots) should also be clean and well maintained.

Properties with negative curb appeal can be rented, but finding a tenant often takes much longer. You may have fewer qualified prospects to choose from or you may have to lower the rent. Because time is money in the rental housing business, the lost revenue caused by poor or negative curb appeal is often much greater than the cost to repair or replace the deficient items. Besides, a well-maintained and sharp-looking property often attracts the type of tenant who will treat your rental property with care and respect and pay a higher rent.

Curb appeal is also important to retaining your current tenants. One of the most common complaints of tenants and a major reason for tenants to move is the failure of the owner or property manager to properly maintain the rental unit. If the tenants are frustrated with the property appearance or if they get the runaround when they need things repaired, the tenants have little reason to remain unless the rent is significantly below market value. Poor curb appeal is the direct result of poor management. There is no excuse for poor curb appeal, and there are no benefits to anyone involved, because the lost revenue is never regained and the property value ultimately declines.

Even the best advertising campaign in the world cannot overcome a poor physical appearance. Making sure your property looks good on the outside as well as the inside significantly improves your chances of finding just the right tenants.

Before you spend money on advertising, take another look at your property with a critical eye or ask someone you know to critique the property. You probably have a relative or friend who has a sharp eye for finding those little details that aren't quite right. So put those people to work helping you identify and then correct those nagging items that will detract from your rental unit.

You don't need to be a Madison Avenue advertising executive to generate interest in your rental unit, but often property managers forget about many of the simple ways they can promote the availability of a rental unit. Although an ad in the local newspaper can be effective, you can generate rental traffic in many other ways as well. I cover some of these later in this chapter.

Being Aware of Fair-Housing Laws in Advertising

Whether you are the owner of a single rental unit or a small- to medium-size multiple unit rental property, when you advertise, you are subject to fair-housing laws. All rental property owners are required to comply with federal (and often state and even local fair) housing laws. You need to know the laws for your area and make sure that you don't violate them, even inadvertently. Check with local tenant/landlord legal experts, your local apartment association, or the National Apartment Association (NAA) for more information about fair-housing laws in your area. To contact the National Apartment Association, write to 201 North Union Street, Suite 200, Alexandria, VA 22314 or call 703-518-6141. You can also visit the NAA online at www.naahq.org. You can locate the NAA-Affiliated Local Association in your area by looking in your Yellow Pages or by visiting the NAA Web site.

The federal fair-housing laws apply throughout the entire country and override state and local laws unless the state or local laws provide more protection of individual rights. Thus, at a minimum, as a rental property owner, the 1988 Federal Fair Housing Act states that you cannot refuse to show a rental unit or rent to someone because of their

- Race
- Color
- National origin or ancestry
- Religion
- Sex
- Familial status
- Physical disability

Any discrimination in rental housing advertising is illegal and can result in very severe penalties.

The 1988 Federal Fair Housing Act also states that the above criteria cannot be used to

- Refuse to rent housing
- Refuse to negotiate for housing

- Make housing unavailable
- Deny a dwelling unit
- Set different terms, conditions, or privileges for rental of a dwelling
- Provide different housing services or facilities
- Falsely deny that housing is available for inspection or rental
- Persuade owners to rent or deny anyone access to or membership in a facility or service related to the rental of housing

If you have a "no pets" policy, keep in mind that the federal Americans with Disabilities Act (ADA) provides that rental property owners cannot have any limitations or discourage occupancy by tenants who have a medically prescribed *companion animal.* This act includes but extends well beyond allowing a visually impaired tenant to have a guide dog. Companion animals can be medically approved for many other physical and/or psychological conditions, and the only requirement is that the tenant must have a written note or prescription from a licensed medical care provider.

If your prospective tenant has a physical or mental disability that substantially limits one or more major life activities or has a record of having such a disability, you must allow the prospective tenant to make reasonable modifications to your rental property, including common areas, if necessary for the prospective tenant to use the rental housing. The law currently defines *physical* or *mental disability* to include mobility, hearing, and visual impairments; chronic mental illness; chronic alcoholism; AIDS or AIDS-related complex; or mental retardation. Many state and local laws are expanding the definition of the protected categories, so be sure to check with legal counsel if you ever have any questions regarding the rights of your tenants under the federal or state fair-housing laws.

Federal fair-housing laws prohibit advertising that indicates any preference, limitation, or discrimination based upon race, color, national origin or ancestry, religion, sex, physical disability, or familial status. If you have any questions, the Department of Housing and Urban Development (HUD) offers free information through their Fair Housing Information Clearinghouse. Contact HUD at 800-343-3442 for brochures that explain the law in detail. You can also find information online at `www.hud.gov`.

Compliance with the federal, state, and local fair-housing laws is critical for all owners of rental property and is discussed in more detail in Chapter 8. Fair housing begins with advertising to all qualified prospects, continues throughout the screening and tenant selection process, and remains a key issue throughout the entire tenancy. If you plan to be in the rental housing business, you need to make sure that all of your advertising, tenant screening, and selection and management policies reflect the intent as well as the letter of the law. Also, be aware that these laws are constantly being redefined and expanded. Ignorance is not an acceptable excuse if you are challenged for your policies.

Whenever you have the space available in your rental advertising, be sure to include the Equal Housing Opportunity logo. This logo may not be an option in certain ads, such as newspaper classifieds, but it should be included in all other advertising, such as flyers, brochures, community bulletin boards, direct mail, and the Internet. You can download the logo for free at the Housing and Urban Development (HUD) Web site. Just go to `www.hud.gov/fheologo.html`.

Looking at Your Advertising Options

When it comes to advertising, you need to think like a tenant. Most rental property owners have been a renter at some point in time. You may have personal experience yourself as a renter looking for the right place to live. You may have found the experience very frustrating, or maybe you developed a successful system for finding quality rental properties at a fair price in your area. Your experience as a renter can be helpful as you place your current ads.

Many rental property owners may remember that, when they began looking for their own rental years ago, they either drove around the area or looked for advertising that was specific to a particular geographic location. That strategy still holds true, because tenants typically look for a unit in a specific location and will try to find property signs, flyers, and local newspaper rental ads that cover just their area of interest.

Most renters dislike moving and although moving is enough of a disruption in your daily routine, adapting to a completely different neighborhood is even worse. Thus, the majority of renters relocate within the same geographic area, unless they're faced with a major change in employment or school or another significant factor that requires a distant relocation.

The following sections outline the different ways you have to reach your prospective tenants, everything from word-of-mouth to the Internet. Use more than one form of advertising, and you'll find a new tenant quicker.

Word of mouth

Often the best source of new tenants is a referral from one of the neighbors near your rental property, one of your other tenants, or possibly even the tenant who has just vacated your rental unit. Many times, referrals also come from coworkers or friends. Word of mouth is often your most effective and least expensive method of finding new tenants, especially if people like your rental property or like where it's located.

In the long run, your best source for new tenant leads is other satisfied tenants.

Many of your tenants or other people who own or rent in the area may have a family member or friend who is looking to relocate or move into the area as well. Creating a sense of community in which your tenants have friends in the immediate area can lead to longer tenancies and lower tenant turnover. This translates directly into improved cash flow for you.

You need to have any rental applicant referred by word of mouth go through the same tenant application and thorough background check as any other applicant does.

Although most of your tenants or neighbors are glad to voluntarily make referrals, you should also consider offering a referral fee, something that makes it worth their time and effort. Typically, referral fees are $50 to $100 and are only paid after the new tenant has paid the full security deposit and the first month's rent and has actually taken occupancy. In a soft rental market, some owners and property managers may even offer referral fees of up to 50 percent of the first month's rent. The market conditions in your area will dictate the appropriate level of referral fee for your rental property. You can also offer a higher amount for multiple referrals.

As with all policies, be sure to offer your referral fees consistently and equally to all tenants to avoid any fair-housing concerns.

Some property managers or owners will give half of the referral fee up front and the other half after the new tenant has lived in the unit for a specified number of months, in order to ensure that the tenant will stay long-term. In my experience, however, the referral fee is more effective if the full amount is paid immediately upon the new tenant taking occupancy. Although on some occasions the referred tenants do not stay for more than a month, this situation is usually nothing that the referring tenant can control, so the referring tenant should not be penalized.

The psychological impact of giving an immediate reward for a referral can be very motivating. You can also adjust the amount of the referral fee for certain rental units that may be more difficult to rent or for certain seasonal times of the year when you have more trouble renting vacancies. For example, if you normally offer a $50 referral fee, you may want to consider offering a $100 fee for any referral given between Thanksgiving and the middle of January, because this time of year is often very slow for rental traffic. (No one likes to move during the holidays or in inclement weather!)

You don't have to pay referral fees in cash. In some states, cash payments may even be illegal unless the referring tenant has a real estate license. In these cases, or if the referral comes from one of your existing tenants, you can offer your tenant a rent credit to be deducted from future rent. (Of course, a rent credit should only be offered to referring tenants who are current on their rent.)

Always screen every referral carefully, but be particularly careful if the referring tenant has a poor payment history or has created other problems. Just as a referral from an excellent tenant often leads to another excellent tenant, a referral from a problem tenant often leads to another problem tenant.

When cash or a rent credit is inappropriate, another option is to offer improvements or upgrades to the tenant's rental unit — maybe installing a new ceiling fan, hanging new wallpaper, cleaning the carpet, or repainting the unit, for example. Certain types of improvements may have a long life, and they will stay with the rental unit after the current tenant leaves, which will make your rental unit more marketable and justify a higher rental rate to a future tenant.

Regardless of the kind of reward you give to referring tenants, the key is to make the tenant feel appreciated for his referral.

Property signs

A property sign is the first step in most rental property advertising programs, because it is one of the most economical ways to promote your vacancies. The use of a simple "For Rent" sign can be very effective and generate great results for only a minimal cost. In certain areas with only limited availability of rental units, a sign on the property is all that you need to generate multiple qualified rental applicants.

Unless your property curb appeal is poor or signs are not allowed, you should immediately put up a property sign when you find out that you will have an upcoming vacancy.

An advantage of the property sign is that callers already know the area and have seen the exterior of the building. The attractiveness and aesthetic qualities or curb appeal of a rental property are essential. The rental property must look good from the street, or rental prospects won't even bother to stop and see the interior of the property.

Use rental signs that are in perfect condition, with large, crisp lettering that is easy to read. The condition of the sign reflects the image of your rental property — whether good or bad. A well-maintained sign provides a good first impression. A faded, worn out, or tacky sign is worse than no sign at all.

Qualified rental traffic is the name of the game

Unqualified applicants can be a major waste of time. You only want qualified rental traffic. Sure, there are always going to be some prospective renters who are not financially qualified or who have a poor rental history. But if you are receiving multiple unqualified prospects from a certain source of advertising, reevaluate either the method of advertising or the message in your ad.

Answering phone calls and showing your rental property are two of the most time-consuming areas of property management. These areas are also two of the most critical for determining your success in the long run. The last thing you need is for unqualified prospects to call and ask numerous questions or even arrange for a personalized showing of the rental property, only to find out that they do not meet your requirements to qualify. In Chapter 7, I cover techniques for using the initial telephone call to determine whether the potential rental applicant is qualified.

A disadvantage of signs is that they announce to the world that you have a vacant rental unit. In some areas, this can lead to vandalism or even people who may want to break into your vacant unit and use it for parties or criminal activity. For this reason, many rental property owners utilize the rental sign while the rental unit is still occupied by the outgoing tenant and then remove the sign when the unit has been vacated. Depending on your tenants and their level of cooperation, you may also want to indicate on the sign that the current tenant should not be disturbed.

Often the current tenant will be very cooperative and will be glad to show the rental unit. But be sure to consider whether the current tenant is your best representative. Obviously, if the current tenant is leaving under difficult circumstances or their housekeeping or demeanor is not the best, then you may be better off waiting and showing the rental unit after the tenant has vacated the rental unit.

To minimize the chances of vandalism when the rental unit is vacant, you can indicate on the property sign that the unit is occupied and include a statement such as, "Please do not disturb the occupant." Although not a guarantee, this simple statement may deter the amateur criminal element who don't want to take the chance of running into any residents.

Make sure that the sign is clearly visible from the street and that the lettering is large enough to read. The two-sided sign should ideally be placed perpendicular to the street so that it is easier for passing vehicles to view the sign. The sign does not need to include too many details about the unit, but the phone number and the date of availability should be very clear. You can also add the number of bedrooms and bathrooms, as well as any special features. Don't get carried away or put so much information on the sign that it cannot easily be read from the street.

Drive by your property from both directions at the usual speed of traffic and make sure that the sign can be seen and understood easily. The main objective is to get the driver's attention with the words "For Rent" or a similar basic message. The driver should pull over and stop to write down the details and the phone number.

Generally, I recommend clearly indicating the rental rate on the property sign, because you need to make sure that the prospective tenants know what to expect. Including the rental rate can even prescreen tenants who are not financially qualified.

However, when the exterior of the property does not do justice to the actual rental unit itself, you're better off *not* including the rental rate on your property sign. Because you will typically not be there to actually show the rental unit at the time the prospective tenant sees the sign, the prospective tenant may think that the rent is either too high or too low and immediately decide not to call. The value of some rental units cannot be appreciated until the prospect has seen the interior of the unit.

Property signs don't work as well if your rental unit is not on a busy street or your property sign is not clearly visible from a main road. Property signs on dead-end streets or cul-de-sacs are still worthwhile, but don't expect the kind of response you would get if your property were on a major thoroughfare or arterial roadway.

If your property is on a side street that is relatively close to a major road, you may also be able to obtain the cooperation of an owner of a nearby property that has a high-visibility location. Approach the owners about the possibility of placing a rental sign for your property on their land — either on a temporary basis only when you have vacancies or on a more formal ongoing basis (with a formal contract drafted by an attorney, outlining the rights and terms and a financial incentive for the owner). Typically, you can expect to pay the landowners from $25 to $100 per month to put your sign on their property, depending on the size and location of the sign.

Any off-site rental sign should clearly indicate the location of your rental property. Make sure that the property where you locate your sign is comparable to your rental property in terms of curb appeal. A property that is vastly superior to your rental property can actually deter potential renters. Naturally, a property that has poor curb appeal will discourage prospective renters from any further inquiry into your rental property, even if your property is in much better condition. As with all signs, first impressions are very important and leave a lasting image in the minds of your prospective renters.

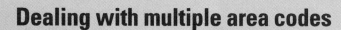

Dealing with multiple area codes

A relatively new challenge faced by many rental property owners in urban areas is the growing proliferation of telephone area codes. Nowadays, every major metropolitan city has at least two or three area codes, and new area codes are being introduced every month.

In some large cities, many rental property owners may find that their rental property is in one area code, their business office is in another area code, and their home is in yet a third area code. This means that when you advertise, your prospective tenants may have to dial a number in a different area code just to reach you and respond to your ad. The telephone companies all claim that long-distance charges are based strictly on the distance of the call and not on the fact that the call is to a different area code. However, many people are skeptical of that claim, and I find that many rental prospects are reluctant to call another area code when inquiring about rentals. They don't want to pay for long-distance or toll calls if they can find another rental property that has a phone number in their same area code. Further, the reality of advertising is that many of your prospects will actually look for reasons *not* to call you, and having a phone number that may be a long-distance call is an easy excuse for some prospective tenants.

One way to address this concern is through the use of an 800 number (or one of the newer toll-free prefixes such as 888 or 877). Most rental prospects immediately recognize a phone number that begins with one of these prefixes as a toll-free call. Having a toll-free phone number can be very helpful when your rental property is located in an area that has multiple area codes.

Toll-free numbers can be established for a specific geographic area. For example, if you have rental properties that are all located within one area, you can set up your toll-free phone number to work only within that area plus any adjacent areas you designate. If you find that many of your rental prospects are transferring to your area from another geographic region, you can expand your toll-free coverage so that you can advertise your toll-free number there as well.

The costs of having a toll-free number can be quite reasonable, with a one-time setup fee and low usage charges. Check with your local telephone service provider as well as the major national phone companies.

Newspapers

The most commonly used medium for advertising rental properties is the newspaper classified ads. These ads can be very effective if you follow some basic rules of advertising:

- Attract the reader's attention.
- Keep the reader's interest.
- Generate a desire to learn more about your property.
- Convince the reader to contact you for more information.

Important considerations when using newspaper advertising include which newspaper to advertise in, the size of your newspaper ad, what to include in the newspaper ad, and how often or on which days the newspaper ad should run. I cover each of these issues in the following sections.

Which newspaper should you advertise in?

In most metropolitan areas, you have several newspapers to choose from for advertising the availability of your rental unit. Typically, you have one major regional newspaper and often one or more neighborhood newspapers as well. Local or neighborhood newspapers are often more reasonably priced and can reach the renters already in the area. Some local or neighborhood newspapers even offer free ads.

So do you advertise in the local weekly throwaway or the regional major daily? Unfortunately, there is no right answer to this question. You need to try each newspaper and see which one works best for a particular rental property.

Often, the local shopper-type newspapers will allow low-cost or even free ads. You may think you can't go wrong with a free ad. But when your phone begins ringing off the hook and none of the callers are qualified, you pay for that ad again and again with your most precious resource: your time. Dealing with unqualified prospective renters can be very time-consuming and frustrating.

Although many newspaper sales representatives proudly speak of their total circulation or readership, the only number that matters to you is the number of qualified prospective renters that see your ad for your rental property. For example, the *Los Angeles Times* Sunday edition circulation is the largest in the country, with well over 1 million readers. Although the potential of 1 million people reading your rental ad may sound enticing and the cost per reader is miniscule, the actual number of qualified renters for your single-family rental property will be measured in dozens.

Evaluate the cost-efficiency of most major metropolitan newspapers by comparing the cost of the ad with the best estimate of the actual number of readers of your specific ad. If the cost per qualified prospect is reasonable, then you may be wise to use the major daily newspaper.

Keep your advertising costs under control, but don't overlook the fact that each day that your rental property sits vacant is another day of lost income that you will never see. Just as the airlines lose money for every vacant seat on the plane at departure, you can end up being penny-wise and pound foolish with your advertising, particularly if your best advertising source is the Sunday newspaper and you need to wait until the following week to place another ad. In that week, you may have lost several hundred dollars (or many times the cost of the ad).

The key to effective advertising is not the overall number of calls that you receive but the number of qualified renters per dollar you spend on advertising. Typically, advertising that costs $20 to $50 per qualified prospect is an effective ad in most major metropolitan areas. So if your Sunday newspaper ad costs $100, you should expect to receive inquiries from two to five qualified prospects every time the ad runs. Of course, you will receive additional inquiries from unqualified prospects, but you can also measure the effectiveness of your ad by noting how *few* unqualified prospects call in response to your ad.

How big should your newspaper ad be?

Newspapers typically offer two different types of rental housing ads: display and classified. Display ads are much more effective and visually eye-catching. However, they are significantly more expensive and beyond the needs and budgets of most small-time rental property owners. Typically, only the owners or property managers of large apartment buildings in your area will use display ads on a regular basis. And most of these advertisers will also use classified ads to augment or supplement the display ads, particularly on the days when their display ad is not running.

Newspapers are in the business of selling space, and large classified ads cost more than smaller ads. The good news is that the larger ads are not always more effective. A large classified ad that fails to attract the reader's attention and keep their interest is a complete waste of money.

Owners or property management companies with multiple properties in a certain geographic area also use display ads, because they are able to combine several of their rental properties into one large display ad, making the ad more cost-effective. If you are a small rental property owner, unless you have multiple properties with vacancies in the same general geographic area, use the classified rental housing advertising section of your newspaper.

The trick is to develop a classified rental ad that is efficient but does not place a higher priority on low cost while sacrificing the ability to attract and keep the attention of the prospective renter. Your rental ad needs to be easily read by the prospect. One of the best ways to make your ad readable is through the use of *white space* in the ad. White space is the blank space that makes your ad stand out from the others, many of which are so crammed with information that readers instinctively skip them.

You will be lucky if a prospective renter spends more than just a few seconds looking at your rental ad. If you cannot attract and keep the attention of the prospect in those brief seconds, they will move on to the next ad. So when it comes to writing your ad, you want to provide as much information as possible, while also keeping the ad readable. But know that the overall size of the ad needs to be kept to a minimum, or you risk a major shock to your advertising budget.

Most renters actually prefer to rent from small-time rental property owners, which is why classified ads can be very effective. Classified ads need to be directed to a specific target market and should stress the particular advantages of a rental property from the tenant's point of view.

What should you include in your newspaper ad?

An effective newspaper ad (like the ones shown in Figure 6-1) provides the basic facts, plus a *hook,* which is a call to action that will help your rental ad to stand out from the rest:

- **The basics:** Every ad should include the following basic information:
    - **General geographic location of the unit:** The most important aspect of promoting your rental unit is to identify the location. Most newspapers sort their rental ads by location, and if your ad isn't listed properly, then all of the rental prospects who want to live in your area will miss your ad. Some newspapers automatically put your ad in a certain geographical area based on the rental property address. In many cities, the name of your neighborhood makes an immediate impression on your prospect. This impression can be very positive or very negative, depending upon the reputation of the particular neighborhood. So if the address would give a negative impression, leave it out.
    - **Number of bedrooms and bathrooms**
    - **Major features or amenities**
    - **Monthly rent:** The monthly rent should be provided in most circumstances, because it lets the prospective renters know your requirements right up front. Most prospective renters are scanning through the newspaper rental ads just trying to eliminate the ads that are not worthy of their time to call. Generally, any ad that does not give the prospective renter enough information to determine their level of interest will be immediately disqualified.
    - **Telephone number where you can be reached**
    - **Who pays the utilities**
    - **Whether the unit is furnished**
    - **Address of the property, unless the rental unit does not have excellent curb appeal (see the nearby sidebar for more information)**
- **The hook:** The hook can be monetary or it can be an improvement to the rental property — anything that will make your ad really grab the prospect's attention. For example, offering the tenant the opportunity to select new tile floor covering in the kitchen or entryway or providing a ceiling fan as an extra bonus are both excellent hooks.

Even in tight rental markets, providing an incentive for the prospect to immediately call on your ad is smart. For example, you could offer to waive the fee for the tenant's credit report if the prospective renter calls the day the ad runs. The credit report typically costs you less than $20, but this kind of offer makes your ad much more interesting to most cost-conscious renters.

#1 Rated Schools!

Hidden Valley executive home. 4 bedrooms, 3 baths, 2250 sq. ft., 3-car garage pool/spa, fenced yard, lush landscaping, a/c, washer/dryer, f/p, gardener incl, pets welcome. $1,995/mo. Avail. 7/1. 423 Sycamore Lane. 555-1212

Cherry Hills Close to Everything

Lg. 1 & 2 BR townhouse apts, on bus route. Walk to schools, stores, medical center. Tennis, pool, spa, no pets. Owner-paid utilities. Furnished units avail. From $575. Maple Grove Apts. 575 Watson Rd. Mention ad for free credit check. Daily 9-6. Call (800) 555-1212

Figure 6-1: Good newspaper ads like these can help you find the right tenant quickly.

If you are in a soft rental market with many of your competitors offering significant rental concessions, you may need to match or even exceed the market. This is when using the upgrades to your rental unit as an incentive comes in handy. Besides providing new floor tile or ceiling fans, common upgrades rental property owners can offer include upgraded kitchen counters or bathroom light and plumbing fixtures. You can also offer new appliances, new or upgraded window coverings, or security screen doors. For rental properties in which the tenants are responsible for yard maintenance, the installation of an outdoor sprinkling system can be a beneficial upgrade for both the new tenant and the owner concerned about absent-minded tenants who may forget to properly water the lawn.

Prospective renters who are looking for the absolute lowest rent or are planning to take advantage of "free rent" and then move along will not be interested in rental unit upgrades. The tenant who is aware of the competitiveness of the rental market and wants to be treated fairly will often appreciate the upgrades even more than the quick cash. Plus, you are making improvements to your own rental unit and these upgrades will make the rental unit more desirable now and for future renters as well.

In addition to the basic information and the hook, be sure to include in your ad every detail that your prospective tenant will want to know. Remember the concept of WIFM (what's in it for me) and be sure to include the features of your rental property from the point of view of the prospective tenant.

Although leaving out some information will save you money in the cost of the classified ad, don't forget that incomplete information will either lead to qualified prospects skipping over your ad or may lead many unqualified prospects to call and ask you every question under the sun.

Be careful with abbreviations in newspaper ads. Although abbreviating some words can stretch your advertising dollar without cutting into your message, the use of abbreviations often discourages tenants from reading your ad. If your ad cannot be understood, it won't generate the phone call you want. And if your ad does not generate phone calls, you've wasted your time and money.

I recommend using only basic abbreviations, and then only if most rental property advertisers in your area commonly use them. Although you can ask your newspaper classified advertising representative, I strongly recommend that you determine which abbreviations are commonly used in your area by reviewing the rental housing ad section yourself. When in doubt, don't use abbreviations. Some common abbreviations used in newspaper ads are listed in Table 6-2.

Table 6-2 Common Newspaper Ad Abbreviations

Abbreviation	*Translation*
a/c	air conditioning
apt	apartment
ba	bathroom
BR, bd, or bdrm	bedroom
d/w	dishwasher
frplc or f/p	fireplace
gar	garage
incl	included
ldry	laundry
lg	large
nr	near
rm	room
sm	small
twnhs	townhouse
w/d	washer/dryer

Considering whether to include the address in your ad

Although there are differences of opinion regarding including a property's address in a newspaper ad, I generally recommend including the address of the rental unit. Including the address allows the prospect to know the exact location and independently determine whether the property is one they are interested in renting. The only situations in which you shouldn't indicate the address in the newspaper ad is when the curb appeal is not yet up to your high standards or when the exterior appearance of the rental unit is deceptive and gives the impression that the unit is small or undesirable in light of the asking rent.

If you include the address in your ad and it is not an easy rental property to locate, you may want to consider including some additional information such as the major cross-streets or a well-known landmark near the rental property. Sometimes including specific directions to assist the prospective renter in locating the property can even be worthwhile. Of course, you also need to consider the potentially significant cost of running additional lines in your ad.

If you do include your address and directions, make sure the directions are correct and easily understood. Ask someone who is not familiar with your rental property or the area to proofread your ad to make sure that the landmarks, cross streets, or directions provided make sense. If the rental prospects can't find your property, you can safely assume that they are not going to be interested in renting there.

This first impression can be very important. Although there may be a more direct route to your rental property that goes past the local landfill, have your prospects take the next freeway off-ramp and backtrack somewhat to your property so they avoid any unpleasant areas of town. The advertising and presentation of your rental property is marketing, and when it's done properly, it will make your job as a rental property owner much easier.

Some newspapers even provide a key of the common abbreviations and print this index right in the rental housing advertising section. This key can be very helpful to the prospective tenants. But remember that you want to attract and keep the attention of the prospect. And one of the best ways to do this is to make your ad one of the easiest to read and provide the most information. If rental prospects are looking to solve a puzzle, they will typically be more interested in the newspaper crossword than trying to decipher the abbreviations commonly found in many rental housing classified ads.

How often or on which days should your newspaper ad run?

Although the Saturday or Sunday editions of many major metropolitan newspapers have the most rental ads, running your ad on these days can be quite expensive. The newspapers often have specials that encourage you to run the ad for longer periods of time, which in turn gives you more exposure.

Check with your newspaper to see if they offer any discounted rates for running consecutive days. Also, if you have many rental properties, look into advertising contracts where you agree to run a minimum number of ad lines over a given period of time at often greatly reduced rates compared to the single insertion ad rate.

Be sure to change your ad at least weekly. Tenants often look for several weeks when they are just beginning to look for a new rental unit. If they see the same ad for more than a week, they could assume that your rental unit is undesirable.

Run a larger ad on the primary rental housing advertising day, and then run a reference ad the balance of the week. For example, if the Sunday edition of your local newspaper is the primary day for rental housing ads, place a large ad on that day. Then on Monday through Saturday, run a small, two-line ad that simply states "Kensington — 2bd/2ba available soon. See last Sunday's ad."

When your ad first appears, be sure to check the newspaper personally to see that it is listed in the proper classification and is worded exactly the way you wrote it. The newspaper ad representatives are very skilled at taking down complicated ads with abbreviations, but mistakes can and do occur. There is nothing worse than not receiving any phone calls because your ad was placed in the wrong classification or because the phone number was listed incorrectly.

Checking your ad for accuracy may be relatively simple if you regularly subscribe to the newspaper. However, if you do not subscribe to the newspaper, be sure to have your newspaper ad sales representative send you a *tear sheet* with a copy of your ad. If the newspaper makes a mistake in your ad, be sure to notify the paper at once, and they will run the corrected ad at no charge. Some newspapers even offer special ads that offer guaranteed results. For example, if your rental property doesn't rent after the ad has run for a week, the newspaper will give you up to an additional week for free. Also, check with your newspaper sales representative for special sections that are run featuring rental housing articles and news features. These special sections are written with the tenants in mind and can increase your ad visibility to prospective tenants.

If your rental unit is located near a military installation, be sure to run an ad in a military newspaper. The military also has housing referral offices at many bases and requires transferees to register with the housing referral office. Contact the housing referral office to let them know about your vacancy.

Flyers

Distributing and posting flyers informs the neighbors that you have a rental unit available, which can be helpful to them because they may know someone who would like to live close by.

You can also distribute flyers to local employers who often have housing referral offices or employee bulletin boards. Your local military installations and educational institutions also often will allow flyers to be posted in the housing referral office.

The cost to reproduce flyers is very nominal and can run about $5 for 100 black-and-white flyers on white paper stock. For an extra $5, consider printing your black-and-white flyer on colored paper. If you really want to stand out, you'll need to pay $25 for 100 color flyers. The extra money is well worth it. Although keeping your costs low is always important for rental property owners, remember that you may be losing $20 to $40 each day that your rental property sits vacant — and that is money you will never get back again! So if you have a rental property that looks great with a four-color flyer, spend the extra $20 and generate those important rental leads today!

You can use flyers to direct people to more information (including maps and additional photographs) on a Web site. See the "Internet" section later for more information on using the Internet to advertise your rental property.

High-tech flyers

Another advantage of flyers is that they allow you a lot more space in which to describe your rental unit. You can go into detail and list many of the features that you couldn't afford to list in a newspaper ad.

With the wide availability of word processing programs, making great-looking rental flyers that contain all of the pertinent information, plus even a photo and a map, is very easy. Although the widely used word processing programs have everything you would need to make basic flyers, I highly recommend that rental property owners invest in a basic desktop publishing software. Several great desktop publishing programs are available, but three of the easiest to use are Microsoft Publisher, PrintMaster Gold, and Broderbund's PrintShop. These programs have templates that simplify the process and can provide you with the graphics and additional features to make your flyer really look sharp.

Another invaluable tool for all rental property owners is a digital camera. A digital camera helps you prepare advertising that works! There is nothing like a photo to separate your rental property flyer from the others that may be circulating at any given time. Check out Figure 6-2 for a great example of a flyer that effectively uses photographs to draw attention to the property.

Some people think that a handwritten flyer actually has greater appeal and implies that the owner is a nonprofessional who has a rental unit at a below-market rental rate. Although this may be true, I believe that the benefits of having a sharp, easy-to-read, typeset flyer with a high-quality photo and detailed map provides superior results.

Executive Home for Rent

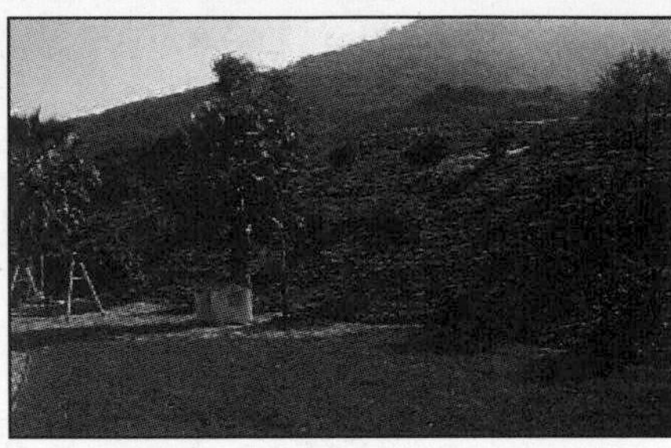

The top-rated Horizon school district and plenty of room! 4-bedroom, 3-bath executive home with over 2,250 square feet of living space and a 3-car garage. Master bedroom suite has over 500 square feet and large walk-in closet. Other bedrooms are oversized with large closets. Plus, a large home office with shelves. Large fenced backyard is perfect for children and pets. Pets are welcome! Separate fenced pool and spa. Lush, mature landscaping, air conditioning, full-size washer and dryer included. Fireplace in family room, formal dining room with bay window, upgraded appliances. Side-by-side refrigerator, double oven, range top, dishwasher, disposal, trash compactor, shutters, intercom, and CD stereo system throughout home, built-in bookcases and lots of storage. Available on 7/1. 423 Sycamore. $1,995 per month. First month's rent plus $2,000 security deposit will move you in!

Call 555-1212 today and mention this flyer for a free credit check.

Figure 6-2: Flyers are a great way to attract attention to your property, giving you the space to highlight the extra details you may not have room for in a small newspaper ad.

Although your goal is to rent your property quickly, the reality is that you'll be marketing your rental unit over a couple of weeks. This is particularly true if you are able to start your marketing during the current tenant's notice period. One of the problems with flyers (just like political placards) is that it is difficult to know which ones are current and which ones are stale. I recommend that you put a date on your flyers and keep them fresh. You should also consider having a series of flyers with a different look, each promoting a different open house. Include the monthly rent on your flyers so prospective renters can immediately determine if your rental property is in their price range.

Flyer distribution

The key to success when it comes to flyers is distribution. Either distribute the flyers personally or consider hiring a reliable individual to distribute flyers door-to-door in the area where your rental unit is located. You can also have the flyers distributed to locations that current and prospective renters are likely to visit. Make sure that your flyers are never placed into the official U.S. mail receptacle, because this is illegal. If you are considering direct mail distribution of your flyer, you should contact a firm that specializes in direct mail services.

Although it is often suggested that renters are looking for a new rental in the last two weeks of the month, I find that in most rental markets there are always renters on the market throughout the entire month. Begin distributing your flyers as soon as you can. Each week, distribute the latest version with the current information and dates so that they are fresh.

Flyers can be targeted to a specific geographic area and can be very effective in reaching good rental prospects. Because they are most often distributed in the area near the rental property, the flyers are effective; renters looking to relocate already live in the local area and want to stay close by or know someone who would also be interested in living in the area. Flyers, like all forms of advertising, are only as good as their distribution, so be sure to distribute the flyers to the high-traffic areas where renters are most likely to see them.

Rental publications

Most major metropolitan areas have one or more rental publications that offer display advertising of rental properties. The most widely circulated rental publications are *For Rent* and *Apartment Guide* (both of which also have a major presence on the Internet, as outlined in the following section). There are also several regional and local rental publications available.

For Rent offers biweekly rental advertising for most major cities in approximately 30 states. Its page format is larger than *Apartment Guide* and it offers ¼-, ½-, and full-page ads; the ads are generally listed by geographic area. The *For Rent* ads are available in four-color or black-and-white, and it also has a handy index that allows prospective tenants to search for certain features. They promote the fact that their biweekly format allows owners and property managers to change the ad content more often.

Apartment Guide is available monthly with over 80 editions for the major metropolitan areas throughout 36 states. Its page format is smaller than *For Rent* and it says that its size is an advantage, because it's easier for rental prospects to carry and use. *Apartment Guide* offers ½- and full-page ads, and it also categorizes the ads in sections that relate to a certain geographic section of a metropolitan area.

The rental publications are primarily designed for the larger rental housing communities and are a cornerstone of their marketing programs. Each of the rental publications offers smaller display ads that are designed for the medium-size rental property. However, unless your rental property has several vacancies at the same time, using a rental publication may not be cost-effective.

The key to success with all advertising is distribution. The rental publications demonstrate this clearly as they battle for positioning on the shelves of major grocery stores and convenience store chains. They race to get the best locations for their curbside racks and make sure that all the major employers and military have a good supply of their latest issue. In certain markets, the rental publications are a dominant source of rental traffic.

If you're thinking about using a rental publication, you need to take the time to determine which one has the best distribution in your area for your target market. For example, you may have determined that the local hospital and medical services facilities just a few blocks from your rental property are potentially a great source for rental prospects. If you find that only one rental publication is distributed on-site to employees, you should start evaluating the publication to see if it can offer you advertising that meets you needs and is within your advertising budget.

Internet

As more and more people have access to the Internet, this medium will be more useful as a source of prospective tenants even for owners of small rental properties. Currently, for small rental property owners, the Internet isn't a good alternative to the more conventional advertising methods discussed throughout this chapter. The problem for the small rental property owner is that the prospective tenants are unlikely to find your specific ad on the Internet, because the Internet is so vast and contains so much information that it is virtually impossible to search for rental ads in specific neighborhoods.

One of the reasons for the difficulty in sifting through the numerous ads is the minimal barriers of entry and low cost of placing information on your rental property on the Internet. Although the likelihood of someone actually finding your specific rental property on the Internet may be minimal unless you utilize the services of a major Internet rental property marketing firm, the Internet still has tremendous potential to assist the small rental property owner.

It seems that everywhere we turn lately the Internet and Internet-based companies are there. And the dot-coms have found property managers. Many of the rental publications are now offering online versions. Although the potential is tremendous, the Internet-based rental publications are still not very cost-effective for many owners of very small rental properties at this time.

Several firms offer owners and property managers assistance in advertising their rental units on the Internet. Here are some of the more popular and successful online advertising venues:

- ***Apartment Guide:*** `www.apartmentguide.com`
- ***For Rent:*** `www.aptsforrent.com`
- **Rentals.com:** `www.rentals.com`
- **SpringStreet.com:** `www.springstreet.com`

Although the online advertising medium is primarily for the major firms, there is one way that the Internet can be invaluable to owners and managers of small to medium rental properties or even a single-family rental home or condo. If you have developed flyers or brochures, you can easily post these marketing pieces online. You can then put the Web page address (or *URL*) right in your rental property advertising and allow prospective renters to gain additional information at their convenience. When a prospective renter calls, you also have the option of referring them to the Web page for more information.

The online rental information you can offer is virtually unlimited. With a digital camera, you can place photos of the rental property online. If you have a wide-angle digital camera, you can even put interior photos online, which is very helpful if the property is currently occupied and you cannot or do not want to bother the current tenant by showing the place. You can also show floor plans and provide detailed directions. If you are really computer-savvy or know someone who is, you can provide a narrative soundtrack that augments your online information or you can just include some music. (Keep in mind that music can be annoying to Web site viewers, however. The last thing you want to do is run potential tenants off with your favorite Barry Manilow song.)

Of course, be careful that the graphics do not slow down the loading of the Web page so significantly that it takes too long to load the page. Just like the short attention span of your prospective tenant when scanning through the newspaper ads, you want to make sure that your Web site will load very quickly with all of the basic information. Use a simple text file format that will load quickly. If you get the attention and interest of the prospect, you can offer links to the graphics of floor plans and property photos.

Community bulletin boards

As with posting flyers, bulletin boards can also be very effective in certain small communities or college towns. Often the local self-serve laundries, pharmacies, hospitals, or grocery stores have bulletin boards that are available at no cost. You may find that you are limited to a 3-x-5 card, but you can tailor your posting to the people who will be most interested in and attracted to your rental property. Post several identical cards so that the interested prospects can simply take a card with them. Posting more than one card with the intention of interested people taking them also allows you to use the back side for more information, including a detailed map and directions to the rental property.

If your rental property has unique features like a garage or large backyard, you may have some additional promotional opportunities. Carefully evaluate your rental property and determine the unique aspects of the property and the specific target market that will be most interested in these specific elements. For example, a rental property with a large yard appeals to renters with pets, so a listing on the bulletin boards often found at the local pet store may reach that specific target market. Likewise, a rental property with a garage appeals to patrons of an auto supply or hardware store.

As with any ad in which the property address is clearly stated, a disadvantage to the public or community bulletin boards is that you may be promoting the fact that the rental unit may be vacant to an element that may be interested in having a party or stealing your appliances. One way to minimize this problem is to use this method only when the unit is still occupied and clearly state that the rental property will be available at a future date. You should also consider indicating that the current tenant should not be disturbed.

Local employers

Another great source for rental prospects are the local employers in your area. Employees of these companies most likely have stable employment and will be looking for long-term rentals.

Many firms have employee assistance or housing referral offices that work with their employees to help them find reasonably priced housing. Most rental properties located in metropolitan areas are located near at least one major employer. As a sharp rental property owner, you may already have determined that the employees of certain major firms are part of your target rental market.

Likewise, the major firms in your area have a vested interest in their employees being able to find good quality and affordable rental housing in close proximity to their location. Progressive employers are always looking for inexpensive ways to assist their employees and improve morale. You can even offer all employees of companies that participate in your corporate referral program an incentive to rent at your property. This incentive can range from waiving the application fee to allowing the security deposit to be paid over the first 90 days or even a discount on the monthly rent.

Direct mailings

The key to success with direct mailing is to have a good flyer or brochure combined with a mailing list that will reach your target market. If you have already developed your flyer or brochure, using this same marketing piece in a direct mail advertising campaign is a natural next step.

Of course, like all advertising, direct mail is only effective and cost-efficient if you can get your specific marketing piece into the hands of a prospective renter for your rental property when they are looking for a place to rent. Use an outside direct-mail firm for the most efficient and cost-efficient handling of direct mail. Often the direct-mail firms have the mailing lists that will reach your target market. But you must be able to provide the firms with specific criteria for your target market as far as geographic location and even the type of recipient you're targeting, so do your market research first.

As always, be very careful that the mailing list does not create any fair-housing concerns through any limitations or restrictions based on the protected categories. If it does, both you and the direct-mailing firm could be in serious legal trouble. One of the benefits of using a major professional direct-mailing firm is that they are well aware of the fair-housing laws and regularly abide by them.

Leasing agencies

One of the recent trends in rental real estate are firms that assist tenants in locating rental units. These services are available in virtually every major metropolitan area. Some offer their services for no charge to the renter and are compensated by the property manager when the prospect signs a rental agreement. Other rental locator firms charge tenants for their service and are only compensated when they find a rental unit that meets the needs of the renter.

Although most owners of small- to medium-size rental properties do not need the services of a leasing agency, there are some definite advantages to consider. Leasing agencies often have close working relationships with major corporations and relocation services and have excellent tenants looking for high-end rentals. These tenants relocating into an area typically do not have the time to search for a rental property and want the leasing agency to handle matters for them. They also are not often candidates for purchasing a home, because they will only be staying for a specific assignment or because they want to rent in the area before making a purchase decision. There is often a trade-off with these renters: They are usually very well qualified, but they are not as likely to rent long-term. But the reality is that not all tenants will stay for a long period of time anyway, and if you know that the tenant will only be with you for a set period (such as a 1-year lease) you can adjust the rental rate to reflect this rental term.

Broker referrals

Besides selling real estate, many real estate agents are also in the business of referring renters to property managers. Many of the calls that real estate agents receive are from individuals relocating from other areas who contact a real estate agent inquiring about a future purchase of a home. Although they may have long-range plans to purchase, they often rent while they become familiar with the area.

Real estate agents don't mind referring renters to an owner or property manager, because they know that today's renter may likely be a home purchaser down the road. Real estate agents are also very interested in referral fees from owners or property managers. Although the referral fee may be a small amount of money compared to the potential commission the real estate agent would earn on a sales transaction, agents are willing to be patient and accept a small reward in the short run knowing the big money will be earned down the road.

Typically, if the real estate agent is dealing with a property manager who is a licensed real estate agent, the referring agent will ask the property manager to sign a non-compete agreement. Often these real estate agents offer a referral fee back to you as an incentive to make sure that the renter works through them when the time comes to become a homeowner. The typical referral fee for a real estate sales transaction can be 20 percent of the earned commission received at the close of escrow by the real estate agent who received the referral. This can be a nice perk for you to soften the loss of your tenant and can even make a short-term rental much more lucrative.

Check the laws in your state, because some states prohibit the payment of commissions to anyone other than real estate licensees.

Property brochure

A property brochure is not necessary for most small rental property owners. However, if you have a rental property with more than ten units, you should seriously consider developing a basic rental property brochure. I recommend a simple tri-fold brochure that can be printed on both sides of 8½-x-11-inch paper. With a basic word processing or desktop publishing program, you can easily make a customized brochure for your rental property. The brochure should include a floor plan and an area map that highlights the key places for employment, shopping, schools, and transportation in the area.

The benefits of a rental brochure are that the prospective tenant can take the information with him and easily share it with another co-applicant. Many rental decisions are not made until after the prospective tenant has had the opportunity to view several properties. After a while, all the properties can begin to look alike, and owners of large apartment properties know that the rental brochure really helps close the sale by reminding the prospective tenant of the positive features of their property. With the dramatic improvement in desktop publishing and much lower cost of producing basic brochures, now owners of even a single-family rental home can tap the advantages of a property brochure.

Television and radio

Major network television advertising in most metropolitan areas is too expensive for even the largest corporate rental property owners, so television is clearly not cost-effective for the small-time rental property owner. However, in some markets the local cable TV provider offers special classified advertising channels that do offer reasonably priced ads. Often the cable TV companies have all real estate sales and rental ads running at certain times. These ads often consist of a series of still photos and a professional spokesperson providing the narrative outlining the features of your property. The challenge with many of these cable TV advertising channels is the relative cost for the limited audience that is likely to see your specific ad.

Don't consider advertising on TV or radio unless you are in a soft rental market or you have already tried the other methods without success. And if you haven't had much success with the other methods of advertising, first take a serious look at your property's curb appeal, the condition of your rental unit, or the monthly rent.

Chapter 7

Handling Prospects and Showing the Rental

In This Chapter

- Using technology to your advantage
- Showing your rental property
- Leasing your rental property
- Taking a look at disclosure issues in rental housing

In virtually all instances, the tenant/landlord relationship actually begins with the initial rental inquiry call. If you successfully master the proper handling and prequalifying of rental prospects and become skilled at selling the prospect on your rental property, you will find owning and managing rental property to be a profitable and even pleasant experience.

Armed with the information in this chapter — and some practice — you will become adept at quickly screening the callers and convincing the qualified prospects that you have the rental unit they want. In this chapter, I explain the importance of preparing for prospect calls, using the telephone as an effective marketing tool, and handling prospects all the way from the first phone call to the completion of the rental application.

Making the Most of Technology

The goal of advertising your rental property is to reach the pool of qualified prospective renters who are currently looking for a new rental property and inform them that you have a rental property that may be of interest to them. When your advertising and promotion generates interest in your rental unit, your phone will ring. But if your rental prospects can't reach you, your prospective tenants will immediately lose any potential interest in you and your rental property. So you need to make sure that you can easily be reached by prospective tenants — and current tenants — at all times.

The telephone's importance in property management

Some property management books recommend never placing your phone number in your rental ads. Instead, they suggest that you market your rental property strictly by advertising and by holding open houses where interested tenants can all view the property at the same time. The concept of an open house is very good, but not until you have prequalified the rental prospects.

In my experience, omitting your phone number from your ads eliminates a large number of qualified rental prospects who don't have the time or interest in racing all over town to attend open houses at rental properties that may not even meet their needs. We live in a world of information, and your most qualified rental prospects are often people who value their time very highly.

You may think that you are able to conserve some of your *own* time by not accepting phone calls, but you will have a different opinion after your first 3-hour open house where only a couple of unqualified rental prospects show up! Or, even worse, you may not get any prospects at all. Now *that* is counterproductive afternoon!

Use the telephone as your primary business tool. Take advantage of all the advances in communications technology to improve your success rate in locating and selling the most qualified renters on the benefits of your rental property.

Advances in telecommunications technology have made the management of rental housing much more efficient today than it was even just a few years ago. However, with so many options, you need to know how to use communications technology effectively and efficiently. In the following sections, I cover the basics of using technology to your advantage. Later in the chapter, you'll find more specific information on using the telephone in particular — because the telephone is still your main link to your prospective tenants.

Using your telephone's special features to your advantage

The telephone is your primary way of staying in touch with your prospective tenants. But using the telephone isn't just about putting your phone number in your classified ad or on your rental sign. The telephone today comes with all kinds of special features that can help you manage your property more effectively. I cover these features in the following sections.

Call forwarding

If you're advertising a property for rent and the only contact number you provide is your home number, for example, but you work outside of the home all day, you won't be available to take the incoming calls you need. If this is the case, you may want to consider using a phone number where you *can* be reached during the day or where you can at least be immediately notified of incoming calls.

But if you don't want to list your work phone number in your advertisements, you can still use your home phone number, a separate rental property phone line at home, or even a pager by using the *call forwarding* feature available through most phone companies. With call forwarding, you simply set up your phone to forward all calls to another phone number — such as your work number, a personal cell phone number, or any other number where you can be reached. And you can turn the call forwarding off when you return home.

Caller ID

Another great phone feature you can use to increase your time management efficiency and lower your costs is caller ID. When you pay for caller ID through your telephone company, you have either a special display unit or a special phone that displays the phone number of the party placing the incoming call. Caller ID is a great way to get the return phone number of your prospective renters in case they neglect to leave their contact information for you.

Why do you need to have the telephone number of a prospective renter? First, having a prospective renter's number allows you to call him back and follow up with more information or get an update on his rental status. You can also use his number to reconfirm an appointment to see the rental property. And later, during the applicant screening process, you can use the phone number as a crosscheck when he submits his rental application, to be sure he's giving you the correct information.

Voice mail

As a rental property manager, you should have a voice mail system or an answering machine that can handle calls 24 hours a day. The outgoing voice mail or answering machine message should provide callers with your digital pager number or your cell number in case of emergencies (this is important for current tenants, and it lets prospective tenants know that you'll be there for them if they need you). You can also record detailed information about the rental property for your prospective tenants; this will help tenants prescreen themselves (they won't waste their time — and yours — if the property you describe is out of their price range, for example).

Most renters spend quite a bit of time looking through various rental housing advertising publications. They typically make many phone calls before actually beginning the process of looking at a rental property. So you want to make the information-gathering process as smooth and efficient for the prospective renters as possible, because you are in competition for the top qualified renters.

The renters are interested in knowing certain basic information up front; this allows them to narrow their choices. Many renters may not even be aware of this, but subconsciously they're often looking for any excuse to eliminate your rental property from their list. You need to develop an information system for your rental property that makes the renter feel relaxed, comfortable, and interested in actually seeing your rental property.

In addition to your name, include on your voice mail system or answering machine recording the following information about your rental:

- Location, including directions
- Number of bedrooms and square footage
- Rental rate and security deposit requirements
- Qualifying information, such as minimum income and whether pets are accepted
- Property features and benefits

As with all forms of communication, if your rental prospect leaves a message, you need to be able to return his call promptly or you will lose the prospect to your competitor. Consider a digital voice mail system or digital answering machine that can forward your calls or page you if you receive a message. And remember: The most qualified renters are the ones who get snapped up first, and these are the tenants you really want! Don't let them get away!

Knowing which additional technological devices you need

In addition to the telephone, standard equipment for many rental property owners includes the following:

- **Digital pager:** A digital pager allows callers to leave either a voice message or an alphanumeric message entered through the caller's telephone or typed into a computer keyboard.
- **Cell phone:** A cell phone is virtually mandatory for owners of rental property. It's an invaluable way to instantly keep in touch with your current tenants as well as prospects responding to your ads or signs.
- **Personal digital assistant (PDA):** When you are planning appointments with contractors or prospective tenants, you can immediately record your schedule on your PDA, which is a small, handheld computer (names you may recognize include the PalmPilot and the Windows CE–based PDAs). With many PDAs, you can download and synchronize your mobile database with your main PC back at your home and/or office.

Working vacation

Recently, my wife and I were in Boston on vacation. We had already seen the traditional sights and had a little extra time to spare, so my wife wanted to do some shopping. Shopping isn't exactly my favorite activity, so I stopped by the Boston Public Law Library and checked my e-mail on my free, Web-based e-mail account. You can get free, Web-based e-mail through a number of services (such as Yahoo! and Hotmail). This allows you to access your e-mail from anywhere in the world, as long as you have access to the Internet.

While I was in Boston, I had all my messages from my primary e-mail account forwarded to my Web-based account. After reading and responding to the most urgent messages, I used my cell phone to call my office and check my voice mail. While listening to messages with requests for meetings, I used my PDA to check my schedule, record the new appointments, and update my to-do list. Technology at work — it's a wonderful thing.

Preparing for Phone Calls

Whether you were ever a Boy Scout or not, you have probably heard about the Boy Scout motto, "Be prepared." This motto applies to the management of rental properties in many ways, but one of the most important is being prepared when the telephone rings. If you handle the rental inquiry call properly, you will not only make your life much easier, you will also get the tenants you want.

In the following sections, I discuss the importance of preparation and the steps necessary to make sure that you are ready when the phone rings. Handling a telephone rental inquiry involves eight basic elements:

- Having the basic tools ready and available
- Answering the telephone professionally
- Providing and obtaining basic information from the caller
- Using open-ended questions and building the conversation
- Selling the rental prospect on your rental property
- Pre-qualifying the rental prospect
- Anticipating and being prepared for objections
- Converting the phone call to a rental showing

The rental inquiry phone call is just the beginning of the rental process, but it is a critical step. Virtually all of your interested renters will first contact you by phone. But the only purpose of the phone call is to get to the next step, the showing of the rental unit. Master the art of the rental inquiry phone call and most of the time you will be able to set appointments with only qualified rental prospects. And that is the name of the game in property management!

Having the basic tools ready

Advertising costs you a lot of time and money, so you don't want to begin to look around for a pen and paper and your notes about the rental property as the phone starts ringing. Rental prospects can tell the difference between the prepared rental property owner and the one who doesn't seem to have a clue. They also form an impression of how you are likely to handle any problems they may encounter with the rental unit in the future. Most sharp renters (and those are the ones you want) are looking for a professional, business-like rental property owner, so that's what you need to be.

The benefits of a professional phone technique are one of the main reasons that I recommend having a separate business location for the management of your rental properties. This does not have to be a separate office in a commercial setting; it could be simply the corner of your bedroom or an office at home. Consider having a separate phone line as well. A separate phone line allows you to quickly distinguish between personal phone calls and rental business phone calls, and to treat each kind of call accordingly.

You can find many great resources on the proper use of the telephone in business, and the very first advice these resources typically offer is how to answer the phone and what to say. But when it comes to the management and leasing of rental properties, I believe that success with the telephone begins with being prepared to use the phone even *before* your first rental inquiry call comes in. In the following sections, I cover some basic tools to have on hand before your first call comes in.

Telephone prospect card

A *telephone prospect card,* like the one shown in Form 7-1, is a useful tool to assist you in gathering from your rental prospects information such as their name and telephone number, how they heard about your rental unit, and their particular needs in terms of move-in date, size, and other requirements. This information can help determine whether your rental property meets the needs and wants of a prospect.

You can also use the telephone prospect card if you show your rental property to a prospective tenant or need to follow up on qualified rental prospects. Finally, you can use it to track the rental advertising source, which allows you to make sure you only continue to use only the advertising media that pay off.

Telephone Prospect Card

Name ______________________ Date of initial call __________ Time ________
Current address ______________________ City ____________ Daytime Phone __________
Rental location (s) discussed ______________________ Cell Phone __________
How did you learn about our rental? ______________________ Email __________
When will you need to move in? ____________ How many bedrooms do you need? ________
How many people will be living in the rental? ________ What size rental are you looking for? ______
What would you feel comfortable with as a monthly rent? ______________________
What do you do for a living? ____________ Where do you work? ____________
Where are you living now? ____________ How much parking space do you require? ______
What is wrong, if anything, with your current rental property? ______________________
Why are you looking to move at this time? ______________________
What types and sizes of pets do you have? ______________________
When can you drive by the rental property? __________ Mentioned Equal Opportunity Housing? ____
What other rental properties have you seen/plan to see? ______________________
Notes ______________________

Follow-up

Rental location(s) shown ____________ Date shown __________ Quoted rent/deposit __________
What did prospect like best about the rental unit? ______________________
Objections, if any? ______________________
Most important features and amenities to prospect ______________________
Rental application completed? ________ Holding deposit? ________ Date to follow-up __________

Form 7-1: Telephone Prospect Card.

One of the primary reasons to track your rental calls is so that you can clearly see the results generated by your advertising. The number of phone calls generated is not the most important factor in determining which advertising medium is the best for your rental property. The key factor is the number of *qualified* rental prospects. In an ideal situation, getting just a few calls from very qualified prospects is much better than getting a number of rental inquiries from unqualified prospects (which is just a waste of your valuable time).

Property knowledge sheets

One of the best ways to have the answers to the questions that may be raised by your rental prospect is to prepare a *property knowledge sheet* for each rental property location. A property knowledge sheet contains all the basic information about your rental property, such as the size and type of the unit and the unit number if it is in a multiple-unit property. Also, you should include on the property knowledge sheet the age, type of construction, and other important details about the rental unit.

A thorough property knowledge sheet also contains important information about the local neighborhood and general area. Just like the Chamber of Commerce or Visitor's Information Bureau, you want to be able to answer questions about the area. Rental prospects are very interested in knowing about employment centers, transportation, local schools, childcare, places of worship, shopping, and medical facilities. You can really make a positive impression on your rental prospect if you can tell them where the nearest dry cleaner or Thai restaurant is located.

You want to have all this vital information from your property knowledge sheet at your fingertips so that you can be ready to answer your rental prospect's questions. The more you know about your property, the better able you will be to find some important reasons for your rental prospect to select your rental over the competition's.

Property knowledge sheets can definitely give you the edge over your competition. Particularly with the advent of the Internet, many rental prospects know more about the area and the other rental options than you may know. Because you will often find yourself competing with large multi-family rental properties, you need to be prepared to answer important questions about not only your rental property but also the area. Often, immediately knowing a detail such as whether there is a certain childcare center in your area can make the difference between success and failure.

Check out Form 7-2 for an example of a property knowledge sheet.

The time you spend answering all of the rental prospect's questions can provide you with useful information. Be sure to take good notes about the source of your rental traffic and any important comments made by rental prospects. Then you can improve your results by incorporating this feedback into your future advertising for that same rental property.

For example, maybe prospective renters indicated that they had trouble finding the property. This is a common problem and one that successful rental property owners know is a serious challenge to success. If your prospective renters cannot find the property, there is very little chance that they will rent. ***Remember:*** You are in competition with a lot of other rental property owners and the best-qualified renters do not need to make extraordinary efforts to find a good quality rental property.

Comparison charts

You may find that you have a vacancy in a soft rental market, when the rental market has a lot of rental units available for prospective tenants. Using a comparison chart can be very helpful in this kind of market, especially if your rental property has distinct advantages over other rental properties in the area. Comparison charts are really just a marketing strategy commonly used by the owners and managers of large rental properties, but the concepts are very helpful for the owners of small- to medium-size rental properties or even a single rental unit as well.

A comparison chart can provide very useful information to prospective renters who may not be aware that they are comparing apples to oranges when looking at various rental properties. Comparison charts are particularly useful to rental property owners who may have a competitive advantage that is not readily apparent to the uninformed prospective renter.

Property Knowledge Sheet

Property Information

Rental address ____________________ Unit # _____ City ______________ Zip code _______
Office hours (if any) ____________ Square footage of unit(s) ____________________
Unit mix—Studios ____ 1 Bedroom ____ 2 Bedroom/1 Bath ____ 2Bedroom/2 Bath ____ Other ______
Rent—Studios _____ 1 Bedroom _____ 2 Bedroom/1 Bath _____ 2Bedroom/2 Bath _____ Other ______
Application fee ________ Security deposit ____________ Concessions ______________
Age of rental __________ Type of construction __________ Parking ______________
Recreational facilities ________________ Laundry ____________ Pets ____________
Storage ________________ Utilities (who pays?) ______________ AC/Heat __________
Appliances ______________________________ Floor coverings ______________
Special features/comments ____

Community Information

School district ______________ Grade school ____________ Jr. high ______________
High school ________________ Jr. college ______________ College ______________
Trade school ______________ Pre-school (s) ______________________________
Childcare ________________ Places of worship ____________________________
Police station ______________ Fire station ______________ Ambulance ____________
Electric ____________ Natural gas ____________ Telephone ____________ Cable ____________
Water ____________ Sewer ______________ Library ____________ Post office ____________
Hospital ________________ Pharmacy ______________ Vet ______________
Other medical facilities ____
Nearby employment centers ____
Transportation ____
Groceries ________________ Other shopping ____________________________
Local services ____
Restaurants ____
Comments ____

Rental Market Information

Rental competitors/rental rates/concessions ___________________________________

Our competitive advantages ____

Our disadvantages ____

Form 7-2: Property Knowledge Sheet.

For example, your rent may be slightly higher than the rent charged by your competition, but you may pay for the utilities whereas tenants at your competition's apartments have to pay for their own utilities. Another potential advantage of your property may be that your rental property has reserved parking, but the competition requires their tenants to scramble for their parking spaces on the street. Or maybe your rental units have much more square footage than the competition. Many older properties are more aesthetically pleasing, with mature landscaping and beautiful shade trees. These are all factors that may not be readily apparent to the prospective renter, and they can give you a competitive advantage. A rental comparison chart levels the playing field and allows you to inform your prospective tenants of the actual costs of your rental housing (and the housing provided by your competition).

Check out Figure 7-1 for an example of a comparison chart highlighting four properties. In looking at the chart, a prospective tenant can see that even though Sunshine Apartments has the lowest rent, when you add in the $75 monthly utilities, they're paying $25 more per month than they would pay at Maple Grove, and they don't get the reserved parking, onsite maintenance, lush landscaping, or free credit check. In this situation, Maple Grove Apartments are the obvious better deal for tenants, even though the monthly rent is higher. Madison Avenue Apartments and Camelot Townhomes, however, when the utilities are taken into consideration, both level out at $700 per month. But Madison Avenue Apartments has better landscaping, and Camelot Townhomes has reserved parking. In this situation, tenants would need to decide which of those two perks — landscaping or parking — is more important to them. The important point is that by providing an honest comparison chart, you're saving your prospective tenants a lot of legwork, and you're highlighting the advantages of your apartment over others.

Comparison Chart

Property	Rent	Owner Paid Water and Heating	Tenant Paid Water and Heating (with estimated costs)	Reserved Parking	Onsite Maintenance	Lush Landscaping	Free Credit Check
Sunshine Apartments	$600	No	Yes ($75/month)	No	No	No	No
Madison Avenue Apartments	$625	No	Yes ($75/month)	No	No	Yes	No
Maple Grove Apartments	$650	Yes	No	Yes	Yes	Yes	Yes
Camelot Townhomes	$700	Yes	No	Yes	No	No	No

Figure 7-1: A comparison chart is a great way to advertise your property's advantages over the competition.

Answering the phone

As your key marketing tool, when your rental phone line rings, you need to stop what you are doing. Take a deep breath and even close your eyes briefly so that you can be focused on this call. Be sure to answer the telephone no later than the third ring; rental prospects generally have a list of calls that they plan to make, so they are rarely patient. If you don't answer in the first few rings, they will begin dialing the next phone number on their list and probably won't take the time to call you again.

First impressions can occur in just a few seconds. If you run your rental management business from your home and your rental prospect calls and hears children screaming in the background or other distracting noises, you will be making a very unprofessional impression. Controlling the atmosphere is essential in order to maintain a professional image.

If you are fortunate enough to have an exciting and chaotic home life, then you need to take steps to make sure that your rental inquiry calls can be distinguished from general household calls. For a nominal charge, many local phone service providers offer a service that gives you two phone numbers for one phone line; a different ringing sound is generated for each phone number so you can identify which number is ringing. You may also want to have your separate rental management line only accessible from a telephone in your home business location. If other members of your household pick up the phone during your conversation, you can easily get distracted.

Have a smile on your face and speak clearly; this is one phone technique that really does make a difference. Your positive attitude and enthusiasm can make a very important first impression. Even if you are not in the best of spirits at the moment the phone rings, don't sound rushed or hurried. You don't want your rental prospects to feel that they are imposing upon you. If you sound disorganized and hesitant on the phone, the prospects will likely feel that you are incompetent and not the type of rental property owner whom they can trust and count on if they have a problem or need a repair.

However, if you come across in your initial contact with the rental prospects as polite, knowledgeable, organized, and confident, they will respect your skills as a rental management professional. Prospects will see that you treat the rental of your property as a business, not a casual hobby.

You may think that if you are not prepared, it may actually be better to let your voice mail system or answering machine take a message. I don't recommend this approach, however, because the majority of rental callers are not willing to leave a message and you will lose an opportunity to personally speak with the rental prospect. Believe me, they won't call back! Remember that the majority of calls made by rental prospects to small rental property owners will require leaving a phone message, and you can really stand out by answering your calls personally.

Because positive first impressions are always very important, remember that it is your goal in your initial contact to project a friendly, helpful, and professional image.

As with any business, you may find that a rental inquiry call comes in when you are right in the middle of another situation that can't wait. I suggest that you still answer the call right away and give your caller the choice to be placed on hold or let them know you can call them right back if they prefer. Asking the caller if they can call back in a few minutes is a very risky strategy and one that I would not recommend because the odds of them calling back are remote. However, this may be an option to consider as well and one that is superior to leaving the caller on indefinite hold.

Providing and obtaining the basic information

Typically, the caller's first comments will indicate that she is inquiring about your rental unit and whether it is still available. Then she will typically ask about the size of the rental and the rental rate. Always answer the questions presented by the caller directly.

One common and effective way to develop rapport with your prospective renter is to address the person by name. People generally liked to be called by their names, and they will appreciate your addressing them accordingly. If the caller has not already volunteered this information, you may want to mention your first name again and ask for her name. If she gives you her name, be sure to ask her permission for you to call her by her first name. Often the prospect will only provide her last name and you should show respect by using an appropriate title when you call her by her surname. It is also a good idea to ask the prospect for her return phone number. (If you have caller ID you should verify that you have the best telephone number to reach her.)

Then prompt the caller for the information that you will both need. For example, you need to know when the rental prospect is looking to move in, how many people (and the number, type, and size of pets, if applicable) will be residing in the rental, and what she is comfortable with as a monthly rent.

It is this basic initial give-and-take of questions and answers that will quickly determine whether there is any point in continuing the rental inquiry conversation. The prospect is looking for the opportunity to eliminate your rental property if you do not have what she needs at the time that she needs it. Likewise, if it appears that your rental property may be a good fit, you still need to explore whether the rental prospect is qualified and will meet your screening requirements.

An easy way to remember the basic questions that you need to ask are to remember the six *w*s — who, what, where, when, why, and how (yes, I realize that's technically five *w*s and one *h,* but you get the point). Remember to use your notes and provide the prospect with immediate feedback so that she knows that you are really interested in her call and are really trying to determine whether your rental unit meets her needs.

Here are some examples of questions that will assist you in determining the needs of the prospect:

- When will you need to move in?
- How many bedrooms do you need?
- How many people will be living in the rental?
- What size rental are you looking for?
- What would you feel comfortable with as a monthly rent?
- How long do you intend to live at this property?
- How much parking space do you require?
- Where are you living now?
- What is wrong, if anything, with your current rental property?
- Why are you looking to move at this time?
- Where do you work?
- What do you do for a living?
- What is your gross monthly income?
- What types of pets do you have?
- When can you drive by the rental property?
- How can I reach you by telephone?

Take notes so that you can summarize the prospect's needs and wants during the initial phone conversation. Bring these notes on each caller to rental showings so that you know what aspects of your rental property are of greatest interest to each prospect. Plus, people will really appreciate the fact that you care enough to write down what they are looking for rather than just try to sell them what you have to offer.

Rental inquiry calls are different from most of the calls we normally make in business. In a rental inquiry call, I often find that both parties are trying to eliminate the other as a prospect and both parties are trying to get as much information without giving out any information of their own. But this is not the best approach. Remember that you are making a telephone presentation of your rental property. You need to have a give-and-take approach whereby you share the basic information that the prospect needs while you make an initial assessment of the prospect's qualifications.

Selling the prospect on your rental property

A key element to success in selling rental prospects on your rental property is your ability to build rapport with the prospect on the phone. As you answer the initial questions presented by the rental prospect, you should take the opportunity to highlight some of the desirable or unique aspects of your rental. For example, if the prospective renter asks about the number and size of the bedrooms, you can reply, “The house has four bedrooms, each with a separate closet. The master bedroom is very large at 15 feet by 12 feet. Will this accommodate your needs?” Or maybe you can say, “The backyard is completely fenced and is very large. Do you have any pets?”

It is your goal to turn the features of your property into benefits for the prospective renters. You need to do this by painting a picture of the property in the mind of your rental prospect. For example, if your rental property has a swimming pool or spa, you can talk about how nice it is to come home at the end of a long day and enjoy the refreshing swim or a favorite beverage poolside.

The entire goal of the telephone call is to get the qualified prospect to see your rental property. You can’t — and shouldn’t — sign a rental agreement on the phone!

As the rental property owner, you definitely want to tell your story about what a great rental property you have. Then when you’ve grabbed their interest and determined that your rental unit meets their needs, you want to begin to evaluate the rental prospect’s qualifications in light of your requirements and needs. If you fail to hook the prospect, you will never get to the next step. Of course, you want to be sure to prescreen the prospective tenant during this initial phone call so that you invest your valuable time only with qualified rental prospects.

Pre-qualifying the rental prospect over the phone

After your prospective tenants have found answers to their initial questions and you have passed their basic need requirements, this is when you need to begin asking your own qualifying questions. You need to confirm when they are looking to move, the size of the rental they require, and their financial qualifications. Both you and the rental prospect need this basic information, and together you go through this ceremonial dance with the goal being to advance to the next stage — the showing of the rental unit.

Rather than presenting a boring monologue or a canned speech, a rental inquiry call should be more like a tennis match, with each side taking a turn presenting their questions and gathering the answers they need to make a decision. Ultimately, both parties need to agree that the rental unit may meet the needs of the rental prospect and the rental prospect may meet the established tenant screening criteria. This is the first step toward achieving your main objective of the rental — getting a commitment from the prospect to make an appointment to see your rental unit in person.

The answers to your basic questions will determine whether you need to go on to the next step. For example, if currently you have only a studio apartment available, there may be no need to show this particular rental unit if the prospect says there are four applicants that will live in the rental.

You also want to make sure that you are not dealing with a *professional tenant,* someone who jumps from rental to rental frequently. Even in your very first phone call, certain red flags may indicate that you are dealing with someone who will be nothing but trouble. Potential signs are a rental prospect who asks very few questions about the rental property and the area but is very interested in things like your move-in special or whether he can get you to lower the rent or whether you will allow him to pay his security deposit over the first 3 months.

Another warning sign is if the tenant seems interested in moving in too quickly. Although you may think that finding someone who wants to move in right away is great and will cut your rent loss, this may be an indication that the person has something to hide or is just looking for his next landlord victim. Maybe his landlord has just served him with eviction papers for nonpayment and he needs to leave before he is physically removed. ***Remember:*** It can take up to 2 or 3 months for eviction actions to become a matter of public record, so your prospective tenant's credit report may turn up clean initially even if he's had recent problems. So you need to be very careful and wary of subtle hints, even as early as the very first phone call.

Using open-ended questions and a pleasant and friendly manner, you need to get the basic information from the tenant to determine if he will meet your rental requirements. It is also important to determine whether you are speaking with the actual decision-maker, or whether this prospect is only making the initial contact and gathering information for someone else. Although you always prefer to deal with the primary decision-maker from the initial contact, you need to be skillful in pre-qualifying all of the prospects without alienating your immediate contact, because the immediate contact is likely to have considerable influence on the decision as well.

You will know that you have a qualified prospect when you have determined that:

- You have a rental of the appropriate type and size available when the prospect needs it.
- The prospects meet your minimum qualifying standards for income, credit history, and employment history.
- They have enough cash to pay the entire first month's rent and the full security deposit.
- At least one of the prospects is of legal age to sign the rental contract.
- The proposed number of occupants is appropriate for the particular rental unit.

- The prospects have an acceptable rental history and are vacating their current living accommodations legally.
- The prospects are willing to live with your property guidelines, such as no pets or no smoking allowed in the rental unit.

Of course, you need to verify this information before making a commitment to rent your property. However, you can begin this pre-qualifying process over the phone instead of having to wait until you meet the prospect when he tours the rental property or completes a rental application. You have already begun the important process of screening your prospective tenant with the very first phone call.

Your goal during the telephone call is to give the caller enough information about your rental property that he can determine whether he has enough genuine interest in the property to make it worth his time to actually see the property in person. Likewise, you want to obtain enough information about the rental prospect and his co-applicants to pre-qualify them for your rental property. Matchmaking is a two-way street.

Naturally, not every rental property will be a match for every rental prospect. Your goal is not to convince *all* the callers that they must see your rental property in person. Showing a rental unit to an uninterested or unqualified rental prospect will be one of the most frustrating experiences of your rental management career. Showing property only to qualified and interested prospects is one of the most important factors in successful time management for rental property owners and managers.

Handling phone objections

If you've done your homework, you're well prepared and you know the answers to questions about the rental unit and the surrounding area. But you'll still have to deal with objections raised by some of your rental prospects during the initial phone rental inquiry. Again, your goal is not to convince the unqualified prospect who truly is not a good match for your property to waste everyone's valuable time and come see the rental unit when it obviously won't work. Instead, your goal is to anticipate some of the more common objections and have information that will allow you and the prospect to determine whether there is enough mutual interest to go to the next step — the showing of the rental unit.

I once owned a rental property with a centralized location, but it was also right under the flight path of a major airport. The ideal location near major employment and recreational centers made our property very desirable, but the proximity to the airport was quite obvious, and it was well known that many rental properties in the area had significant problems with airport noise. Virtually all of our rental prospects who visited the property raised this concern, but even many of the callers brought up the noise, because they were familiar with the area. When the property was built, the architects had designed the rental units with special double-pane soundproof windows and extra insulation so interior noise was not a problem. Knowing the perception of rental properties in the area, we began to incorporate our soundproofing design features right upfront in our telephone rental presentation.

You may hear the complaint or concern that your older, 20-unit rental property does not have individual washers and dryers in every unit, as found in competitive properties in your area. Instead, your property features a centralized laundry room with new washers and dryers and a large folding table for the tenant's convenience. Anticipating that some prospects will be looking for individual washers and dryers and will raise an objection when you do not have this feature, you are prepared and have done your homework. You know that the competitors also have smaller units with less storage, because the washer/dryer takes up important closet and storage space. You also know that your competitor's tenants have to pay for the water, whereas you pay for the water usage at your property. These are important facts that you can politely mention to the prospect over the phone. When showing the rental unit to a prospect, you can provide them with the comparison chart discussed earlier in this chapter.

Being prepared for rental inquiries for your rental unit includes anticipating reasonable objections and providing an honest answer to the rental prospect.

Converting phone calls to rental showings

If your initial phone conversation goes well, the prospects will want to tour your rental property. You have already invested a lot of time and energy into the rental inquiry calls. This is the moment of truth when you find out whether the rental prospects are really interested in your rental. Maybe they are just gathering information for a future move, or maybe they're checking out similar rental properties to determine if the rent increase they just received from their current landlord is justified.

You have answered a lot of their questions, taken careful notes highlighting their needs and wants, and you have built up a rapport with each prospect. You wouldn't have invested this much time in a prospect unless you felt that your rental met his needs and that he was very likely to pass your tenant screening criteria. So now is not the time to become passive and tell him to call you back if he's interested. And it's not the time to sheepishly suggest that he "stop by the open house this weekend, if you're in the neighborhood."

You need to be assertive and come right out and ask him to come to your rental property so that you can personally show him your rental unit. If the tenant shows any signs of hesitating, you need to directly ask him if there is a problem. The tenant may then admit that he actually has just filed bankruptcy or he plans to use your rental property for an iguana farm. Asking questions is one of your best tools — be sure to use it.

Creating a sense of urgency

When you ask your prospect to come out and see your rental property, you may get a non-committal response or an excuse that she can't make it no matter how many different appointment times you offer over the next week. Of course, the most popular excuse you will hear is that that she has just begun calling and your rental ad is the first one she called. This may be true, so you need to be polite and patient. But if you are truly her first call, then it is likely she called you first for a reason — your advertising made your rental sound like their best option. So patience can be a virtue as long as you are not *too* patient.

Be honest, but don't hesitate to let the prospect know that you already have or will soon be receiving many more rental inquiry calls. Let her know that it is your intent to sign a rental agreement with the most qualified rental prospect, but you process the rental applications in the order in which they are received, so if there are two or more qualified applicants you may lean toward the first qualified rental prospect who submitted an application. This creates a sense of urgency for the prospect.

If you anticipate receiving interest in your rental property from multiple callers, set up one or two open houses so that you can show the rental property to several interested prospects in just a couple of hours rather than making multiple trips. In tight rental markets, the open house method often creates a competitive or even an auction-like environment, in which the tenants don't want to lose out to another rental applicant. There's nothing like a little competition to instill the call to action for potential renters.

The rental prospect may indicate that he's interested in the rental property based on your conversation, but he would like to drive by the property before actually making an appointment for a rental showing. This is fine and can be another useful tool in maximizing your efficiency as a rental property owner. Two things can happen if the prospect wants to do his own drive-by before scheduling a rental showing:

- He will call back and ask for an appointment or ask for the time of your next open house, and you can rest assured that he will show up.
- He will drive by the property and find that it is not suitable for him.

In both cases, this was a positive step. In the former case, the prospect is not pre-sold on the area and curb appeal of your rental property alone; in the latter, the prospect won't waste your time scheduling a personal tour.

Many rental management advisors suggest you improve your efficiency by allowing the prospects to tour your rental property on their own. They suggest giving the prospect the combination to a lockbox at the rental property or allowing the rental prospect to drop by and pick up a key. They usually suggest that you ask for a $25 cash deposit or that you hold the prospect's driver's license (I hope they aren't driving to your property!) as an incentive to return the key. However, I would be extremely careful in this kind of situation, because you could find that your prospective tenant has stripped the appliances or severely damaged the property while he's been there. Even a worse result could be that he decided he liked your rental property so much that he just moved right in!

In my experience, many prospects make a rental showing appointment only to drive by the property a few minutes before the actual appointment and then skip the appointment if they don't like what they see. Another common scenario is one in which the prospect has already decided that your rental is not going to be his next home no matter how great the interior and how competitively you price the rental. But they feel guilty and don't want to skip out on you, so they show up for the appointment and go through the motions of looking at everything for close to an hour. Imagine how many hours are wasted because the prospect could have taken the opportunity to see the neighborhood and the curb appeal of the rental property before scheduling a rental showing.

Planning Ahead for Open Houses and Walk-Throughs

One of the most time-consuming aspects of owning and managing rental property is the time spent filling vacancies. And the biggest time trap for most owners who do not have a system already in place is the rental showing. If you were to schedule a separate appointment with every interested rental prospect, you would be making trips constantly back and forth to the property. Unless you live or work very close to your rental property, you can quickly find that you're spending hours showing the rental to one prospect after another. That's why having a strategy for showing your rental — whether you plan to have an open house or set up individual appointments — is the best way to go.

Holding an open house

Because your time is valuable and you will have many qualified prospects interested in seeing your rental property, you may want to consider holding an open house. An open house can allow you an opportunity to efficiently show the rental property to several interested rental prospects within a couple of hours. A successful landlord won't make a dozen trips to show her property to a dozen different rental prospects.

Select a time for your open house that is convenient for you and most working people (preferably during daylight hours). For example, an open house on Saturday from 11:00 a.m. to 2:00 p.m. usually gives rental prospects a good opportunity to see the rental property at a convenient time for them, while saving you from having to make multiple trips. In the summer months, a weekday afternoon from 4:00 p.m. to 7:00 p.m. may also be a good option. Combining a weekday afternoon open house with one on the weekend can also be very effective. That way, virtually all prospects can fit the rental showing into their busy schedules.

One of the other benefits to holding an open house is that many rental prospects feel more comfortable touring a rental property when there are other prospects around. Many rental prospects may be concerned about meeting someone they don't know in a vacant rental property. And you, too, should be very concerned about your own personal safety for the same reasons. Holding an open house can eliminate or at least reduce any safety concerns you — and the prospects — may have.

Open houses are also beneficial because having multiple prospects viewing the property can create a sense of urgency and competition, which will often generate multiple applicants for your rental property.

An open house promoted strictly in a newspaper ad is not a good idea, because you may end up with many unqualified renters walking through your property. But an open house where you invite all qualified prospects whom you have spoken with in response to your ad is a good way to efficiently lease your rental and even create a sense of urgency and competition among the rental prospects.

Scheduling individual appointments

If you are in a depressed rental market or find that you need to fill a vacancy during the holidays, you may not be able to generate enough interest from prospects to schedule an open house for multiple prospects. In this case, you need to be prepared to show your rental units in the evenings and on weekends, because that is often when your prospects are available. Of course, you can still try to consolidate your appointments to a certain timeframe, but don't push this too far. Asking the prospects to conform to your schedule may turn them off.

If you have to schedule individual appointments to show your property, be sure you have the phone numbers for your rental prospects. Call each person to verify the rental showing before making a special trip to the property. By calling, you are also reassuring the prospect that you will be there and are not going to be delayed.

Crime is a concern in virtually all parts of the country. Making an appointment to show a stranger your rental property can be an opportunity for someone criminally inclined. Be alert, and take reasonable steps to protect yourself. If you ever have an uneasy feeling about a rental prospect, just decline to show the rental rather than risk personal injury. If you can, bring someone with you to the showing, and limit your rental showings to daylight hours. You can also tell your rental prospect that you will meet him outside, right in front of the property or at another public location and require a picture ID before showing the rental property. You then can use your cell phone to call a family member or friend and tell that person the name and driver's license number of your rental prospect. You can also have someone call you on your cell phone to check in throughout the showing. Of course, if you ever feel uncomfortable, be polite yet firm, end the rental tour, and leave immediately. Don't ever put yourself in a dangerous situation!

Providing directions to the property

When you have a commitment from the rental prospect to come to the property for an open house or rental showing, you need to make sure that you can provide clear and easy-to-follow directions from anywhere in your area. Giving directions may not be quite as simple and effortless as you may initially think. So you need to carefully consider the best route for your rental prospect. Take into consideration the traffic conditions your prospect will face at the time of the open house or appointment. Think about which route will present the neighborhood in the best light. You want the route to be direct, but don't hesitate to have the tenant come in from a different direction if doing so will provide the prospect with important information, such as the great shopping, schools, or other benefits of the area near your rental property.

If you are not good with directions, seek the input from someone who has a knack for giving them. Be sure to avoid someone who knows the area too well. Someone too familiar with the area may know how to drive the route by memory, but he may be completely unable to provide any street names or the details that a first-time visitor needs. Remember that the directions need to spell out each road and turn and should be very precise.

Showing Your Rental Unit

When your rental prospects arrive, be sure to greet them and introduce yourself. Ask for their names and shake their hands. Refer to your notes on the telephone prospect card from your initial phone conversation to let them know that you remember speaking with them. This will give the prospective tenants a good feeling that you are not just going through the standard rental spiel.

Listen to any questions or concerns that may have come up since you spoke on the phone or during their travel to your rental property. Ask them if they found your directions accurate and easy to use. Also, ask them if they have any other needs that they are looking for in a rental property that haven't already been discussed.

Don't just let the prospects wander through the rental unit by themselves. (Of course, this is particularly true if you are showing an occupied rental unit.) Listen carefully to your prospect and anyone they brought with them as you informally guide them through the rental unit. Pay close attention to the features that your tenants have indicated are of particular interest or comments made during the walkthrough.

For more information on preparing your rental for walkthroughs, see Chapter 4.

Showing a vacant rental

If you're showing a vacant rental, begin the tour of the rental unit and act as a tour guide. Don't be too controlling; instead, let the prospects view the rental in the manner that suits them. Some prospects go right to a certain room, which gives you a clue about the importance they place on that aspect of your property. Of course, if the prospects hesitate or are reluctant to tour on their own, you can casually guide them through the rental property yourself.

Encourage your rental prospect to see the entire rental property, including any garage or storage areas and the exterior grounds or yard, if there are any. You want to be sure that the prospect had the opportunity to observe the condition of all portions of the rental property and ask any questions. This minimizes claims that you may have discriminated against a prospect by selectively showing the rental property.

There are as many different ways to show a rental unit as there are rental property owners. Keep in mind the information provided by the prospect and customize the tour by beginning with the feature or room that you feel has the most interest for the prospect. This is not the time to head straight to *your* favorite feature. When in doubt, start with the kitchen, then transition to the living areas and the bedrooms.

As you begin to show the interior of your rental, avoid making obvious statements such as "This is the living room" or "Here's the bathroom!" Instead, listen and observe the body language and facial expressions of your prospects as they walk through the property. You don't need to oversell if they seem pleased, but you should feel free to point out the benefits of your rental property (for example, "It sounds like this neutral colored carpet will go great with your living room furniture" or, "The view from the kitchen of the sunsets is so relaxing").

Rental units look smaller when they are vacant. If your prospects express concerns that their furniture won't fit in your rental, you can consider a strategy used by property managers and owners of large rental properties: Set up a partially or fully furnished model rental unit to demonstrate what furniture will fit. Although this may not be feasible for most single-family home or condominium rental units, it can work quite well for medium to larger apartment properties that regularly have units vacant or have a market for furnished rentals. Smaller rental properties can use a *vignette,* which is a rental unit that has been decorated with towels, books, and knickknacks to give the unit personality. Sometimes you can even close the sale by offering to give the new renter these small items.

If you are holding an open house, you can quickly find yourself dealing with multiple prospects who all seem to have better timing than a synchronized swimming team. Do your best to courteously greet and speak with each prospect individually. At least cover the basic information and get the prospects started on the property tour before beginning to work with the next prospect. Be sure to communicate clearly that you will answer all of their questions, and be sure to treat all prospects openly and fairly to avoid any allegations of favoritism or discrimination.

Showing an occupied rental

If you will be showing an occupied rental unit, be sure to consider the inherent advantages and disadvantages.

If your current tenant is being evicted, is not leaving on good terms, or has an antagonistic attitude for any reason, don't show the rental unit until the property is vacated. Be sure to complete your rent-ready preparation work and any rental unit upgrades. This strategy also works best if your current tenants have not taken good care of the rental property or their lifestyle or furnishings may be objectionable to some rental prospects.

In most states, if the current tenants are at the end of their lease or they have given a notice to vacate, the rental property owner is specifically allowed to enter the rental property in order to show the unit to a prospective tenant. Of course, you must comply with state laws, which require you to give your current tenant advance written notice of entry prior to showing the rental unit. Your tenant could agree to waive the notice requirement, but make sure that you have that agreement in writing.

Try your best to cooperate with the current tenants when scheduling mutually convenient times to show the rental. Be sure to respect their privacy and avoid excessive intrusions into their lives. To ensure the cooperation of your tenant, you may even want to offer the current tenant a small bonus after they vacate, as a part of their security deposit disposition.

Although the current tenant may legally be required to allow you and your prospects to enter the rental unit for a showing, they do not have to make any efforts to ensure that the property is clean and neat. They also are not required to help you in your efforts to impress the prospect. Keep this fact in mind when deciding whether you want to show your rental unit while it is still occupied.

Showing a vacant rental unit is generally much easier, but touring your prospect through an occupied rental property does have some distinct advantages. Your current tenant can actually be a real asset if they are friendly and cooperative and take care of the property. The rental prospects may want to ask the current tenant questions about their living experience at your property.

If you can, get copies of recent utility bills from your current tenant, in case your prospective renters have any questions about utility costs. Utility costs for electric, natural gas, water and sewer, and trash are becoming significant items in the budgets of many renters. You don't want your tenant to be unable to financially handle the typical monthly utility costs, because that may impact their ability to pay your rent. You may also be able to use low utility costs as a marketing tool.

Pre-qualifying your prospects during the rental showing

While you are touring the rental, you can verify the information that the rental prospect provided during your initial phone conversation. Refer to your notes and verify the prospect's desired move-in date, the number of occupants, the rental rate, their employment and other important information. Also, make sure the tenant is aware of your rental policies and any limitations on pets or other important issues.

You don't want to be abrupt or refuse to let the prospect and the other rental applicants begin looking at the property until they answer numerous questions, but verifying the basic information upfront can save a lot of time if there was a misunderstanding or if the prospect's needs have changed.

If you don't take the time to review the information a prospect provided to you on the phone as well as your rental terms and expectations, you may find that some prospects had glossed over certain problems or indicated your rental policies were just fine when really they're not. Of course, their strategy is to wait until you think you have successfully rented the unit and you are just about to sign on the proverbial dotted line when they spring the truth on you. Maybe their dying aunt has suddenly asked them to care for her 300-pound Doberman or their paycheck was delayed and they can only pay your security deposit in installments. These are surprises that you don't need!

Resolving objections

Almost every rental prospect will express some concerns or reservations about some physical aspects of the rental property, your rental rate or other terms, or about the area. This is to be expected, because no rental property will exactly meet the needs of the prospective tenant.

There are different types of objections. Some prospects will use objections as an effort to test you and see if you will lower the rent or make some improvements to the rental property. The other forms of objections are sincere issues that are generally more tangible and specific in nature.

If you have been listening carefully to the prospect and taking notes, then some objections can be anticipated and handled even before they are raised by the prospect. In many instances, objections can actually present the opportunity to reassure your prospect that your rental property meets their needs.

If the prospect raises a question and you do not know the answer, make a note and promise to get back to the prospect as soon as possible. Most objections can be overcome if they are openly discussed with the prospective tenant and you give them honest feedback. Giving the prospect a response and attempting to answer positively is important.

Convincing your prospect

After you have qualified the prospect, you need to convince her that you have the best rental unit available. People want more than just a place to live. They want to feel they can communicate with you if a problem arises. They also appreciate it when someone shows an interest in their lives. And by showing an interest, you are clearly setting yourself apart from other property managers. I believe that prospects will even accept a rental unit that is not exactly what they are looking for if they have a positive feeling about the rental property owner or manager.

Very early in my career in property management I realized how important the property manager can be to renters when I transferred a popular manager from one property to another. Ginny had been our onsite manager at a 300-unit rental property for nearly 5 years before we gave her a promotion to a 400-unit rental community a few miles away. I was shocked when over 50 of Ginny's current residents decided to give notice and move with her to the larger property (in spite of the fact that the rents were higher and the area was much hotter in the summer).

I have never seen a rental unit that can "rent itself." So *you* need to make the difference. No matter how close your rental unit meets the stated needs and wants of your prospects, they will often hesitate and doubt their own judgment. You don't need to be pushy, but you should be prepared to actively convince the rental prospects that your rental property is right for them.

The best way to avoid problem tenants who pay late, damage your property, or disrupt the neighbors is not to rent to them in the first place. Screening your next tenant begins with the very first phone call.

Inviting your prospects to lease

When you've convinced your prospects that your unit is the right one for them, it's time to close the sale. This is one area where many rental property owners and managers suddenly get cold feet. They can do a great job handling the initial telephone rental inquiry, the preparation and showing of the rental property, and even objections, but when it comes right down to asking the tenant for the order — they become shy and freeze.

Your goal is to receive a commitment from the prospect to rent by having him complete your rental application and pay the credit screening fee, his first month's rent, and a full security deposit on the spot. Of course, you still need to thoroughly screen the prospect and confirm that he meets your rental criteria before signing a lease or rental agreement.

If despite your best efforts, the prospect is still undecided, you should make sure that he gives you a holding deposit. Remind him that you may make a deal with the very next prospect and he'll be out of luck. Of course, if you have a lot of demand for your rental units, you should develop a priority waiting list, covered later in this chapter.

Having the prospect complete a rental application

You need to offer every interested prospect the opportunity to complete a written rental application (like the one shown in Form 7-3). There are two important reasons for this policy:

- **You want to have all of the information so that you can begin the screening process and select the best tenant for your rental property using objective criteria and your rental requirements.** The rental application is the key document you will use to verify information and conduct your entire tenant screening procedures. I discuss tenant screening in more detail in Chapter 8.
- **You want to avoid having prospects accuse you of discriminating against them by not permitting them to fill out the rental application.** It is important not to prejudge an applicant. The prospect may have already volunteered enough information about his financial situation and tenant history that you believe it would be a waste of time and effort for him to complete an application. But even in these situations, always be sure to offer your rental application form to every rental prospect of legal contracting age.

Have several rental applications and pens available at the property. Although you want to make sure that you offer a rental application form to every prospect, you don't just want to hand them out and let the prospects leave without making a commitment.

Here are some important guidelines to remember when accepting rental applications:

- **Every prospective tenant who is currently 18 years of age or older should completely fill out a written application.** This applies whether the applicants are married, related in some other way, or unrelated roommates.
- **Before accepting the rental application, carefully review the entire form to make sure that each prospective tenant has clearly and legibly provided all requested information.** Pay particular attention to all names and addresses, employment information, social security numbers, driver's license numbers, and emergency contacts. Any blanks should be marked with an "N/A" if not applicable so that you can tell that they were not inadvertently overlooked.
- **Each prospect must sign the rental application authorizing you to verify the provided information and to run a credit report.**
- **Ask each prospective tenant to show you his current driver's license or other similar photo identification so that you can confirm that the applicants are providing you with their correct names and current addresses.**

You may be asked by the prospect — or you may determine on your own — to go over the rental application with the prospect and assist him in providing the information. If you do so, be very careful to ask only questions that are part of the rental application. Avoid asking questions that may directly or indirectly discriminate. Do not ask the rental applicant about his birthplace, religion, marital status or children, or a physical or mental condition. You can ask him if he has ever been convicted of a crime and whether he is at least 18 years of age, however.

Holding a deposit

Some rental prospects are willing to make a firm commitment, but they will not or cannot give you the full security deposit and first month's rent. Maybe they just don't have the funds at the time or maybe they want to reserve your rental while looking for a better property. In these situations, you may want to ask for a holding deposit to allow you to take the rental unit off the market for a limited period of time while you obtain a credit report or verify other information on the rental application.

GRISWOLD REAL ESTATE MANAGEMENT

RENTAL APPLICATION AND APPLICATION FEE RECEIPT

VERIFIED BY

NAME ______ First ______ Last ______ Middle ______ CO-APPLICANT ______ First ______ Last ______ Middle ______

PRESENT ADDRESS ______ Street ______ City ______ State ______ Zip Code ______

TELEPHONE(____) ______ DATE OF BIRTH ______ CO-APPLICANT DATE OF BIRTH ______

SOCIAL SECURITY NO. ______ DRIVERS LIC.# ______

CO-APPLICANT SOCIAL SECURITY NO. ______ CO-APPLICANT DRIVERS LIC. NO# ______

NAMES AND AGES OF ALL PERSONS TO RESIDE IN APARTMENT ______

EMPLOYMENT HISTORY (Last Five Years) • USE REVERSE SIDE IF NECESSARY

PRESENT EMPLOYER ______ SUPERVISOR'S NAME ______ TELEPHONE (____) ______

ADDRESS ______ Street ______ City ______ State ______ Zip Code ______

GROSS SALARY ______ JOB TITLE ______ DATE EMPLOYED ______

FORMER EMPLOYER ______ TELEPHONE (____) ______

ADDRESS ______ Street ______ City ______ State ______ Zip Code ______

GROSS SALARY ______ JOB TITLE ______ PERIOD EMPLOYED From ______ To ______

CO-APPLICANT'S EMPLOYER ______ SUPERVISOR'S NAME ______ TELEPHONE (____) ______

ADDRESS ______ Street ______ City ______ State ______ Zip Code ______

GROSS SALARY ______ JOB TITLE ______ DATE EMPLOYED ______

OTHER INCOME ______

AUTOMOBILE Year ______ Make ______ Color ______ License ______ Year ______ Make ______ Color ______ License ______

HOW MANY PETS DO YOU HAVE? ______ WHAT TYPE? ______ DO YOU HAVE A WATERBED? ______

Have you or any proposed occupant listed above ever:
been convicted or pled guilty to a misdemeanor involving violence, sexual misconduct, or honesty? ____
been convicted or pled guilty to any felony? ____; been evicted or asked to move out? ____
broken a lease or rental agreement? ____; declared bankruptcy? ____; been sued for nonpayment? ____
been sued for damage to rental property? ____; had a recorded lien, garnishment or judgment? ____
If yes to any of the above, please indicate year, location and details: ______

Form 7-3: Rental Application (Page 1 of 2).

Don't allow the prospective tenant to reserve your rental property with a small holding deposit for more than a couple of days. This will give you more than enough time to screen the prospect, and any additional time the rental unit is off the market often translates into rent that you will never see. After you approve the rental prospect, you should have the prospect sign the lease or rental agreement. If the prospect still insists he needs additional time, he should agree to pay the daily rental rate or you should refund his holding deposit and continue your leasing efforts.

By taking the rental unit off the market you are forgoing the ability to rent the property to someone else. If the prospective tenant fails to go forward and rent your property for any reason, you will have potentially lost revenue while the unit has been vacant and reserved. On the other hand, rental prospects don't want to pay rent while you're running them through your tenant screening process. The solution is to use a written holding deposit agreement and receipt, like the one shown in Form 7-4 which outlines the understanding between you and the prospective tenant.

IN CASE OF EMERGENCY NOTIFY ____ Name ____ Relationship ____

ADDRESS ____ Street ____ City ____ State ____ Zip Code

PHONE ____ REFERRED BY ____

TOTAL INCOME $____ /MO.

QUALIFIED? YES ____ NO ____

$____ RENT

$____ SEC. DEP.

$____ APPLICATION FEE

$____ OTHER CHARGES

$____ TOTAL CHARGES

$____ LESS DEPOSIT ALREADY PAID

$____ TOTAL DUE ON MOVE-IN

LAST THREE PLACES OF RESIDENCE (MANDATORY)

	DATES FROM/TO	NAME OF APT. BLDG. AND MANAGER	ADDRESS	MGR'S PHONE NO.
1.				
2.				
3.				

CREDIT REFERENCES

NAME	ADDRESS	ACCOUNT NO.	PAYMENTS

BANK ____ BRANCH ____ Checking Account No. ____

BANK ____ BRANCH ____ Savings Account. No. ____

In consideration of the Application Fee in the sum of $____. Management will conduct verification of rental appliction information, including obtaining consumer credit information. Management reserves the right to unilaterally deny this application should there be any change or new information available regarding employment, compensation or any other significant item provided or requested herein between the time of the acceptance of this application by management and the move-in date; and/or if this application is not accepted by Management within seven (7) days from the date of this application, said amount shall be refunded in either case.

PROOF OF RENTER'S INSURANCE? YES ____ NO ____

Falsification or unverifiable information will be grounds for denial of said rental application. Applicant represents that all the above statements are true and correct and hereby authorizes verification of the above items including, but not limited to, the obtaining of a credit report and agrees to furnish additional credit references on request.
Applicant agrees that Management shall not be liable for any delay in the date said apartment unit is ready for occupancy. First month rent and security deposit, must be paid by cashiers check or money order prior to move-in.

M.I. DATE: ____

APPROVED BY ____ OWNER/AGENT

OWNER/AGENT

Applicant (1) ____ DATE

BY ____ TITLE ____ DATE

Applicant (2) ____ DATE

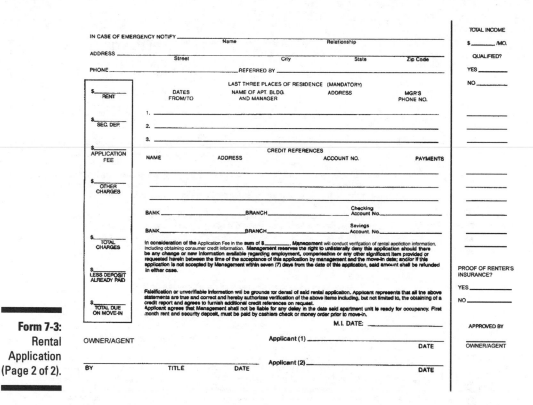

Form 7-3: Rental Application (Page 2 of 2).

If you use a holding deposit you must have a written agreement or you are very likely to encounter a misunderstanding or even legal action. State laws regarding holding deposits vary throughout the country, yet they are almost uniformly vague and can easily lead to disputes.

Developing priority waiting lists

If you have several qualified rental prospects who are interested in your rental unit, you will only be able to rent to one of them. Use the tenant selection criteria covered in Chapter 8 to select the tenant who is the most qualified.

If you have other qualified tenants, you may have other rental units at the same property or in close proximity that would interest them. If those other units aren't available right at the moment, instead of turning away the qualified rental prospects, you may be able to offer them a spot on your *priority waiting list,* which is just a way for you to keep track of qualified tenants for whom you simply don't yet have available rentals. Being in this situation is a dream come true for many rental property owners or managers.

Holding Deposit Agreement and Receipt

On the date below, ____ (Owner) received $ _______________ from

____ (Applicant) as a Holding Deposit for the premises located at:

____ (Rental unit) on the terms and conditions set forth herein.

1. Rent of $ __________ per month shall be payable in advance on the first of each month. The tenancy will begin on the _____ day of _______________, 20____, but subject to any present tenant vacating or the unavailability of the rental unit.
2. Of the total funds hereby received by Owner, the sum of $ ________ is an Application Fee that the Applicant understands and agrees is nonrefundable. The Application Fee represents the estimated costs incurred by the Owner in obtaining and verifying the credit information, employment and references of the Applicant and similar tenant screening functions.
3. Of the total funds hereby received by Owner, the sum of $ ________ represents a Holding Deposit.
4. The Applicant has paid the Application Fee and Holding Deposit to the Owner in the form of cash, cashier's check, money order or personal check. Owner is free to deposit all funds received herein and shall maintain this Holding Deposit in liquid funds subject to review by Owner or its agents of the Applicant's rental application.
5. Applicant shall be entitled to a full refund of the Holding Deposit within ________ days if the Owner determines that:
   a) The Owner does not approve the Applicant's rental application; and/or
   b) The premises are not available on the agreed date
6. Upon notification by the Owner to the Applicant that their rental application has been accepted, the Applicant agrees to execute all lease or rental agreement and related documents and pay any balance still due for the first month's rent and full security deposit. Applicant understands that once their rental application has been approved, the rental unit is being taken off the rental market and reserved for the Applicant and any or all other potential Applicants will be turned away.
7. If after acceptance of the Applicant's rental application, the Applicant fails to comply, the Owner may immediately deduct from the amount received the sum of $ ________ per day (daily rate) for each day the rental unit is vacant from the date the Applicant's tenancy was to begin through the date the rental unit is rerented to another tenant, but not in any event to exceed 30 days. It is agreed that the daily rate is calculated as an amount equal to 1/30th of the above monthly rental rate. In addition, the Owner shall be entitled to retain reasonable administrative fees and advertising expenses associated with remarketing the rental unit. The Applicant agrees that the daily rate plus the actual incurred administrative expenses and advertising costs are reasonable and liquidated damages since the actual damages would be difficult or impossible to ascertain.
8. The Owner, within ______ days after the rental unit is rerented, shall return to Applicant, to the Applicant's address shown below, any remaining balance of the Holding Deposit and shall include an itemization of the Owner's damages.
9. If any legal action or proceeding is brought by either party to enforce any part of this agreement, the prevailing party shall recover, in addition to all other relief, reasonable attorneys fees and costs. By signing below, both the Owner and Applicant acknowledge and accept all terms contained herein.

______________________ Applicant's Signature	______________________ Applicant's Signature
______________________ Applicant's Name (print)	______________________ Applicant's Name (print)
______________________ ______________________ Applicant's Address	______________________ ______________________ Applicant's Address
______________________ Date	______________________ Owner/Agent

Form 7-4: Holding Deposit Agreement.

If potential tenants express a desire to rent your property at a future date, and if you know that there are other rentals available in the area, it may be because your rents are lower than market value. (Otherwise, they would simply find another comparable rental somewhere else instead of having to wait.) If you have a long waiting list, make sure it's just because your rental property is desirable — not because you're charging too little in rent.

Some prospective tenants are simply looking for a great rental property several months in advance. Although you can't hold your rental property vacant and off the market until they're ready to rent, you can lock them in for one of your rental units that may be coming available in the future at the time they are prepared to move. This situation is especially typical for prospects who are relocating from out of town and make a trip to look for a rental a few weeks or months before they officially make the move. You may be able to pre-rent your rental units even before they become vacant (and that's a great position for any property manager to be in).

When you create a priority waiting list, don't just write the prospective tenants' names on a piece of paper, because this give you no commitment, and the chances of that prospect returning to rent from you are slim. However, prospective tenants' level of commitment will increase if you pre-qualify the prospects, take a partially refundable deposit, and give them a written confirmation that they are on your priority waiting list. You may even want to offer that you will lock in a rental rate if they rent from you within a certain number of months.

Be sure to let your prospective tenants know where they are on the waiting list. Also be sure to let them know that you can't guarantee that a certain rental unit will be available, because you can't control when your current tenants will actually vacate. Give prospective tenants the right to cancel, and let them know that the portion of their deposit not used for the tenant screening process is fully refundable at any time.

As with all rental policies, you need to apply them uniformly to all rental prospects. So if you have a priority waiting list, be sure to let all prospective tenants know about it and do not restrict anyone from being added to the list. Otherwise, you could be accused of discriminating.

Handling Mandatory Disclosures and Environmental Issues

One of the major challenges to being a successful rental property owner is keeping abreast of the constantly-evolving health and safety requirements across the country that affect rental properties. In addition to providing your tenants with a clean and habitable rental property, you need to take precautions to ensure that the rental is a safe and healthy environment.

Although there are definitely legal implications and substantial liability for failing to meet required state and federal disclosures, most rental property owners would not want to see their tenants get sick or injured. In the following sections, I cover some of the most common issues facing rental property owners today.

New federal and state legislation is constantly under consideration, and rental property owners must stay current with all requirements or face serious consequences.

Lead-based paint disclosures

Although lead-based paint is not a hazard when in good condition, it can be a serious problem (particularly for young children) when it cracks, peels, or turns to chalk due to age. Lead has been banned from paint since 1978, but even to this day older rental housing units may contain paint that was manufactured before that time. You cannot tell if paint contains lead just by looking at it; a special lead test is the only way to verify the existence of lead.

In pre-1978 properties, lead is usually found on:

- Exterior painted surfaces
- Interior trim
- Windowsills and horizontal painted surfaces
- Doors, door jambs and frames, railings, and banisters

Lead-based paint is not easy to remove. Hire a licensed contractor to address concerns about lead. Unfortunately, the removal of lead can be quite expensive. Often the best solution is to manage the lead in place rather than completely remove it as the removal processes of sanding and scraping can release large amounts of lead dust.

As a rental property owner, you need to be aware of the dangers of lead and the federally required disclosures. Over 35 states now have lead hazard reduction laws in place, some of which do require testing and careful maintenance in addition to the federal disclosure requirements.

The federal Residential Lead-Based Paint Hazard Reduction Act of 1992 covers all dwellings built before 1978 and requires rental housing owners or their property managers to notify tenants that the rental property may have lead-based paint. Testing for lead-based paint or removal is not currently required under federal law, however, you must disclose any known presence of lead-based paint or hazards and provide all tenants with copies of any available records or reports pertaining to the presence of lead-based paint and/or hazards.

In addition to all housing constructed after January 1, 1978, there are some limited rental property exemptions from federal lead-based paint disclosure regulations. Exempt properties include the following:

- Housing for the elderly or persons with disabilities (unless children who are under the age of 6 will be living there)
- Short-term rentals of 100 days or less
- Certain university housing
- Studio or efficiency units
- Housing that has been inspected and certified as "lead-free"

Be sure to contact the EPA or your state health and environmental agency for specific information. If you are advised that your property is exempt, you should be sure to receive written verification before ceasing to follow the federal requirements.

The Residential Lead-Based Paint Hazard Reduction Act also requires that you provide the tenant with an information pamphlet by the federal Environmental Protection Agency (EPA) entitled "Protect Your Family from Lead in Your Home." You can get this pamphlet online at `www.epa.gov/opptintr/lead/leadpdfe.pdf`. You can request a printed brochure (in English or Spanish) and clarification on the law from the National Lead Information Clearinghouse (NLIC) at 800-424-5323. If you need to order bulk copies of the pamphlet, you can do so through the Government Printing Office (GPO) at 202-512-1800 (you'll pay $26.00 for 50 brochures).

California and Massachusetts are currently the only states that have their own pamphlet on lead-based paint hazards that the EPA has authorized to be distributed in lieu of the EPA pamphlet.

For tenants on leases, the federal regulations require property owners or managers to notify the tenant the first time the tenant renews a lease that was made prior to December 6, 1996. Nearly all tenants should have received the required notification, because virtually all residential leases have renewed or rolled over to month-to-month rental agreements since December 6, 1996. For month-to-month rental agreements, the regulations require the disclosure statement to be given when the first rent check is collected after December 6, 1996. Immediately give your rental prospect or tenant the disclosure statement if you do not have written verification that they have already received one.

Most rental property owners use a lead-based paint disclosure form (see Figure 7-2) to ensure that they have complied with this law. You can print this form online at `www.epa.gov/opptintr/lead/lesr_eng.pdf` or contact the NLIC at 800-424-5323 for more information.

Disclosure of Information on Lead-Based Paint and/or Lead-Based Paint Hazards

Lead Warning Statement

Housing built before 1978 may contain lead-based paint. Lead from paint, paint chips, and dust can pose health hazards if not managed properly. Lead exposure is especially harmful to young children and pregnant women. Before renting pre-1978 housing, lessors must disclose the presence of known lead-based paint and/or lead-based paint hazards in the dwelling. Lessees must also receive a federally approved pamphlet on lead poisoning prevention.

Lessor's Disclosure

(a) Presence of lead-based paint and/or lead-based paint hazards (check (i) or (ii) below):

(i) _____ Known lead-based paint and/or lead-based paint hazards are present in the housing (explain).

____

____

(ii) _____ Lessor has no knowledge of lead-based paint and/or lead-based paint hazards in the housing.

(b) Records and reports available to the lessor (check (i) or (ii) below):

(i) _____ Lessor has provided the lessee with all available records and reports pertaining to lead-based paint and/or lead-based paint hazards in the housing (list documents below).

____

____

(ii) _____ Lessor has no reports or records pertaining to lead-based paint and/or lead-based paint hazards in the housing.

Lessee's Acknowledgment (initial)

(c) _______ Lessee has received copies of all information listed above.

(d) _______ Lessee has received the pamphlet *Protect Your Family from Lead in Your Home.*

Agent's Acknowledgment (initial)

(e) _______ Agent has informed the lessor of the lessor's obligations under 42 U.S.C. 4852(d) and is aware of his/her responsibility to ensure compliance.

Certification of Accuracy

The following parties have reviewed the information above and certify, to the best of their knowledge, that the information they have provided is true and accurate.

Lessor	Date	Lessor	Date
Lessee	Date	Lessee	Date
Agent	Date	Agent	Date

Figure 7-2: As a property owner, you are required by law to give a lead-based paint disclosure form like this one to any tenants or prospective tenants if your property was built before January 1, 1978.

Courtesy of U.S. Environmental Protection Agency

Whichever pamphlet you provide your tenants, be sure that you comply with the federal law and keep a copy of the disclosure form signed and dated by the tenant. This written record of compliance with the disclosure requirements must be kept and available for review in case of an investigation or audit for a minimum of 3 years. Remember that you only need to make the required disclosure once, even if a tenant renews an existing lease.

Significant fines can be applied for rental property owners or property managers who fail to follow the federal regulations for lead-based paint. To enforce the regulations, the federal Housing and Urban Development (HUD) agency and the EPA are working together to investigate complaints from prospective tenants and/or current tenants who believe they may have been exposed to lead-based paint. If the tenant does not receive the required EPA or approved state information pamphlet or the disclosure statement, the owner or property manager may be subject to:

- A notice of noncompliance
- A civil penalty of up to $11,000 per violation for willful and continuing noncompliance
- An order to pay the injured tenant up to three times their actual damages
- A criminal fine of up to $11,000 per violation

Recently the EPA and HUD have begun to aggressively enforce these regulations and have levied very significant and well-publicized fines against the owners and managers of rental properties who have not complied with the federal law. Government testers will even pose as prospective tenants, and federal agents will scour all of your leasing and maintenance records looking for evidence that you knew or should have known about the existence of lead-based paint hazards on your property. This is not an area where you want to tempt fate. Make sure that you comply with this law and keep the required documentation on file and easy to retrieve for at least 3 years.

Asbestos

Asbestos has received a lot of media coverage over the last 20 years. You may remember the federal government's concerns about asbestos in schools and the major efforts to remove asbestos-containing materials from those facilities. Despite this concern, there are currently no federal disclosure rules for asbestos in rental housing and there is no federal requirement to investigate or remove asbestos. However, be sure to check with your local and state officials for any disclosure requirements they may require.

Asbestos is a mineral fiber that historically was added to a variety of products to strengthen them and to provide heat insulation and fire resistance. In most products, asbestos is combined with a binding material so that it is not released into the air. As long as the material remains bonded so that fibers are not released, there is no health risk. There are several types of asbestos fibers, and asbestos can only be positively identified with a special type of microscope.

Studies of people who were exposed to asbestos clearly show that breathing high levels of asbestos fibers can lead to an increased risk of lung cancer;

mesothelioma, a cancer of the lining of the chest and the abdominal cavity; and *asbestosis,* a condition in which the lungs become scarred with fibrous tissue.

Although there is no known safe exposure level to asbestos, the small exposure that we receive in our daily lives is not a problem. However, the risk of lung cancer and mesothelioma increases with the number of fibers inhaled. The risk of lung cancer from inhaling asbestos fibers is also greater if you smoke. People who get asbestosis have usually been exposed to high levels of asbestos for a long time. The symptoms of these diseases do not usually appear until about 20 to 30 years after the first exposure to asbestos.

The concern in most rental properties is that asbestos-containing materials will be disturbed. If disturbed, asbestos-containing material may release asbestos fibers, which can be inhaled into the lungs. The fibers can remain there for a long time, increasing the risk of disease. Unfortunately, some asbestos materials are *friable,* meaning they crumble into small particles or fibers. Asbestos-containing materials can also crumble easily if mishandled, and asbestos can be released into the air if it is sawed, scraped, or sanded into a powder. A common cause of the release of asbestos in rental housing is inappropriate or unsafe handling of asbestos-containing materials during remodeling or the renovation of the rental property.

Products containing asbestos are not often labeled. Until 1981, asbestos was commonly used, and it is estimated that there are over 3,000 products still in use contain asbestos or asbestos-containing materials and can be found in many rental properties. These include acoustic ceilings, vinyl flooring and tile, building insulation, wall and ceiling panels, carpet padding, roofing materials, pipe and duct insulation, patching and spackling compounds, and furnaces.

The federal Occupational Safety and Health Administration (OSHA) has developed regulations that apply to any building constructed prior to 1981. These pre-1981 buildings are presumed to have asbestos unless the owner affirmatively tests to verify that asbestos or asbestos-containing materials are not present.

According to the American Lung Association, if you have asbestos-containing substances in your rental property and the material is in good condition, leave it alone. If the material is damaged, you may want to have the material repaired or removed. Always seek the advice of a professional environmental firm to evaluate and recommend the best course of action concerning asbestos.

Repair usually involves either sealing or covering asbestos material. Sealing is also commonly referred to as *encapsulation* and involves coating materials so that the asbestos is sealed in. Encapsulation is only effective for undamaged asbestos-containing material. If materials are soft, crumbly, or otherwise damaged, sealing is not appropriate. Covering involves placing something over or around the material that contains asbestos to prevent the release of fibers.

The removal of asbestos-containing materials is an expensive and hazardous process and should be a last resort. Removal is complex and requires special training, tools, and techniques. A licensed contractor who specializes in asbestos-containing materials should be used, because improper removal could very easily increase the health risks to the workers, yourself, and your future tenants.

Asbestos is a very dangerous material if disturbed. Do not attempt to test for asbestos on your own. Hire a professional environmental testing firm because the act of breaking open potentially asbestos-containing material to obtain test samples could release asbestos into the air and create a very dangerous situation.

Radon

Radon is a radioactive gas, and a known cancer-causing agent, that is found in soil and rock in all parts of the United States. It is formed as a byproduct of the natural decay of the radioactive materials radium and uranium. Radon gas is invisible; it has no odor or taste. Its presence in the interior of buildings has been found to cause lung cancer. However, most radon found in buildings poses no direct threat to human life because the range of concentration is generally below the minimum safe level.

Although there are currently no federal requirements to disclose or even test for radon gas, it is potentially a serious health issue and one that is receiving more attention. Be aware of radon levels in your rental units, and check with local authorities for more information about the prevalence and appropriate precautions that should be taken to avoid radon exposure. Florida and New Jersey have been particularly aggressive in addressing the radon problem. But be sure to check with your local authorities for any specific disclosure requirements in your area.

Although radon may be found in all types of homes and buildings throughout the U.S., it is more likely to occur in the lower levels of tightly-sealed, energy-efficient buildings where insulation limits the flow of air from the inside to the outside and ventilation is poor.

The only way to know whether your rental property has radon at unhealthy levels is to conduct short-term and/or long-term radon testing. The good news is that radon tests are inexpensive and easy to use. The quickest way to test for radon is with a short-term test. Short-term tests remain in your home anywhere from 2 to 90 days, depending on the device. Long-term tests remain in your home for more than 90 days. Because radon levels tend to vary from day to day and season to season, a long-term test is more likely to tell you your home's year-round average radon level than a short-term test.

You can test for radon yourself or hire a professional. The do-it-yourself radon test kits are available in hardware stores. Some laboratories provide kits through mail order. Make sure you get one that meets the EPA standards or your state's requirements — the test kit will usually say so on the package. The price of a simple short-term radon test kit starts at about $10 and generally includes the cost of having a laboratory analyze the test. If you cannot find a radon test kit in your community, you can contact the EPA National Radon Hotline by calling 800-767-7236 or by visiting the EPA Web site at `www.epa.gov/iaq/radon/`.

If your tests reveal radon in one particular unit of an apartment building, have all the other units tested immediately, and notify all other tenants in the building of the problem promptly. Remember that even if your radon test shows low radon levels, there may be high levels in other parts of the building.

Fixing a radon problem usually involves repairs to the building. Therefore, you as the building owner, not your tenant, should have this work done. If your rental property has high radon levels, you can take steps to see that the problem is fixed including the installation of equipment such as fans, blowers, and ducts that are available to reduce the radon gas levels. The EPA advises that radon reduction costs between $500 and $2,500 for a single-family home. For a larger rental property, the costs depend on the size and other characteristics of the building.

Radon reduction work generally requires a trained professional. To find out which radon reduction system is right for a building and how much those repairs will cost, consult with a professional radon contractor. The EPA and many states have programs set up to train or certify radon professionals. Look in the Yellow Pages for your state radon office, because they can provide a list of individuals who have completed state or federal programs. They can also provide a list of EPA-approved radon mitigators in your state.

Sexual offenders

Almost every state has a version of Megan's Law, which requires certain convicted sexual offenders to register with local law enforcement. The local law enforcement then maintains a database on the whereabouts of the registered sex offenders, and they often make this information available to the public.

Megan's Law is named after 7-year old Megan Kanka of Hamilton, New Jersey, who was raped and murdered in the summer of 1994 by a convicted child molester who was living in her neighborhood without her parents' knowledge. In 1996, this federal crime prevention law was passed, requiring the Federal Bureau of Investigation (FBI) to keep a national database of all persons convicted of sexual offenses against minors and violent sexual offenses against anyone. Prison officials are required to inform convicted sex offenders of their legal obligation to register with state law enforcement authorities. The state agencies are required to inform local law enforcement and the FBI as to the registered addresses for each convicted sex offender. Local law enforcement agencies are then permitted to release the collected information as necessary to protect the public.

Unfortunately, the states are not very consistent in their efforts to maintain and make this database available. The federal law allows each state to decide how to use and distribute the database information. The three options are:

- **Widespread notification with easy access.** This allows notification to the public, including methods such as posting the names and addresses on the Internet or on a CD-ROM.
- **Selective notification with limited access.** This allows notification to only those most at risk, such as schools and daycare centers.
- **Restricted notification with narrow access.** This allows access only for a particular name or address.

Although registration is mandatory, often the addresses provided are not verified or the convicted sex offender may move and fail to reregister at his new address. Also, the accuracy of this database can vary widely based on the age of the information.

Some states require property owners or managers to provide a disclosure statement to each tenant advising him of the availability of the Megan's Law database. Whether you are required by state law to give your tenant a Megan's Law disclosure, if you are ever asked by a prospective renter about Megan's Law, be sure to refer the prospect to local law enforcement and make a written and dated note for your file. For specific information on the requirements of Megan's Law for your state, call your local law enforcement.

Chapter 8

Eenie, Meenie, Miney, Mo: Selecting Your Tenants

In This Chapter

- Setting up written criteria for your tenant screening process
- Verifying your applicants' information
- Knowing the laws surrounding fair housing

When you own rental property, one of your most important tasks is screening and selecting tenants. Because the process of screening tenants is time-consuming, you need to have a system in place for doing it efficiently, so in this chapter, I help you navigate these unfamiliar waters with ease.

Actually tenant selection and screening can be summed up very simply:

- Develop and use objective, written tenant selection criteria.
- Consistently screen all rental applicants against these minimum criteria.
- Select the most qualified tenant based on your review.

With a system, tenant screening really isn't that difficult; it just requires assertiveness, diligence, and patience. Even after you've been managing your rental properties for many years, you still won't be able to just look at a rental application and know whether the applicant is qualified. You have to check the tenant's references, credit history, employment income, job stability, and history as a tenant. And you can't cut corners. Selecting a bad tenant is much worse than having a vacant rental unit. So take the time to choose your tenants wisely, and you'll profit in the long run.

Another critical part of choosing your tenants is making sure you handle the selection process without bias, abiding by all fair-housing regulations. This can be a murky issue, but it's an important one, and one you need to pay attention to no matter what your situation, so you're not slapped with a lawsuit charging you with discrimination.

Understanding the Importance of Screening

If you're like many rental property owners, you may be thinking, "Screening? Isn't that just a waste of time? After all, I trust my gut instinct when I meet people. I know which ones are good and which are just trouble." Although it does take time to verify all the information on your prospective tenant's rental application, it's time well spent. Relying on your instincts is very inaccurate, arbitrary, and above all, illegal.

In order to increase your chance of finding a long-term, stable tenant, and in order to avoid charges of discrimination, your tenant selection criteria and screening process should be clear, systematic, and objective. Put it in writing to ensure that the process is applied consistently and fairly to *all* rental applicants.

Setting up a systematic screening process is particularly critical if you only own a single rental or a small, multi-unit rental property. *Professional deadbeat tenants* (people who go from property to property damaging the units or not paying rent) are experienced and shrewd. They know that the large, professionally managed rental properties have detailed and thorough screening procedures that attempt to verify every single item on their rental application. If certain items don't check out, the professional property manager doesn't just trust her feelings on the prospective tenant. The professional deadbeat tenants, who always have something to hide, know that small rental property owners are easier targets, because the novice property owner is more likely to bend the rules than the professional.

Sometimes the mere mention of the tenant screening process is enough to make the rental prospect fidget and then shift into the classic "I'm just looking" mode. Don't rush or allow a prospect to hurry you through the tenant screening and selection process. The wrong decision can be financially devastating, particularly if you have just a couple of rental units with monthly debt payments.

Establishing solid tenant-selection criteria and performing a thorough tenant screening process does not guarantee a good tenant, but it does significantly improve your odds.

Establishing Tenant Selection Criteria

Tenant selection criteria are written standards that you use to evaluate each prospective tenant's qualifications as a tenant for your property. You should determine your exact minimum qualifications and adhere to them. Of course, your written criteria cannot be discriminatory or violate any federal, state, or local fair-housing laws.

In order to establish your tenant selection criteria, review what you are looking for in a tenant. Your idea of the ideal tenant may be different from someone else's, but here are five important traits to look for:

- Someone who will be financially responsible and always pay his rent on time.
- Someone who will respect and treat the property as if it were her own.
- Someone who will be a good neighbor and not cause problems.
- Someone who will be stable and be likely to renew his lease.
- Someone who will leave the premises in a condition the same as or better than she found it.

In order to have the best results in selecting your tenants and make sure that rental prospects understand your tenant-selection criteria, develop a *statement of rental policy,* which is a formal, written statement explaining your screening criteria.

Giving all prospective tenants an overview of your rental screening procedure and requirements up front lets them know exactly what you're looking for in a qualified rental applicant. Because these are the minimum standards you will accept, prospective tenants will know why their rental application may be rejected.

If you make an exception for one applicant and not another, you could find yourself accused of discrimination in your tenant selection process.

Form 8-1 shows a sample statement of rental policy that you can develop for your rental property and provide to each and every rental applicant over the age of 18. Your policy standards may be more or less stringent depending on your rental market and experience. But no matter what, be sure that they comply with all state and local laws.

Developing your own statement of rental policy has several benefits:

- **The rental applicant knows that you are aware of and comply with all fair-housing laws.**
- **Rental applicants understand that rental activity and getting units ready to rent are dynamic processes.** Certain units will or will not be available even within the same day and there are legitimate business reasons behind this. Outlining this policy and maintaining good records can minimize accusations of discrimination.
- **Rental applicants are aware that you abide by the reasonable limits suggested by most federal and state standards, while being aware of the limitations of the rental unit.**

- **You have explained your process of evaluating rental applications so the applicant knows what to expect.** The applicant knows that all applications are thoroughly verified, that the process takes one or two days, and that you charge an application fee to cover some of your costs for the screening process.
- **Your objective tenant screening criteria show that all applicants are evaluated consistently and fairly.** The rental prospect can review your requirements and evaluate their own qualifications to see whether it's even worth their time to apply.

Your statement of rental policy should be given to each and every applicant with the rental application. If you have a multi-unit rental property with an office, clearly post the policy where all applicants can see it. If you do not have an office, insert the policy in an acrylic or similar holder and place it in clear view on the rental unit's kitchen counter or another area where all prospects can see it as they walk through.

You are not required to provide your rental prospects with a copy of your written tenant selection criteria. Although you must offer all prospects a rental application and process each one received, there is a benefit to prospects making their own decision not to apply for your rental based on the criteria you've set up. The key is to follow the criteria without exception and have the information available if you are challenged.

Some rental property owners feel more comfortable discussing the tenant-selection criteria right from the first rental inquiry call, whereas others will wait and distribute copies only to those who actually apply. You need to decide which policy works best for you and then apply it consistently.

Always be very thorough when you perform tenant screening, and use the same process with all rental applicants. You run the risk of a charge of illegal discrimination if you deviate from your written standards for certain applicants. There are many legally acceptable reasons to deny a rental application. Be sure that your requirements are clearly understood and followed.

The fact that you carefully pre-screen all prospects is a positive factor not only for you, but also for your rental applicants, your current tenants, and even the neighbors. In fact, you have a responsibility to your current tenants to weed out the unqualified tenants with a track record of disrupting the neighbors everywhere they go. The good rental prospects will appreciate the fact that their neighbors had to meet your high standards, too.

Over 90 percent of your rental applicants will be good tenants, pay their rent on time, take good care of their homes, and treat you and their neighbors with respect. You just need to carefully guard against those few bad apples, and don't hesitate to deny prospects who cannot meet your standards.

Statement of rental policy

We are glad you are interested in our rental property. For your convenience, we have prepared this overview of our guidelines used in processing all rental applications. Please feel free to ask any questions.

We are an equal opportunity housing provider: It is our policy to rent our units in full compliance with the federal Fair Housing Act and all state and local fair-housing laws. We do not discriminate against any person because of race, color, ethnic background, religion, sex, age, marital or family status, physical disability or sexual orientation.

Rental unit availability: Rental units only become available when they are completely ready to rent, including cleaning, painting, and the completion of all maintenance work and planned improvements. Rental unit availability can change as units become available during the day or are removed from the rental market based on rentals, cancellations or maintenance issues.

Valid photo identification and written authorization: You must be able to present a current photo identification such as a driver's license, military or state identification card, or passport so that we can verify your identity. If your rental application is approved, we will require a photocopy of your identification at the time of your move-in to be kept in your tenant file. You must authorize us to verify all information provided in your rental application from credit sources, credit agencies, current and prior landlords and employers, and personal references, and allow us to run a criminal background check.

Occupancy guidelines: In compliance with all applicable fair-housing laws we have established restrictions on the total number of persons that may occupy a given rental unit. Our guidelines allow two persons per bedroom plus one additional person per rental unit. These guidelines are to prevent overcrowding and are in keeping with the limitations of the rental unit and its building systems. Occupancy will be limited to the persons indicated on the original rental application and lease only unless otherwise agreed in writing. Any proposed additional tenants must complete a rental application and be processed and approved through this same tenant-screening process prior to occupying the rental unit.

Application process: All rental applications are evaluated in the same manner, and each adult applicant must voluntarily provide his or her social security number for us to obtain a consumer credit report. Every adult applicant must complete a separate rental application form and pay the nonrefundable application fee in advance. Any false or incomplete information will result in the denial of your application. If discovered after you are approved and have moved in, we reserve the right to terminate your tenancy. We will verify the information provided on each rental application through our own screening efforts and/or with the assistance of an independent tenant-screening firm. A credit report, criminal history, and employment and rental references for each and every applicant in a given rental unit will determine whether our rental criteria has been met. Unless we need to verify information by regular mail, we are usually able to process a

Form 8-1: Statements of Rental Policy (Page 1 of 2).

rental application in one or two days.

Rental criteria

Income: The total combined monthly gross income of all rental applicants in a given rental unit must be at least three times the monthly rental rate. Only income that can be verified will count. We expect rental applicants with income to prove at least one year of continuous employment. Full-time students are welcome if the total income of all applicants combined is sufficient or with a lease guarantor. You must provide proof of a source of income if you are unemployed. Remember: All adult tenants are joint and severally liable, which means that each one can be held responsible for the payment of all funds due regardless of ability to pay.

Credit history: You must be able to demonstrate fiscal responsibility. If you have any charge-offs, unpaid debts, or a pattern of delinquent payments, your application may be denied.

Rental history: Each rental applicant must be able to demonstrate a pattern of meeting their rental obligations, leaving prior rental properties in good condition and not having a pattern of complaints from neighbors. We will require satisfactory rental references from at least two prior landlords. If you have ever been evicted for any lease violation, your application may be denied.

Criminal history: If you have ever been convicted of (or pled guilty or no contest to) a felony, or a misdemeanor involving violence, sexual misconduct or honesty, your application may be denied.

Guarantors: If you do not meet one or more of the above criteria, you may be able to qualify for a rental unit if you have a third party located within the state that will guarantee your lease. The guarantor must pass this same application and screening process except that we will deduct the guarantors own housing costs before comparing his or her income to our income criteria.

Form 8-1: Statement of Rental Policy (Page 2 of 2).

Verifying Rental Applications

Bad tenants don't walk around with the word *deadbeat* printed on their foreheads. The tenant screening process requires you to be a detective, and all good detectives verify each fact and take thorough notes. You want to ensure that the rental prospect meets your minimum standards as outlined in your statement of rental policy.

I recommend that you use a rental application verification form, like the one shown in Form 8-2, to collect and review the necessary information that will allow you to properly evaluate the qualifications of your rental applicant.

Keep copies of all rental applications, the corresponding rental application verification forms, credit reports, and all other documentation for both accepted *and* rejected applicants for at least three years. That way, if anyone ever makes a claim that you discriminated against him, your best defense will be your own records, which will clearly indicate that you had legal rental criteria and you applied it consistently.

Verifying the identity of all adults

The very first step you should always take in verifying a rental application is to personally meet each prospective adult tenant. You should require each prospective adult tenant to show you his or her current driver's license or other similar (and official) photo ID so that you can confirm that the applicant is providing you with the correct name and current address. Advise the rental applicants that if their application is approved, you will need a photocopy of their ID to be kept in their tenant file. Initial the rental application to record that you did indeed verify this information.

Inquire about any discrepancies between the application and the ID provided. Even if the explanation seems reasonable, be sure to write down the new information. Maybe an old address appears on the photo ID, which you can check out further through a credit reporting agency.

Having a photocopy of the ID for each adult tenant can be very important if a dispute concerning the tenant's identity arises in the future. In these situations, you need to be able to clearly show that you positively identified the tenant upon move-in.

Reviewing occupancy guidelines

Take a look at the rental application information provided by the tenant concerning the number of persons they plan to have occupy your rental property to ensure that the anticipated use is within your established occupancy guidelines.

One of the major concerns of property managers is excessive wear and tear of the rental unit. Clearly, the greater the number of occupants in a rental unit, the more possibility for wear and tear. Unfortunately, there are no simple answers when it comes to occupancy, and the laws and regulations concerning occupancy standards are not universally accepted. For example, the HUD guidelines state that property managers can limit occupancy to two individuals per bedroom. However, state and local restrictions must be followed as well. And in California, for example, the Department of Fair Employment and Housing has formulated the *2 + 1 occupancy standard guideline,* which states that a property manager must allow 2 individuals per bedroom, plus an additional occupant for the unit. In other words, 3 individuals may occupy a 1-bedroom rental unit, and 5 individuals a 2-bedroom rental unit, and so forth.

Contact your local or state housing agency for information on their regulations concerning occupancy. You must always apply the most generous occupancy standard.

Rental Application Verification Form

Name of Applicant ______________________________

Address of Rental Unit ______________________________

Rental History (*Note:* Use separate sheets to verify at least two prior landlords.)

Name and Phone of Prior Landlord ______________________________

Prior Address ______________________________

Is the applicant currently living in your rental unit? ____________

What is/was the applicants monthly rent in your unit? ____________

Are you related to the applicant? ______________________________

Was the applicant a roommate or guest? ______________________________

When did the applicant move in? __________ Move out? __________

Did the applicant pay rent on time? ________ If late, describe __________

Did you ever begin legal proceedings against the applicant or other occupants? ________ If yes, what was the outcome of those proceedings? __________

Why did the applicant leave? ______________________________

If the applicant moved voluntarily, did the applicant give proper notice? ______

How many days? ________

Did the applicant or other occupants damage the rental unit (beyond normal wear and tear) or damage the common area? ________ If yes, please describe

____

____

Did the applicant pay for any damage? ______________________________

Did the applicant maintain their rental unit in a clean and sanitary condition?

____

What types of pets did the applicant have? ______________________________

Were there any problems with the pets? ______________________________

Would you rent to this applicant again? ______ Why or why not? __________

Form 8-2: Rental Application Verification Form (Page 1 of 3).

Other Comments ____

____

Employment Verification

Contact Name ____________________ Company ______________________

Contact's Job Title ____

Contact Phone ______________________ Date contacted ______________

Dates of Employment ____

Applicant's Job Title ____________________ Compensation ______________

Stability of employment ____

Comments ____

Credit History

Credit report obtained from ____

Date of credit report ____

Information consistent with rental application? __________________________

Summary of pertinent results ____

Criminal History (if any)

Criminal history report obtained from ______________________________________

Date of criminal history report ____

Criminal convictions, if any ____

Personal reference

Contact Name ____

Contact Phone ______________________ Date contacted ______________

Relationship to Applicant ____

How long have you known applicant? ______________________________________

Form 8-2: Rental Application Verification Form (Page 2 of 3).

Comments ____

Additional Information

____

____

Reason for Rejecting Applicant (if applicable)

____

Form 8-2: Rental Application Verification Form (Page 3 of 3).

In addition to the occupancy standards, there are also maximum occupancy limits that are usually set by state and local health and safety boards, or building codes based on the size of the rental unit and the number of bedrooms and bathrooms. The maximum occupancy that would be permitted under these code sections is often as high as 7 persons in a 1-bedroom rental unit. The occupancy of your rental unit should stay closer to the minimum rather than the maximum.

Unless you have a more generous state or local requirement, I recommend using the 2 + 1 minimum occupancy guideline. Although the federal and most state and local occupancy standards will allow a more restrictive policy, the burden of proof is on the rental property owner. If you feel that you have a legitimate basis for having a more restrictive occupancy standard, hire a consultant and have him make an independent evaluation and recommendation.

Checking rental history

Contact the rental applicant's current landlord and go through the questions on the rental history portion of the rental application verification form. When you first contact the prior landlord, you may want to listen to his initial reaction and let him tell you about the applicant. Some landlords will welcome the opportunity to tell you all about your rental applicant. Listen carefully.

Some rental applicants will provide you with letters of reference from their prior landlord or even a copy of their credit report. This is particularly true in many competitive rental markets where only the prepared tenants have a chance to get a quality rental property. Although the more information you have the better decision you can usually make, be very careful to evaluate the authenticity of any documents provided by the rental applicant. Accept any documents that the prospect provides, but always perform your complete tenant screening process to independently verify all information.

If the information you receive on your applicant from the current landlord is primarily negative, you may not need to check with any other prior landlords. However, be wary that the current landlord may not be entirely honest; he could be upset with the tenant for leaving his property or not say anything bad about a problem tenant so that he can get the tenant out of his property and into yours.

Current or prior landlords may not be entirely forthcoming with answers to many of your questions. Most likely they are concerned that they will have some liability if they provide any negative or subjective information.

When a current or prior landlord is not overly cooperative, try to gain his confidence by providing him with some information about yourself and your rental property. If you are still unable to build rapport, try to get him to at least answer the most important question of all — "Would you rent to this applicant again?" He can simply give you a "yes" or a "no" without any details. Of course, silence can also tell you everything that you need to know.

Another useful screening tool is to request all tenants to provide copies of their water and utility bills for the past year. This will verify the tenant's prior address and also give you an idea if they pay their bills on time. (A rental prospect who cannot pay their utility bills in a timely manner is very likely to have trouble paying your rent.) You may also want to inquire with local law enforcement to see if their records show any complaints at the tenant's prior address.

Verifying employment and income

Although credit reporting agencies may provide information on your rental applicant's employment and income, they typically will not have all the information you need to properly evaluate this extremely important rental qualification criteria.

Independently verify the company information and phone number the applicant puts on her application if you have any doubts about the authenticity of it. You may have reason for concern if the employer is a major corporation and the telephone is not answered in a typical and customary business manner, for example. You also need to be careful that you confirm the sensitive compensation and stability of employment questions only with an appropriate representative of the employer.

Occasionally, you may find that an employer or the current or prior landlord will not verify any information over the phone. So be prepared to send letters requesting the pertinent information and include a self-addressed, stamped envelope. Be sure to tell your rental prospect that you may have a delay in providing her with the results of your tenant screening process.

In addition to your credit report information and the results of your verification calls, your rental applicant should provide you with proof of her employment and income such as recent pay stubs. No matter how strong the information is, you must still verify it directly with the employer or source of the income.

Always require written verification of all other sources of income that a rental applicant is using to meet your income qualification requirements. If you cannot verify the income, you do not have to include it in your calculations to determine whether the applicant meets your minimum income requirements.

When you have a rental applicant that relies on sales, commission income, or bonuses, make sure you review at least six consecutive months of pay stubs. Of course, the best policy is to require all applicants with any income other than salary to provide a copy of their signed tax return for the last two years. Although you must be careful it is an authentic document, I have yet to find a rental prospect who overstates her annual income on her tax return.

As a detective, you need to pay close attention to applicants who seem to actually be overqualified or anxious to be approved and take possession of your rental unit. Remember the old saying, "If it sounds too good to be true, it *is* too good to be true"? That definitely applies in the world of rental property, so keep it in mind at all times.

Be particularly careful of rental applicants who seem to have plenty of cash to pay your security deposit and first month's rent, but who do not have verifiable sources of income that seem consistent with their spending patterns. The applicant may be involved in illegal activity, and you may need to evict her later at considerable expense and loss of income. Rental property owners can even lose their properties under certain circumstance if they fail to take action to eliminate the source of illegal activity on their property.

Reviewing the applicant's credit history

You can and should check out an applicant's credit history by getting a credit report on each applicant. A credit report will show all current and previous credit cards and loans with rating information on the timeliness of payments when due, plus all public record entries such as bankruptcy and judgment. You can figure out whether an applicant has been late or delinquent in paying his rent or other living expenses.

So what are you looking for on a credit report? You want someone with a pattern of financial responsibility and prudent or conservative spending. You want to avoid rental applicants who seem to be using excessive credit and are living beyond their means. If they move into your rental property and have even a temporary loss of income due to illness or a job situation, you may be the one with an unexpected loss of income because of it!

If it looks too good to be true, it probably is!

I once managed a large rental property in a major city. I regularly visited the property and performed an inspection of both the physical aspects as well as the rental office procedures. One area of ongoing review was the new rental applications, which I reviewed to ensure that they were being properly completed and that the tenant screening process was being applied uniformly.

During one of my visits, I reviewed a rental application for a 1-bedroom apartment that was in the process of being reviewed. The onsite manager spoke very highly of this younger person who had just graduated from high school, was looking for his first apartment, and listed an income of $500 per week. The manager then told me how, with over $2,000 per month in income, this applicant was financially qualified.

Having been in rental management for many years, I was curious about the weekly income, so I took a look at the rental application and noticed that the individual listed the local sports facility as his employer. Sure enough, upon our subsequent inquiry of the employer and then the prospect, it became apparent that the rental prospect did indeed earn $500 per week. The only problem was that this was only during the six months of the professional baseball season and only in the two weeks per month that the local team was playing games in town. We were reminded of the importance of looking at the income of an applicant over a long period of time.

Carefully compare the addresses contained on the credit report to the information provided on the rental application. If there is an inconsistency, ask the rental prospect for an explanation. Maybe they were temporarily staying with a family member or they simply forgot about one of their residences. Of course, be sure to contact prior landlords and ask all the questions on the rental application verification form just to make sure that the applicant didn't neglect to tell you about that residence for a reason.

Information obtained in credit reports must be kept strictly confidential and cannot be given to any third parties. In some states, the rental applicant is entitled to a copy of his own credit report upon request, and federal law allows anyone denied credit on the basis of his credit report to obtain a free copy of their report.

Credit reports can have their limitations. So make sure that you are reviewing the credit report of your actual applicant. People with poor credit or tenant histories have been known to steal the identity of others, particularly their own children by using the child's social security number. One solution is to make sure that your credit reporting service provides a social security search.

The cost of a credit report varies widely. On an individual basis, credit reports can run between $30 and $50. If you join a credit reporting agency, you can get discounts of 50 percent or more on each credit report. Some agencies offer memberships with minimum monthly fees. But only owners of multiple rental properties who run at least one credit report per month will really benefit from membership. If you run less than a dozen credit reports annually, you'll usually find it cheaper to just pay a higher fee per report.

If you own just a few rental units, you may find that joining your local apartment association is a better deal than paying $30 to $50 per credit report. Not only will you have easy access to reasonably priced credit reports through your local apartment association, but as a member you can also take advantage of its education, publications, and forms.

The three largest credit reporting agencies are:

- **Experian,** Web site: `www.experian.com`, phone: 888-397-3742
- **Equifax,** Web site: `www.equifax.com`, phone: 800-997-2493
- **Trans Union,** Web site: `www.tuc.com`, phone: 800-888-4213

What's in a name?

I have served as an expert witness in many interesting litigation matters concerning real estate. One of my more memorable assignments was to consult with the Legal Aid Society of Alameda County, based in Oakland, California. It had received complaints from several people who claimed they were being repeatedly denied rental housing even though they had excellent jobs and perfect credit.

After a brief investigation, it became obvious that the problem was a particular Bay Area tenant screening service that was not careful to accurately identify the rental applicant. When a rental applicant with a fairly common name was run through their database, they would provide the rental property owner with negative information on evictions and poor credit patterns. Unfortunately, their information was not carefully screened and verified and was not information on the actual rental applicant.

Some very responsible and qualified applicants were turned down when they submitted rental applications, because they have the same name as an individual with a very poor credit report. The case was resolved and the tenant screening company implemented new crosschecking procedures to greatly improve the accuracy of its database.

The lesson for rental property owners is this: Be sure to verify the applicant's name, social security number, and several former addresses to ensure that you are using the correct information in your screening efforts. Compare the social security card number provided by the applicant with information showing the approximate date and general geographic location of issuance. You know you have a problem if your applicant is over 40 years old and was born and raised along the East coast, yet the credit reporting agency indicates that the social security card was originally issued in Arizona in the last few years.

Charging an applicant for a credit report if you do not actually run one is illegal. If you receive a large number of rental applications, review them first and then only run the credit report on the most qualified applicants. Check your state laws to make sure that you do not exceed any legal maximum charges, and be sure to return any unused credit check fees to those for whom you don't run the credit check.

The Internet is quickly changing the tenant screening procedures for many rental property owners. Credit reports, tenant history, and limited criminal background information are now available from your computer in a matter of seconds and often this allows you to approve your rental applicant in a single day, which can be a strong competitive advantage. Many firms are entering this market locally and nationally, and all offer very impressive services designed to save you time and help you fill your vacancies faster. Using technology can improve the efficiency of the information collection for tenant screening and provide you with more information to make a better decision. However, don't rely strictly on computers and forget to personally contact past landlords, verify the applicant's income and employment, or consider your own dealings with your prospective tenant. Rental property ownership and management is still and always will be a people business.

Although the Internet companies have some very slick marketing and impressive claims, be very careful when you hear a pitch that an online tenant screening service will respond to you with recommendations to "accept," "accept with conditions," or "decline" a rental applicant. These systems assign points for length of employment or income and allow for additional points or deductions for bad credit or negative references. Although touted as a way to objectively evaluate rental applicants, these systems are very subjective based on the weight assigned to each criterion. Thus, they are potentially discriminatory, and you could be challenged to explain your criteria for denying the rental applicant. For these reasons, I recommend that you avoid tenant screening and selection methods that assign points in order to rank tenants based on their financial stability, tenant history, and other factors.

Many types of applicant screening products are available to rental property owners. With the wide choice of tenant screening services, you may have a hard time deciding exactly what you need. So I recommend that you use a tenant selection service that offers a retail or consumer credit report, an eviction search or tenant history, an automated crosscheck of addresses, a social security search, and an employment or reference verification.

Checking the applicant's criminal history

The liability for rental property owners is increasing all the time. One area of particular concern is criminal acts committed by tenants. In most states, rental property owners have no legal duty to ask about or investigate the criminal background of applicants or current tenants.

In many areas of the country, only a county-level criminal records search is possible, because the statewide criminal records are not accurate or up-to-date. Plus, many states only indicate felony records and do not even list misdemeanors involving violence, sexual misconduct, or honesty.

Although the technology to cost-effectively perform a criminal background records search is improving each year, it is still of limited use. Currently only half of the states in the U.S. offer statewide database searches, and they can cost between $5 and $11 per state. County-level searches are available in all 50 states but the cost can run from $10 to $25 per county. Remember that these charges are *per rental applicant.*

With many tenants moving from area to area, performing a thorough criminal background records search is generally cost prohibitive. So many rental property owners only request a criminal records search if the rental applicant indicates that he has been convicted of (or pled guilty or no contest to) a felony, a misdemeanor involving violence, sexual misconduct, or dishonesty. Be diligent in looking for any indications that may provide a clue to possible criminal activity, such as gaps in rental history while the prospect was incarcerated.

Consistency is the key to all tenant screening activity, including your efforts to minimize the chances of renting to someone who may present a direct threat to the health or safety of others. You need to establish a policy of either inquiring about past criminal history or of running a criminal background check on *all* rental applicants to ensure that your rental screening process is applied uniformly.

Talking with all personal references

Although you could expect that all personal references will only tell you glowing comments about how lucky you are to have the prospect as your new tenant, investing the time and making the calls is important for several reasons.

First, you will occasionally find someone who will tell you that the rental applicant is her best friend but she would never loan the applicant money or let him borrow her car. Plus, if you call the references given and find that the information is bogus, you can use this information as part of your overall screening of the applicant.

Dealing with guarantors

If your rental prospect does not meet the criteria outlined in your statement of rental policy, you may consider approving his application if he provides a cosigner or *guarantor.* The guarantor needs to sign a Guarantee of Lease or Rental Agreement form (shown in Form 8-3); however, a guarantor must be financially qualified and screened or the guarantee is worthless.

Require your guarantor to complete a rental application, pay the application fee, and go through the same tenant screening process as the applicant. Keep in mind that the guarantor will not actually be living at the rental unit and thus will have his own housing costs. So in order to ensure that the guarantor can meet all of his own obligations and cover your tenant's rent in case of a default, you need to deduct the guarantor's cost of housing from his income before comparing it to your income requirements. For example, if the proposed guarantor has a gross monthly income of $4,000 with a $1,000 mortgage payment, he has an adjusted gross income of $3,000. So assuming you have an income standard that requires the tenant to earn three times the monthly rent (and assuming the guarantor meets all of your other screening criteria), the person could be the guarantor for your prospect as long as the rent does not exceed $1,000 per month.

Although a lease guarantor can be very important and can give you the extra resources in the event of a rent default by your tenant, out-of-state lease guarantors are not as valuable as in-state ones. Enforcing the lease guarantee against an out-of-state party can be very difficult or even financially unfeasible.

Notifying the Applicant of Your Decision

Rental property owners are legally allowed to choose among rental applicants as long as their decisions comply with all fair-housing laws and are based on legitimate business criteria.

One of the most difficult tasks for the rental property owner is informing a rental applicant that you have denied his application. You obviously want to avoid an argument over the rejection, but even more importantly, you want to avoid a fair-housing complaint based on the applicant's misunderstanding about the reasons for the denial.

Regardless of whether your rental applicant is accepted or rejected, be sure to notify the applicant promptly when the decision is made. If you have approved the applicant, contact him and arrange for a meeting and a walk-through of the rental unit prior to the move-in date. Do not notify the other qualified applicants that you have already rented the rental property until all legal documents have been signed and all funds due upon move-in have been collected in full.

Guarantee of Lease or Rental Agreement

On the date below, in consideration of the execution of the Lease or Rental Agreement, dated ________________, 20 _____,

for the premises located at: ____ (Rental unit) by and between

____ (Tenant)

____ (Owner) and

____ (Guarantor);

for valuable consideration, receipt of which is hereby acknowledged, the Guarantor does hereby guarantee unconditionally to Owner, Owner's agent, and/or including Owner's successor and assigns, the prompt payment by Tenant of any unpaid rent, property damage and cleaning and repair costs or any other sums which become due pursuant to said lease or rental agreement, a copy of which is attached hereto, including any and all court costs or attorney's fees incurred in enforcing the lease or rental agreement.

If Tenant assigns or subleases the Rental unit, Guarantor shall remain liable under the terms of this Agreement for the performance of the assignee or sublessee, unless Owner relieves Guarantor by express written termination of this Agreement.

In the event of the breach of any terms of the Lease or Rental Agreement by the Tenant, Guarantor shall be liable for any damages, financial or physical, caused by Tenant, including any and all legal fees incurred in enforcing the Lease or Rental Agreement. Owner or Owner's agent may immediately enforce this Guarantee upon any default by Tenant and an action against Guarantor may be brought at any time without first seeking recourse against the Tenant.

The insolvency of Tenant or nonpayment of any sums due from Tenant may be deemed a default giving rise to action by Owner against Guarantor. This Guarantee does not confer a right to possession of the Rental unit by Guarantor, and Owner is not required to serve Guarantor with any legal notices, including any demand for payment of rent, prior to Owner proceeding against Guarantor for Guarantor's obligation under this Guarantee.

Unless released in writing by Owner, Guarantor shall remain obligated by the terms of this Guarantee for the entire period of the tenancy as provided by the Lease or Rental Agreement and for any extensions pursuant thereto. In the event Tenant and Owner modify the terms of said Lease or Rental Agreement, with or without the knowledge or consent of Guarantor, Guarantor waives any and all rights to be released from the provisions of this Guarantee and Guarantor shall remain obligated by said additional modifications and terms of the Lease or Rental Agreement. Guarantor hereby consents and agrees in advance to any changes, modifications, additions, or deletions of the Lease or Rental Agreement made and agreed to by Owner and Tenant during the entire period of the tenancy.

If any legal action or proceeding is brought by either party to enforce any part of this agreement, the prevailing party shall recover, in addition to all other relief, reasonable attorney's fees and costs. By signing below, Owner, Tenant and Guarantor acknowledge and accept all terms contained herein.

______________________	______________________	______________________
Tenant's Signature	Guarantor's Signature	Owner's Signature
______________________	______________________	______________________
Tenant's Name (print)	Guarantor's Name (print)	Owner's Name (print)
______________________	______________________	______________________
______________________	______________________	______________________
Tenant's Address	Guarantor's Address	Owner's Address
______________________	______________________	______________________
Date	Date	Date
______________________	______________________	______________________
Daytime phone number	Daytime phone number	Daytime phone number

Form 8-3: Guarantee of Lease or Rental Agreement.

If you reject an applicant based on his credit report, you are required by the federal Fair Credit Reporting Act to notify the applicant of his rights. Although it is not *required* to be in writing, you should provide the denied applicant with a letter containing the mandatory disclosures so that you have proof that you complied with the law. You must also provide this information even if you have approved the applicant but have required him to pay a higher security deposit, higher rent, or have a cosigner. Your rejection letter should include:

- The names, addresses, and phone numbers of all credit reporting agencies that provided you with information.
- A notice that the credit reporting agency only provides information about credit history and they take no part in the decision process and cannot provide the reasons for the rejection.
- A notice that the applicant has the right to obtain a free copy of the credit report from the credit agency if he requests it within 60 days of your rejection.
- A notice informing the applicant that he has the right to dispute the accuracy of the information on the report. He can also demand a reinvestigation or provide the credit reporting agency with a statement describing his position.
- A notice that if information was received from a person or company other than a credit reporting agency, the applicant has the right to make a written request within 60 days of receiving this notice for a disclosure of the nature of this information.

Keep a copy of all rejection letters for at least three years.

Using a notice of denial to rent form (shown in Form 8-4) to inform the applicant in writing of your decision as well as outline the valid reasons is an excellent idea. This form helps you to document the various legal reasons for your rejection of the applicant. It is a simple checklist that also allows you to provide the applicant with the required information per the federal Fair Credit Reporting Act.

Notify your denied rental applicant in writing. If you notify the applicant only by phone, you may have difficulty giving all of the details and required disclosures. The written notice of denial to rent avoids a situation in which the applicant may unintentionally (or sometimes intentionally) form the opinion that you are denying his application in a discriminatory manner and file a complaint with HUD or a state or local fair-housing agency.

Some of the new Internet tenant screening services offer *risk scoring* of your rental applicant based on scoring models that they claim are designed to objectively predict an applicant's likelihood of fulfilling his lease obligations. If you use one of these services, make sure you can meet the disclosure requirements of the federal Fair Credit Reporting Act. Only use a tenant screening service that is willing to provide your denied applicants with a written, detailed notice of denial to rent that meets the requirements of the federal Fair Credit Reporting Act.

Although you need to carefully follow fair-housing guidelines, never compromise your tenant screening criteria or allow yourself to be intimidated into accepting an unqualified rental applicant. HUD and state fair-housing agencies have consistently ruled that rejecting an applicant who doesn't meet your tenant screening criteria isn't discrimination, even if the applicant belongs to a legally protected class.

NOTICE OF DENIAL TO RENT

To: ______________________ [Full Names of All Applicants Listed on Application] ______________________

Thank you for applying to rent at: ____

We have carefully and thoroughly reviewed your rental application. We are hereby informing you of certain information required by the Federal Fair Credit Reporting Act. Based on the information currently in our files, your application has been denied for the following reason(s):

I. Rental History

_____ Could not be verified _____ Unpaid or delinquent rent reported _____ Property damage reported

_____ Disruptive behavior reported _____ Prior eviction reported _____ Other ____________________

II. Employment and Income

_____ Employment could not be verified _____ Local employment could not be verified

_____ Irregular or temporary employment _____ Income could not be verified _____ Insufficient income

_____ Other ____

III. Credit History

_____ Could not be verified _____ Unsatisfactory payment history _____ Collection activity

_____ Bankruptcy filing _____ Liens, garnishments, or judgments

_____ Other ____

IV. Criminal History

_____ Conviction for (or pled guilty or no contest to) any felony, or a misdemeanor involving violence, sexual misconduct or honesty

V. Personal Reference

_____ Could not be verified _____ Lack of non-related references _____ Negative reference

_____ Other ____

VI. Application

_____ Application unsigned _____ Application incomplete _____ False information provided

_____ Rental unit rented to prior qualified candidate _____ Other ______________________

When a credit report is used in making this decision, Section 615(a) of the Fair Credit Reporting Act requires us to tell you where we obtained that report. The credit reporting agency that provided information to us was:

Form 8-4: Notice of Denial to Rent Form (Page 1 of 2).

Name ______________________________

Address ______________________________

Telephone ______________________________

This agency only provided information about you and your credit history and was not involved in any way in making the decision to reject your rental application, nor can they explain why the decision was made. Pursuant to the Fair Credit Reporting Act, if you believe the information they provided is inaccurate or incomplete, you may call the credit reporting agency at the number listed above or communicate by mail.

You have the right to obtain a free copy of your consumer report from the credit reporting agency indicated above if your request is made within 60 days of the date of this notice. If you dispute any of the information in your report, you have the right to submit a consumer statement of up to 100 words into your report explaining your position on the item in dispute. The credit reporting agencies offer assistance in preparing your consumer statement.

If information was received from a person or company other than a credit reporting agency, then you have the right to make a written request to us within 60 days of receiving this notice for a disclosure of the nature of this information.

You may have additional rights under the credit reporting or consumer protection laws of your state or local municipality. For further information contact your state Attorney General or consumer affairs office.

______________________________ ______________________________

Signature of Owner or Agent for Owner Date

Form 8-4: Notice of Denial to Rent Form (Page 2 of 2).

Avoiding Housing Discrimination Complaints

If you're in the rental housing business for long, you'll hear about a shocking settlement or award against a rental property owner for violating a fair-housing law. Many of these awards or settlements can exceed $100,000. In a recent ten-year period, fair-housing discrimination cases investigated by HUD alone resulted in awards of over $42 million.

You may even have read about the facts of certain fair-housing cases and thought to yourself that the defendants deserved to lose and that a discrimination case will never happen to you. That is probably true — if you are an educated owner and you know and abide by all federal, state, and local fair-housing laws. The problem arises when rental property owners are unaware that their policies or practices are discriminatory. For example, you may think that you are just being a courteous and caring landlord by only showing rental applicants with children your available rental units located on the ground floor. But not giving applicants with children the same treatment you give your other applicants is a form of discrimination — even if that wasn't your intent.

There are two types of fair-housing discrimination:

- **Treating members of protected classes differently from the way you treat others who are not members of that protected class.** For example, if you had two applicants with similar financial histories, tenant histories, and other screening criteria, but charged one applicant who is a member of a protected class a larger security deposit, you may be subject to a fair housing discrimination inquiry or complaint on the basis of different treatment.
- **Treating all prospects equally, but having a different impact because of an individual's minority status.** If your occupancy standard policy is two persons per bedroom, you may be accused of familial status discrimination based on disparate impact. Although you have set an occupancy standard policy that is applied equally to all tenants, your restrictive policy will discourage applicants with children. This is an example of *disparate impact.* The policy is the same for all applicants, but the policy has a much different effect on certain applicants and essentially creates an additional barrier to rental housing for families.

Some rental property owners illegally use the occupancy standard as a subtle tool to limit the number of rental applicants with children. HUD and state and local fair-housing agencies receive a large volume of calls concerning familial status discrimination. In some areas, these complaints outnumber claims on the basis of all other protected classes combined. One reason is that the majority of rental housing was categorized as "adults only" until federal and state fair-housing laws were changed in the 1980s to require most rental property owners to accept children. You may be able to have your rental property officially acknowledged by HUD as a senior's property; however, there are specific requirements and you must have this HUD designation in writing.

There are three main exemptions to the federal fair-housing laws.

- An owner-occupied rental property with four or fewer units.
- Single-family housing rented without the use of discriminatory advertising or without using an agent to facilitate or handle the leasing.
- Housing reserved exclusively for seniors that is intended for and solely occupied by persons 62 years of age or older, or HUD-certified seniors properties where 80 percent or more of the households are occupied by at least one person 55 years of age. Here the exemption is only against claims of age discrimination.

Many states and even local governments have passed their own legislation that may apply to your rental property. Don't count on an exemption, and be sure to abide by all fair-housing laws even if you are positive that you are exempt. Abiding by all fair-housing laws not only eliminates any potential complaints, but it's also simply the right thing to do.

Federal and state laws prohibit discrimination against certain protected classes in rental housing. These laws impact your tenant screening and selection process, and I cover the issues surrounding these laws in the following sections.

Discrimination

Discrimination is a major issue for rental property owners and has serious legal consequences for the uninformed. If you don't know the law you may be guilty of various forms of discrimination and not even realize it until you've been charged with discrimination. That's why knowing the law is so important.

The Federal Fair Housing Act prohibits discrimination on the basis of race, color, religion, national origin, sex, age, familial status, and disability. Be sure to check the state and local fair-housing laws in your area; some additional state and local protected classes include occupation, educational status, medical status, and even physical body size.

Be careful that you don't inadvertently favor one sex as renters. For example, some rental property owners may have the perception that male tenants aren't as clean or quiet as female tenants. Conversely, some owners with a rental property in a rough area may believe that male tenants are less susceptible to being victims of crime. Don't allow any stereotypes or assumptions to enter into your tenant selection criteria.

If you have a rental unit in an area where a significant portion of the local population speaks a language other than English, get fair-housing posters in that particular language. HUD offers free fair-housing posters in many different languages.

Although the federal Fair Housing Act does not specifically state that age is a protected category, there are many states and localities with laws that directly address the issue of age. Typically, you will be able to deny rental applicants who are under 18 years of age. The exception is if they are legally married, in the military, or emancipated. In these cases, you must treat them just like any other adult rental applicant.

You cannot refuse to rent on the basis of gender nor can you have special rules for tenants based on gender, such as limiting female tenants to upper-level rental units only.

There are other issues that are not specifically protected under federal fair-housing laws. However, several states and many major cities have laws to protect individuals. Examples include marital status, sexual orientation, and source of income. Although there are still several states with laws prohibiting unmarried couples from living together, the majority of states have very broad fair-housing laws that forbid all arbitrary discrimination on the basis of an individual's personal characteristic or trait. Always be sure to fully understand the fair-housing requirements and limitations that apply to your rental property.

Steering

Steering means to guide, or attempt to guide, a rental applicant toward living where you think he should live based on race, color, religion, national origin, sex, age, familial status, disability or handicap, or another protected class. Steering is an illegal act that deprives persons of their right to choose to rent a rental unit where they want. HUD has clearly indicated that not showing or renting certain units to minorities is one form of steering; however, so is the "assigning of any person to a particular section or floor of a building, because of race, color, religion, sex, handicap, familial status, or national origin."

Rental property owners often have only good intentions when they suggest that a rental prospect with children see only rental units on the ground floor or near the playground, however, the failure to offer such an applicant an opportunity to see *all* available rental units is steering — and a violation of the fair-housing laws.

Steering can be subtle or very direct. Some examples of steering include:

- Limiting families to ground floor units or undesirable units in the hope that they don't rent.
- Offering families only units near the playground or by the laundry room or elevator because noise makes these units less desirable.
- Relegating families to certain buildings or sections of a building or having separate family and adult buildings.

Be very careful not to even make any suggestions or comments that could be misinterpreted as steering. All rental applicants should receive information on the full range of rental units available and be able to decide which units they want to see, making the choice themselves.

Children

Federal and state legislation has virtually eliminated "adult only" housing except for certain HUD-certified seniors properties.

Until 1993, the HUD Handbook that provides the operating policies and guidelines to the owners and managers of federally assisted housing indicated that "children should not share a bedroom with a parent." Many owners and managers of *nonassisted* housing adopted this policy, thinking that it was a standard or law that applied to them. Some rental property owners knew that this HUD directive was only for federally assisted housing yet they used this policy as a way to either deny rental applicants with children or require them to take a larger and often more expensive apartment.

In 1993 HUD clarified this issue with a modification of the guideline that stated, "A child may share a bedroom with a parent if the parent so wishes, often depending on the child's age. This is, however, a decision to be made by the parent." Rental property owners should make sure that any apartment that is available to a certain number of adults is also available to the same number of adults and children. Rental property owners cannot cite moral reasons or concerns about additional wear and tear, because it effectively discriminates against children.

Some rental property owners are concerned about renting to children because there are hazards on the property that may be dangerous for children. For example, the property may not have any safe areas for the children to play. Although you may truly only have the children's best interests in mind, it is the parent's right to decide if the property is safe for their children. Of course, you do need to take steps to make your property as safe as possible by posting speed limit signs in your driveway or reminding parents to not let their children play in unsafe areas or to play while unattended.

Be careful not to discourage applicants with policies and guidelines for the conduct of children unless they are *safety-related.* For example, don't institute a policy against children riding bicycles on the property. Instead, you can have a policy that says that *no one* is allowed to ride bicycles on the property. (This way, the policy doesn't discriminate against children; it is uniformly applied to all.) Make sure all of your policies are age-neutral except for health and safety issues. For example, some states have specific laws that allow you to have a policy that states that, in order to use the swimming pool, children under 14 must be accompanied by an adult.

Charging rental applicants with children higher rents or higher security deposits than applicants without children is also illegal, as is offering different rental terms, such as shorter lease terms, fewer unit amenities, or different payment options. The property facilities must also be fully available for all tenants, regardless of age, unless there is a clear safety issue involved.

I always recommend that rental property owners openly accept renters with children. Families tend to be more stable, and they are looking for a safe, crime-free, and drug-free environment in which to raise their children. Along with responsible pet owners, who also have difficulty finding suitable rental properties, families with children can be excellent, long-term renters. And typically, the longer your tenants stay, the better your cash flow.

Reasonable accommodations

The Federal Fair Housing Act requires property owners to make reasonable accommodations at the owner's expense for tenants with a disability, so that they are able to enjoy the rental property on an equal basis with tenants who are not disabled. The fair-housing regulations state:

"It shall be unlawful for any person to refuse to make reasonable accommodations in rules, policies, practices or services, when such accommodations may be necessary to afford a handicapped person equal opportunity to use and enjoy a dwelling unit, including public and common areas."

Rental property owners are also required to make reasonable adjustments to their rules, procedures, or services upon request. Examples of reasonable accommodations that the rental property owner may be required to offer include:

- Providing a parking space that is wider and closer to the rental unit of a wheelchair-bound tenant.
- Arranging to read all management communications to a tenant with poor vision.
- Allowing a tenant who receives income from a government agency to pay on a biweekly rather than monthly basis.

Reasonable modifications

Federal law also provides that rental property owners are required to allow the disabled tenant the right to modify her living space at the tenant's own expense. The modifications can only be to the extent necessary to make it safe and comfortable, and only as long as the modifications will not make the unit unacceptable to the next tenant, or only if the tenant agrees to return the rental unit to its original condition upon vacating the property. Rental property owners can also require the tenants to pay the funds necessary to perform the needed restoration into an interest-bearing escrow account.

Reasonable modifications that tenants may request to make at their expense include:

- Ramps at the rental unit entry or in the common area to provide access to public areas.
- Lower light switches and removal of doors or widening of doorways to allow for wheelchair access.
- Grab bars or call buttons in bathrooms.

The modifications must be reasonable. You can require the tenant to obtain your prior approval and ensure that the work will be done in a workmanlike manner, including any necessary government approvals or permits. You can also require the tenant to provide proof for the need for the modification from a medical provider or social worker. But you cannot ask about the specific handicap of the tenant that necessitates these changes.

Americans with Disabilities Act

Discrimination against the disabled in residential housing is covered in the Federal Fair Housing Act. However, the Americans with Disabilities Act (ADA) was implemented in 1992 and has far-reaching impact on most commercial and retail real estate. The ADA has only limited requirements for many rental property owners, because it does not apply to private residential properties built prior to 1991, except to the extent that the rental property has facilities that are open to the public or qualify as "public accommodations."

The ADA addresses the accessibility of public areas. For example, a rental property with a rental office, clubhouse, or pool area must be accessible to the handicapped, and the removal of existing physical barriers at the rental property owner's expense is required whenever it can be done at a reasonable cost.

Many local municipalities have very specific parking requirements for multi-unit rental properties. Check with your local building and code enforcement office for details.

The ADA requirements are more stringent for new residential rental properties constructed since 1991, which must be designed to provide for the access and use by handicapped persons. For more information on ADA requirements for residential rental property owners, visit the federal Department of Justice ADA Web site at `www.usdoj.gov/crt/ada/adahom1.htm`.

Companion or service animals

Many rental property owners have policies that prohibit tenants from having pets in their rental unit. But service animals that assist tenants with daily life activities are exempt and must be allowed in all rental properties, regardless of any no-pet policies.

However, you must also allow a tenant to have a pet if requested under the "necessary and reasonable accommodation" provisions of the Americans with Disabilities Act (ADA). Some tenants do seek the accommodation of a companion animal based on their need for comfort or companionship, and federal law requires owners and managers to consider the tenant's claim and grant the request if it is true and reasonable. The best method of determining whether a request is reasonable is to get verification from the tenant's health care provider or other professional such as a medical doctor, therapist, or social worker. To avoid claims of discrimination or favoritism, requests for verification must be a consistent policy that is required for all requests. Of course, like all potential housing discrimination issues, the failure to consider a tenant request could lead to serious legal consequences.

The determination of what is reasonable in the eyes of governmental fair-housing officials is always murky. However, you need to look at each request individually to make a proper determination. For example, a tenant in a 1-bedroom apartment who requests to keep two large dogs as companion animals is being unreasonable, but the same request from a tenant in a large, single-family home with a yard is most likely a reasonable request. If you are uncertain as to whether a particular request is reasonable, whenever possible, seek direction from local fair-housing agencies. Ask them to provide you with their written opinion or send them a letter outlining their verbal directive and be sure to keep copies in your rental files.

Sexual harassment

Sexual harassment, in the world of property management, occurs when you refuse to rent to a person who refuses your sexual advances or when you make life difficult for or harass a tenant who resists your unwanted advances. Most rental property owners understand the concern and find such behavior unconscionable; however, the problem often arises when rental property owners hire someone to assist them with the leasing, rent collection, or maintenance requirements at their properties. The rental property owner is accountable, because these individuals are the employees or agents of the owner.

Make sure that you have a clear written policy against sexual harassment, provide an open-minded procedure for investigating complaints, and conduct thorough and unbiased investigations that lead to quick corrective action, if necessary.

Part III

The Brass Tacks of Managing Rentals

"It's an eviction letter from the Ray Charles Realty Co. It says, 'Hit the road, Jack, and don't you come back no more no more no more no more...'."

In this part . . .

Managing rental property involves a lot more than just managing the property itself. Working with tenants — from fielding the first call of a prospective tenant to having the paperwork in order when the tenant moves out — is what you'll spend a huge chunk of your time doing. So the chapters in this part take you through that relationship step by step. I show you how to help tenants at move-in and move-out times, how to increase the rent without losing your tenants, and how to retain the good tenants and deal with the bad. Chances are, you'll find the answer to any question you may have about your tenants in this part.

Chapter 9

Moving In the Tenants

In This Chapter

- Agreeing on a move-in date
- Walking your tenant through the policies and procedures of your property
- Noting the condition of the unit before the move-in date
- Keeping all the paperwork organized
- Making your new tenants feel welcome in their new home

After you've have selected your new tenants, you still have to complete one very important step to ensure that you establish a good tenant/landlord relationship: moving in the tenants. In order to ensure that the tenants' move-in process goes smoothly, you need to hold a tenant orientation and rental property inspection meeting, which allows you the opportunity to present the rental property and your ownership and management skills in the best possible light. You also need to ensure that your new tenants understand and agree to the policies and rules you have established for the rental property.

If you're organized and prepared, you'll be able to quickly and efficiently handle the administrative steps to get the tenants into their new rental unit. Tenants are very excited and motivated to begin moving in to their new home, and you want this process to be smooth and pleasant for everyone.

In this chapter, I outline the important steps to ensure that your tenant/landlord relationship gets off to a good start, including: scheduling the move-in date and the tenant orientation meeting; the pre-occupancy inspection and the move-in/move-out checklist; important policies in the tenant information letter; and creative ideas to welcome your tenants on move-in day.

Establishing the Move-In Date

When you have informed your prospective tenant that his rental application has been approved, you need to determine a mutually agreeable move-in date. You and the tenant may have discussed this during your initial telephone conversation or when you showed the rental property, but be sure to raise the issue again to make sure that you're in agreement of the date.

After new tenants have been approved, some tenants suddenly stall on setting the move-in date. They may stall because they are still obligated under a lease or 30-day notice at another rental property and they don't want to double pay. Unless you're willing to suffer additional rent loss that you can never recover, insist that the tenant begin paying the rent on the originally scheduled move-in date. The time for your new tenant to negotiate the move-in date was *before* you approved him.

In some situations, your rental unit may not be available at your mutually agreed move-in date. Perhaps the prior tenants didn't vacate as they said they would, maybe the rental unit was in much worse condition than you anticipated, or maybe you just weren't able to complete the work required in time. If it becomes apparent that there will be a delay in having the rental unit available as promised, you need to communicate with your new tenant immediately. Often, new tenants can adjust their move-in date as long as you give them reasonable notice. If they can't adjust their move-in date, communicate with them and try to work out other possible arrangements.

Sometimes new tenants ask if they can begin moving just a few items into the rental unit before your pre-occupancy conference. Don't allow it! You will create a tenant/landlord relationship simply by letting the new tenants have access to the rental unit without being there or by allowing them to store even a few items in the unit. If you need to cancel the rental for any reason, you would then need to go through a formal legal eviction that could take several weeks.

Although the rental property should be in rent-ready condition before being shown to rental prospects, the property can quickly get dirty or dusty if there is any delay between showing the property and the actual tenant move-in. So before meeting with your tenant prior to move-in (covered in the following section), make one last visit to the rental unit and go through your rent-ready inspection checklist (covered in more detail in Chapter 4) again just to make sure that there will be no surprises when move-in day arrives.

Moving is very stressful for most people, and if your new tenants have a bad move-in experience it can last for months, or even stay in their minds throughout their entire tenancy. Many aspects of the tenant's move are beyond your control. Although you can't guarantee your new tenant a simple and painless move, you can take steps to ensure that you are organized and ready to handle any complaints or concerns about their new home. If at all possible, arrange to be on the premises during their move-in so you can answer any questions for them.

Meeting with Your Tenant Prior to Move-In

After you and your tenant have decided on a move-in date, you need to get together to deal with some of the technicalities, like walking through the property, signing some paperwork, and giving the tenant the keys. Getting together to do this is a very important step, and you need to do it before your new tenant actually moves in and takes possession of the rental unit.

Schedule a meeting with the tenant either for the day of the scheduled move-in or within just a few days before the move-in date.

At this meeting, you will review your property policies and rules, review and sign all the paperwork, collect the move-in funds, and conduct a thorough property inspection with your new tenant, including the completion of the Move-In/Move-Out Inspection Checklist (covered later in this chapter).

Going over the rules with your new tenant

When you meet with your new tenant, start by giving him a copy of your house rules (see Form 9-1 for an example of this kind of document). Give him a chance to read over the rules and ask any questions, and provide clarification as necessary. Then ask for his signature, indicating that he has received and understands the rules and agrees to abide by them.

Many owners and managers of single-family or small rental properties do not worry about detailed rules and regulations, because they think the lease or rental agreement covers it all. But setting up some basic rules that can easily be changed as necessary upon proper written notice to the tenants is a good idea, because it ensures that you and your tenants are on the same page and it gives you flexibility as you manage your property.

The term *rules and regulations* tends to sound rather imposing to most tenants. So I recommend using the term *policies and rules* or simply *house rules* whenever possible. Your policies and rules are separate from the lease or rental agreement, which is drafted by an attorney using lots of formal and hard-to-understand terminology. The rules you draft should be more informal and conversational in tone than your lease. Be sure to use clear language that is neither harsh nor demeaning.

Policies and Rules

We are proud of this property and we hope that your living experience here will be pleasant and comfortable. The support and cooperation of you, as our tenant, is necessary for us to maintain our high standards.

This is your personal copy of our Policies and Rules. Please read it carefully as it is an integral part of your rental agreement. When you sign your rental agreement, you agree to abide by the policies and rules for this rental property, and they are considered legally binding provisions of your rental agreement. If you have any questions, please contact us and we will be glad to help.

This document is an addendum and is part of the Lease or Rental Agreement, dated ___________, by and between ______________________________, Owner, and ______________________________Tenant, for the premises located at: ____.

New policies and rules or amendments to this document may be adopted by Owner upon giving 30 days written notice to tenant.

Guests: Tenant is responsible for their own proper conduct and that of all guests, including the responsibility for understanding and observing all policies and rules.

Noise: Although the Premises are well constructed, they are not completely soundproof and reasonable consideration for neighbors is important. Either inside or outside of the Premises, no tenant or their guest shall use, or allow to be used, any sound-emitting device at a sound level that may annoy, disturb, or otherwise interfere with the rights, comforts, or conveniences of other tenants or neighbors. Particular care must be taken between the hours of 9:00 p.m. and 9:00 a.m.

Parking: No vehicle belonging to a Tenant shall be parked in such a manner as to impede passage in the street or to prevent access to the property. Tenant shall only use assigned and designated parking spaces. Tenant shall ensure that all posted handicap, fire zones, or other no-parking areas remain clear of vehicles at all times. Vehicles parked in unauthorized areas or in another tenants designated parking space may be towed away at the vehicle owners expense. Vehicles may not be backed in, and repairs and maintenance of any sort are not allowed on the premises. All vehicles must be currently registered and in operative condition. No trucks, commercial vehicles, recreational vehicles, motorcycles, bicycles, boats, or trailers are allowed anywhere on the Premises without advance written approval of the Owner. All vehicles must be parked properly between the lines of the parking space. Tenant shall ensure that their guests abide by all of these parking policies and rules.

Patios/Balconies and Entry Areas: Patios/balconies and entry areas are restricted to patio-type furniture and are to be kept clean and orderly. No barbecues or similar cooking devices may be used on the Premises without advance written approval. No items may be hung from the Premises at anytime, and all entryways and walkways must be kept free from items that could be a hazard. Owner reserves the right to require that items that detract from the appearance of the Premises be removed immediately upon request. No unauthorized storage is allowed at any time.

Wall Hangings: Pictures may be hung on a thin nail. Mirrors, wall units, hanging wall or light fixtures, etc. need special attention and professional installation. Please contact the Owner for approval in advance as damage to the Premises will be the responsibility of the Tenant.

Trash: Tenant is responsible for keeping the inside and outside of the Premises clean, sanitary, and free from objectionable odors at all times. Tenant shall ensure that all trash, papers, cigarette butts, and similar items are sealed in trash bags and placed in appropriate receptacles. No trash or other materials shall be allowed to accumulate so as to cause a hazard or be in violation of any health, fire, or safety ordinance or regulation.

Form 9-1: Policies and Rules (Page 1 of 2).

Tenant shall refrain from disposing of any combustible or hazardous material and all trash shall be disposed of routinely per the local trash collection procedures.

Animals or Pets: No animals or pets may be kept or are allowed on the Premises by the Tenant or their guests unless the Tenant and Owner have approved an Animal Agreement in advance.

Maintenance: Tenant agrees to promptly notify Owner of any items requiring repair at the Premises. Requests for repairs or maintenance should be made by contacting the Owner or their agent during normal business hours, when possible. Emergencies involving any immediate health and safety matter should be handled by the appropriate governmental agency (police, fire, paramedic) and the Owner shall be contacted as soon as practical thereafter. Costs for any repairs, including repair or clearance of stoppages in waste pipes or drains, water pipes, or plumbing fixtures caused by the negligence of the Tenant or their guests are the responsibility of the Tenant.

Inclement Weather: Tenant shall close all windows, doors, and other building openings tightly when leaving the Premises to prevent damage from the elements to the Premises. When the Tenant will be away from the Premises during the heating season, the thermostat shall be placed at a minimum of 50 degrees to avoid freezing of pipes and other damage.

Keys: If you lose your key and need a new one, there will be a minimum replacement charge during normal business hours for the first request. Subsequent requests or after-hours lockout service will be handled at a charge of $20.

Key Release: Owner will not give a key to the Premises to anyone unless their name is on the Rental Agreement or Tenant has provided Owner in advance with a written key release request. This is for the Tenants protection. If you are expecting guests or relatives, please be sure they will have access to the Premises.

Window Treatments: Tenant is not allowed to make any alterations to the existing window coverings without the advance written approval of the Owner. Only white or neutral color window treatments will be allowed and Tenant shall refrain from using aluminum foil or any other material visible from the exterior of the Premises.

Insurance: The Owners insurance coverage offers no protection for the Tenants personal property or any liability claims against the Tenant. The Tenant should obtain Renters Insurance coverage for fire, water, wind, vandalism, theft, earthquake, hurricane, tornado, or other damage. This includes your vehicles, furnishings, and all other personal property.

Right to Enter: Owner reserves the right to enter the Premises with 24 hours notice with or without the Tenants permission at any reasonable hour for any lawful reason or without notice in the event of an emergency.

Safety/Security: Safety and security is the sole responsibility of each Tenant and their guests. Owner or their agent assumes no responsibility or liability, unless otherwise provided by law, for the safety or security of the Tenant or their guests, or for injury caused by the criminal acts of other persons. Tenant should ensure that all doors and windows are locked at all times, and Tenant must immediately notify Owner if any locks become inoperative. Tenant should turn off all appliances when departing from the premises and notify Owner when leaving for an extended period. Tenant shall not smoke in bed or use or store any combustibles on the Premises.

Form 9-1: Policies and Rules (Page 2 of 2).

You want your tenants to actually read and follow your rules, so try not to be too overbearing. Review your rules with several of your friends and colleagues and see if there is a better way to say the same thing. Be clear, direct, and firm, yet not condescending. And watch out for something called the *no index.* The no index happens when many of your rules are too blunt and negative, such as "No cash," "No glass in the pool area," "No storage on your balcony," or "Don't ride bikes on the grounds." Although each of these rules is reasonable and important to the safe and efficient operation of your rental property, you can say the same thing in a much more positive way. For example, instead of saying, "Don't ride bikes on the grounds," you could say, "Please walk your bikes in the common area." Or instead of saying, "No cash," you can say, "We gladly accept your checks or money orders." Phrasing the rules in a more positive tone and minimizing the no index makes the rules — and you — seem friendlier to your tenants.

Make sure your policies and rules are reasonable and enforceable. They must not discriminate against anyone in a protected class. The term *protected class* refers to the federal antidiscrimination laws that "protect classes" of people because of race, gender, ethnicity, religion, and so on.

Be particularly careful to review your house rules to avoid any reference to children unless it is related to health and safety issues. For example, you can have a rule that states, "Persons under 14 must be accompanied by an adult while using the spa," because there are legitimate safety concerns for unattended children in spas. But a rule that says, "Children are not allowed to leave bicycles in the common area" would be inappropriate, because it singles out children (implying that adults can leave bikes in the common area if they want). A better way to handle this issue would be to use wording that isn't age specific, such as "No one is allowed to leave bicycles in the common area." That way, it applies to everyone and doesn't discriminate based on age.

And then there was light. . . .

Tenants are usually not very anxious to begin paying for utilities so you need to be sure that your procedures verify that your new tenants immediately contact the utility companies and put the utilities that are their responsibility in their name. Most rental property owners have the utilities revert to their name when the rental unit becomes vacant for unit turnover and rental showings. So if your new tenants don't change the utility billing information, then you may end up paying for some of their electric and natural gas bills. Confirm that the tenants have dealt with the utilities prior to releasing the mailbox key to them.

One way to avoid paying for the tenant's utilities is to immediately contact the utility company as part of your tenant orientation meeting. The new tenant can then establish the utilities in their name.

With the high cost of utilities, you need to make sure that you and your tenants are on the same page when it comes to who is financially responsible for the rental unit's utilities. In many states, rental property owners are required to disclose if the tenant is financially responsible for payment of any utility services outside of their rental unit. For example, exterior common area lighting may be connected to the rental unit, or a common area natural gas barbeque may be connected to the gas meter of the tenant. Besides disclosing this fact, rental property owners are required in many states to give the tenant an appropriate rent credit for the common area utilities paid by them. Check the laws in your area and be sure to disclose this kind of information if you're so required.

Regularly review and make improvements in your policies and rules based on situations that you've encountered. But remember that you're not running a prison camp and you don't want to alienate your tenants by harassing them with rules or controlling their day-to-day life.

As you revise your policies and rules, indicate the latest revision date in the lower left corner of the document so your tenants know which rules are the most current. When you distribute the revised rules, be sure to remind your tenants that these policies and rules supersede any prior versions. Get signatures from all of your tenants, indicating that they have received and will comply with the rules.

Reviewing and signing documents

Tenants and property owners alike are usually aware of all the legal paperwork involved in renting a home. And although sifting through all that legalese isn't fun for anyone, it is important. Rental property owners and tenants each have specific legal rights and responsibilities that are outlined in these documents, and being aware of what you're agreeing to — and being sure that your tenants know what they're agreeing to — is crucial.

In this section, I outline the documents you'll need to go over with your new tenant and get his signature on.

The lease or rental agreement

Be sure that your tenant understands that, when he signs your lease or rental agreement, he is entering into a business contract that has significant rights and responsibilities for both parties. Before your tenant signs the document, carefully and methodically review each clause of the rental agreement or lease.

Certain clauses in the lease or rental agreement are so important that you should have the tenant specifically initial them to indicate that he has read these points and understands his rights and responsibilities in relation to them. For example, the clause concerning the need for the tenant to obtain his own renter's insurance policy to protect his property and cover him for liability claims should be initialed by the tenant.

Also have your new tenant initial that he has received the keys for the rental property and acknowledge that you had the locks rekeyed or changed since the last tenant vacated.

Be sure to have the tenant review and sign any other lease or rental agreement addenda before taking possession of the rental unit.

After the tenant has been given the keys and taken possession of the rental property, getting him to sign your required legal documents can be very difficult. Even if the tenant failed to sign the lease or rental agreement, an oral tenant/landlord relationship is established when you give the tenant the keys to the unit — and when you're relying on oral agreements, you and the tenant are likely to disagree on the terms. Regaining possession of your rental unit can be a long and expensive process, so be sure that every adult occupant signs all documents prior to giving your new tenant the keys.

Environmental disclosure forms

If you have not already done so, be sure to give the tenants a copy of the required environmental disclosure form and the EPA pamphlet for lead-based paint and lead-based paint hazards, which is required under federal law. (Turn to Chapter 7 for more information on disclosure of environmental hazards.)

Smoke detector agreement

Inform your new tenant of the importance of smoke detectors. You may even want to create a separate smoke detector agreement, like the one shown in Form 9-2, to be sure your tenants fully understand the importance of this vital safety equipment and realize that they must take an active role in ensuring that the smoke detectors remain in place, operate properly, and have electrical or battery power in order to protect the tenants in case of smoke or fire.

Many tragic instances have occurred in which fires broke out and tenants had completely removed or disabled the smoke detectors because they were annoyed with false alarms triggered by smoking or cooking. Some tenants fail to regularly test the smoke alarms or replace the batteries as needed. They need to understand that you can only address conditions brought to your attention, so the tenants must be actively involved in ongoing inspections of the rental unit to ensure their own safety.

Animal agreement

Marketing your rental property to tenants with pets can be very profitable, because you usually have lower turnover and higher rents. If your new tenant has pets, you need to have him complete and sign an animal agreement, like the one shown in Form 9-3. The animal agreement outlines the policies and rules at your rental property for your tenant's animals or pets.

Dogs, cats, birds, and fish are not the only species that people keep in their homes. With the broad variety of animals that tenants are known to keep, I have broadened the concept from merely pets to animals in general. A good pet or animal policy clearly outlines exactly which animals are acceptable. It may just be semantics, but you don't want to get to court and have your tenants argue that the large iguana that damaged your rental unit is not subject to your rules because it is not their "pet."

The importance of smoke detectors

I once managed a great 70-unit apartment building that looked like it was pulled straight from a Gene Autry movie set. It had a complete western motif, featuring wood everywhere — covered wooden walkways, completely enclosed wooden carports, and wood decks. This property was a termite's dream! But it was also a significant fire risk. And that is exactly what one crazed friend of an evicted tenant must have thought when, in the middle of the night, he doused one of the apartments with gasoline and lit a match.

The fire was intense and spread quickly. Luckily, the onsite manager was walking back into the property from a movie and saw the fire soon after it started. He immediately alerted all of the adjoining tenants before calling the fire department. The property manager truly saved the tenants' lives. One tenant had taken her smoke detector down because of false alarms from cooking, and another tenant admitted that his smoke detector didn't go off in the fire because he had taken the batteries out just a few days ago when his radio needed batteries!

It was amazing that no one died. This event will always be a vivid reminder to me that smoke detectors can save lives, but the only way they can do so is if they're properly maintained.

Keep current photos of each animal living on your property in the individual files of their owners. This may seem ridiculous, but no matter how large your security deposit or how strict your rules, animals have the potential to cause significant damage. Determining the source of the problem can be difficult if you cannot accurately identify the guilty animal.

After the initial move-in, tenants may be tempted to take advantage of your policy and bring in additional animals or pets. I have seen the goldfish in the small glass bowl succumb only to be replaced by a 200-gallon aquarium. Your tenant may decide that the small Poodle you agreed to is lonely and needs the company of a Great Dane in your studio rental unit! Often tenants have very good and heartwarming stories about how they've ended up adding new animals to the mix, but you need to retain control over the number, type, and size of the animals on your property. One way to do this is to actually meet and photograph the animal so there is no doubt as to what you have approved. Also, remember that small puppies can grow into large dogs. Make sure that your policies anticipate the animal at its *adult* size.

Collecting the money

In your meeting prior to move-in, be sure to get the first month's rent and the security deposit. You need to collect this money *before* you give the tenants the keys to the rental unit. Payment may be in the form of cash, a cashier's check, or a money order. But don't accept a personal check (because you have no way of knowing whether the check will clear). Be sure to give your tenants a receipt for their payments.

Smoke Detector Agreement

This document is an addendum and is part of the Lease or Rental Agreement, dated ____________________,

by and between __________________________, Owner/Agent, and ________________________Tenant,

for the premises located at: ____.

In consideration of their mutual promises, Owner/Agent and Tenant agree as follows:

1. The premise(s) is (are) equipped with a smoke detection device(s).

2. Each Tenant acknowledges the smoke detector(s) was (were) tested and its operation explained by management in the presence of the Tenant(s) at the time of initial occupancy and the detector(s) in the unit was (were) working properly at that time.

3. Each Tenant shall perform the manufacturers recommended test to determine if the smoke detector(s) is (are) operating properly at least twice a month.

4. Initial here ONLY if the smoke detector(s) is (are) **BATTERY OPERATED:** _______________

By initialing as provided, each Tenant understands that said smoke detector(s) and alarm is a battery-operated unit and it shall be each Tenants responsibility to:

a. Ensure that the battery is in operating condition at all times;

b. Replace the battery as needed (unless otherwise provided by law); and

c. If, after replacing the battery, the smoke detector(s) do not work, inform the Owner or authorized Agent immediately in writing.

5. Tenant(s) must inform the Owner or authorized Agent immediately in writing of any defect, malfunction, or failure of any detectors.

6. In accordance with the law, Tenant shall allow Owner or Agent access to the premises for the purpose verifying that all required smoke detectors are in place and operating properly or to conduct maintenance service, repair or replacement as needed.

________	______________________	________	______________________
Date	Owner/Agent	Date	Tenant

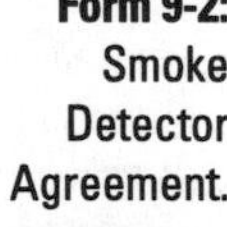

Form 9-2: Smoke Detector Agreement.

Although cash is legal tender, have a firm policy *against* accepting cash, and only accept cash for the move-in or the monthly rent payment when absolutely necessary. Regularly collecting cash for your rents can make you a target for crime. Because you will often have tenants moving in on the weekends and in the evenings, you don't want to have cash on you or at your home until you can get to the bank. Of course, if you have someone assist you in your rent collections, he is also at risk (not to mention the fact that cash is harder to keep track of and your assistant may be tempted to skim off some of the cash for his own needs).

Animal Agreement

This document is an addendum and is part of the Lease or Rental Agreement, dated ____________________,

by and between ____________________, Owner/Agent, and ____________________Tenant,

for the premises located at: ____________________.

In consideration of their mutual promises, Owner/Agent and Tenant agree as follows:

1. The Lease/Rental Agreement provides that without Owner/Agents prior written consent, no animals whatsoever shall be allowed in or about the premises. Tenant shall not keep or feed stray animals in their rental unit or anywhere on the grounds. Tenant may not allow an animal to be in their rental unit or on the premises even temporarily. Tenant must advise their guests of this policy prohibiting animals or secure advance approval from the Owner/Agent.

2. Tenant desires to keep the following described animal (see attached photo), herein after referred to as Pet, and represents it is a domesticated dog, cat, bird, fish, or ____________________. Said Pet is: Breed: ______________; Size (Current and Adult Height/Weight): ____________________; Color __________________. Tenant represents to Owner/Agent that said Pet is not vicious, and has not bitten, attacked, harmed, or menaced anyone in the past.

3. Tenant agrees to comply with all applicable ordinances, regulations, and laws governing pets. If the Pet is a cat, it must be spayed or neutered and Veterinary proof is required. Tenant must provide and maintain an appropriate litter box and not dispose of litter in the toilets. If the Pet is a bird, it shall not be let out of the cage. If the Pet is a fish, the water container shall not exceed ________ gallons and will be placed in a safe location in the rental unit. Pet shall not be fed directly on the carpet or any floor covering in the rental unit. Tenant shall prevent any fleas or other infestation of the rental unit or other property of Owner. Tenant shall not permit, and represents that Pet will not cause any damage, discomfort, annoyance, nuisance or in any way inconvenience, or cause complaints from, any other Tenant.

4. Tenant acknowledges and agrees that Owner/Agent may, at any time and in Owner/Agents sole and absolute discretion, revoke its consent by giving Tenant written thirty (30) day notice, if Owner/Agent receives complaints from neighbors or other residents about Pet, or if Owner/Agent, in Owner/Agents sole discretion, determines that Pet has disturbed the rights, comfort, convenience, or safety of neighbors or other tenants. Tenant shall permanently remove Pet from Owners property upon Owner/Agents written notice that consent is revoked.

5. If any rule or provision of this Animal Agreement is violated, Owner/Agent shall have the right to demand removal of Pet from the community upon three (3) day written notice. Any refusal by Tenant to comply with such demand shall be deemed to be a material breach of the Lease or Rental Agreement, in which event Owner/Agent shall be entitled to all the rights and remedies set forth in the Lease or Rental Agreement for violations thereof, including but not limited to eviction, damages, and attorneys fees.

6. Tenant shall be strictly liable for the entire amount of any wrongful death, or injury to the person or property of others, caused by Pet, and Tenant shall indemnify Owner/Agent for all costs resulting from same, including but not limited to litigation costs and attorneys fees.

7. Tenant agrees that Pet will not be permitted outside Tenants unit unless restrained by a leash, cage or other appropriate animal restraint. Tenant shall not tie Pet to any object outside the rental unit or premises. Use of the grounds or premises for sanitary purposes is prohibited and Tenant agrees to promptly clean up after Pet, if necessary. Pet shall be allowed or walked only in the exterior area(s) designated by the Owner/Agent. Tenant shall not permit Pet in swimming pool areas, laundry rooms, management offices, clubrooms, playgrounds, other recreation facilities, and other dwelling units.

________	____________________	________	____________________
Date	Owner/Manager	Date	Tenant

Form 9-3: Animal Agreement.

Most convenience stores offer money orders for a nominal cost and are open at all hours, so let your tenant take the risk of carrying the cash to the bank or convenience store to get a money order. Tell your new tenant that your policy is to accept only a bank cashier's check or money order upon move-in. Also, let him know whether your rent collection policy will allow him to pay his future monthly rent payments with a personal check.

Pythons and piglets and bears, oh my!

In managing rental properties over the years, I have seen just about every type of pet you can imagine. I once took over management of a small rental property where the owner allowed the tenants to have pets. I wasn't too concerned until it became obvious that the prior management company didn't have any limitations. I soon found out that we had everything from the usual dogs and cats to a large Burmese python and a pot-bellied pig. One tenant even had two goats on his patio. Be sure to strictly define exactly which animals are acceptable — or you could be in for a big surprise.

Prior to giving the keys to your new tenant and allowing him to take possession, you need to insist on having the cash in hand through *good funds* (as opposed to *insufficient funds,* where a person writes a check and doesn't have the money to cover it in his account). Most owners do this by requiring cash, a bank cashier's check, or a money order. But many rental property owners aren't aware that both bank cashier's checks and money orders can be stopped. Financial institutions and convenience stores allow the purchaser to obtain a stop payment, because these financial instruments can be lost or stolen. However, the bank cashier's check and money orders are superior to personal checks because they do represent good funds and will at the very least not be returned to you because there was no money to cover them.

If despite my strong advice, your tenant persuades you to accept a personal check, then at least don't give him access to the rental property until you have called and verified with his bank that the check will be honored. Your best bet is to physically take the check to the tenant's bank and cash it or at least have it certified. If the bank will certify the check, they are guaranteeing that there are sufficient funds available and the bank will actually put a hold on the funds. Of course, cashing the check is the only sure way to collect your funds, because a devious tenant can always stop payment on even a certified personal check.

Inspecting the property with your tenant before the move-in

The number one source of tenant/landlord disputes is the disposition of the tenant's security deposit. Many of these potential problems can be resolved with proper procedures even before the tenant takes possession of the rental unit by using a move-in/move-out inspection checklist, like the one shown in Form 9-4. This form is an excellent tool to protect you and your tenant when the tenant moves out and wants the security deposit returned.

You can't judge a book by its cover

I once had a resident manager who had been in the rental management business for many years. She had probably rented to literally hundreds of tenants and consistently was one of my best managers, with very high occupancy and rarely any uncollected rent. She used to tell me how, over the years, she began to feel as though she could "read" a person and had even developed a sort of sixth sense to weed out bad applicants as she reviewed their rental applications.

One Saturday afternoon a very well-dressed man in his 30s came into see an apartment. He drove a fancy car and wore several pieces of expensive jewelry. He looked at a couple apartments and then said he would take the larger unit at the back of the property, because he preferred privacy. He said that he had just arrived in town and had been staying at a nice hotel in the area, but he was anxious to get settled and wanted to know if he could move in the next day, on a Sunday afternoon. The man was quite charming and very smooth. So charming, in fact, that this seasoned resident manager didn't wait for the results of the credit screening and accepted a personal check for all of his move-in funds, even though it was clearly against company policy. Unfortunately, his personal check bounced and it took over two months to evict this "gentlemen" from the rental unit. When we finally got possession of the unit after a lengthy eviction action, we found that this individual was quite a salesman — he had installed over a dozen phone lines in his apartment for his telemarketing operations.

The first column of the checklist is where you can note the condition of the unit before the tenant actually moves in. The last two columns are for use when the tenant moves out and you inspect the unit with the tenant again. Often, you won't immediately know the estimated cost of repair or replacement, so you can complete that portion of the checklist later and then include a copy when you send your tenant his security deposit disposition form.

When properly completed, the inspection form clearly documents the condition of the rental property upon acceptance and move-in by the tenants and serves as a baseline for the entire tenancy. If the tenant withholds rent or tries to break the lease claiming the unit needs substantial repairs, you may need to be able to prove the condition of the rental unit upon move-in. When the tenants move out, you'll be able to clearly note the items that were damaged or were not left clean by the vacating tenants so you can charge them the maximum allowed under your state or local laws.

The move-in/move-out inspection checklist is just as important as your lease or rental agreement. The purpose of the inspection is not to find all the items that you or your maintenance person forgot to check, because you should have already been through the rental unit looking carefully to ensure that it met your high standards. The purpose of the inspection is to clearly demonstrate to the tenant's satisfaction that the rental unit is in good condition except for any noted items.

Move-In/Move-Out Inspection Checklist

Tenant Name(s) ____

Rental Unit Address ____

Move-in Date ____________________ Move-out Date ____________________

Tenants have inspected the entire premises both interior and exterior, including but not limited to, each item listed on this form. The condition of each item is clean, undamaged, in good working order and adequate for usual and customary residential use unless otherwise noted. Tenants understand and agree that the Condition on Arrival versus the Condition on Departure comments will be compared and that all Tenants will be joint and severally liable for all discrepancies in an items condition. Tenants also understand that upon move-out, the Owner/Manager may make all legally allowed deductions from the security deposit for cleaning, repairing, or restoring said items to their move-in condition except for damage caused by ordinary wear and tear. Tenants note that the premises must be returned completely clean and that cleaning is not subject to allowance for ordinary wear and tear. Cross out items that are not applicable. Use additional sheets for bedrooms and bathrooms as necessary.

	Condition on Arrival	Condition on Departure	Estimated Cost of Repair/Replacement
Kitchen			
Floors/floor covering			
Walls & ceiling			
Windows/locks/screens			
Window coverings			
Doors/knobs			
Light fixtures/bulbs			
Cabinets/cupboards			
Drawers/countertops			
Sinks/stoppers/faucets			
Drains/plumbing			
Shelves/drawers			
Other			
Other			
Appliances			
Stove/oven			
Outside			
Burners			
Drip pans			
Hood vent			
Timer/controls			
Broiler pan			
Light			
Other			
Refrigerator			
Outside			
Inside			
Ice trays/Icemaker			
Other			
Dishwasher			
Outside			
Rack			
Other			
Garbage disposal			
Trash compactor			
Laundry equipment			
Other appliances			
Living Room			
Floors/floor covering			
Walls & ceiling			
Windows/locks/screens			
Window coverings			
Doors/locks			
Light fixtures/bulbs			
Closet/shelves			
Fireplace			
Other			
Other			

Form 9-4: Move-In/ Move-Out Inspection Checklist (Page 1 of 4).

The move-in/move-out inspection checklist is unique in that you will use the form throughout the entire tenancy — upon initial move-in, during the tenancy (if there are any repairs or upgrades to the rental unit), and when the tenant finally vacates the rental unit. Be sure to give your tenants a copy of the completed and signed form for their records.

	Condition on Arrival	Condition on Departure	Estimated Cost of Repair/Replacement
Dining room			
Floors/floor covering			
Walls & ceiling			
Windows/locks/screens			
Window coverings			
Doors/locks			
Light fixtures/bulbs			
Closet/shelves			
Other			
Other			
Other room			
Floors/floor covering			
Walls & ceiling			
Windows/locks/screens			
Window coverings			
Doors/locks			
Light fixtures/bulbs			
Closet/shelves			
Other			
Other			
Entry/Hall/Stairs			
Floors/floor covering			
Walls & ceiling			
Windows/locks/screens			
Window coverings			
Doors/locks			
Light fixtures/bulbs			
Closet/shelves			
Utility room			
Other			
Other			
Front entry/porch			
Light fixtures/bulbs			
Doorbell			
Other			
Back/side entry			
Light fixtures/bulbs			
Other			
Garage/carport			
Floor type/condition			
Doors/locks			
Light fixtures/bulbs			
Cabinets/shelves			
Other			
Storage			
Exterior			
Interior			
Attic/basement			
Other			
Grounds			
Lawn/Trees			
Flower beds			
Garden			
Sprinklers/Hose bibs			
Walkways			
Driveway			
Parking area			
Patio/terrace/deck			
Swimming pool			
Spa			
Other			

Form 9-4: Move-In/Move-Out Inspection Checklist (Page 2 of 4).

You need to physically walk through the rental unit with your new tenants and guide them through the inspection form. Let the tenants tell you the conditions they observe and make sure that your wording of the noted conditions and comments are detailed and that they accurately describe the conditions.

	Condition on Arrival	Condition on Departure	Estimated Cost of Repair/Replacement
Bathroom 1			
Floors/floor covering			
Walls/tile/grout/ceiling			
Windows/locks/screens			
Window coverings			
Doors/knobs/locks			
Light fixtures/bulbs			
Exhaust fan/heater			
Counters/shelves			
Mirrors/cabinets			
Sink/basin/faucets			
Drains/plumbing			
Tub/Shower/caulking			
Shower head/tub faucet			
Shower door/curtains			
Shower tracks			
Towel racks			
Toilet bowl/seat			
Toilet paper holder			
Other			
Bathroom 2			
Floors/floor covering			
Walls/tile/grout/ceiling			
Windows/locks/screens			
Window coverings			
Doors/knobs/locks			
Light fixtures/bulbs			
Exhaust fan/heater			
Counters/shelves			
Mirrors/cabinets			
Sink/basin/faucets			
Drains/plumbing			
Tub/Shower/caulking			
Shower head/tub faucet			
Shower door/curtains			
Shower tracks			
Towel racks			
Toilet bowl/seat			
Toilet paper holder			
Other			
Bedroom 1			
Floors/floor covering			
Walls & ceiling			
Windows/locks/screens			
Window coverings			
Doors/knobs/locks			
Closets/shelves			
Light fixtures/bulbs			
Other			
Bedroom 2			
Floors/floor covering			
Walls & ceiling			
Windows/locks/screens			
Window coverings			
Doors/knobs/locks			
Closets/shelves			
Light fixtures/bulbs			
Other			
Bedroom 3			
Floors/floor covering			
Walls & ceiling			
Windows/locks/screens			
Window coverings			
Doors/knobs/locks			
Closets/shelves			
Light fixtures/bulbs			
Other			

Form 9-4: Move-In/Move-Out Inspection Checklist (Page 3 of 4).

Print legibly and be as detailed and specific as possible noting the condition of each item. Be sure to indicate which items are in new, excellent, or very good condition as well as noting any items that are dirty, scratched, broken, or in poor condition.

	Condition on Arrival	Condition on Departure	Estimated Cost of Repair/Replacement
Other items			
Hot water heater			
Heating/thermostat			
Air conditioner (A/C)			
A/C filters & vents			
Cable TV/Antenna			
Electrical system			
Telephone/Intercom			
Laundry equipment			
Fire extinguishers			
Other			

Keys/Openers/Alarms	**Received**	**Returned**	**Charge for missing/ damaged key/opener**
Door			
Mailbox			
Laundry/Amenity			
Garage/Parking			

Additional items/comments

____

____

Move-in comments

____

____

Move-out comments

____

____

Smoke Detector(s)

____ By initialing here, Tenants acknowledge that all smoke detectors were tested in their presence and found to be in proper working order. Tenants have been advised as to the proper testing procedure and agree to test the smoke detector(s) at least monthly and to immediately report any problems to the Owner in writing. Tenants agree not to remove, disable, or disconnect the smoke detector(s) for any reason and Tenants agree to immediately replace/install all smoke detector batteries as necessary.

Alarm system

____ By initialing here, Tenants acknowledge that the alarm system was tested in their presence and found to be in proper working order. Tenants have been advised as to the proper operating instructions and testing procedure and will immediately contact the Owner if there is any malfunction of the system. Tenants have also been given an instruction manual that they have or will read.

Move-In/Move-Out Inspection Checklist completed upon **move-in** on ______________ at _________, and approved by:
Date Time

______________________________ and ______________________________
Owner/Manager

____
Tenants

Move-In/Move-Out Inspection Checklist completed upon **move-out** on ______________ at _________, and approved by:
Date Time

______________________________ and ______________________________
Owner/Manager

______________________________ ______________________________
Tenants Forwarding Address(es) Tenants

Form 9-4: Move-In/ Move-Out Inspection Checklist (Page 4 of 4).

For example, rather than generally indicate that the oven is "broken," be specific and note that the "built-in timer doesn't work." The oven works fine but the tenants know that they need to use a separate timer and that they will not be held responsible for this specific item upon move-out.

Be particularly careful to note any and all mildew, mold, pest, or rodent problems, because these are health issues that must be addressed immediately before the tenant takes possession. If the problems persist after move-in, then consult with the appropriate licensed professional to evaluate any potential health risk to the tenants and for the necessary response and remedial action.

Although a good inspection checklist clearly documents all damaged or substandard items, you should not overlook the importance of noting a detailed description of the items that are in good condition. If the flooring in the kitchen is new, be sure to indicate that on the form. Many disputes can be resolved if the inspection checklist specifically notes the condition of the item. If you only comment on dirty or damaged items, a court may conclude that you didn't inspect or forgot to record the condition of a component of the rental unit that you are now claiming was damaged by the tenant. You may think that everyone knows and agrees that all items without any notation are in average or "okay" condition, but the tenant will likely tell the court that the item was at least somewhat dirty or damaged and that you should not be able to collect for that item.

You and the tenant should complete the inspection form *together* prior to or at the time of move-in. If it is impossible for you to do this walk-through with your tenant, then you should complete the move-in/move-out inspection checklist and ask that all adult tenants review and sign the form as soon as possible upon move-in. Inform the tenants that you will be glad to deliver the mailbox key after you have the approved form in hand. I never seem to get anything but bills and junk mail myself, but I have learned that the mailbox key is very important to tenants and is a useful tool to motivate the tenant to promptly review and approve the inspection form.

When used properly, your move-in/move-out inspection checklist will not only prove the existence of damage in the rental unit, but it can pinpoint when the damage occurred. Don't fall for one of the oldest tenant ploys in the book. Tenants often try to avoid walking the rental unit with you upon move-in because they want to wait and be able to avoid charges for damage that occurs during their actual move-in. You must require the tenants to walk through the rental premises and agree that all items are in clean and undamaged condition *before* they start moving in their boxes and furnishings.

If you discover any problems during your inspection walkthrough, note them on the inspection form and take steps to have them corrected, unless it is not economically feasible. For example, you may have a hairline crack along the edge of the bathroom countertop. If you have determined that it would be too costly to refinish or replace the countertop, just note the condition on the inspection form so that your tenant is not charged in error upon move-out.

Be sure that your move-in/move-out inspection checklist reflects any repairs or improvements made after the initial walkthrough inspection. For example, if you and your tenants noted on the form that the bathroom door didn't lock properly, you would have that item repaired and you would need to update the inspection form and have your tenants initial the change. Or you may install new carpeting or make other improvements to the property that should be reflected on the inspection form.

Always be sure to note the condition of the carpets and floor coverings, because this is one of the most common areas of dispute with tenants upon move-out. Although tenants should not be charged for ordinary wear and tear, if they destroy the carpet they should pay for the damage. Indicate the age of the carpet and whether it has been professionally cleaned as part of your rental turnover process. When a tenant leaves after only six months and has destroyed the carpet, you can be sure that their memory will be that the carpet was old, dirty, and threadbare. The tenant's selective memory will not recall that the carpet was actually brand new or at least in very good condition and professionally cleaned upon move-in!

Another excellent way to avoid disputes over security deposits is for you to take photos or videotape the rental unit before the tenant moves in. In addition to your inspection form you will have some photos to help refresh the tenant's memory or show the court if the matter ends up there.

If you videotape the rental unit, be sure to get the tenant on the tape stating the date and time. If your tenant is not present, then bring a copy of that day's newspaper and include it in your video. With all detailed photography it is not always easy to understand exactly what the picture is showing unless specifically stated. So be sure to include a caption or descriptions with all still photos and provide a running detailed narrative with the video.

Do not assume that your tenants are familiar with the appliances and how they work. Provide your tenants with the appliance manuals or at least copies of the basic operating instructions.

If you have natural gas appliances or gas heat, instruct your tenants to contact the local utility company if they have any questions or concerns. This is particularly true if they detect the sulfur smell commonly associated with a gas leak. They should also contact the utility company or your maintenance person if there is a need to relight a pilot light.

Part of your new tenant orientation should include showing your tenants exactly where and how to shut off the utilities in case of a water leak, electrical short, or fire on the property. If you have a serious storm or earthquake, your tenants will need to be able to immediately turn off the natural gas supply as well. Provide your tenant with an inexpensive special wrench available from the natural gas utility company. Attach it to the gas meter with a simple cable so that your tenant or maintenance person will have it handy in case of an emergency.

Giving your tenant an informational letter prior to move-in

The key to success in managing rental properties is to develop an efficient system that reduces the time you spend managing your rentals. A good way to minimize your phone calls from tenants is to provide them with a *tenant information letter* (see Form 9-5), outlining all your policies and procedures that are too detailed to include in your lease or rental agreement. You can also attach information on the proper operation and care of appliances, plus other important information that they should know about the rental unit.

Customize the letter to present the policies and procedures you have implemented for each rental property. Although the letter should be customized for each property, here are some of the items to include:

- Property manager name and contact number
- Procedures to follow in case of emergency
- Rent collection information, including when rent is due, how payment is to be made, where to pay or mail rent, and how late fees and other charges are handled
- Requirements for ending tenancy, including notice requirement
- Procedures for the return of the security deposit
- Handling of new or departing roommates
- Proper procedure for requesting maintenance and repairs
- Lockout procedure and charges for lost keys
- Renter's insurance requirements
- Guest occupancy policy
- Annual safety inspection information
- Utility shut-off locations, including a separate diagram for the individual unit
- Trash collection and recycling program information
- Parking policies

Tenant Information Letter

Tenant Name(s) ______________________________
Rental Unit Address ______________________________

Dear ______________________________,

We are very pleased that you have selected our property to be your home. We hope that you enjoy living here and would like to share some additional information that will explain what you can expect from us and what we will be asking from you:

1. Owner/Manager:

2. Rent Collection:

3. Notice to End Tenancy:

4. Security Deposits:

5. New or Departing Roommates:

6. Maintenance and Repair Requests:

7. Lockout Procedure/Lost keys:

8. Renters Insurance:

9. Guest Occupancy Policy:

10. Annual Safety Inspection:

11. Utility shut-off locations:

12. Trash collection or recycling programs:

13. Parking:

Please let us know if you have any questions.

Sincerely,

______________________ Owner/Manager ______________ Date

I have read and received a copy of this Move-in Letter.

______________________ Tenant ______________ Date

______________________ Tenant ______________ Date

Form 9-5: Tenant Information Letter.

Distributing the keys

Key control is a very serious issue, with significant liability for rental property owners and managers. A problem in key control can allow access to a tenant's rental unit, and theft or serious bodily injury crimes can occur. Keys require careful handling and should be stored only in a locking metal key cabinet or safe.

As the property owner, you're responsible for ensuring that the rental property can be properly secured. Include an entry lock set and a sturdy deadbolt with at least a 13⁄16-inch throw on all exterior entry doors. Peepholes should be provided on the main or primary exterior entry door as well.

Some states have laws that specifically require the rental property owner to provide window locks as well. Whether legally required or not, I recommend that you provide locks for all windows that can be opened. Although not legally required in most states, I recommend installing window locks on upper level windows as a safety device and to minimize the chance that young, unsupervised children could fall from an open window.

For the convenience of your tenants, have a single key that works all entry locks for their particular unit while being able to also operate common area or laundry room locks.

One of the least desirable aspects of managing rental property is handling tenant lockout calls. Tenants rarely seem to get locked out of their rental unit during normal daylight hours, and you need to inform your new tenants about your lockout and lost key policies and charges. Set up a policy that acknowledges the difference between a lockout during reasonable business hours and non-working hours. For example, you could charge the tenant $20 for a lockout Monday through Friday from 9:00 a.m. to 6:00 p.m. and $40 for a lockout at all other times.

Changing the locks between tenants is extremely important. Prior tenants may have retained copies of the keys and could return to steal or commit some other crime. You can purchase and install an entirely new lock, or you can have your maintenance person or a locksmith rekey the existing lock. If you have several rental units, it makes economic sense to substitute the existing lock set with a spare lock set. Keep several extra lock sets in inventory so that you can rotate locks between units upon turnover. Your new tenant should sign a statement indicating that they are aware that the locks have been changed or rekeyed since the prior tenant vacated. Give them a copy of the locksmith receipt for their records.

The importance of changing locks between tenants

As the host of a live weekly radio show on real estate, I am often amazed at some of the stories I hear from callers. I will never forget the call I received from a tenant in a small multi-unit rental property who was shocked to find out that another tenant had a key to his rental unit. Apparently, one of the tenants had loaned his key to a family member who got confused and inadvertently entered the rental unit of my caller. When the caller confronted the property owner, the owner was not very concerned at all and didn't understand or share the concern of the tenants. He stated that he always used the same locks so that he didn't have to carry around extra keys if he needed access to a rental unit in case of emergency!

If you have a master key system for your rental properties, be extremely careful with it. Don't have any extra copies or loan the master key to anyone whom you don't trust implicitly. Although locksmiths are required by law to have written authorization prior to duplicating a key marked "Do not duplicate," remember that an individual who wants a copy of your key to commit a crime is not likely to be concerned that he is breaking the law by illegally copying the key.

Setting Up the Tenant File

You need to be able to immediately access important written records, and one way of doing that is to have an organized filing system to ensure that you don't waste time searching aimlessly for a lost or misplaced document. The best way to accomplish this goal is to immediately set up a new tenant folder for tenants at the time of their move-in.

Set up a file folder for each rental property with individual files for each tenant. Your tenant file should include the following:

- Rental application
- Rental application verification form
- Credit report
- Background information
- Holding deposit agreement and receipt

- Signed lease or rental agreement
- Lead-based paint disclosure form
- Smoke detector agreement
- Any other addenda to the lease or rental agreement
- Move-in/move-out inspection checklist
- Photos or videos of the unit, taken at move-in

You'll continue to turn to this file throughout the tenancy, adding to it all new documents such as rent increases, notices of entry, maintenance requests, and correspondence. Keep tenant files for three years after the tenant vacates.

Preparing a Welcome Package for Your New Tenant

Tenant satisfaction and retention are critical to success in rental management. One way to make a positive first impression is to provide your new tenants with a move-in package. Move-in packages can be very elaborate or just a few inexpensive but thoughtful items.

Give your new tenants a simple move-in package with a few useful items that they will need. For example, a couple of bottles of spring water in the refrigerator, a bar of soap and paper towels in the kitchen, change of address forms, a pad of scratch paper and a pen by the telephone, and a roll of toilet paper in the bathroom can be very handy in the first couple of days when your new tenants have everything packed away in boxes. A discount coupon or a gift certificate for a free pizza is another great way to impress your new tenant buried in moving boxes.

Another simple idea that will really impress your new tenants is to offer them one or two hours of free maintenance assistance when they first move in. Every new tenant needs to hang a few pictures or install a paper towel holder or some other minor maintenance work that will make your new tenant feel at home.

All your efforts to make a great first impression can backfire if there is not a clear understanding of the limitations of your offer or if the maintenance person is rude or does not do quality work. Provide your new tenants with a list of suggested items for your maintenance person and be sure to have your tenants sign a simple disclaimer form waiving their right to sue you or make a claim if your maintenance person damages their favorite picture while hanging it on the wall.

Although the tenants can handle many of the typical plumbing problems, be sure to instruct your tenant to call immediately if the plumbing backup results in any amount of sewage overflow, because this can be a significant health and safety risk. If plumbing clogs become common, it is likely the result of damaged pipes, roots in the waste line, or a blocked vent pipe, and you should immediately have a professional correct the problem at your expense.

Chapter 10

Collecting and Increasing Rent

In this Chapter

- Establishing a rent collection policy
- Handling late payments
- Knowing what's involved with pursuing legal action
- Increasing the rent without losing your tenants

If location is the most important element in real estate investing, then collecting rent in full and on time is the most important element in managing rental property. But how can you make sure that your tenants will pay their rent on time every month? The reality is that most tenants do not have significant cash resources, and many live from paycheck to paycheck. So if a tenant's paycheck is delayed or her car breaks down or she has an unexpected major expense, then her ability to pay the rent in full and on time is in jeopardy. And since the tenant's funds are so tightly budgeted, when she falls even one month behind on rent, catching up again is even more difficult.

However, you can take some steps to increase the likelihood that you'll always get your rent money in full and on time. The key to success when it comes to rent collection is establishing policies and procedures and being firm with your enforcement of collecting your rent.

You can begin laying the foundation for successful rent collection even before your property is rented. The best preventive measures you can take to ensure that your tenants have the ability to pay rent include targeting your advertising to responsible tenants and establishing a thorough and careful tenant screening and selection process.

Review your rent collection procedures with each adult occupant of your rental unit. Make rent collection a featured topic of your meeting with the tenants prior to the move-in date, when they review and sign the lease or rental agreement. Include your rent collection procedures in the informational letter you give to all new tenants as well. This way you can at least be sure the tenant is informed.

Collecting the rent is a key part of property management, as is keeping the rent competitive in your market. Raising the rent to reflect the trends in your area is a necessary part of managing rental properties. Many property owners hesitate to raise the rent for existing tenants, but it can be done well, without risking the loss of your tenants.

In this chapter, I fill you in on what you can do to ensure that you're getting paid on time and that your rent is competitive in your area.

Creating a Written Rent Collection Policy

The fundamentals of property management are very straightforward: You provide the tenants with a clean and comfortable place to live; and they pay the rent, live quietly, and keep the rental unit clean. Problems and confusion can arise, however, if you and your tenant do not understand the rights and responsibilities that come with the tenant/landlord relationship.

Setting up a successful rent collection policy, putting it in writing, and giving it to your tenants in the tenant information letter is the best way to avoid confusion. No single rent collection policy works for *all* rental property owners, but every policy should cover certain key issues, which I outline in the following sections.

When rent is due

I recommend that you require your tenants to pay the full monthly rent, in advance, on or before the first of each month. This method is the most common, and many state laws require it unless the lease or rental agreement specifies otherwise.

Although rent is traditionally paid in full at one time, it is perfectly legal for you and your tenant to agree that the rent will be divided up and paid twice a month, every week, or in any other mutually agreed timeframe. Generally, however, try to avoid accepting more frequent payments, because your goal is efficiency and handling the rent collection process only once each month is definitely more efficient.

You and your tenant can agree that the monthly rent will be paid on any mutually agreeable date during the month; rent does not have to be paid on the first of the month. This may make sense if your tenant receives income or assistance payments on certain dates. For example, you may have a tenant who receives an income check on the 10th of each month so you set the monthly rent due date for the 15th of each month.

Think about the ramifications of accepting rent based on the tenant's scheduled receipt of income rather than your usual rent due date. By accommodating the tenant, you are tacitly acknowledging that the tenant needs that payment in order to afford the rent. But one of the most fundamental issues in the management of rental housing is to avoid tenants who cannot afford the rent. If your tenant needs that income in order to pay your rent that month, no safety net is in place if the tenant's check is lost in the mail, or his car breaks down, or he is temporarily laid off from his job. To avoid surprises and delinquent rent, you do not want your tenants to have their finances so tight that they need this month's income to pay this month's rent. Your tenant screening process should provide you with the information so that you can effectively select tenants with enough financial cushion that they are paying this month's rent from cash already on hand as of the first of each month.

Some owners make the rent payable each month on the date the tenant first moved in. For example, if the tenant moves in on the 25th of the month, then her rent is due on the 25th of each future month. This policy is legal and may be acceptable if you have only a few tenants and are willing to keep track of each due date. But having all of your rents due on the first of the month makes life simpler and avoids confusion or the chance of making an error on legal notices for nonpayment of rent.

If your rent due date falls on a weekend day or a legal holiday, the tenant is allowed to pay it by the next business day in most states. Even if this is not required in your state, adopting this policy is a good idea.

Prorating rents

Life would be simpler if all your tenants moved in and out only on the first of the month, but they won't. If your tenant's occupancy begins in the middle of the month and you have a rent collection policy that all rents are due on the first of each month, then you need to prorate the rent at move-in. There are two basic ways to prorate the rent at the beginning of your new tenant's occupancy.

If your tenant moves in toward the end of a month, collect a full month's rent (for the next month), plus the rent due for the additional prorated portion of the current month. For example, if your tenant takes occupancy on July 25, upon move-in collect 7 days' rent for the period of July 25 to July 31 plus a full month's rent for the month of August. Your new tenant will usually be glad to do this if there are only a few days to prorate.

However, if your tenant moves in early in a month, expecting your tenant to pay a full month's rent plus the prorated rent upon move-in may be unreasonable. If your tenant moves in on July 10, he will most likely balk at your request for payment of seven weeks' rent upon move-in. In these situations, collect a full month's rent prior to move-in and then collect the balance due for the prorated rent on the first of the next month. For example, prior to your tenant taking occupancy, collect a full month's rent covering the period of July 10 through August 9. Then on August 1, collect the balance of the rent due for August 10 through August 31 or 22 days. By September 1, the tenant is on track to pay his full rent on the first of each month.

Unless otherwise agreed, rent is normally uniformly apportioned from day to day using a 30-day month. Take your monthly rental rate and divide it by 30 to determine the daily rental rate. This formula applies to February as well.

Providing a grace period

Many rent collection policies allow for a grace period that provides the tenants with a few extra days to make the monthly rent payment in full before incurring late charges. And most tenants incorrectly believe that if they pay rent within the grace period, their payment is legally on time. However, the rent is due on or before the rent due date and is delinquent from a legal perspective regardless of the terms of the grace period.

Make sure that the lease or rental agreement and the tenant information letter are very clear and unambiguous about the fact that the rent is due on or before the first of the month and is technically late even if paid during the grace period.

Grace periods are optional and can be any number of days in length. A few states have mandatory grace periods, so be sure to check your local and state laws. I recommend that your grace period expire on the third of the month regardless of whether the third falls on a weekend, but some states have laws that require you to give the tenant an additional day if the third of the month falls on a weekend or holiday.

You do not have to wait until the grace period expires to begin your collection efforts. Contact tenants who show a pattern of being late. You can even serve legal notices demanding the rent payment. Your lease or rental agreement should contain a specific provision that you have the right to refuse payment after the expiration of your legal demand notice, so that you are not obligated to accept an offer of rent from the tenant and can move forward with the eviction.

Where rent is paid

You can collect your rent in several ways, but unless otherwise agreed, many states require that rent be collected at the premises. The burden is on the rental property owner to stop by the rental property each month and personally collect the rent.

Although stopping by the unit allows you the opportunity to see your rental property, it is not very time-efficient unless you live on or very close to your rental property, especially if you have to make multiple trips. Tenants in low-rent properties often expect the owner or property manager to come by and collect the rent in person, whereas renters at middle- to higher-rent properties will think you are too nosy if you personally come by for the rent.

You can also have the tenant bring the rent to your home or office. Although this may be very convenient for you, many tenants object to having to personally deliver their monthly rent to you. For this reason, asking the tenants to deliver the rent to you in this way is not conducive to getting the rent on time and only places an additional burden on your tenant when your goal is to simplify the rent collection process for everyone involved.

For most rental property owners and tenants, the most popular way to remit the monthly rent payment is to have the tenants mail their monthly rent to you. Because collecting rent by mail is only effective if your tenants pay on time, I strongly suggest that you make it extremely simple for your tenants by providing them with stamped, pre-addressed envelopes. Giving tenants several envelopes at once is more efficient as long as the tenants are responsible and will not lose them or use them to pay other bills.

If you and the tenant agree the monthly rent will be mailed, you may run into some questions about when the rent is actually considered paid. Is rent considered paid when it is postmarked or when it is received? Check your local laws and have a clear written agreement in your rent collection policy. Absent any legal requirements, I recommend that you consider the rent paid when the payment is postmarked. By mailing the rental payment on time, the tenant is acting in good faith, and you don't want to unfairly penalize your tenant if the mail is delayed.

How rent is paid

Your lease or rental agreement should clearly indicate how rent is to be paid: by cash, personal check, cashier's check, or money order. Give your tenants a receipt for all money received, including checks.

Checks

For many rental property owners, the acceptance of checks is routine. Most tenants have a personal checking account, and paying by check is easy for them.

Some rental property owners request post-dated checks in advance from their tenants with the idea that they will already have the rent payment in hand and the tenant just needs to make the funds available to cover the check. I strongly advise against accepting post-dated checks. Often these checks are not good, and the laws of many states consider a post-dated check a promissory note. You could actually be unable to bring an eviction action for nonpayment of rent while the note is pending.

Payment by check is conditional. If the check is not honored for any reason, it is as if the tenant never paid and late charges and returned check charges should apply.

Never accept second-party checks, such as payroll or government checks. Have a policy that all rent payments made after the grace period must be in the form of a cashier's check or money order.

Cash

Avoid cash whenever possible. Turning down cash is always difficult, and your tenants may remind you that cash is legal tender. However, you have the legal right to refuse to accept cash. What's wrong with cash?

- **You become a target for robbery.** Even if you use a safe, you have an increased risk.
- **If you have employees and you accept cash, there is an added risk of employee theft.** Plus you are potentially putting your employees in danger.
- **Accepting cash attracts tenants that may be involved in illegal businesses that deal primarily in cash.** These tenants don't want to have their activities tracked and prefer rental properties where cash payments are allowed. Don't make your rental property more attractive to the criminally inclined.

Do not accept even small amounts of cash for rental application fees and late charges.

Clearly state in your lease or rental agreement that cash is not accepted under any circumstances.

Good accounting practices suggest that all of your income and expenses be clearly documented. The Internal Revenue Service may become interested in auditing your rental housing if they become aware of frequent cash transactions at your rental properties.

Electronic payments

Technology is making the rent collection process much more efficient and timely. Rental owners and property managers can now process hundreds of rent payments each month in a matter of minutes. Because of improvements in software automation and *security encryption,* which prevents the theft of confidential information, the process is actually more secure than the conventional method of paying rent with a personal check.

Several companies now offer technology for the electronic transfer of funds in order to allow tenants to pay their rent. These companies provide you with software for your computer that enables you to download all the information on all the payments processed each month. You are automatically notified if your tenant did not have sufficient funds to cover the electronic transfer, so you can enforce your regular rent collection policies. Check with your local IREM chapter or apartment association for referrals.

Some tenants may be reluctant at first to try the new technology; however, after they are hooked, they will not want to go back to their old method of paying rent. Instead of the tenant having to manually write out and mail a check each month, she simply fills out a form one time, and the preauthorized amount is deducted on a designated day (usually the first of each month) from her bank account and deposited directly into your account.

Dealing with Rent Collection Problems

As a rental property owner, you're not in the banking business. So your tenants must always pay the entire rent due in good funds on or before the due date. However, you need to establish policies for the most common problems you will encounter in collecting rents.

Dealing with multiple rent checks

When you have multiple tenants or roommates in one of your units, you will probably receive several checks for portions of the total rent due. And you may not receive all the rent checks at the same time or for the proper amount. When you call the tenants, you may hear from one of the roommates that he paid his share and you need to track down one of the other tenants. How your tenants choose to decide to divide the rent between them shouldn't be your problem, however.

Accommodating your tenants and accepting multiple checks can cause administrative nightmares and lead roommates to erroneously believe that they are not responsible for the entire rent. I recommend that you have a firm policy of requiring one check for the entire month's rent.

Besides the administrative convenience for you, there are other benefits to this policy. Legally, each roommate in your rental property is "joint and severally" liable for all lease or rental agreement obligations. This means that if one skips out, the others will owe you the entire amount. If you allow them to pay separately, they may forget that they are each responsible for the entire amount.

You also want to have your tenants assume responsibility and take the lead in getting the delinquent roommate to pay rent. Let the responsible tenant know even if they have already paid a portion of the rent, they will be on the hook for the balance of the unpaid rent. After all, they are in a better a position to track down their elusive roommate than you are.

These policies outline the specific penalties that are enforced for tenants who bounce a check, fail to pay in full, or occasionally pay after the due date and the expiration of the grace period, if any. I cover some of these key issues in the following sections.

Collecting late rent

One of the most difficult challenges for a rental property owner is dealing with a tenant when the rent is late. You don't want to overreact and begin serving threatening legal rent demand notices, because that will definitely create tension and hostility if there is a legitimate reason for the delay. On the other hand, late rent can be a very serious issue.

If you are having trouble collecting rent on time, consider mailing your tenants a monthly payment reminder or an invoice. Some owners have also found that a rent coupon book (just like a mortgage payment coupon book) can be helpful in improving their rental collections.

You can also call your routinely slow rent payers and remind them that the rent is due on or before the first of the month. You can remind your tenants that you expect your rent to be their top priority among their various financial obligations. However, I don't recommend that you call and remind tenants indefinitely, because your time is too valuable to look after your tenants. If they consistently fail to pay the full rent on or before the due date, you should not renew the lease or give a 30-day notice to terminate the tenancy.

The key to keeping your response in line with the magnitude of the problem is to communicate. You need to remain calm and businesslike and determine why the rent is late before taking any action.

The most effective way to collect rents and determine whether you should exercise a little patience is to contact your tenant directly. Simply mailing a rent reminder or hanging a late notice on the front door typically won't get the job done.

Your goal in personally contacting your tenant is not to harass them but to remind them, or to be solution-oriented and work out an agreement to get your rent. Whatever agreement you reach, make sure that it is in writing and signed by the tenant.

Call your tenant at home *and* at his place of business. Although you may not want to bother the tenant at work, you have a right to know when to expect your rent. You can also go to the rental unit and speak with your tenant directly. Don't be shy, or paying the rent will quickly become a low priority for your tenant.

If you're having trouble locating your tenant, check with the neighbors or call the emergency contact listed on their rental application. Check to see if the utility company has been notified to cancel the utilities; maybe the tenant has skipped town and not notified you.

Charging late fees

Charging tenants late fees when they don't pay their rent on time is one of the most effective ways to encourage on-time payments. Although many rental property owners have late charges, they are often enforced inconsistently and therefore become ineffective. Other rental property owners have very long grace periods or set their fees so high that they are unenforceable if challenged in court, so they are often waived.

Late charges are very controversial and many state courts have ruled that excessive late fees are not enforceable. Implementing and enforcing a late charge policy makes sense, as long as it is reasonable and relates to your actual out-of-pocket costs or expenses incurred by the late payment.

Don't allow tenants to form the impression that your late charge policy approves of late rent payments as long as the late charges are collected. Your late charge should be high enough to discourage habitual lateness, but not so high as to be unreasonable. Send a written warning to those tenants who regularly pay late (even if they pay the late charges) clearly indicating that their late payments are unacceptable and a legal violation of the terms.

You can assess late charges in one of several ways:

- **Flat fee:** The most common late charge is a flat fee due immediately after the grace period and can be any set amount. Typical amounts range from $20 to $50 and are usually set at 4 to 6 percent of the monthly rental rate. The problem with the flat fee late charge is that many tenants are only 1 to 2 days late and the late charge is not reasonable. Rental property owners end up waiving the late charge or, if the matter is ever heard in court, the late charge fee is usually challenged by the tenant and may be thrown out by the court.
- **Percentage of the monthly rent fee:** Percentage late fees are calculated as a percentage of the periodic or monthly rent payment and range from a low of 4 percent to as high as 8 percent of the monthly rental rate. The usual and customary late fee percentage for late rent payments is either 5 or 6 percent. Some states even have legal limits on late charges expressed as a percentage of the rent.

- **Daily late fee:** If you use a daily late charge, you set a daily late charge with a reasonable cap or maximum late fee. A late charge of $5 per day with a maximum of $50 works very well. A tenant who is only one day late is charged a nominal $5. A tenant who is eight days late will pay a more hefty $40 late charge. The purpose of the cap is to keep the late charge reasonable. By the time you get to the cap (at ten days late), you will have already sent the proper legal rent demand notices.

The flat fee and the percentage of the rent method both fail to provide an incentive for the tenant to pay their rent promptly. Once the late charge has been incurred, the tenant often finds other financial obligations more important than your rent. Assessing a daily fee offers the incentive some tenants need to get their rent in sooner rather than later.

Waiving the late charge is excusing the late payment of rent and can send the wrong message to all your tenants. If you routinely accept late payments and waive the late charges, you cannot suddenly change your attitude and begin eviction proceedings the next time your tenant pays late. You need to give your tenant a written notice that you will once again actively enforce the strict rent collection terms of your lease or rental agreement. You also need to be consistent in applying your late charge policy to all tenants equally — or you could face claims of discrimination.

If you receive a late payment by mail, always keep the envelope with the postmark in case the tenant wants to dispute the late charge.

In order to determine what a reasonable late charge should be for your rental property you need to evaluate your own increase in costs as a result of late rent payments. Put this in writing and be prepared to explain your policy if challenged in court. Additional costs may include phone calls and in-person meetings with the tenant; the preparation and sending of warning letters and required legal rent demand notices; time and costs spent preparing delinquency lists; and additional accounting and bank deposits when the funds are received.

Handling returned checks

Returned rent checks can cause major problems for your rent collection efforts, so you need to charge tenants a fee when one of their checks is returned.

Often, when you contact your tenant, he will have some excuse for the returned check and tell you that his check is now good. I recommend that you don't redeposit the check, however. Go to the tenant's bank and cash the check immediately or get it certified, which means the bank will reserve the funds for payment when you deposit it in your bank.

Some states have laws that allow you to charge interest and penalties on returned checks.

Early-payment rent discounts

Some landlords have tried to get around the late charge problems by using early-payment rent discounts to entice their tenants to pay their rent on time. They set the rent in the lease or rental agreement slightly higher than the market rent, and then offer tenants a reduced rent if the rent is paid in full on time. For example, if they really want to have a $900 rent and a $75 late charge, they set the lease rent at $975 with a $75 discount if the tenant pays on or before the third of the month.

Although this may be creative, the courts have consistently determined that the actual rent is the discounted amount. The courts have ruled that giving a large discount for an on-time payment is the same as charging an excessive late fee.

Don't play this game. If you're challenged, your case will be thrown out of court. There have been at least two large class-action lawsuits specifically on this practice and landlords got creamed with major legal costs and severe financial penalties. The whole thing is a scam, and the courts have seen right through it. If you want more rent, raise your rent. If you want tenants who pay on time, carefully screen your tenants. Establish a reasonable and fair late charge policy, and apply it uniformly to all tenants.

The best policy is to demand your tenant immediately replace a returned check with a cashier's check or money order. After a tenant has a second returned check, regardless of the tenant's excuses, require all future payments be made only with a cashier's check or money order, which are guaranteed to have sufficient funds. But tenants can still request a stop-payment on a cashier's check or money order, claiming they were lost or stolen, so be sure to deposit the money right away.

Like late charges, returned check charges should be reasonable. Try setting the fee at $15 to $25 per returned item, or slightly higher than the amount your bank charges you for the returned check.

Unless the returned check is replaced with good funds before the end of your grace period, your tenant is also responsible for late charges.

Dealing with partial rental payments

Occasionally, you'll encounter a tenant who won't be able to pay the full rent on time. The tenant may offer to pay a portion of the rent that is due with a promise to catch up as the month proceeds. Your written rental collection policy should not allow partial payments of rent, and deviating from this policy is generally not a good idea.

However, in some instances, allowing for partial rent payments may make sense. If your tenant has had an excellent rental payment history and you can verify that this will be a one-time situation, then you are probably safe in accepting a partial rent payment. Of course, you need to be careful and watch for the tenant who is delaying the inevitable and stalling you from pursuing your legal options.

If you do accept a partial payment, prepare the proper legal rent demand notice for nonpayment of rent or draw up a written notice outlining the terms of your one-time acceptance of the partial rent payment, including late charges. Then give the legal rent demand notice or written agreement when the tenant gives you the partial payment. This way, you can be sure that the tenant understands your terms.

In most areas, the acceptance of a partial payment will void any prior legal notices for nonpayment of rent. If your tenant is causing trouble besides the delinquent rent, do not accept any partial payments or you will have to begin your eviction proceedings from scratch — and you can be sure that they will be difficult to serve again.

Rental payments should always be applied to the oldest outstanding past due rent amount even if the tenant tries to indicate the payment is for a different time period.

Be sure to apply your rent collection policies, including your late charges, partial payment, and returned check policies consistently with all tenants. If you don't, you could be accused of discrimination by simply allowing some tenants to pay late or by accepting multiple checks from some roommates and not from others.

Serving legal notices

If you're having trouble collecting the rent from one of your tenants, you may need to pursue legal action. In most states, you don't need to wait until the end of the grace period to serve a legal rent demand notice. The notices should be served personally whenever possible; but the laws of each state do offer alternative means of achieving legal process service. Contact your local affiliate of the National Apartment Association for local requirements for process serving.

Legal notices for nonpayment of rent and similar breaches of the lease or rental agreement vary widely from state to state. The generic 50-state forms available from office supply stores may be ineffective or even invalid in your area. Contact your local affiliate of the National Apartment Association or the local affiliate of the National Association of Realtors for current and legally correct forms.

Offering incentives for paying on time

Because timely rent collection can make or break your career as a rental property owner, you may want to offer your tenants incentives to pay on time. If you have several rental units, one good way to motivate your tenants is to offer a monthly prize drawing for all tenants who have paid rent in full by your due date. Of course, you need to carefully outline your rules in writing and make sure that you do not violate any local or state laws.

The drawing should be simple and easy for the tenants to understand. Eligibility should be limited to tenants who are current with their rent, and tenants should be automatically entered when you receive their full rent on or before the due date. Inform the tenants of the time and place for the drawing, and try to hold it in a common area at one of your rental properties.

Another idea is to give a second entry to tenants who pay early and be sure your rules disqualify a winner whose rent check is later returned because of insufficient funds.

The prize can be a gift certificate to a local store or restaurant. Many times the merchant will even discount or donate the prize if they get some good publicity from your drawing. You may even want to offer a rent discount off the next month's rent.

Consider sending out a written announcement congratulating your monthly drawing winner. This can be a great motivator and reminder for other tenants to get the rent in on time so they can be eligible for the drawing each month.

Increasing the Rent

Raising the rent is one of the most difficult challenges rental property owners face. If you need to raise the rent, you may be worried that the tenant will leave, or you may not even know how much to increase the rent.

Even if you're raising the rent for the first time in several years, most tenants will naturally have a very negative reaction to the rent increase. So you need to do your homework and make sure that your rent increase is reasonable and justified. When the rental market is tight, you should adjust your rents by small amounts with greater frequency rather than a very large increase more sporadically. Most tenants will not leave over a small rent increase.

Before increasing the rent, be sure to determine what improvement you will make in the common area of your rental property or, better yet, in the tenant's rental unit. I suggest that you set a budget that is equivalent to three to six months of the rent increase and plan on making an immediate upgrade to the tenant's rental unit. Often, just painting and cleaning or replacing the carpet will help your tenant accept the rent increase. Installing new plumbing or light fixtures are usually appreciated as well.

Unless you are in a rent-control area, there is no limit on the amount or how often you can increase the rent of a month-to-month or periodic tenant with proper legal notice. If your tenant is on a lease, you need to wait until the lease expires. You can raise the rent as much and as often as your good business judgment and the competitive rental market will allow. Of course, don't be too aggressive, or you will lose your best tenants. Trying to get that last $25 per month can cost you a vacancy with significant turnover costs plus the lost rent of over $25 per day!

The best policy is to regularly review and survey the rental market to determine the current market rental rate for comparable rental properties — ones that are of similar size and condition and that have the same features and amenities. Turn to Chapter 5 for more information on evaluating the competitive rental market and setting rents.

Many wise rental property owners intentionally keep their rents slightly below the maximum the competitive rental market will allow as part of a policy to retain the best tenants. Unless you are planning a major upgrade of your rental units with a new tenant profile and much higher rents across the board, tenant turnover is usually bad business.

Although you are only legally required to give a 30-day notice in many cases, I recommend a minimum rental increase notice of 45 days. If the rent increase is significant (10 percent or more), a 60-day written notice is advisable. Some owners fear that giving their tenant notice will also give them plenty of time to find another rental. However, if you've set your increased rent properly, you want your tenant to have the opportunity to compare the new rental rate to the market conditions rather than just overreact with a notice to vacate.

If possible, inform your tenant personally of the pending rent increase and be sure to follow up by legally serving a formal written notice and keeping a copy in the tenant's file. The letter doesn't have to be a literary work, but you may consider attaching any market information obtained from your market survey so that your tenant can see that you have made an informed decision.

Be careful when raising the rent so that you are not accused of giving rent increases in retaliation. An increase immediately after the tenant complains to the Health Department or an increase that is much higher than other tenants received is likely to lead to problems. As always, your best defense is to have a sensible rent increase policy, keep good records, and be consistently fair and equitable with all of your tenants.

You don't have to worry about rent control limiting your rental rates unless you are a rental property owner in California, the District of Columbia, Maryland, New Jersey, or New York. In these five states, many of the larger cities and certain surrounding communities have rent-control laws that regulate many aspects of the tenant/landlord relationship. Although the local rent control ordinances are different in each area, they all have limitations on setting and adjusting rental rates. They also have very specific requirements that must be met prior to increasing the rent, if allowed at all. If you own rental property in a city with rent control, you should always have a current copy of the rent control ordinance and be sure that you have a good understanding of all regulations or procedures that you must follow.

Chapter 11

Keeping the Good Tenants — and Your Sanity

In This Chapter

- Retaining your tenants by knowing what they want and making sure they get it
- Knowing whether renewing a lease is the best option for you and your tenant

The key to your success as a property manager is an occupied rental unit. But this basic fact is something many rental property owners quickly forget.

Although advertising your vacancy, having a well-polished presentation, knowing all the latest sales closing techniques, implementing a thorough tenant-screening program, and moving in your prized tenant with amazing efficiency are all important parts of your job, the reality is that the day your tenant moves in is the day your most important job — keeping your good tenants satisfied and happy — begins.

Your goal is to have your tenants stay and pay. If you offer a quality rental experience at a reasonable price, you will have lower turnover than other rental properties in your area.

You can retain your quality tenants and have a lower turnover rate by treating tenants with the same personal attention and courtesy you demonstrated when you first spoke to them on the phone or gave them a tour of the vacancy.

Knowing what your customers want is really the key to success in any business, and as a rental property owner, your tenants are your customers. In this chapter, I let you know what most tenants are looking for in a rental experience so you can make sure you're meeting those needs. I also give you some tips on getting to the point where your tenants not only enjoy their experience at your property but want to renew their lease.

What Tenants Want

If you're trying to raise your level of tenant satisfaction (and that should always be your goal), you need to determine what your tenants want and figure out how to deliver that to them. Your tenants are basically looking for the following:

- Timely and effective communication
- Professional maintenance of the interior and common areas
- Respect for their privacy
- Fair and consistent policies and rules, as well as equal enforcement of them
- Reasonable rent in relation to what they're getting

I cover each of these in the following sections.

Timely and effective communication

A variety of issues concern most tenants — and those issues are usually fairly obvious. Good tenants don't like loud or noisy neighbors, unkempt common areas, broken or unserviceable items in their rental unit, or unsubstantiated rent increases. But the good news is that most of these problems can be solved if you have good communication and follow-through.

The one problem that tenants will not ignore is a landlord's apathy. If you seem uncaring or nonchalant about your tenant's concerns, he will get the message that you don't value his business. The perception of apathy is often created by an unwillingness or failure to communicate. If you give your tenants the impression that you only care about them when their rent is late, you're headed straight down that apathy path.

Keep your tenants informed. No one likes surprises, and tenants are no different. If the pest control company cancels its service call, let your tenant know right away. If the walkthrough with your new lender has been changed to earlier in the day, call or e-mail your tenant instead of arriving unexpectedly with a weak apology. Common courtesy goes a long way.

Quick responses to maintenance requests

One way to set *your* rental management apart from your competition is to handle tenant maintenance requests quickly and professionally. Getting prompt resolution to your tenants' problems will keep them happy.

After a new tenant moves in, if he notes any problems, don't view these complaints as negatives. Instead, think of them as opportunities to let your tenant know that you care. By quickly and professionally addressing the problem, you will actually improve your tenant relations. Successful rental owners don't have to be perfect; they just need to admit the mistake or problem, communicate openly and candidly, and take the necessary steps to resolve it.

One of the most common complaints about rental owners is that they are unwilling to maintain, and especially upgrade, their rental units for the current tenants. In my experience, tenants have a valid complaint. Refusing to repaint, recarpet, or upgrade the appliances for a great tenant makes no sense. Because if you don't do it for the great tenant you already have, and that tenant is frustrated with your lack of effort and moves out, you'll have do the work anyway in order to be competitive in the rental market and attract a new unproven tenant.

Rental property owners often also overlook punctuality when it comes to making repairs. Undoubtedly, you're a very busy person, but it's easy to lose sight of the fact that your tenants are busy, too. If you tell your tenants that you will call or meet them at a certain time, be sure to be there when you said you would — or at the very least, call and let them know if you're running late. Require your property manager, maintenance personnel, or contractors to treat your tenants with the same level of respect as well.

Treating your tenants as important customers can be the best decision you ever make. When working with a tenant concern or complaint, try to ask yourself how you would want to be treated. Treating your tenants as you would want to be treated will make your tenant relations much more pleasant, and you will dramatically decrease your tenant turnover and improve your net income — a win-win situation for all!

Respect for their privacy

One of the biggest complaints most tenants have is a rental owner who fails to respect the tenant's privacy.

In most states, the property manager or owner can only enter the premises with advance written notice or the tenant's permission, except in the event of an emergency.

Your notice of entry should only be during normal business hours. Some state laws offer specific day and time parameters, but many don't. Without the guidelines, some rental owners feel that as long as they give proper legal notice, they can enter the rental whenever they want. But I recommend limiting your request for entry to Monday through Saturday from 8:00 a.m. to 7:00 p.m., unless the tenant requests or voluntarily agrees to a different time.

Although legally you may only have to post a notice on the door a few days in advance of when you want to be able to enter the rental unit, that isn't enough to maintain a positive and mutually respectful relationship with your tenants. Even though you own the rental property, the last thing you want your tenant to feel is that their home isn't really theirs. If you don't respect the privacy of your tenants in their own home, they will be less likely to show respect for you or your rental property during or at the end of their tenancy.

Enforcement of house rules

A frequent source of tenant complaints is the rental property owner's failure to enforce reasonable policies and rules.

Good tenants actually *want* and *appreciate* fair and reasonable policies and rules. They know that they are going to be quiet and respectful of their neighbors, and they want to know that their neighbors will be required to reciprocate. Establishing standard policies and house rules for your rental properties and enforcing them fairly is all part of the job of managing rental property.

Tenants talk to one another, and they will quickly discover if you have different rules for different tenants. Inconsistent or selective enforcement of rules has fair-housing implications. For example, you may think that waiving a late fee for a tenant you've known for years but charging the late fee to a new tenant in similar circumstances is okay. After all, you've known the first tenant longer, and you're willing to forgive that oversight once in a while, right? Wrong. You can't have different interpretations of the rules, because the legal consequences you may face are severe.

Fair rental rates and increases

Rent increases are always unpopular, and if you don't handle them properly, they can easily lead to increased tension and tenant dissatisfaction. No one likes to pay more, but we all know that the good things in life aren't cheap. Most tenants don't mind paying a fair and competitive rent as long as they're sure you're not gouging them with unnecessary rent hikes.

Although they may initially be upset with the increase, your tenants may be thinking to themselves that you will now finally be able to address the peeling paint and missing window screens. And if your rental property has peeling paint and missing window screens and you've just increased the rent, you'd better be sure to address those problems right away, not months down the road, if you want your tenants to be satisfied.

There is nothing wrong with increasing your price — after all, you're running a business, not a charity. But common sense and prudence dictate that you explain to your tenants the reasons for the rent increase and what benefits are in it for them.

Renewing Leases

Lease renewals are a sign that you're doing a good job at keeping your tenants satisfied and meeting their needs, not to mention the fact that they are one of your most productive activities as a rental property manager. Of course, not all tenants are good candidates for lease renewal, but renewing a lease with a current tenant clearly has an additional benefit over a lease with a new tenant. After all, you have a track record with your current tenant; you know her rent payment history and whether she treats the property and her neighbors with respect. And you can never be 100 percent sure of that kind of information when you're starting from scratch with someone new.

Plus, your tenant knows what to expect form you as a rental property owner. She knows your standards for maintaining the property, your interest in and response to her requests, your policies and rules (and whether they're fairly enforced), and the level of courtesy and respect you have for her privacy. Your tenant has a certain comfort level with you, and as long as you're willing to be competitive with your rental rate, it's in her best interests to stay.

Unless your lease agreement contains an automatic renewal clause, it will expire on the date specified. If you want your tenant to stay, don't be afraid to approach her and ask her to sign another lease effective when the current one expires. Contact your tenant at least 60 days prior to the lease expiration.

If the tenant moves out, you'll have to incur extensive turnover costs for maintenance, painting, and cleaning, plus you'll lose rent for every day the rental unit sits vacant. So why not make a few upgrades to the rental unit a couple months before the tenant's lease expires, just as a reminder that you care about the tenant's satisfaction.

Give your tenant a list of comparably priced service items or unit upgrades and let the tenant choose which upgrade she wants. This way, you send the message that you value her input and strive to reward her business.

In a competitive rental market with increasing rents, most tenants who intend to stay will be glad to renew their current lease or even sign a new lease at a higher, but still reasonable rent. Renewing a lease in a strong rental market may not be in your best interest, however, because a lease prevents you from raising the rent or changing any terms. Plus, with a lease in place, evicting a problem tenant is much more difficult.

One of the most common reasons tenants leave or don't renew their lease is their intention to purchase a home. Although home ownership is a very worthy goal, you may want to advise your tenants about other options. For example, if you want to entice your tenant to stay, you may offer them a lease option (see Chapter 19 for more information) or a long-term lease at a fixed amount that offers them rent stability. A number of calculators are available on the Internet to help people determine whether they'd be better off renting or buying, given their overall financial situation. Letting your tenants know about their options — without discouraging them from buying if that's really best for them — makes sense.

Chapter 12

Dealing with Problem Tenants

In This Chapter

- Knowing how to handle common tenant problems
- Using mediation or arbitration to resolve conflicts with your tenants
- Making your way through the eviction process
- Being prepared for everything — from tenant bankruptcy to tenant death

Although the proper tenant screening and selection techniques greatly improve your success in picking good tenants, they aren't a guarantee, which means that at some point in your rental property management tenure, you're sure to come across a problem tenant or two. Some tenants don't pay their rent, disturb the neighbors, damage the property inside and out, or keep a growing collection of inoperative cars on the front lawn, and you need to take steps immediately to remove them from the rental unit and replace them with someone else. But other tenants — like the one who pays his rent a few days late every single month, or the one who sneaks in an animal even though pets aren't allowed — are more subtle in the problems they present, and their behavior may not warrant eviction. In this chapter, I give you tips for handling some common tenant problems and let you know about valuable alternatives to evictions. Plus, I prepare you for some unusual situations that you may encounter with your tenants and let you know how to deal with them.

Recognizing and Responding to Common Tenant Problems

The level of response you have toward a problem tenant depends on how severe the problem is and how frequently it occurs. Some issues — including nonpayment of rent, additional occupants not on the lease, noise or disturbances, and threats of violence or intimidation — are breaches of the lease or rental agreement and clearly call for serving a legal notice. Specific legal notices are available in most states to deal with the issue of nonpayment of rent, but you should document other violations of the lease or rental agreement in writing using a Lease or Rental Agreement Violation Letter, like the one shown in Form 12-1.

Whenever you have a problem with a tenant, documenting the problem is critical. Even minor problems are worth documenting, because over time, they may add up or increase in severity. If you find yourself needing to evict a tenant, having written proof of the entirety of the problem is necessary, especially if the matter gets into the legal system.

Late payment of rent

One of the toughest issues you'll encounter is how to deal with a tenant who is consistently late in paying her rent. In other respects, the tenant may not create any problems, but she just can't seem to get the rent in on time. You may have even had to serve a Notice of Nonpayment of Rent in order to get the tenant to pay — and even then, she may have not included the late charge. In my experience, this nagging problem won't go away unless you put a stop to it.

When you're faced with a tenant who just can't seem to get her rent check in on time, you have many factors to consider (such as whether the tenant is creating any other problems for you or your other tenants). But the strength of the rental market is usually the most important issue. If it's a renter's market and you know that finding another tenant to rent the property will be difficult, you may be willing to be more flexible and tolerant.

Even if you know you'd have trouble finding another tenant, you shouldn't ignore the problem of a tenant who consistently pays late. Clearly inform the tenant in writing that she has breached the lease or rental agreement — and be sure to do so each and every time she pays late. If you fail to enforce your late charges, the tenant can later argue that you've waived your rights to collect future late charges. Be sure to let the tenant know in writing that chronically late payments are grounds for eviction — even if you're not necessarily willing to go that route just yet.

Additional occupants

Tenants frequently abuse the guest policy by having additional occupants in their rental unit for extended periods of time. But you may have trouble determining the difference between a temporary guest and a new live-in occupant.

If you suspect that your tenant has added an additional occupant to his rental unit, your first step should be to talk with your tenant to find out what's going on. Be sure to get your tenant's story before jumping to any conclusions. This policy is sound not only because it's considerate, but also because you need to be careful to avoid claims of discrimination, particularly if the additional occupants are children.

Lease or Rental Agreement Violation Letter

____
Date

____
Name

____
Street address

____
City/state/zip code

Dear ______________________________________,

This is a formal legal reminder that your lease or rental agreement does not allow:
____
____.

It has come to our attention, that recently or beginning __________________________ and continuing to the present, you have broken one or more terms of your tenancy by:
____
____
____
____

It is our sincere desire that you will enjoy living in your rental unit, as will all of your neighbors. To make sure this happens, we enforce the Policies and Rules and all terms and conditions of your Lease or Rental Agreement. So please immediately:
____
____
____
____

If you are unable to promptly resolve this matter, we will exercise our legal right to begin eviction proceedings.

Please feel free to contact us if you would like to discuss this issue.

Sincerely,

____
Owner/Manager

Form 12-1: Lease or Rental Agreement Violation Letter.

If you find that the tenant is not in compliance with your guest policy, immediately send him a Lease or Rental Agreement Violation Letter indicating that he must have the additional occupant leave as soon as possible or be formally added to the lease or rental agreement as a tenant. If the new occupant is an adult, that person must complete a rental application, go through the tenant screening process, and sign the lease or rental agreement if approved. If the tenant fails to cooperate, you may need to take legal action.

Inappropriate noise level

You'll usually hear about a noisy tenant from one of the tenant's neighbors. Let the tenants who are complaining know that they should always contact law enforcement and file an official complaint as soon as the noise level becomes a problem. Then they should let you know that they've done so.

Have a policy requiring all complaints tenants might have about their neighbors, especially for noise, to be in writing. Neighbors usually don't want to go to court to testify; they just want you to quickly solve the problem and allow them to keep their anonymity. But if the noisy tenant disputes the charges, the courts are usually reluctant to accept your unsubstantiated testimony — and the neighbor's testimony becomes critical. A report from law enforcement and a written complaint made contemporaneously by a neighbor carry a lot of weight.

Unsupervised children

Under federal law, with the exception of the limited number of HUD-certified senior housing properties, you must accept children at your rental property. Unfortunately, one of the toughest dilemmas you'll face is dealing with a tenant's young child who may be unsupervised on the grounds of your rental property. If the child is unsupervised, you don't do anything, and the young child gets hurt, you will likely be sued for failing to take reasonable action. But if you don't handle the matter properly, the tenant may claim that you're discriminating against families with children, and you will need to be able to prove that you acted reasonably and consistently.

If you become aware of an unsupervised child at your rental property, immediately take the child home to the child's parents. If the problem happens again, take the child home again, and send a letter to your tenants warning them of the seriousness of the matter. If the written notice isn't effective, you can always call the police or social services while advising your tenant in writing that an eviction may be warranted.

If your tenants fail to properly supervise their children and the children damage your rental property, don't just talk to the children about the problem. Immediately contact the tenant and officially advise him of the problem, stressing the fact that property damage by tenants of any age is unacceptable. This kind of action is usually sufficient, but if the damage is severe or continues, notify the tenant in writing and bill him for the damage; warn him that any continued problems will result in eviction.

Exploring Alternatives to Eviction

Evictions are not only expensive but emotionally draining as well. They can be costly in terms of lost rent, legal fees, property damage, and turnover expenses. And they can earn a negative reputation for your rental property with good tenants in the area. So be sure to evaluate each situation carefully and only turn to eviction as a last resort.

When you're looking for an alternative to evicting a problem tenant, don't underestimate the importance of communicating with your tenant. And remember to document any conversations you have or agreements you reach.

If the most likely outcome of a problem with a tenant is an expensive and time-consuming eviction, do your best to minimize or cut your losses. A court judgment against a tenant without any assets won't help your cash flow, but a non-paying or bad tenant is much worse than no tenant at all. Your primary goal should be to regain possession of the rental unit and find a new tenant as quickly as possible.

Negotiating a voluntary move-out

You may be able to negotiate a voluntary move-out with your tenant. Some rental owners have negotiated agreements with their problem tenants, in which they forgive the unpaid rent if the tenant agrees to leave by a mutually agreed upon date. Other owners have agreed to refund the tenant's full security deposit immediately after the tenant has vacated the property (as long as no significant damage has been done to the property). Although you may feel strongly that your tenant should keep up his end of the lease, you may come out ahead by avoiding legal action and not having to worry about the problem anymore.

Never count on a verbal agreement. Any voluntary move-out must be in writing.

Using mediation or arbitration services

If you aren't able to reach an agreement with your tenant on a voluntary move-out, consider taking your dispute to a neutral third-party mediator or arbitration. *Mediation* is an informal opportunity for both parties to resolve their disputes with the assistance of a local mediation group at little or no cost. Often confused with mediation, *arbitration* is legally binding and enforceable and can be a relatively quick and inexpensive alternative to litigation. Mediation typically involves only the parties to the dispute (you and your tenant), whereas arbitration often uses attorneys, witnesses, and experts. Many organizations offer both mediation and arbitration services, so if mediation does not resolve the issue, you can always try arbitration.

Taking your tenant to court

The small claims or municipal courts in most areas deal only with monetary demands; the issue of possession of the rental unit in an eviction can only be determined in a higher court. However, the small claims court can play an important role in resolving disputes that don't concern an eviction.

For example, you may have a dispute with your tenant regarding the tenant's failure to properly maintain the rental property grounds. The tenant may have let the lawn die, and you want him to pay to resod the lawn. But he claims that it isn't his fault that the lawn died, because the sprinkler system timer mysteriously failed. The issues of responsibility and damages can be handled in small claims court, preferably after you've reached an agreement with the tenant whereby he will vacate the rental unit.

Evicting a Tenant

Unfortunately, some tenants just don't pay their rent; others violate the rules or are involved in criminal activities. In these situations, after you've explored your other options, you may have no other reasonable alternative but an eviction. The eviction process can be intimidating and costly, but keep in mind that allowing the tenant to stay will only prolong the problem.

The eviction process varies greatly from state to state and many attorneys who specialize in representing rental property owners offer guidebooks that outline the specific legal steps in an eviction action in your area. Your local Institute of Real Estate Management (IREM) chapter or affiliate of the National Apartment Association (NAA) can provide attorney references.

Serving legal notices

In order to evict a tenant, you have to first terminate the tenancy by giving an appropriate legal Notice of Termination. Month-to-month tenancies generally can be terminated with a written notice of 30 days, whereas leases only expire at the end of their term (unless they are renewed or contractually converted to a month-to-month rental agreement).

Although the terminology varies from state to state, three basic types of legal notices are required, depending upon the circumstances:

- **Pay Rent or Quit notices:** These notices are given to tenants who have not paid rent. The notices require the tenants to pay the rent or move out. The tenant is allowed from three to seven days to pay in full (depending on the law in your state).

- **Cure or Quit notices:** These are given to tenants who have violated one of the terms or conditions of the lease or rental agreement. They give the tenant a limited number of days (determined by state law) to cure the violation, vacate the premises, or be subject to an eviction action.
- **Notice to Quit or Unconditional Quit notice:** These are the most severe notice and require the tenant to vacate the premises without the opportunity to cure any deficiency. Most states discourage the use of these notices unless the tenant is conducting illegal activity, has repeatedly violated a significant term or condition of the lease or rental agreement, or has severely damaged the premises.

If, after receiving the appropriate legal notice, your tenant doesn't cure the violation or otherwise leave the rental property, your tenant will not be *automatically* evicted. Instead, you must begin a formal eviction action by filing the required forms with your local court and arranging to have the tenant properly served with a summons and complaint. The complaint is usually a pre-printed form, and you can only seek unpaid rent and actual damages, not late charges or other fees.

Serving legal notices is not simply a matter of mailing the notice or slipping it under the tenant's door. You must have an authorized person serve the legal notice by actual physical hand delivery or through constructive service. Every state has specific rules and procedures as to what exactly constitutes *proper legal service,* including who can serve notices, the method of delivery, the specific parties who can be legally served, and the amount of time the tenant has to respond to the legal notice. Check with your local attorney for the requirements in your area.

By law, a trial date is set and your tenant has a certain number of days to file an answer to your summons and complaint. Tenants usually either deny the allegations you have made in your eviction action or claim that they have an *affirmative defense* (a legal justification for their actions). The tenant may deny your allegations, for example, if he has a cancelled check showing that the rent was paid and your records are in error. An affirmative defense could be that you failed to maintain the premises and the tenant legally used some of the rent to make the needed repairs.

Frequently, tenants know that you are correct and that they have materially breached their lease or rental agreement and will voluntarily leave the premises. Or you may be able to reach a settlement or agreement with the tenant without going to court. If you reach this kind of agreement with your tenant, you must formally dismiss your court eviction action. Not only is dismissing your court eviction action under these circumstances the proper way to treat your tenants, it also preserves your reputation with the court. After all, courts have limited resources and don't respond well to parties who resolve their matter and fail to file a timely dismissal.

If your tenant doesn't file an answer in a timely manner and the eviction action proceeds to court, you will have what's called an *uncontested eviction.* The court will require you to prove your case just as you would have had to do if the tenant had appeared, but the tenant isn't there to respond to or deny your charges. Typically, you'll easily prevail in these situations, as long as you have good documentation.

A *contested eviction* occurs when your tenant files an answer and appears at the trial. Just as in a small claims court, each side will be given the opportunity to present its evidence to the court, and the court will make a ruling. If you are prepared and you professionally present the facts in a well-supported case, you will generally win. However, the courts can be very harsh if you have acted illegally or in a retaliatory or discriminatory manner toward the tenant.

Tenants may be able to make an argument that they are entitled to additional time to either work out a payment plan for the unpaid rent or that they have a hardship that requires the court's leniency. Although not legally required in most states, courts have been known to allow tenants an extension due to inclement weather, while the tenant appeals the ruling, or until the tenant's health or other personal situation improves.

If you win the eviction lawsuit, you must generally give the judgment to a local law enforcement department, and they will give the tenant one final notice before they will go to the rental unit and physically remove the tenant and the tenant's possessions. If it comes to this, arrange to have someone meet the law enforcement officers at the premises at the designated time, and have the locks changed after you have been given legal possession of the rental property.

Although the eviction process is rather straightforward in most areas, I recommend using an attorney to handle evictions. There are very precise and detailed rules regarding filing and serving eviction actions, and the smallest mistake can result in delays or even the loss of your case on technicalities, regardless of the fact that the tenant hasn't paid rent or has otherwise violated the lease.

Even if you're in the middle of an eviction process with a tenant, don't fail to properly respond to that tenant's maintenance requests. You are *always* responsible for properly maintaining the premises, regardless of the status of the tenant. If someone gets hurt because of your failure to keep the rental property in good condition, you could be sued. Tenants and their attorneys are very sensitive to maintenance issues. Any failure to respond to a tenant's request for maintenance will be used as a defense in the eviction action even though there may be no basis.

Don't get too emotionally involved in an eviction process and make an irrational decision that can be construed as a self-help eviction. A *self-help* or *constructive eviction* is a situation in which the owner takes illegal actions to effectively force the tenant to vacate the premises. Although veteran rental property owners love to tell stories about the "good old days" when they could just change the locks or shut off the electricity or water to encourage the tenant to immediately vacate the premises, the reality is that there are no states in which any of these aggressive tactics are legal, regardless of how bad the tenant is. In many states, even the reduction or elimination of "free" services such as cable television can create a serious problem, because the court could consider these illegal self-help measures, and the tenant could sue you for significant penalties.

Collecting judgments

When you win in court and your tenant owes you for unpaid rent, damages, or legal fees, you've received a *money judgment* against the tenant. But the judgment isn't worth much to you unless you're able to collect. If you know that the tenant has a job or other unencumbered assets, in most states you may be able to obtain a court order to garnish his salary or have local law enforcement seize the assets and sell them, with the net proceeds of the sale given to you.

The majority of deadbeat tenants aren't easy to locate, so your best bet may be to hire a licensed collection agency to attempt to locate and collect your judgment from the tenant. These agencies are typically paid on a contingency basis and receive a portion of the collected amount, typically ranging from one-third to one-half of the amount they collect. Although you may want to make your own efforts to enforce the judgment, remember that collection agency success rates and fees are often tied to the age of the bad debt. So the sooner the judgment is submitted for collection, the easier it is for the agency to collect, and the lower the fee.

Your success in collecting judgments often depends on how hard you worked at the beginning and throughout the tenancy. The rental application typically contains very valuable information for a collection agency, including the tenant's social security number, prior addresses, current and prior employment information, banking and credit card accounts, vehicle information, and emergency telephone numbers, so if you required your tenants to complete the application and verified its accuracy, you have a great place to start.

Knowing What to Do in Unusual Tenant Situations

After a year or so as a rental property owner, you may begin to think that you've seen it all, but there are always some new and interesting twists that keep rental management challenging. Knowing how to handle these unusual, yet surprisingly common, situations, some of which I cover in the following sections, can make life much easier.

Bankruptcy

One last-ditch effort some tenants make when they're in financial trouble is to file bankruptcy. Although the rental housing industry continues to lobby for changes in the federal bankruptcy code, many rental owners are dealt a severe financial blow when a tenant files bankruptcy during the eviction process.

When the federal bankruptcy action has been filed, your state court eviction proceeding cannot be filed or completed because the bankruptcy results in an automatic *stay* (halting) of the eviction. As soon as you become aware of the bankruptcy, you must stop any collection or eviction efforts, because there are severe penalties for rental owners who violate the stay. You will be required to file pleadings with the federal bankruptcy court requesting the issuance of a Relief from Stay in order to proceed with the eviction.

Even if you routinely handle your own legal work, have an attorney handle all tenant bankruptcy matters.

Illegal holdovers

Another difficult challenge often faced by rental owners is when a tenant fails to vacate the rental property as mutually agreed or at the end of the lease. Unless you accept rent, tenants who continue to live at the property are referred to as *holdover tenants.* Many states require you to give holdover tenants a legal notice to vacate immediately; other states allow you to proceed directly with an eviction action.

If you accept rent, you have agreed to a continuation of the tenant's rental, generally on at least a month-to-month basis, unless state law indicates differently.

Broken leases

Although you may occasionally be faced with a tenant who won't leave as agreed, you will certainly encounter a tenant who leaves before the expiration of his lease and doesn't want to pay the balance of his financial obligation to you. In these cases, in practically all states, you don't have the right to demand that the tenant pay the rent due each month for the balance of the lease.

First confirm that the tenant has indeed given up his right of possession. Then take reasonable steps to mitigate or limit the ongoing rent and other charges to the departed tenant by preparing the rental unit for rerenting. In most states, you must make a reasonable effort to promptly rerent the property, including advertising or using other usual rental marketing methods, or the tenant may be released from any further legal obligation to pay the balance of rent owed under the lease.

Handle the marketing of this rental unit just like any other unit. You don't need to lower the rent, lower your tenant selection standards, or give this rental priority over any other available rental unit. Of course, you can't be vindictive and attempt to enrich yourself either.

Tenants frequently dispute whether your efforts were reasonable in mitigating the former tenant's financial obligations. If challenged in court, you need to be able to show the court that you maintained detailed records clearly indicating the dates and actions you took to rerent the property, including copies of all documents. The tenant generally has the burden of proof, but the courts are often sympathetic to tenants who may have a hardship, so be prepared.

Tenants sometimes have legitimate reasons for breaking their leases, and in these situations, they don't have any further obligations to you. These legitimate reasons are all subject to state and even local laws, but they can include the rental owner harassing the tenant or violating a significant lease provision or a rental unit that is uninhabitable. Some state laws allow the tenant to leave under certain specified circumstances, like job transfer, military transfer, or health reasons. Make sure that you know the laws in your area.

Assignments or subleases

A tenant may approach you and request the right to assign or sublease her interest in the rental unit. Tenants usually only do this because they must suddenly relocate for personal or professional reasons. Typically, leases, like the one shown in Chapter 5, prohibit subleases or assignments because you should have a direct relationship with the occupant (meaning, you screen them and approve their application).

Subleases needlessly complicate the tenant/landlord relationship and prevent you from directly taking legal action against the occupant of your premises. If the proposed occupant meets all your rental criteria, propose terminating the current lease and entering a new lease with the new prospective tenant.

Departing roommates

On occasion, you may receive a notice that a particular tenant or roommate will be leaving the rental property in the middle of a lease. The departing tenant will usually request a refund of a portion of the security deposit, even though not all of the individuals on the lease or rental agreement are vacating the premises. But as discussed in chapter 13, you should retain the entire security deposit until all occupants on the lease have vacated the property.

If one tenant chooses to vacate early, then the tenants need to resolve any security deposit issues between themselves. For example, if there is a new roommate moving in, that individual can inspect the premises and pay the departing tenant an agreed amount for her share of the security deposit. Or the remaining tenant can reach some other agreement with the departing tenant that they agree is fair and equitable.

If there is going to be a change in the lease, require the departing tenant to complete a Deposit Assignment and Release Agreement (see Form 12-2). This will release you from liability.

Domestic problems

Another difficult challenge faced by rental property owners comes in the form of couples who rent the premises together and then have domestic disputes. Just as with disputes between neighbors or any roommates, you need to avoid getting involved. You lack the authority to side with one party or the other, so staying neutral, encouraging them to resolve their problems between themselves, and continuing to treat both parties fairly and equally is best.

Unfortunately, some disagreements between couples involve domestic violence, and you may receive a request from one member of the couple to change the locks or remove one of the co-tenants from the lease. Do not agree to any such changes, regardless of the strength of the tenant's argument, without first seeking legal advice and requiring a copy of a restraining order or other appropriate court order. Require a verifiable letter or agreement and consent of the other party as well.

Death of a tenant

If you have reason to suspect the death of a tenant who lives alone, try calling the tenant or bang loudly on his door, check with the neighbors, and call the tenant's place of employment as well as the emergency contact number from the rental application. If you still aren't sure, exercise your right to inspect the rental unit in an emergency or contact the police or fire department.

When the death has been confirmed and the body has been removed, you must immediately take reasonable steps to safeguard the deceased tenant's property, including not allowing access except for obtaining personal effects for a funeral. Secure the property and only allow access to legally authorized persons or law enforcement. If you have any doubts about the authority or actions of the tenant's relatives or friends, contact your attorney for further advice.

Deposit Assignment and Release Agreement

This agreement is entered into this _______ day of _________, 20 _____, between _________________________ (Tenant) and _________________________ (Owner).

WHEREAS, on or about _________________, 20 _____, Tenant delivered to Owner a written notice of termination stating an intention to vacate the Premises located at: ____, effective on the _______ day of ______________, 20 __.

In consideration for Owner releasing Tenant from the obligations under the Lease or Rental Agreement dated the ______ day of __________________, 20 _____, Tenant hereby assigns to _______________________________________ any and right or claim to the security deposit held by Owner for said rental unit.

As further consideration for the execution of this Agreement by Owner, Tenant agrees to waive and release any and all right or claim to said security deposit.

_____ ____________________ _____ ____________________
Date Owner/Agent Date Tenant

Form 12-2: Deposit Assignment and Release Agreement.

In addition to the impact of having your tenant die, you may find yourself in the middle of a dispute as to who properly has access to the rental unit. Although you should be sympathetic to the grieving relatives of your tenant, you need to make sure that you don't allow access to the rental unit to an unauthorized person, or you may be held liable if anything is missing.

Chapter 13

Moving Out Tenants

In This Chapter

- Confirming the move-out with a Notice of Intent to Vacate form
- Setting up move-out procedures for your tenants
- Keeping your tenants informed of your policies and procedures
- Dealing with security deposit disputes
- Knowing what to do when a tenant abandons your property

Although hanging on to your great tenants forever would be nice, the reality is that all tenants leave at some point. Your goal is to make the experience as straightforward and painless as possible, maintaining clear communication and having procedures in place.

Don't assume that your tenants will be familiar with the proper move-out procedures. You need to have a proactive plan that gets your tenants involved in the process of preparing the rental unit for the next tenant.

A good way to motivate your tenants to comply with your move-out procedures is to give them a simple reminder that they will receive the full return of their security deposit if they leave the rental unit in clean condition, with no damage beyond ordinary wear and tear.

Start preparing for your tenants' eventual move-out when they first move in. The Tenant Information Letter (covered in more detail in Chapter 9) provides the tenants with the legal requirements of move-out as well as your expectations for giving proper notice. The Move-In/Move-Out Inspection Checklist (again covered in more detail in Chapter 9) is completed upon move-in to establish the baseline condition of the rental unit. Use this same detailed checklist to evaluate the condition on move-out and calculate the appropriate charges, if any.

Security deposit disputes are the number one problem in tenant/landlord relationships. Although the proper use of the Move-In/Move-Out Checklist eliminates many of these disputes, the definition of "ordinary wear and tear" is one of life's greatest mysteries. You can minimize arguments with former tenants and avoid small claims courts by making only fair and reasonable deductions and providing the security deposit accounting and any refund within legally required time limits.

This chapter covers the importance of having a written notice (the Move-Out Information Letter) and proper procedures in place for the return of the security deposit. I also cover the definition of "ordinary wear and tear." And I help you handle special move-out situations.

Requiring Written Notice of Your Tenant's Move-Out Plans

When giving notice that they plan to move, most tenants often just call or verbally mention it when they see you — even though your lease or rental agreement most likely contains clauses that require written notice. (Many states have laws that specifically require the tenant's notice to be in writing, with the exact date the tenant plans to move out.)

Some tenants put their notice in writing by sending you a simple letter. Often these written notices are only one or two sentences and can be ambiguous, leaving out critical information or important details. Although any type of written notice from the tenant is usually legal, a proper notice should provide much more information.

To be sure that you're complying with the law in all regards, require your tenants to use a Tenant's Notice of Intent to Vacate Rental Unit (like the one shown in Form 13-1). This form contains important information, including the tenant's approval of your ability to enter upon reasonable notice to show the rental unit to workers, contractors, and prospective tenants.

When you receive verbal or written notice, go ahead and honor the date of the notice but still ask the tenant to complete the form. Even if you're not required to do so by law, insisting that the tenant give you a written Notice of Intent to Vacate is a good policy. If you don't have this information in writing, many opportunities for misunderstandings arise. You may not remember the move-out date and be caught by surprise. Or you may schedule a new move-in only to find that the tenant won't be out until the following week. Surprises are not a good thing for rental property owners!

Time is truly of the essence when it comes to an occupant's move-out. In Tennessee and Georgia, for example, landlords are required to send the vacating tenant advance notice of the proposed security deposit deductions within only three days of move-out. Over a dozen states have deadlines of only 14 days. Virtually *all* states require the security deposit accounting to be completed within three to four weeks.

Tenant's Notice of Intent to Vacate Rental Unit

____
Date

____
Owner/Manager

____
Street Address

____
City, State and Zip code

Dear ______________,

This is to notify you that the undersigned tenant, ____________________________________
hereby give your written notice of intent to vacate the rental unit at ____________________________
on ______________________.

I understand that my Lease or Rental Agreement requires a minimum of _________ day's notice before I move. This Tenant's Notice of Intent to Vacate Rental Unit actually provides _________ days notice. I understand that I am responsible for paying rent through, the earlier of: (1) the end of the current lease term; (2) the end of the required notice period per the Lease or Rental Agreement; or (3) until another tenant approved by the Owner/Agent has moved in or begun paying rent.

(Optional Information)
We are sorry to learn that you are leaving. We would appreciate a moment of your time to tell us the reason for your move:

____ Moving to a larger rental unit _____ Moving to a smaller rental unit _____ Buying a home _____ Moving out of area
____ Dissatisfied with rental unit or common area (explain) ____________________________
____ Dissatisfied with management (explain) ____________________________________
____ Other (explain) ____
Is there anything we can do to encourage you to continue as our tenant? __________________________

Other comments ____

In accordance with our Lease or Rental Agreement, I agree to allow the Owner/Agent reasonable access with advance notice in order to show our rental unit to prospective renters or workmen and contractors.

Sincerely,

____
Tenant

Form 13-1: Tenant's Notice of Intent to Vacate Rental Unit.

Providing Your Tenants with a Move-Out Information Letter

Many tenants are afraid that you'll cheat them on their security deposit refund. Security deposit disputes are the number one issue in many small claims courts. Just as the Tenant Information Letter (covered in Chapter 9) helps to get the tenant/landlord relationship off to a good start, the Move-Out Information Letter (shown in Form 13-2) can help end the relationship on a positive note.

Move-Out Information Letter

Tenant Name(s) ____
Rental Unit Address ____

Dear ___________________________,

We are pleased that you selected our property for your home and hope that you enjoyed living here. Although we are disappointed to lose you as a tenant, we wish you good luck in the future. We want your move-out to go smoothly and end our relationship on a positive note.

Moving time is always chaotic and you have many things on your mind, including getting the maximum amount of your security deposit back. Contrary to some rental property owners, we want to be able to return your security deposit promptly and in full. Your security deposit is $_______________. Note that your security deposit shall not be applied to your last month's rent as the deposit is to ensure the fulfillment of lease conditions and is to be used only as a contingency against any damages to the rental unit.

This move-out letter describes how we expect your rental unit to be left and what our procedures are for returning your security deposit. Basically, we expect you to leave your rental unit in the same condition it was when you moved in, except for ordinary wear and tear that occurred during your tenancy. To refresh your memory, a copy of your signed Move-in/Move-out Inspection Checklist is attached reflecting the condition of the rental unit at the beginning of your tenancy. We will be using this same detailed checklist when we inspect your rental unit upon move-out and will deduct the cost of any necessary cleaning and the costs of repairs, not considered ordinary wear and tear, from your security deposit.

To maximize your chances of a full and prompt refund, we suggest that you go through the Move-In/Move-Out Inspection Checklist line by line and make sure that all items are clean and free from damage, except for ordinary wear and tear. All closets, cabinets, shelves, drawers, countertops, storage, refrigerator, and exterior areas should be completely free of items. Feel free to check off completed items on this copy of the Move-In/Move-Out Inspection Checklist, as we will use the original for your final inspection.

Some of our tenants prefer to let professionals complete these items. You can contact your own professional or, upon request, we will be glad to refer you to our service providers so that you can focus on other issues of your move. You will work directly with the service provider on costs and payment terms, knowing that you are working with someone who can prepare the unit for the walkthrough inspection. Call us if you would like contact information or for any questions as to the type of cleaning we expect.

Please be sure to remove all personal possessions, including furniture, clothes, household items, food, plants, cleaning supplies, and any bags of garbage or loose items that belong to you. Of course, please do not remove any appliances, fixtures, or other items installed or attached to your rental unit unless you have our prior written approval.

Please contact the appropriate companies and schedule the disconnection or transfer of your phone, cable, and utility services in your name. Also, cancel any newspaper subscriptions and provide the U.S. Postal Service with a change of address form.

Please contact us when all the conditions have been satisfied to arrange an inspection of your rental unit during daylight hours. To avoid being assessed a key replacement charge; please return all keys at the time you vacate.

You have listed ____________________ as the move-out date in your notice. Please be reminded that you will be assessed holdover rent of $________ per day for each partial or full day after the above move-out date that you remain in the rental unit or have possession of the keys. If you need to extend your tenancy for any reason, you must contact us immediately. Please be prepared to provide your forwarding address where we may mail your security deposit.

It is our policy to return all security deposits either in person or at an address you provide within __________________ after you move out **and** return all keys. If any deductions are made for past due rent or other unpaid charges, for damages beyond ordinary wear and tear, or for failure to properly clean, an itemized explanation will be included with the security deposit accounting.

If you have any questions, please contact us at ____.

Thank you again for making our property your home. We have enjoyed serving you, and we hope that you will recommend our rental properties to your friends, family, and colleagues. Please let us know if we can provide you with a recommendation letter. Good luck!

Sincerely,

____
Owner/Manager

Form 13-2: Move-Out Information Letter.

The Move-Out Information Letter thanks your tenants for making your rental unit their home and provides them with the procedures to follow to prepare the rental unit for the final move-out inspection. It also informs them of your policies and method of returning their security deposits after any legal deductions.

Provide your tenants with a Move-Out Information Letter as soon as they give their written notice to vacate. Although state law and your lease or rental agreement may contain information on the security deposit refund process, most tenants appreciate receiving this information so they know what to expect without having to search for their lease while they're trying to pack.

The Move-Out Information Letter includes language that reminds the tenants that their security deposit cannot be applied to the last month's rent and is only to be used as a contingency against any damages to the rental unit or for other lawful charges. If no portion of the tenant's deposit was called "last month's rent," you are not legally obliged to apply it in this way. Unless your lease or rental agreement uses this wording, don't allow your tenants to try to apply their security deposit toward their final month's rent, or you may not have enough money on hand to cover any legally allowed charges.

If the tenant moving out is a good one, ask him if you can provide him with a letter of recommendation. A positive reference can be very helpful to tenants, whether they are moving to a new rental property or buying a home. This kind of offer is welcome and courteous — and one that most tenants have never received from prior landlords. If you make this kind of offer, the tenant will often work extra-hard to make sure that the rental unit is clean and undamaged in order to thank you for your positive comments and offer to provide that letter.

Many owners see the tenant's security deposit as a source of additional income that is theirs for the taking. However, as a business practice, the return of the full security deposit is actually much better for the owner. Although each state law varies, typically the only lawful deductions from the tenant's security deposit are for unpaid rent, damages beyond ordinary wear and tear, keys, and cleaning. Therefore, the actual out-of-pocket costs for the renovation of the rental unit for the next tenant will be greater than the legally allowed deductions, because you must pay for all damage that is within the scope of ordinary wear and tear.

Excessive deductions almost always lead to acrimonious discussions with the former tenant that could end up in small claims court. Spending your day in court can be very counterproductive, particularly because the courts often seek a compromise that requires at least a partial return of the security deposit to the aggrieved tenant. You may feel that there are no legal bases for a judge to find in the tenant's favor, but the court may rule merely to compensate the tenant for their time and costs of going to court.

Encourage tenants to earn the return of their full security deposit. They can use the money, and if there is no major damage you can quickly begin to show the rental property to new prospective tenants. Typically, you can't charge the outgoing tenant for lost rent days incurred while maintenance and cleaning are being done. So if you can quickly prepare the rental unit and get it back on the rental market, you're well ahead of the game.

Walking through the Unit to Check Its Condition at Move-Out

Try to schedule the move-out inspection with your vacating tenants just *after* they have removed all their furnishings and personal items, turned in all their keys, and had the utilities disconnected. The only way to determine the condition of some parts of the unit is to wait until the rental unit is vacant. Also, you want to make sure that the tenant doesn't do additional damage after the inspection while they're removing their possessions.

Unfortunately, you can't always arrange to do the inspection with the tenant at this time. If that's the case, conduct the move-out inspection as soon as possible and preferably with a witness present. If you wait too long to inspect the unit and then discover damage, the tenant may claim that someone else must have caused the damage and you may face an uphill battle in court.

Tenants have been known to show up for the walkthrough but deny that they know anything about the damaged items you find. Refer to your Move-In/ Move-Out Inspection Checklist in these situations. If the item is clearly indicated on the checklist as being in good condition when the tenant moved in, the tenant doesn't stand much of a chance. However, if the move-in remarks are blank or vague, you may have some problems justifying a deduction. ***Remember:*** As the rental housing professional, the courts hold you to a higher standard and interpret your vague documents in favor of the tenant.

Although the tenant should be present for the move-out inspection, you may not know the actual charges for certain items until later, when the work is completed and you receive the final invoice from a contractor. Plus, damages are often not discovered until the rental unit preparation work is being done. So just note that the item is damaged on the checklist and advise the tenant that you reserve the right to deduct the actual repair costs. When you know the actual charges, you can fill in the column on the checklist for the estimated cost of repair or replacement and include a copy of the completed checklist with your security deposit itemization.

Tenants often are counting on the return of their full security deposit and will request the chance to do some more cleaning or make repairs if you indicate that deductions will be made. If they can act quickly and you feel that they are capable of the work, you may want to give them a second chance at cleaning or simple repairs. However, be wary of tenant repairs that could cost you more to correct later or that create liability issues. Even a simple paint touch-up by your tenants can become a disaster if they are sloppy painters or color-challenged and mismatch the paint. When it comes to the majority of repairs, you're better off refusing the tenant's request to fix them himself.

Defining "ordinary wear and tear"

Legally you are entitled to charge your tenant for damages beyond "ordinary wear and tear." But virtually all disputes over security deposits revolve around this elusive definition. It's your job to be able to tell the difference between ordinary wear and tear and more serious damage that you can legally deduct from your tenant's security deposit.

The standard definition of "ordinary wear and tear" in most states is deterioration or damage to the property expected to occur from normal usage. The problem then is what is considered to be "normal usage." Court decisions vary from state to state and even court to court. If you ask 100 small claims court judges or commissioners you will likely get nearly 100 different interpretations of this definition.

The bottom line is that there are no hard and fast rules on what constitutes ordinary wear and tear and what the tenant can legally be charged. Table 13-1 gives you some room for comparison; however, to help you determine what's ordinary wear and tear, and what goes beyond ordinary into damage you can charge for.

Table 13-1 Ordinary Wear and Tear versus Damage

Ordinary Wear and Tear	*Damage beyond Ordinary Wear and Tear*
Smudges on the walls near light switches	Crayon marks on the walls or ceiling
Minor marks on the walls or doors	Large marks on or holes in the walls or doors
A few small tack or nail holes	Numerous nail holes that require patching and/or painting
Faded, peeling, or cracked paint	Completely dirty or scuffed painted walls
Carpet worn thin from normal use	Carpet stained by bleach or dye
Carpet with moderate dirt or spots	Carpet that has been ripped or has urine stains from pets
Carpet or curtains faded by the sun	Carpet or curtains with cigarette burns
Moderately dirty mini-blinds	Bent or missing mini-blinds
Doors sticking from humidity	Broken hinges or doorframes

If you make deductions from the security deposit, be sure that your paperwork is accurate and detailed. Because property damage deductions are only for damages beyond ordinary wear and tear, you need to be sure that your description of the item explains why the damage exceeds that.

If you merely indicate, "Pet damage — $100" on the security deposit itemization form, you may very well be challenged. However, if you provide details like "Steam cleaned carpeting in living room to remove extensive pet urine stains — $100," you greatly improve your chances if the matter gets to court or, better yet, of not even being challenged in the first place.

Here are some guidelines to follow when listing the charges on your security deposit itemization form:

- **Indicate the specific item damaged.** List each damaged fixture, appliance, or piece of furniture separately.
- **Indicate the specific location of the damaged item.** Note the room and which wall, ceiling, or corner of the room the damaged item is located in. Use compass directions, if possible.
- **Note the type and extent of the damage.** Be sure to describe the damage in detail using appropriate adjectives, like *substantial, excessive, minor, scratched, stained, ripped, cracked, burned,* or *chipped.*
- **Note the type and extent of repair done.** Describe the repair using adjectives such as *spackle, patch, paint, steam clean, deodorize,* or *refinish.* Indicate if an item was so damaged that it had to be replaced and, if so, why.
- **Indicate the cost of the repair or replacement.** List exactly how much you actually spent or plan to spend based on a third-party estimate.

Some rental property owners give all vacating tenants a pricing chart with a list of prices that will be charged for different services or damaged items. These owners believe the pricing charts minimize disputes because the charges are predetermined and are given to the tenants in advance. Further, they argue that the tenants will see how expensive repairs are and will take care of some of the work on their own. There is some logic to this method, but it also poses some potential problems. For example, prices frequently change, and most courts insist on actual, not estimated, charges. So the price chart would have to be consistently updated. Plus, many items can't possibly have preset prices for repair, and different contractors may charge different amounts. You can be assured that the tenant won't pay up if your actual charge turns out to be much higher than the preset charge indicated on your pricing chart. But if the tenant challenges your deductions and your actual invoice shows you paid less than what you charged the tenant, you'd better have your checkbook ready.

Using a Security Deposit Itemization form

After you have inspected the rental unit and determined the proper charges, you need to prepare the Security Deposit Itemization form (shown in Form 13-3). You need to complete this form and give the vacating tenant a check for any balance due within the maximum time guidelines of your state. Most states allow rental property owners 14 to 30 days to complete the accounting, but several states have no specific legal deadline. Make sure that you don't wait until the last minute, because the consequences in most states are severe, including forfeiting your rights to any deductions and even punitive damages.

Send the security deposit accounting and refund as soon as you are sure of the final charges. Tenants need this money, and the longer they wait the more impatient and upset they get — and the more likely they are to challenge your charges. Of course, you need to make sure that your maintenance personnel has been through the entire rental unit carefully and found all tenant damage beyond ordinary wear and tear. In theory, you can always seek reimbursement for items discovered after you refund the security deposit, but your chances of collecting would be slim.

Some tenants want to personally pick up the security deposit as soon as possible whereas others won't even tell you where they can be reached. Generally, you will mail the Security Deposit Itemization form to the address provided by your tenants on their Tenant's Notice to Vacate form. If you do not have your vacating tenant's forwarding address, send the security deposit itemization to their last known address, which may be your own rental unit. There's a chance they've had their mail forwarded to their new address; if not, the check will just be returned to you.

If your Security Deposit Itemization form and refund check are returned undeliverable, be sure to save the returned envelope in case the former tenant claims you never sent the legally required accounting. Many states have very severe penalties for improper deductions or failure to provide the security deposit accounting in a timely manner. Check with your state laws to determine the proper disposition of the tenant's uncashed security deposit fund refund check.

Be sure you are able to prove that you've met the legal requirements in terms of returning the security deposit in a timely manner. Otherwise the small claims courts may rule against you because you are in the rental housing business and held to a higher standard.

You can send the deposit via certified mail in order to prove the date you sent it; however, it is much more cost-effective to go to the post office and ask for a *certificate of mailing,* which just records the date you sent the check (and doesn't require the recipient's signature for delivery).

Security Deposit Itemization Form

Deductions for unpaid rent, damages beyond ordinary wear and tear, and cleaning

____
Date

____
Name

____
Forwarding address

____
City/state/zip code

Rental unit address: ____

Move-in date __________ Date that Notice to Vacate was received __________ Actual date vacated __________

Rent paid through __________ Monthly rental rate __________ New tenant move-in date, if applicable __________

1. Security deposit received $ __________
2. Excess balance of pre-paid rent (if any) $ __________
3. Interest on deposit (if required by lease or law) $ __________
4. Total credit (sum of lines 1–3) $ __________

5. Defaults in rent not covered by any court judgment $ __________

6. Court judgment for rent, costs, attorney fees $ __________
7. Itemized property damage and repairs/replacements $ __________

8. Necessary cleaning of rental unit upon termination $ __________

9. Other deductions $ __________

10. Total deductions (sum of lines 5–9) $ __________

11. Balance due

____ Total amount Owner owes Tenant (check # __________) $ __________

____ Total amount Tenant owes Owner (must be paid within 14 days) $ __________

Comments ____

Form 13-3: Security Deposit Itemization Form.

Tenants, particularly roommates or married couples in the midst of a separation or divorce, may fight amongst themselves over the security deposit. Legally, the security deposit belongs equally to all tenants who signed the lease or rental agreement, unless otherwise agreed in writing. If you arbitrarily split the check between the tenants, you can find yourself liable to the other party. So always make your security deposit refund check payable jointly to all adult tenants. Then mail copies of your Security Deposit Itemization form to each of the tenants at their respective forwarding addresses. Include the security deposit refund check to one of the tenants with a copy of the check to the others. Leave it up to the tenants to handle the endorsement of the check. However, if you have a court order or a written agreement or instructions signed by all tenants, you can handle the deposit as directed.

Handling Special Move-Out Situations

Although you may have worked very hard to make sure everything goes smoothly during your tenant's move-out, a few special situations inevitably arise. And the more you know as a rental property owner about how to handle these situations, the less likely they are to become significant problems.

When damage and unpaid rent exceed the security deposit

As a rental property owner, you will probably encounter a situation in which a tenant's security deposit is not sufficient to cover the unpaid rent and the damage caused by the tenant. Unless legally prohibited, you should first allocate the security deposit to cover the damage and then to cover the unpaid rent, because it makes sense to apply the security deposit to items that would be more difficult to prove in court.

For example, let's say you're holding a $500 security deposit from a tenant when she vacates, owing $350 in delinquent rent. When you inspect her unit, however, you find $400 in damage beyond ordinary wear and tear. The total of the rent owed and the damages done is $750, but you only have $500 in the form of a security deposit. What should you do? First, apply the $500 security deposit to cover the full $400 in damage, and allocate the remaining $100 toward the unpaid rent. You then can pursue the $250 delinquent rent balance with your rent collection ledgers and records as evidence to clearly prove this amount is owed.

If instead of resolving the costs for damages first you choose to cover the delinquent rent and then bill the tenant for the $250 in damages, you can be assured the tenant will challenge the validity of the charges. And it's harder to prove the damages than it is to prove the unpaid rent.

Be sure to always keep track of the actual costs for damages even if you don't intend to pursue the tenant for the balance owed. This way you can prove your expenses in court if you ever need to.

In most states, even if your lawful deductions exceed the departing tenant's security deposit charges, you must provide the tenant with a full accounting of the damages. This is true even if you file a small claims lawsuit for the balance due. So be sure to always follow the required procedures for the accounting of the security deposit.

When disputes arise over the deposit

No matter how fair and reasonable you are with your security deposit deductions, sooner or later you are bound to have a former tenant challenge your deductions. Even if your deductions were proper and you are sure that you're right, going to court over the security deposit deduction may cost you more than the amount in dispute. Often, the actual disagreement is over a relatively small amount of money.

For example, you may have deducted $100 for painting touchup, but your former tenant may believe that the charge should be only $50. So you're only arguing over a $50 difference. Explore possible negotiations to resolve the matter before going to court. If you're sure that your charges were fair, be sure to always maintain that in your discussions with your former tenant, even if you want to see if a settlement is a possibility.

If you charge your tenants for damage to the rental unit either during their tenancy or by deducting from the security deposit, you need evidence to back up your claim, in case your tenant disputes the damage. Videotaping the damage can be an effective tool to resolve disputes with tenants or prove your position in court. Many courts now have video monitors that you can use to show the judge or jury your evidence. Be sure that you have possession of the unit or have given proper legal notice before entering the unit to videotape, however.

When the rental is abandoned

Occasionally tenants will abandon your rental unit without notice. This can be good news if you're taking legal action against the tenant, because you will definitely save lost rent days and you may be able to reduce your legal costs.

Each state has its own definition of abandonment, so make sure that you comply with all state legal requirements before you try to determine that the rental unit is abandoned. The best way to know for sure is to contact the tenants and have them give you a statement in writing relinquishing their rights to possession of the rental unit.

Have a policy in place saying that your tenants must inform you if they will have an extended absence of more than one or two weeks from the rental unit. This policy can be helpful in determining whether the property is abandoned or the tenant is just on a long vacation.

If you begin to see a pattern indicating that a tenant has abandoned your property, consider giving the tenant a legal notice complying with the requirements of your state law in order to enter the rental unit. After you're inside the rental unit, look for additional evidence, including furniture removed, clothing removed, toiletries removed, a lack of food or only stale or spoiled food, and missing pets.

If you have already started an eviction action, your legal counsel may just suggest that you continue the legal process until you have been granted possession because you can minimize your potential liability in the event the tenant shows up later and claims the right to the rental unit. Or, if no eviction action is in progress, be sure to serve the required legal notice of belief of abandonment. When you have met your state requirements, you can take possession of the rental unit and begin your turnover work to put it back on the rental market.

Dealing with abandoned personal property

One of a rental property owner's worst nightmares is discovering that one of their tenants has suddenly abandoned the rental unit and left all of his furnishings and household items behind. More common, however, is finding that a tenant has moved out and returned the keys, but left behind a few items of personal property. Often these items are junk that even your favorite charity will refuse to accept.

State laws vary widely in terms of the standards for establishing that the personal property has been abandoned. Your duty and obligation in handling the personal property of the tenant also varies from state to state.

When you first discover that your tenant appears to have left abandoned personal property, immediately try to locate the tenant and ask him to reclaim his property. Serve the appropriate legal notices as required by your state.

If you are unable to locate the tenant or the tenant refuses to claim the items, you need to have an impartial witness assist you in preparing a written and photographic inventory of the abandoned items. If possible, carefully move and consolidate the abandoned items into a secure storage area until you can proceed with the sale or disposal of the property per state law. If the personal property is extensive, it is often a good idea to have a third-party firm that specializes in handling these situations prepare appraisals and conduct the sale or disposition. Keep copies of all appraisals and photos for your records.

Several states allow the owner an automatic lien on the property to use toward unpaid rent or storage costs. This means that after the expiration of legal notices, you can attempt to sell the items and generate funds to offset your expenses in transferring the items to storage and the costs of sale, with any balance applied toward unpaid rent. Any excess funds beyond those items belong to the tenant. Be sure to check your state laws to be sure you're always in compliance with them.

In some states, the disposing or sale of the tenant's abandoned property requires advance court approval. Be extremely careful that you have followed the specific legal requirements for your area before you sell, give away, or keep any of the tenant's abandoned personal property, because the penalties can be very stiff.

Part IV

Techniques and Tools for Managing

"Don't worry, Mrs. Morse. As soon as the plumber's done patching the roof I'll have him call the electrician to finish wallpapering the dining room."

In this part . . .

A big part of managing rental property has to do with people other than your tenants — everyone from employees you hire to contractors you work with. And just as owning your own home involves a lot of maintenance work, the same holds true for owning rental property. Plus, as a landlord, you have to be aware of the safety and security of your property — and your tenants. In this chapter, I cover all these issues, so that whether you're managing a painting contractor or thinking about a new security system for your property, you have the information you need.

Chapter 14

Working with Employees and Contractors

In This Chapter

- Knowing what to look for in an employee
- Firing an employee fairly
- Assembling a team of contractors

As your rental property business grows, you will find that there are limits to how much you can handle yourself, and you may begin to consider hiring employees. But before you jump into being an employer, you need to fully understand your responsibilities and the financial consequences. You also need to determine how much hiring an employee will cost, and then compare that amount to how much that employee is worth to you based on the time-consuming aspects of rental management the employee will be able to take off your plate.

Extensive legal requirements and responsibilities also come with being an employer. So you may find that using independent, self-employed contractors or hiring companies that have employees who can handle your maintenance and service needs, is easier. In fact, you may actually be better off financially to pay the higher cost of an independent contractor or service company than to employ your own onsite manager or maintenance person.

In this chapter, I touch on the benefits and burdens of hiring employees to assist you in the management of your rental properties, plus the proper way to locate, hire, and supervise contractors. Property management is a time-consuming job, but you can lessen the burden a bit by hiring people to help you.

Hiring Employees

If you own only a few rental units, you probably won't need any employees, because you can handle all of your duties yourself or with the help of contractors. However, when you begin to acquire a large number of rental properties, whether they are many small rental properties in different locations or one or two larger apartment buildings, you will most likely need to hire employee.

For most rental owners, the very first employee they will hire is an onsite manager. In some areas of the country, laws actually require rental property owners to have an onsite manager if there are a certain minimum number of rental units at a single location. For example, rental properties with 9 or more units in New York City or properties with 16 or more rental units in California require an onsite manager or responsible party.

Onsite managers offer many advantages. They can handle many of the day-to-day problems, make sure that the property is properly maintained, and notify you or your maintenance person if an emergency occurs. They can also assist in marketing the vacant rental units and resolving a budding conflict between tenants. However, there are some disadvantages to having onsite managers, namely the added expense and the difficulty finding and retaining good qualified help. But don't let these challenges stand in your way if a manager will be an asset to you.

Establishing job duties, work schedule, and compensation

Before you begin looking for a new employee, you need to determine what that employee's job duties, work schedule, and compensation will be.

Most rental property owners don't create written job descriptions for their onsite managers and maintenance personnel, but this is a mistake you don't want to make. If you rely solely on verbal agreements, disputes are sure to occur — and they are usually resolved in the employee's favor.

Many local affiliates of the National Apartment Association offer great onsite manager employment agreements that are written specifically to comply with federal and state employment laws. Use these forms to formally record your mutual agreement regarding duties, limits on authority, compensation, hours, and rental unit credit, if any. Check state laws concerning limits on the rent credit. Also, take particular care to ensure that the employee has set scheduled hours and that the compensation meets the federal or state minimum wage. Require any overtime to be approved in advance.

You should also have your employees fill out a time card every day and be sure to pay overtime or allow compensating time off within the same pay period or within the limits of your state law. Failing to have a clear contract, carefully document the hours worked, and strictly enforce limits on extra hours could lead to exorbitant claims for back pay and overtime from a disgruntled employee in the future.

Screening employees

Screening employees is very important, because your employees will have close contact with your tenants. Be sure to have all prospective employees complete an employment application that lists their education, experience, and references; plus, specifically have them authorize your right to investigate the information provided. If you are hiring an employee who will live onsite, you should also require that he or she complete a separate rental application and rental agreement.

The evaluation and selection of your onsite manager is one of your most critical tasks, and you should make every effort to be diligent and objective. As my good friend, rental industry educator Dorothy Gourley, has advised owners for many years, your onsite manager needs to be fair, firm, and friendly — not always an easy combination to find in one person. But your ideal manager candidate will combine honesty and integrity, perseverance, and good communication or people skills. The employee should also have a good employment history, the ability to work with you, and a professional, stable demeanor that will be compatible with your tenant profile. Prior experience is not necessary if you are willing to train or to provide educational opportunities from the Institute of Real Estate Management (IREM) or the local apartment association.

Begin by pre-screening your prospective employees on the phone. Describe the job requirements, hours, and compensation. Then discuss the applicant's current employment status, review his qualifications and experience, and reconfirm his interest in the position with the proposed work schedule and compensation. If there seems to be mutual interest, schedule an in-person interview and a tour of the rental property.

The employment screening process is much more difficult than tenant screening because of the numerous state and federal laws to protect prospective employees. These extensive laws make it very difficult for the small rental owner to meet all the legal requirements of hiring. If you're an owner of just a few rental properties, use outside employment firms for locating and screening potential employees.

Screening rental applicants primarily focuses on income, plus credit and rental history, whereas pre-employment screening should focus on education, job history, personal references, plus a criminal background search and drug/alcohol screening. Be sure to check with an employment law specialist for the laws in your area before initiating a pre-employment screening policy.

For example, the job applicant's credit history can be important if the employee will be handling money, yet the federal Fair Credit Reporting Act (FCRA) was amended to cover employee background checks, and several mandatory disclosures are required. Consult an employment law specialist. Alternatively, a pre-employment screening firm can usually assist you in ensuring that your employment application form meets the federal and state requirements. Also, the Americans with Disabilities Act (ADA) severely restricts an employer's ability to seek information about an applicant's medical history. The employee can volunteer information, but you cannot ask questions concerning physical limitations, prior workers' compensation claims, lost time due to illness or injury, and prior drug and alcohol addictions. Be very careful, because there are significant penalties for employers who violate the FCRA or ADA regulations.

Some small rental property owners find using employment agencies or at least employee screening firms when hiring employees is actually easier and cheaper in the long run. You can no longer rely on a resume, an interview, and a list of references when making hiring decisions. And the rental housing industry and building maintenance trades have historically been relatively easy for individuals with poor work history, problems with alcohol or substance abuse, and even serious criminal convictions to find employment. But many managers and maintenance personnel are in a position of trust; they often assist in rent collection and have ready access to building equipment and supplies. When combined with the regular contact with tenants, and keys that provide access to the rental units, the liability for a rental owner who fails to properly screen his employees or contractors is very high.

The ever-changing and more restrictive employment-screening regulations are creating a strong demand for employment-screening firms. I recommend using these firms whenever possible, particularly those that specialize in the rental housing industry. Be sure to specify that you want them to conduct a criminal background check in every county where your prospective employee lived, attended school, and worked. This will cost more up front, but it's a good investment that will pay dividends and offer peace of mind in the long run.

Be wary of employee screening firms that claim to be able to conduct a single national criminal database search. Only half of the states offer statewide searches, and the data is often inaccurate or out of date. Also, the statewide data typically only includes felony records, not serious misdemeanors, so the most thorough information still must be gathered on a county-by-county basis.

Be sure to ask your rental applicant about any gaps in employment or tenant history, because that may be your only clue about a deceptive applicant with a criminal history.

Knowing your responsibilities

Being an employer has very serious legal obligations and requirements. Besides the responsibility for wages and employment taxes and reporting, you are also responsible for proper supervision and liability for the acts of your manager. So you want to make sure that your manager abides by all fair housing laws, stays within his level of authority, and has knowledge of the basics of tenant-landlord law.

The right onsite manager can make all the difference in the world. Make sure that you are very competitive with your compensation, and use recognition rewards and financial incentives that acknowledge positive results such as low turnover, minimal lost rent due to vacancy and bad debt, and efficient control of expenses. A competitive compensation package is a wise investment that will allow you to hire and retain the best onsite manager.

Employees are typically paid based on a salary or hourly wages. The exact amount will vary based on the manager's responsibilities and work schedule, but be sure to meet the minimum wage requirements in your area. You can often obtain information on the wages and benefits you'll need to offer in order to be competitive from other rental property owners or your local apartment association.

You are also responsible for your employee's withholding taxes, social security, federal and/or state unemployment insurance, and workers' compensation insurance.

Federal law requires all employers even with a single employee to post signs explaining legal rights of their employees, including information posters on the Federal Labor Standards Act, Job Safety and Health Protection, and the Employee Polygraph Protection Act. If you have 15 or more employees, you must also have the Equal Employment Opportunity Act poster. The Family and Medical Leave Act notice is required if you have more than 50 employees. Many states have additional requirements or have posters that supersede federal law. The law also states that these notices "must be posted in a prominent and conspicuous place in every establishment of the employer where it can readily be observed by employees and applicants for employment." This requirement can be a challenge for many rental property owners with small rental properties, but they are mandatory federal laws that must be followed. These posters are all available at no charge online at: `www.dol.gov/dol/osbp/public/sbrefa/poster/main.htm`.

You must provide your employees with workers' compensation insurance that pays employees and covers their medical expenses if they are injured or become ill as a result of their job. Employee safety must always be a top priority, but workers' compensation is a no-fault system that provides benefits regardless of the safety of your workplace, or even if the employee's own negligence contributed to his injury or illness. There are workers' compensation laws in all states; be sure to fully comply with them. In some states, this insurance coverage is available through a government agency, whereas private insurance companies also offer coverage in other areas. Although some states may not require you to carry this coverage unless you have a minimum number of employees, I advise carrying workers' compensation coverage even if you don't have *any* employees.

For example, any contractor you hire to perform work on your rental property should have his own workers' compensation insurance policy to cover all of his employees. However, if someone gets hurt and the contractor has limited or even no coverage, you can be certain that his injured employee will come after you for compensation. Don't take chances; this coverage can often be added to your standard insurance policy for a nominal cost.

Many rental owners prefer to have payroll handled by an accountant or a firm that specializes in this service. However, there is another option to avoid all of the bureaucracy of being an employer. You can use an employee leasing company that will be the employer of record, and thus responsible for payroll, withholding taxes, workers' compensation, benefits, deductions, regulations, and reporting. You can pay the firm with a single check and let them deal with the paperwork. Check with your local IREM chapter or apartment association for referrals.

Working with your manager

You have to walk a fine line between being an involved and caring rental owner and an overbearing micromanager who inhibits your onsite manager from properly running the property. Good managers treat the property as if it is their own and often will make a major effort to keep the property in excellent condition and maximize your net income. Of course, there are many incompetent managers who will only do what they are literally forced to do. Stay out of the way of the good manager, and terminate the bad or uncaring manager.

Your onsite manager must have the respect of the tenants in order to collect rents, deal with problems, and respond to maintenance service requests. As the owner or property manager, you should back up the onsite manager whenever possible. However, your onsite manager must earn respect from you and the tenants. Backing up a manager when he is wrong can create a much larger problem.

When dealing with tenant complaints about your onsite property manager, remain neutral and then calmly investigate the facts before getting back to the tenant with a formal response. Never ignore the tenant's concerns, but always be sure to balance the need to investigate the tenant's complaint with well-reasoned trust of your employee.

Although fortunately it doesn't happen often, be very careful if you ever have any indication that your employees are abusive, make threats, or show any signs of violent or disruptive behavior. You are not always liable if one of your employees threatens or harms someone. But workplace violence is a concern throughout the country, and rental housing employees are often in positions of authority, with access to personal information and access to rental units.

Watch for any signs or indications of threats or illegal possession or use of weapons. If you become aware of any of these signs, or if you find out about previous attacks or prior convictions for violent crimes, immediately contact your employment law specialist for advice on the proper response, which may include a written warning or the employee's immediate termination.

Claims of sexual harassment of tenants by managers or other employees, contractors, or even other tenants are a growing concern for rental property owners. You need to have a clear, firm, written zero-tolerance policy against sexual harassment and promptly and fairly investigate any complaints. Cases of employee or contractor misconduct have been a problem for years; however, recent litigation against owners includes cases where one tenant accuses another tenant of sexual harassment and it is alleged that the owner or manager condones such actions or fails to take proper steps to address the concerns. This is dangerous territory, so don't jump to conclusions, because balancing the need for a prompt and accurate investigation against the rights of the accused individuals can be difficult. Immediately contact your attorney for advice when you're told about any allegations of sexual harassment.

Firing an employee

You have the right to terminate an employee at any time, as long as you do not have an illegal reason such as discrimination or retaliation. As with any employment situation, always document any concerns about job performance in writing and discuss them with the employee as soon as possible.

If you need to terminate the employee, be prepared to show that the termination was for cause and was carefully documented. Reasons for terminating an employee include poor job performance, failure to follow the written job description, dishonesty or theft, or engaging in any illegal or criminal activity.

Although the details of terminating your employees are probably not on your mind when you hire them, you need to have clear written documentation about the process of parting company, particularly with onsite employees. Rental property owners often have legitimate concerns that the terminated onsite manager or other onsite employee may cause problems. Because they typically receive a rent discount, they will also take their time relocating unless you have a clear policy upfront.

Keep a written agreement clearly indicating that the rental unit is a condition of and incident to their employment. Any rights to occupy a rental unit cease upon the employee's termination. Although some people advise giving onsite employees only 24 hours notice to vacate, I believe that one week is reasonable to find a new place and make the move, particularly because they are now unemployed. You can always be flexible, but you should also have a holdover rent clause that calls for rent at the rate of 125 percent of the current market rent for the rental unit as an incentive for them to relocate quickly. Although the utilities and telephone service should be in the name of the employee, if these items are included in their compensation for any reason, be sure you're able to require the former employee to put them in his name immediately.

Building Your Contractor and Vendor Dream Team

Every rental property owner depends on contractors and vendors to assist him in the proper management of his rental units. The real challenge for many rental property owners is finding the right people or companies for the job and ensuring that they are paying a competitive price for the services or materials.

Independent contractor versus employee status

As a rental property owner, you may routinely have assistance from workers who perform jobs like cleaning, painting, and landscaping. These workers are classified as either independent contractors or employees. You are responsible for the employment taxes for your employees, but independent contractors pay their own employment taxes. The advantage of having these workers classified as independent contractors is obvious; however, the IRS is actively investigating businesses that traditionally use independent contractors to be sure that they're not classifying employees as independent contractors incorrectly.

The IRS has established very detailed and comprehensive requirements to qualify as an independent contractor. For example, workers must provide their own tools and equipment, offer services to the public at large, perform their services in such a manner that the workers have control over the process and the outcome, and they must be in a position to potentially incur a loss as a result of their work.

Most onsite managers, and possibly other maintenance workers, cannot meet these and the other stringent requirements. They are usually being paid a salary or hourly wage, under the guidance and control of the rental owner or property management firm, and they have set hours and specific job responsibilities.

Check with your attorney or accountant, but my advice is to not even try to structure your relationship with your onsite manager as anything other than an employer-employee relationship. If the IRS or a state agency later determines that your "independent contractor" was really your "employee," you will be liable for back withholding taxes, penalties, and interest. To make matters worse, you also must retroactively pay the employee's share of these employment taxes.

Other owners or the product service council of your local apartment association or IREM chapter can be a great source for contractors and vendors. Be sure to obtain several references, and actually call them before signing the contractor on. Look for a contractor or vendor with a proven track record and a minimum of three to five years of experience.

Although it is always nice to see new companies enter the field, if you own one or only a few rental units you have too much at stake and can't afford any problems or delays. When you have selected a qualified contractor, start him on a relatively simple job initially and supervise him carefully so that you can see firsthand the quality of his work and avoid surprises in his billing.

You typically pay a major portion of your overall expenses to contractors and service providers, so it is important that these dollars are spent wisely. Just like the importance of screening and supervising your own employees, care must be taken to ensure that the contractors are honest, dependable, and competent.

Giving a contractor unlimited and unsupervised access to a rental unit can be dangerous, because you usually have very little, if any, personal background information on the contractor or his employees.

In addition to good work, dependable response, and competitive pricing, when you hire contractors you must insist that they provide a copy of their certificates of insurance, including current and adequate workers' compensation and liability insurance coverage. Contact the state contractor's licensing board to ensure that their license is current and that they have any required bonds.

When hiring a contractor on a service contract, be very careful to avoid some common pitfalls. Some contractors or vendors will propose a multiyear contract or one with an automatic renewal clause. I strongly recommend avoiding any service contract that cannot be cancelled with or without cause upon a written 30-day notice. Even if you must pay a penalty to prematurely terminate the contract, you always want this option. Also, although they will initially say otherwise, all terms of the service contract should be negotiable. Unless they have a monopoly in your area, you should seriously consider another contractor if the one you're talking with refuses to negotiate.

Be sure to get competitive quotes and make sure that all bidders are using identical specifications. Have the firm with the best reputation and qualifications set the scope, specifications, and proposed time schedule of the bid. Then you can let the other competitors bid using the same information, with the pricing deleted. ***Remember:*** Good quality and service cost money.

Have a clear understanding about the billing and the contractor's expectations about payments. The payments should be made in arrears and due generally in 30 days; however, even more prompt payments should coincide with the completion and your approval of the work. If you are having a very large project completed, you may want to authorize progress payments, but always withhold at least a 10 percent retainer for your final walkthrough upon final completion.

Make sure that your contractors properly supervise their employees and require them to clean up upon completion and remove all debris from your property. And hold them accountable if they do any damage.

Never pay for services in advance unless the work requires some special order or customized product, and then pay only a small deposit. Unethical contractors have been known to demand large payments up front and then suddenly file bankruptcy or leave town. Don't be a victim. Check with your state contractors licensing board for any dollar limits on advance payments required by contractors.

Be sure to issue an IRS Form 1099, Statement of Miscellaneous Income, at the end of each calendar year to each independent contractor or vendor that is not incorporated and was paid more than $600.

Chapter 15

Maintenance

In This Chapter

- Setting up a maintenance plan for your rental property
- Knowing what types of maintenance issues you're likely to face
- Responding to your tenants' maintenance requests professionally

Maintenance — the work required to keep something in proper condition or upkeep — is just part of the territory when you own rental property. Although maintenance isn't anyone's favorite job, you can enhance your investment by making needed repairs promptly and maintaining the entire property in the best possible physical condition.

Although owning and operating rental property clearly requires ongoing physical maintenance, many rental owners are not prepared for the work involved. If you have a background and experience in maintenance and repairs, you may welcome the opportunity to do some of the work yourself. But maintenance requests do not always work around your schedule. And many needed repairs require special tools, skills, and training that only a professional would have.

Whether you do the maintenance work yourself or hire and oversee a contractor or maintenance person, take the time to know enough about basic maintenance that you can make sure they're doing a good job. Many fine books cover the specific repairs required in most rental units, including *Home Maintenance For Dummies* by James Carey (Hungry Minds, Inc.).

Besides the benefits in marketing and keeping your property full, you are required by law to properly maintain and repair your rental properties to meet all building, housing, health and safety, and habitability codes. In legalese, this is called the *implied warranty of habitability.* In plain English, it means that, from the day the tenant moves in until the day the tenant moves out, you must keep the rental property in a safe and habitable condition. Check the state and local laws or statutes in your area for specific habitability requirements that apply to your rental property.

In this chapter, I cover the reasons that a good maintenance plan is essential for all rental properties, the most common types of maintenance, and some sound procedures for handling rental property maintenance and saving money.

Recognizing the Importance of a Maintenance Plan

One of the most common reasons that dissatisfied tenants leave a rental property is the failure of the rental owner to respond to the tenants' basic requests for maintenance. But you can use this to your advantage when you show your well-maintained rental unit by informing your prospective tenants about your system for promptly addressing maintenance issues. If you have a solid maintenance plan in place, you will consistently get higher rents and have much lower turnover.

Plus, when you're working with a maintenance plan, you can control your expenses and keep them to a minimum. You greatly reduce the need for emergency or extraordinary repairs (which always cost more money). And you have the names of contractors and suppliers on hand so that you can have the proper repair done the first time (instead of having to fix a botched repair).

Because long-term, satisfied tenants are the key to financial success in managing rental properties, you need to establish a responsive maintenance system that properly maintains the premises in order to avoid operating losses and potential legal problems. A poorly maintained property will lead to higher tenant turnover and tenants of progressively lower caliber, who are willing to accept the poor condition of the property. A tenant can also use the poor condition of the property to call the local housing inspector, withhold rent, vacate in the middle of a lease, defend an eviction, or even sue under slumlord statutes found in most urban areas.

Take a proactive approach to maintenance. At least once a year, conduct an annual rental unit safety inspection walkthrough. Most tenants will cooperate fully, but a few states prohibit you from entering just to inspect the unit without the tenant's advance permission. In these cases, or as an additional tool to improve your tenant relations, you can send your tenant a non-intrusive note and maintenance checklist that allows a quick response. This standard policy will protect you from claims of poor maintenance, allow for repairs when problems are small, and keep your good tenants satisfied.

A good maintenance plan includes regularly scheduled exterior property inspections. A customized property inspection checklist for each rental property is a good management tool. The frequency of the inspections will vary, but they should be performed at least quarterly and upon each tenant turnover.

Your tenant has a responsibility to maintain the premises in a clean and sanitary manner and to properly use the premises in a usual and customary fashion. You should always hold the tenant financially accountable for any damage caused to the property by their negligence or misuse of the property.

Being Prepared for the Different Types of Maintenance Issues

Maintenance isn't just a matter of fixing a leaky faucet here and there — rental properties require several different types of maintenance, and you're sure to run into each of them at one time or another. Although each type of maintenance is critical, you need to respond to and handle each type in a unique way.

My first employer in property management taught me the saying, "To own is to maintain." It's something worth keeping in mind when you find yourself having to do maintenance work on your rental property.

Emergency maintenance

Part of being a rental property owner is being prepared for emergency maintenance requests at all hours of the day. Although your tenants should contact the appropriate authorities for life safety matters, you will still receive your share of emergency maintenance requests.

When you get a maintenance call from a tenant, first you need to determine whether the urgent maintenance request really is an emergency. An emergency repair is work that must be done *immediately* in order to prevent further property damage or minimize the chance of endangering people. The most common maintenance emergencies typically involve plumbing or electrical problems.

In a maintenance emergency, immediately advise the tenant of what steps to take to limit any further damage. For example, if a pipe is leaking, tell the tenant to shut off the water at the angle stop under the sink or at the water meter; this can prevent further water damage. Instruct tenants not to use appliances or electrical systems that are malfunctioning until they have been inspected or repaired.

If a fire, flood, or gas leak emergency ever occurs at your rental property, or if a natural disaster hits the area, immediately shutting off the utilities may be imperative. Prepare charts and simple diagrams for each rental property indicating where to find all utility shutoff locations and the tools necessary to operate them — as well as instructions letting tenants know which situations warrant shutting them off.

In many parts of the country, you may need to remind tenants that freezing outdoor temperatures can lead to water damage in unheated rental units. Tenants may want to turn off the heat when they go to work or when they're on vacation as a way to save money, but turning the heat off completely or setting the thermostat below 40 degrees can lead to the freezing and bursting of pipes. Make heating the rental unit to a minimum of 40 degrees a requirement in your lease or rental agreement, and send out a newsletter or reminder letter as the seasonal weather begins.

Preventive maintenance

A sound preventive maintenance program can increase your cash flow and reduce the number of maintenance emergencies at your property. *Preventive maintenance* is the regularly scheduled inspection and maintenance performed to extend the operating life of the building systems of a property. This often includes annual maintenance surveys or inspections of the interior of the rental units.

One great example of preventive maintenance is regularly lubricating the motors and replacing the filters in heating and air-conditioning systems. When performed annually on a service contract, this preventive maintenance is very inexpensive, and the lubricated motors and clean filters lessen the strain on the equipment so they will last longer and operate with greater energy efficiency.

Preventive maintenance can often address problems when the conditions are still minor, thus saving significantly over future emergency repairs or replacement. The cost of maintenance labor is also reduced because maintenance personnel can work more efficiently by having all the necessary tools, parts, and supplies on hand. According to a study by the Institute of Real Estate Management (IREM), 80 percent of the cost of most maintenance repairs covers labor, and only 20 percent covers the actual parts and supplies.

For even further savings, schedule the preventive maintenance work during the contractor's slow season.

Be sure to give all tenants written notice before beginning maintenance work that will require the discontinuance of any utility service. A temporary shutoff of utilities (particularly water) will often be necessary in emergencies or while performing preventive maintenance and repairs at your rental property. Advising your tenants in advance can minimize the inconvenience for your tenants. The courts will generally allow reasonable utility shutoffs as long as you're diligent in making the necessary repairs in a timely manner.

Corrective maintenance

Although planning and performing preventive maintenance work is usually cheaper than fixing or replacing items, the reality is that if something breaks it must be fixed or replaced in a timely manner. The most common maintenance requests from tenants are for corrective maintenance. If you respond professionally and in a timely manner, you'll earn a reputation as a good rental property owner.

Even with the best preventive maintenance programs, corrective maintenance is a normal part of any maintenance program. Anything in a rental unit can, and eventually will, break or need attention in normal usage, including toilets and sinks that become clogged, doors that stick, and appliances that malfunction. The key to tenant satisfaction is often dependent upon whether you have a system for efficiently accepting and responding to tenant maintenance requests.

Although the telephone, a pager, or even an answering service or machine are still the best ways to communicate an urgent maintenance request, e-mail is becoming more popular with both owners and tenants for many non-emergency maintenance situations. E-mail works well for owners, who often prefer not being interrupted by a phone call at a potentially inconvenient time, and it works well for tenants, who appreciate being able to send the e-mail at any time of the day or night instead of having to wait until normal business hours to get ahold of you. Upon receipt of the e-mail, you can reply with a confirmation or ask for more details. You can even forward the e-mail directly to the maintenance contractor who will be handling the service request.

Custodial maintenance

Custodial maintenance is the regular day-to-day upkeep of the rental property and the most frequently occurring type of maintenance. The curb appeal and physical appearance of your property and grounds depend on regular patrolling and cleaning. In single-family rentals, the tenant typically handles this duty, and the specific responsibilities should be included in your lease or rental agreement. In larger rental properties, an onsite manager should be responsible for daily inspection and cleaning of the property.

Keep a list of routine maintenance items, including washing windows; hosing down parking areas, driveways, and walkways; and doing other tasks that will keep the interior and exterior of the rental property clean and presentable. Don't forget to keep the trash bin areas clean and free of litter as well.

The number one complaint of tenants, and the bane of all rental owners, is deferred maintenance. Not really a type of maintenance at all, *deferred maintenance* is the result of obvious repairs that are not properly addressed in a timely manner. Common examples are peeling paint, broken screen doors, overgrown landscaping, and minor roof leaks in the garage. Although every property has some deferred maintenance, your goal as an owner is to keep it to a minimum.

Cosmetic maintenance

Properties with great curb appeal are easier to manage and generate higher returns on your investment. So if you're willing to spend money to improve and upgrade the appearance of the exterior and the individual rental units, you'll reap the rewards. Examples of cosmetic maintenance or upgrades include replacing old countertops, installing new light fixtures, repainting, installing new window coverings, and decorating with wallpaper.

One of the most common complaints tenants make is that their landlord refuses to paint the interior of the rental property every few years. Except for local rent-control ordinances or to mitigate lead-based paint, no federal or state laws require you to repaint the rental unit after any certain period of time for strictly cosmetic reasons. Of course, repainting the rental unit to keep your tenant satisfied if he is willing to pay more rent may be a good idea.

Handling Rental Property Maintenance

Even though you may be assertive in properly maintaining your rental property through regular property inspections and diligent interior maintenance upon tenant turnover, there will always be an ongoing need to make repairs.

Responding to a tenant's request for maintenance

Your first knowledge of a maintenance problem or needed repair will likely be when you are contacted by your tenant. In many businesses, the companies with the best reputation and customer loyalty are those that are respected for the positive attitude and efficiency with which they address complaints. The rental property business is no different.

Typically, you will receive the request for service by telephone, and while you need to be respectful of your tenant's time, you also need to ask questions to gather a detailed description of the necessary maintenance and the precise

location of the problem. This information allows you to make an informed decision as to the urgency of the problem and determine the proper person to handle the work. It also gives you the chance to make sure that the proper tools, equipment, and parts will be available at the first service call, if possible.

Be sure that your tenants know that they cannot contact your maintenance person or contractor directly. Tenants may think they're doing you a favor by contacting the maintenance person directly by not hassling you with their problem. Or they may remember another problem when the maintenance person is in their rental unit working on something else. But either way, require all service requests to be routed through management. Then, whenever a tenant contacts you with a maintenance problem, you can properly record all information in writing on a Tenant's Maintenance Request Form (see Form 15-1) regardless of how insignificant the problem.

Having proof that the tenant gave permission to enter the rental unit, either by signing the Maintenance Request Form in person or by giving approval on the telephone, is essential. If the tenant cannot sign the request in person, make a specific note indicating the date and time, and who gave permission to enter. If the tenant did not specifically give permission for a maintenance person to enter the unit, serve a Notice of Intent to Enter Rental Unit (see Form 15-2), as legally required in your area.

All tenant maintenance requests should be entered in a master maintenance log in chronological order. (See Chapter 18 for more information on computer software programs and manual maintenance tracking systems that simplify the paperwork.) A good tenant maintenance tracking system does much more than just record the request for service and the fact that the tenant granted permission to enter. The system can provide proof that the repairs were actually made, record the parts and materials used in the repair, and serve as the basis of a billing record if the tenant caused the damage and will be charged for the service call.

Copies of Tenant Maintenance Request Forms should always be filed in the tenant file and in a separate permanent maintenance file for each rental unit. If the tenant complains to authorities or makes allegations of a breach of habitability, Tenant Maintenance Request Forms provide a repair history that you can use to document that tenant complaints were properly addressed.

Your maintenance personnel and contractors are key in giving your tenants a positive or negative impression, because they have direct contact with your tenant and are a reflection on you. Remind them that they are entering your tenant's home and they must immediately identify themselves with proper identification, such as a photo I.D. They must always be well groomed, respectful, and courteous, and they should never smoke in an occupied or unoccupied rental unit. They must be businesslike and stick to the facts while keeping the tenant informed about the status of the service request. They should always completely clean up after themselves as well.

Maintenance Request Form

Maintenance Request Number __________

____
Date

____
Name

____
Street Address Unit number, if any

____
City/State/Zip Code

____________________________ ____________________________
Home Phone Work or Alternate Phone

Service Requested (Describe very specifically):

____
____
____
____
____
____

Best time to perform service (Day and time): ____

Authorization: Owner/Agent/Service personnel are authorized to enter rental unit if Tenant is not present unless specific instructions have been given in advance to the contrary.

____
Signature of Tenant

If verbal approval received, given by: ____________________. Received by: ____________________

Report of action taken
____ Completed, by ______________ (Upon completion, describe problem/work done/materials used)
____
____
____
____ Unable to complete on ______________, because ______________________________
____ Outside professional assistance required, because ______________________________
____ Will return to complete on ______________________________

Charge cost to Tenant: _____ Yes _____ No If Yes, Reason ______________________
____

Comments: ____
____
____

Received: ________________ ________________________________
Date Owner/Agent

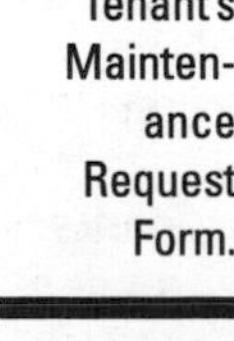

Form 15-1: Tenant's Maintenance Request Form.

Although responding to tenant maintenance requests can lead to excellent tenant relations, some tenants may have excessive demands. The best way to handle these tenants is to remain calm and courteous and to address all legitimate health and safety items or maintenance repairs that preserve your investment. When the tenant demands become unreasonable, politely explain that providing extra service calls or cosmetic upgrades will necessitate an increase in the tenant's rent to cover your additional expenditures.

Notice of Intent to Enter Rental Unit

____
Date

____
Name

____
Street Address

____
City/State/Zip Code

This notice is to inform all persons in the above Premises that on the ____ day of ____________, 20 __, beginning approximately between the hour of _______ a.m./p.m. and until ___________ a.m./p.m., the Owner, Owner's agent or Owner's employees or representatives, will enter the Premises for the following reason:

____ To perform or arrange for the following repairs or improvements:
____
____
____

____ To show the premises to:

____ a prospective tenant

____ a prospective or actual purchaser or lender

____ workers or contractors regarding the above repair or improvement

____ Other:
____
____
____

Naturally, you are welcome to be present. Please notify us if you have any questions or if the date or time is inconvenient.

Sincerely,

____
Owner/Manager

Form 15-2: Notice of Intent to Enter Rental Unit.

Reimbursing tenants if repairs aren't made in a timely manner

In most states, if you fail to properly maintain the rental property in a safe and habitable condition after proper notice of a defect from the tenant, the tenant has the right to have the defect repaired and then deduct some or all of the cost of the repairs from the following month's rent.

If your state provides for the repair and deduct remedy, you need to fully understand the limitations and the rights and responsibilities of both you and the tenant. In most states, the tenant must follow a prescribed procedure to use the repair and deduct remedy, including proper notification to the rental owner and allowing a reasonable time to respond. There are also limits on the number of times this remedy can be used, specific guidelines as to the types of defects covered, and limitations regarding how much can be deducted (either in a set dollar amount or in a set percentage of the monthly rent).

Your goal as a rental owner should be to promptly respond to legitimate complaints about the rental property and to make sure that all maintenance work is done properly and for a reasonable cost. When the tenant resorts to the repair and deduct remedy, you can face unpleasant consequences. The tenant may attempt to make the repair himself or herself or hire a contractor who is not skilled. Even worse, the tenant may hire a contractor who is very skilled but also quite expensive, and then have the bill sent to you.

The bottom line? Always make repairs in a timely manner and you won't have to face these problems to begin with.

Keeping tenants from fixing things themselves

In most states, you can legally delegate some of your maintenance and repair tasks to the tenant, often in exchange for a reduction in rent. However, you remain responsible for ensuring that the rental unit is habitable. Even if your tenant is qualified and capable of handling many routine repairs, you should retain control of even the minor maintenance problems.

Initially, allowing your tenant to handle certain minor repairs seems to offer significant savings in cost and aggravation. However, most tenants unfortunately lack the proper skills, training, special tools, or even motivation to do the job properly. They may be willing to ignore or live with a problem that can be resolved inexpensively. But that little problem may soon become a major problem — and a major expense — and you will be left with the responsibility to pay for it.

One of the main advantages of renting is that someone else is responsible for the maintenance and repair of the property. Most tenants are relieved to know that you appreciate the opportunity to properly maintain the rental property and that they won't have to do a thing except alert you to problems when they come up.

Disabled tenants may have the right to modify their living space at their own expense after obtaining your approval.

Purchasing maintenance parts and supplies

As a new rental property owner, you will suddenly find that you are interested in wandering through your favorite hardware store looking for obscure parts, or flipping through a huge catalog for the latest sale on disposals. Don't underestimate the importance of having reliable vendors with competitive pricing, because the ongoing maintenance and repair of a rental property will greatly exceed the original construction cost.

You can receive trade discounts from most rental housing industry vendors and suppliers just by setting up an account in the name of your rental property or management business. These discounts usually apply to all purchases, but there are often special volume or bulk discounts for commonly used items.

Don't fall into the trap of buying items in greater quantities than you immediately can use if the items don't have a long shelf, regardless of the great savings offered at the time. A common mistake property owners make is buying the latest discontinued paint on sale, only to have to completely repaint their rental unit upon turnover because the excess paint has gone bad in storage. Instead, use the same standard color on all rentals so that the color will always be available, you can buy in bulk, and you can do touchups when you need to.

Another growing trend is the purchasing of parts and supplies online. Web sites offer a wide variety of items, from appliances to plumbing and electrical fixtures to even tools and hardware parts. They make the purchasing process very easy and typically offer free delivery. If you own just a few rental units, however, you may find that the savings are nominal unless you purchase in quantity.

All new appliances come with manufacturer's warranties covering the cost of replacement or repairs if the appliance breaks down during the warranty period. Be sure to keep all appliance and equipment warranties plus copies of all purchase receipts in a readily accessible file for each rental property. Read the warranty before attempting a repair yourself, or you may inadvertently void your rights to have the manufacturer replace or repair the appliance or equipment for free. After the basic warranty expires, many manufacturers offer extended service contracts for an annual fee, but these contracts generally aren't worth it, as long as you have good quality appliances and a reliable service technician at your disposal.

Chapter 16

Safety and Security

In This Chapter

- Handling and preventing crime in and around your rental property
- Taking precautions to keep your tenants and your property safe
- Protecting against environmental hazards, including fire and carbon monoxide poisoning

As a rental property owner, you need to take an active role in implementing policies and security measures for the safety of your tenants and their guests. Even if your property is located next-door to the local police station, you still need to implement proper building security measures. Crime can strike anywhere, even in so-called "good" neighborhoods. And even if crime is not a problem in your area, you may face potential safety challenges from Mother Nature. Take the lead in working with local experts to prepare for the most likely natural disasters that may occur in your area, including severe storms, wildfires, floods, hurricanes, tornadoes, and earthquakes.

Whether you're trying to ward off criminals or you're looking for ways to keep your rental property and tenants protected from an earthquake, I give you the suggestions you need in this chapter.

Tackling Crime in and around Your Rental Property

Crime is a fact of life for all of us, rental property owners or not. But part of your responsibility as a rental property owner is to make your property as safe as possible for your tenants and to alert your tenants to their responsibilities as well. In this section, I give you some tips for keeping crime to a minimum in your area and responding to it if and when it does occur.

Participating in the Crime-Free Multi-Housing Program

One of the best crime prevention programs for rental property owners is available through most local law enforcement departments. The Crime-Free Multi-Housing Program incorporates rental property owners, your local law enforcement, and tenants in a combined effort to fight crime and raise the standard of living. Law enforcement representatives work with and train owners and managers in how to keep illegal activity out of their rental properties. The training is comprehensive and covers applicant screening techniques, proper preparation of rental agreements, the warning signs of drug activity, crisis resolutions, and ongoing management responsibilities. Tenants are also given instruction on how to identify criminal and suspicious behaviors, and they are strongly encouraged to take responsibility to prevent crime from occurring.

After the training is completed and the owners and managers demonstrate that they are screening prospective tenants, evicting problem tenants and using the Crime and Drug-Free Housing Addendum (see Form 16-1), they can become certified as a Crime-Free Multi-Housing Community. When you're certified, you can display signs at the entrances to the rental property to alert any prospective tenants that your rental property will not tolerate any criminal or drug-related activity.

A large number of local law enforcement departments are actively supporting this new program in conjunction with a traditional neighborhood watch program. Like neighborhood watch, they train tenants to recognize crimes or suspicious activity and report it to police. Law enforcement is working one-on-one with the owners, managers, and tenants by sharing information regarding criminal activities that have occurred in their community. Their goal is to help these rental communities become certified and help improve the overall quality of life for all.

A great resource for information is the Burglary Prevention Council, which offers a free brochure with advice and suggestions to help you evaluate your rental unit's current safety features, the most likely points of entry, factors that will attract or discourage criminals, tips on implementing a cost-effective security program, plus a vacation checklist. This information can also be useful for your home or office and is available online at `www.burglaryprevention.org`.

Paying attention to tenant questions and complaints about safety-related issues

When a tenant directly inquires about safety or security at your rental property, always provide an honest answer and inform them of any recent confirmed

serious or violent criminal incidents, while also referring them to local law enforcement for specific information. Rental owners are not routinely advised or aware of crime in the area or often even in their own rental property. You obviously cannot disclose information that you don't have, but you should refer prospective or current tenants to local law enforcement for more information.

Crime- and Drug-Free Housing Addendum

This document is an addendum and is part of the Lease or Rental Agreement, dated ____________________,

by and between ________________________, Owner/Agent, and ________________________Tenant,

for the premises located at: ____.

In consideration of the execution or renewal of a lease of the Premises identified in the Lease or Rental Agreement, Management and Lessee agree as follows:

1. Lessee, any member of Lessees household, or a guest or other person under the Lessees control shall not engage in criminal activity, including drug-related criminal activity, on or near said Premises. Drug-related criminal activity means the illegal manufacture, sale, distribution, use, or possession with intent to manufacture, sell, distribute, or use a controlled substance (as defined in section 102 of the Controlled Substance Act (21 U.S.C. 802).

2. Lessee, any member of Lessees household, or a guest or other person under Lessees control shall not engage in any act intended to facilitate criminal activity, including drug-related criminal activity, on or near said Premises.

3. Lessee or members of the household will not permit the Premises to be used for, or to facilitate criminal activity, including drug-related criminal activity, regardless of whether the individual engaging in such activity is a member of the household or a guest.

4. Lessee or members of the household will not engage in the manufacture, sale, or distribution of illegal drugs at any location, whether on or near said Premises or otherwise.

5. Lessee, any member of Lessees household, or a guest or other person under Lessees control, shall not engage in acts of violence or discharge firearms on or near said Premises.

6. Violation of any of the above provisions shall be a material violation of the Lease or Rental Agreement and good cause for termination of tenancy. A single violation of any of the provisions of this addendum shall be deemed a serious violation and a material noncompliance with the Lease or Rental Agreement. It is understood and agreed that a single violation shall be good cause for termination of the Lease or Rental Agreement. Unless otherwise provided by law, proof of violation shall not require criminal conviction, but shall be by a preponderance of the evidence.

7. In case of conflict between the provisions of this addendum and any other provisions of the Lease or Rental Agreement, the provisions of the addendum shall govern.

________	______________________	________	______________________
Date	Owner/Agent	Date	Tenant

Form 16-1: Crime- and Drug-Free Housing Addendum.

Although describing your building's security devices can be an effective marketing technique, you must take care to avoid inadvertently increasing your liability. The problem arises when you represent or even imply that your rental property is safer and more secure than other properties. If you make those kinds of claims, it had better live up to your statements. In reality, crime can happen anywhere, and no rental property is immune.

Exclude the words *safe, secure, security,* or any variations from your vocabulary and all advertising and marketing materials. Don't use these words in your advertising, on the phone, or when showing your rental property, because if your tenant ever becomes a crime victim he will certainly claim that your ads or comments gave him the expectation of security. Be honest with people, but be sure they understand that neither you nor the law enforcement officials can guarantee any level of safety or security for them, their family and guests, or their personal possessions or vehicles. When discussing any building features, be sure to speak generically without embellishment. For example, if you happen to have an alarm device in your rental unit, do not refer to it as a "security protection system" or add or imply that they will be safe and secure because of this or any other building feature.

Make sure that you test any alarm, demonstrate the proper use of all security devices in the presence of the tenants, and have them sign an acknowledgement. Remind your tenants in writing to test these devices as they can fail or malfunction, and to call immediately for repairs or replacement.

Some rental property owners put disclaimers in their lease and rental agreements that say the owner is not responsible if a tenant suffers damage or an injury, regardless of the cause. Because they have this disclaimer in place, owners get careless and slow in responding to tenant complaints about lighting or malfunctioning doors or window locks. But what the property owners don't realize is that these disclaimers are almost certainly unenforceable. Many states have laws that invalidate these broad clauses that attempt to shift the owner's duty to properly maintain the premises in order to avoid responsibility for a tenant's injuries or damage. However, it is a good idea to include language in your lease or rental agreement informing tenants of the following:

- You have not promised security of any kind.
- The tenants acknowledge that you do not and cannot guarantee the safety or security of the tenants or their guests.
- You don't guarantee the effectiveness or operability of security devices.

See your local legal counsel for assistance in preparing the proper legal documentation.

Responding to crimes when they occur

If a serious or violent crime occurs at your property, be sure to give your tenants written notification as soon as possible, along with any warnings or safety tips provided by law enforcement. Some rental owners are concerned that telling tenants about crime at the property or in the immediate area will lead to increased vacancies. Although on occasion you indeed may lose a tenant this way, warning your tenants so that they can be more conscious of safety and security issues is important and helps prevent other similar crimes from occurring.

There are no specific rules about what crimes should be reported to your tenants. But you should notify them about any crime concerning physical attack or bodily injury, and also any attempted or actual rental unit break-ins, burglaries, or robberies. A random car break-in or minor isolated vandalism on the property usually does not rise to the level of notification unless there are repeated incidents. You can use a letter or memo to inform tenants about criminal activity, or larger rental properties can use the community newsletter or tenant meeting as a forum for discussing the issue.

The written notification should be dated and tell your tenants that a crime has occurred. Be sure to include any information, composite sketches, or safety tips provided by law enforcement. Do not include the victim's name or address unless they have requested that you do so or unless you have advance approval. Remind tenants to be careful regarding security and safety and to call law enforcement immediately if they suspect a crime. Also, remind tenants that security is their responsibility. And be extremely careful that you, your onsite manager, or any other employees avoid making any statements that could be used against you in any future legal action.

You have personal information on your tenants, including where they live and work, what cars they drive, and all of their personal identification and financial information. You have a tremendous responsibility to keep this information confidential. Have a policy of not providing any information to anyone unless the tenant has specifically given you advance written authorization. You must also securely lock all of your property and tenant files in unlabeled file drawers to prevent intruders from rifling through these documents to target vulnerable tenants, such as the elderly or single women. You may also want to consider eliminating tenant rosters, or at least limiting the information to only their last names on controlled access directories. See your mail carrier about putting the tenant's names only on the inside of the mailbox.

Taking Security Precautions

One of the best ways to keep crime from occurring at your rental property is to make security a top priority. In this section, I cover some important security issues worth considering, not only for the safety of your property but for your tenants' well-being, too.

You can't guarantee your tenants that your property will be safe. But you can and should do what you can to increase the likelihood that they'll be free of problems.

Keys and access-control systems

Rental unit locks are useless as security devices when there's no effective control over keys. Some properties have a master key system where one single key works on all locks. Although this is convenient, I strongly recommend against using a master key system, because one lost key can require you to completely rekey the entire property. Instead, use a duplicate key system with different keys for each lock.

Always arrange to have someone you know provide needed access to contractors or suppliers rather than giving them a key.

All owner or manager keys should be kept in a metal locking key cabinet or key safe. The keys should not be labeled with the tenant's address or unit number but should be coded so that if they become lost or are stolen they cannot easily be used. If a tenant reports a lost or missing key, change or rekey the lock rather than just giving him a duplicate key, unless they are sure the key is irretrievably lost. Charge the tenant a reasonable fee to cover your costs of getting a new key made.

Although you must always change or rekey all entry locks upon tenant turnover, some tenants will want to change, rekey, or install additional locks. This is fine as long as they give you a duplicate key so that you can enter the rental unit during emergencies and to make agreed-on repairs. If you become aware that a lock has been added or changed, verbally explain your policy and request a copy of the key. If the tenant doesn't want to give you a copy of the new key, send a polite but firm letter informing him of your policy. Ultimately, you may need to consider eviction if you aren't able to get a copy of the key.

More sophisticated card key and other access control systems are now available and regularly used in the hospitality industry. When combined with full-perimeter fencing, these card systems can be effective in controlling access as long as your tenants cooperate and do not let anyone follow them in. Unfortunately, these systems are generally not cost-effective except for larger rental properties.

Be sure to invalidate any lost or stolen card keys.

Access control is an important element of building security that is benefiting from improvements in technology. New systems will soon be affordable for the owners of small rental properties. I have personally installed smart card access-control systems with great success. Smart cards are the size of a credit card and contain a small microchip that provides a unique identification number that is almost impossible to forge. Smart card readers can be installed at all access control points on the property, such as vehicle and pedestrian gates, as well as common area facilities. Another great feature of smart cards is that, with the use of an ATM-type station, they can store monetary value and be used for laundry machines, tennis court lights, or any other amenity that you want to charge for or control.

In addition to keys and/or access-control systems, use standard rental unit security devices such as deadbolts (preferably with a minimum 1-inch throw) and locking passage sets. All wood entry doors should be solid core and have wide-angle peepholes or door viewers. Window locks and safety pins for all sliding glass doors or even simple wood doweling for window tracks are also extremely cost-effective yet valuable security devices. Make sure that your tenant initials that all these security devices are operative on her move-in checklist and knows to contact you immediately if any locks or security devices are inoperative. Repair any broken locks or security devices immediately upon being notified.

Make sure that any security devices you install are easy to operate and difficult to disable. A determined criminal can clearly break in to any rental community, but you want to make your property a more difficult target. Also, avoid installing security devices that create an illusion of security, because they can actually lower a tenant's guard and make him more vulnerable to crimes. For example, don't install phony security cameras or monitors in an attempt to deter criminal activity. Courts have routinely held that if such security measures are installed, the owner is required to employ the appropriate staff to oversee them. ***Remember:*** You are in the rental housing business, not in the business of installing security services.

Lighting

Outdoor lighting has many benefits. Proper lighting is an extremely cost-effective way to protect your property and your tenants. It can serve as a deterrent to vandalism while illuminating your building walkways and the common areas to help prevent injuries to tenants and guests. The right lighting plan can also beautify your buildings and improve your property curb appeal.

Lighting is only effective if it is operative, properly located, and has the right type of fixture and light bulb for the intended purpose.

To keep your property well lit, replace any exterior lighting on clock timers with photocells that automatically detect darkness. This eliminates the need to constantly adjust the timers as the daylight hours vary with the seasons, plus photocells will turn on the exterior lights on dark stormy days. You can easily inspect and test your lights during the day by blocking the photocell sensor with tape to simulate darkness and cause the lights to go on.

Establish a regular schedule for inspecting the common area exterior lighting and immediately repair broken fixtures and replace any bulbs that are out. The best method for inspecting and testing your lights is at night, when you can see that all fixtures are working properly and providing sufficient illumination in the correct locations. Proper lighting in parking lots is very important because many of your tenants will routinely use the parking areas after dark. Be sure to log your lighting inspections and repairs or bulb replacement in your maintenance records.

Security firms

Most owners of small rental properties do not need onsite security firms or even random patrols of their property. However, if you own rental properties in areas where security firms are needed, there are generally two common types of security services offered: standing guard or drive-through service. Standing guard services can be quite expensive, particularly if you use it full-time. A drive-through and property lock-up service that makes a predetermined number of random checks of the premises each evening (either strictly by vehicle or also on foot) and includes securing of common area facilities is another less expensive alternative.

If you need a security service, you may want to have guard services part-time, with a schedule that constantly shifts the days and hours of the guards. This way, you're balancing the high cost of security guards with a limited, but random schedule to keep the criminal element deterred and guessing. Another option is having standing guards on some shifts interspersed with drive-throughs.

If you decide to hire a security firm, carefully interview and screen the company, including the actual guards that will be assigned to your property. Always reserve the right to request a different guard, and make sure they understand your expectations and behavior guidelines, including a strict policy against socializing with tenants.

Check their references and the status of all required state and local licenses or permits, including a business license, security protection firm permits, or guard cards. Require a current certificate of insurance with general liability coverage of at least $3 million, with both you (the owner) and your rental property manager (if you have one) named as additional insureds. You also must be notified at least 30 days in advance of any lapse in coverage. Require proof of workers' compensation and employer's liability insurance, plus auto liability insurance and a fidelity bond.

Your agreement should be in writing and should clearly indicate that the security firm is an independent contractor. The agreement should also have a short termination notice requirement, because service from security firms can deteriorate very quickly.

Avoid armed guards unless absolutely necessary for your area. If a security firm indicates that armed guards are required for your area, immediately contact local law enforcement for confirmation of that opinion. And think seriously about whether you want to own this type of property in the first place.

Local law enforcement officers in some areas are allowed to offer their off-duty services to patrol your property, and some are even allowed to take their law enforcement vehicles home at night. This can be a powerful deterrent to the criminally inclined; however, you need to be extremely careful in establishing any such arrangement. Even if you offer a rent discount, you should use your standard lease or rental agreement. But you should add an addendum that clearly indicates the officer is an independent contractor, and outline the general services provided and the exact financial terms. Consult with your legal counsel to draft the proper legal documents. See Chapter 17 for more information on working with independent contractors.

Addressing Environmental Issues

Although crime is usually the first safety concern that come to mind for rental property owners, important tenant safety topics also include fire protection, environmental challenges, and the potential for natural disasters.

Fire safety

Fire safety is a critical issue for rental owners. Every year several thousand Americans die in fires and over 100,000 are injured. Fires can spread quickly and fully engulf a room or even an entire rental unit in a matter of minutes. The fire also produces poisonous gases and smoke that are disorienting and deadly.

Work with your local fire department to develop an evacuation plan for your property, including written notification to authorities of any rental units occupied by tenants with children, or tenants with physical or mental challenges who may require assistance in an emergency.

Fire inspections are conducted regularly in most areas; when your property is inspected, you will receive written notification of any deficiencies. These noted items must be addressed immediately, and you must contact the appropriate officials in writing to acknowledge that the items have been corrected and to request a reinspection. Be sure to get written confirmation that all items have been satisfactorily corrected.

In some areas, rental owners are required by law to provide fire extinguishers and to properly inspect and service or recharge them upon rental unit turnover. A multipurpose dry chemical fire extinguisher can be a valuable and effective tool to quickly extinguish a small fire. If not required by law, evaluate your potential liability in the event the fire extinguisher is defective, used improperly, or even improperly maintained by your tenant. If your tenant gets hurt because the fire extinguisher you provided wasn't working properly when she needed it, you could be held liable and be sued. Your local fire department will often offer your tenants instruction on the proper use of extinguishers.

Fires are always serious, but the most dangerous fires are the ones that start while the tenants are asleep. That is one of the reasons that virtually all states require rental owners to install smoke detectors in all rental units. Even if not legally required in your area, I strongly recommend installing smoke detectors in all rental unit hallways and near or preferably just inside all sleeping areas in compliance with local fire codes and the manufacturer's specifications.

Always inspect and test the smoke detector according to the manufacturer's instructions upon tenant turnover. If a fire hurts a tenant because the smoke detector wasn't working properly when he moved in, you could be sued and held responsible. So be sure to keep written records of your inspection and testing of the smoke detector and have your tenant initial his lease indicating that the smoke detector was tested in his presence and that he can perform his own tests.

Also, be sure to immediately address all tenant requests for smoke detector inspections and repairs. These requests should be noted in your maintenance log along with the date that the smoke detector was repaired or replaced. If the tenant is present, have him sign acknowledging that the smoke detector now works properly. Smoke detector complaints are always a top priority requiring immediate attention, so keep new smoke detectors on hand for this reason.

Carbon monoxide

Carbon monoxide, a colorless, odorless, and poisonous gas produced when fuel burns incompletely, can quickly build up in a rental unit in just hours. If the leak occurs when the tenants are asleep, they could easily lose consciousness and suffer a serious injury or even die before noticing anything was wrong.

Appliances such as natural gas and oil furnaces, gas water heaters, wood-burning stoves, fireplaces, and gas or kerosene space heaters can all emit carbon monoxide. When these appliances are working properly, the carbon monoxide is vented to the chimney or other venting system and there is no danger. However, if the appliances or fireplace are not vented properly, then carbon monoxide can build up within a rental unit.

Naturally, carbon monoxide poisoning is a particular concern for rental owners with properties in cold weather areas of the country where tenants rely on one of these appliances to heat their rental unit. Carbon monoxide detectors are only legally required in certain areas; however, I strongly advise installing a carbon monoxide detector if your rental unit has a fireplace or uses carbon monoxide-producing heating appliances. Even if you don't, have your onsite manager and maintenance personnel look out for any tenant misuse of a portable gas or kerosene heater, because they are major cause of carbon monoxide poisonings and death.

Take steps to have a professional from your oil or natural gas supplier inspect all heating systems annually in the fall. If they do not offer this service, hire a professional heating appliance repair company. If you have fireplaces, you need to have a chimney cleaning company periodically inspect your chimney, chimney connections, and insulation for cracks, blockages, or leaks. Have the recommended work done as soon as possible and quickly respond to any complaints from tenants about possible carbon monoxide poisoning.

Electromagnetic fields

Electromagnetic fields (EMFs) are a relatively new environmental hazard with varying scientific opinions regarding the potential danger to humans. Electric power lines, electrical wiring, and even appliances all create some level of EMFs. Although the forces created by these sources is minimal when compared to even the normal electrical activity found within the human body, scientists cannot agree definitively as to whether exposure to EMFs can or does increase a person's chance of developing certain types of cancer, particularly childhood leukemia.

This potential problem is well beyond your control, but although there is little conclusive scientific evidence that EMFs cause cancer, you should be aware of this issue in case you receive a tenant complaint. The bottom line is that because you cannot insist that the electric utility remove its power lines and transmitters, the only viable solution for a tenant with legitimate concerns about EMFs is to move. Evaluate the legitimacy of your tenant's concerns to determine if it is in your mutual best interest to release a tenant from his lease.

Natural disasters

Every area of the U.S. experiences its own set of challenges from Mother Nature. Make sure that you and your tenants are prepared for whatever natural disaster may be possible at your rental property. Every state and many local jurisdictions have emergency preparedness offices that can provide information and tips so that you and your tenants can take the appropriate steps now, before an emergency happens. You can find these offices in the front of your local telephone directory.

The Federal Emergency Management Agency (FEMA) has many great resources available online to identify and assess your risk to hazards that could potentially impact you and your community. They even have a Hazard Information and Awareness section that allows you to see exactly what natural disasters or hazards have occurred historically in your area. Visit the FEMA Web site at `www.fema.gov`.

In many parts of the country, snow and ice accumulations can create dangerous conditions. Many areas have state or local laws that require owners to remove snow and ice from walkways or driveways, whereas others don't. However, in most states, you are not responsible if a tenant slips and falls on natural accumulations of snow and ice.

Part V
Money, Money, Money!

"In going over your figures, you calculated your rental property has depreciated 9 percent over the year. However, by trying to do your own taxes, we've calculated your brain has depreciated by nearly 72 percent."

In this part . . .

Keeping track of your money is important no matter what business you're in, but it's especially important in property management. In the chapters in this part, I make two not-so-fun issues you'll have to deal with as a rental property owner — insurance and taxes — easy to understand. I also give you some great tips for keeping records and managing your finances. So for all issues monetary, read on.

Chapter 17

Two Necessities of Property Management: Insurance and Taxes

In This Chapter

- Insuring yourself against loss and liability
- Wading through the tax laws

As a rental property owner, two of the major financial responsibilities you have to deal with are insurance and taxes. Getting into the game knowing the rules ahead of time is the best way to play, and in this chapter, I let you know what to expect.

Cover Me, I'm Going In!: Making Sure You Have the Insurance You Need

There are insurance companies that will sell you coverage against any possible danger or loss in the world. And a sharp insurance agent is a master at describing all sorts of horrible problems that could befall your rental property. If you want to make sure you're covered at a reasonable cost, you need to sift through the sales pitch and decide which coverage is right for you. ***Remember:*** Your goal is to pay only for coverage for events and losses that are most likely to occur at your property. The right insurance coverage is worth a lot, but buying hurricane insurance in Minnesota may not make a whole lot of sense.

You also need to be concerned about lawsuits and having the proper insurance coverage to defend yourself and protect your assets. According to a recent national study by Liability Consultants, a national consulting firm for security issues, apartment complexes were sued more than any other type of business entity with allegations regarding inadequate premises security (see Figure 17-1).

As intimidating as these statistics may be, you'll most likely be okay if you have sound ownership and management policies combined with an insurance coverage program that has been customized for your specific needs.

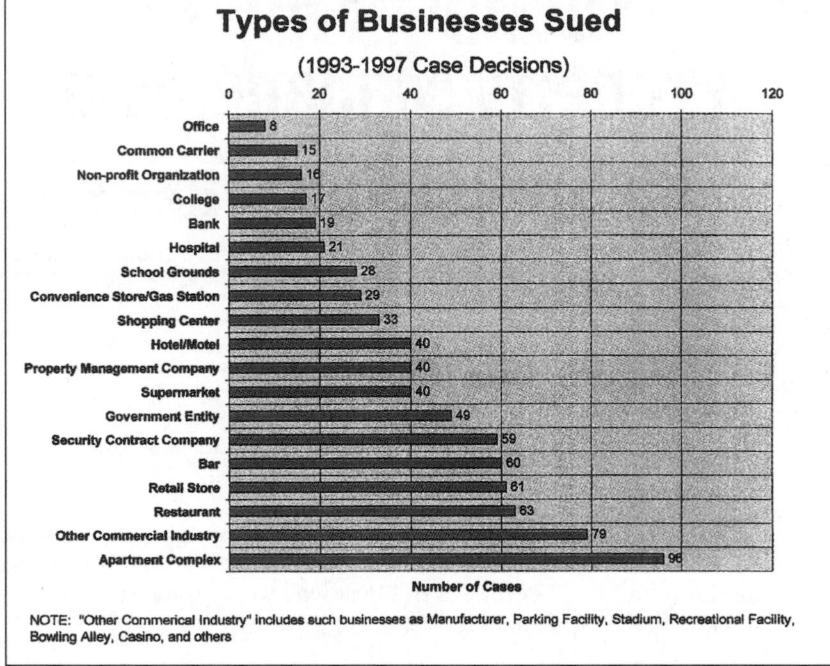

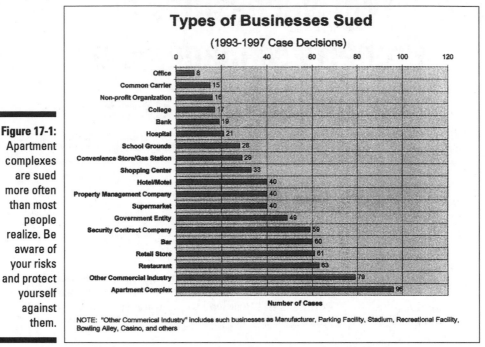

Figure 17-1: Apartment complexes are sued more often than most people realize. Be aware of your risks and protect yourself against them.

© Liability Consultants, Inc.

Knowing the difference between the different types of insurance coverage you can get

One of the first steps in getting the right insurance is understanding the different types of insurance that are available. The proper insurance coverage can protect you from losses caused by many perils, including fire, storms, burglary, and vandalism. A comprehensive policy also includes liability insurance, covering injuries or losses suffered by others as the result of defective conditions on the property. Liability insurance also covers the legal costs of defending personal injury lawsuits; because legal defense costs are commonly much greater than the ultimate award of damages, if any, this is a valuable feature.

The coverage you can get as a rental property owner varies from insurance company to insurance company. Be sure to interview and select a qualified insurance broker or agent who understands your unique needs. The insurance professional can then provide you with information on the kinds of coverage worth considering.

When selecting an insurance company, look at the company's ratings and its reputation for quickly and fairly handling and paying claims. Although there are several rating firms, the most widely known is A.M. Best Company. The top companies have an A or preferably an A+ or A++ rating (A++ is as high as the scale goes). You can visit A.M. Best online at `www.ambest.com` and search for ratings on insurance companies you're considering.

Insurance professionals are either independent brokers or exclusive agents that just write policies for one company. Talk with an insurance broker and a couple of company agents to ensure that you are receiving the insurance coverage you need at the best value. Keep in mind that the lowest premium is often not the best policy for your needs. Ask a lot of questions, and insist on evidence that the insurance company has provided coverage with a *written binder* as soon as you have coverage; your best proof of coverage is a formal certificate of insurance.

Basic, broad-form, and special-form coverage

Most insurance companies offer a basic coverage package that insures your rental property against loss from fire, lightning, explosion, windstorm or hail, smoke, aircraft or vehicles, riot or civil commotion, vandalism, sprinkler leakage, and even volcanic action. This coverage often does not include certain contents, such as boilers, equipment, and machinery unless specifically added as an endorsement. They will also offer you a *broad-form coverage,* in which you get all of the basic package, plus protection against losses of glass breakage, falling objects, weight of snow or ice, water damage associated with plumbing systems, and collapse from certain specific causes.

The broadest coverage available is *special form,* which covers your property against all losses, except those specifically excluded from the policy. This coverage offers the highest level of protection but is typically more expensive. Many insurance companies, however, offer competitive insurance packages especially designed to meet the needs of rental owners, so remember to shop around.

Flood, hurricane, and earthquake insurance are examples of coverage available for a separate cost. This coverage can be critical in the event of a natural disaster. However, these policies often are very expensive with extremely high deductibles, making them uneconomical for the average small rental property owner. Get quotes nonetheless, and see whether it's something you think you can afford.

Seriously consider replacement cost coverage. An insurance company can pay owners for losses in two ways: *actual cash value* pays the cost of replacing property less physical depreciation; *replacement cost* pays the cost of replacing the property without subtracting for physical depreciation. The standard policies most insurance companies offer provide for actual cash value coverage only, and you must specifically have an endorsement and pay extra for replacement cost coverage.

If you decide to rent out your personal residence, immediately contact your insurance agent and have your homeowner's policy converted to a landlord's policy. A landlord's policy contains special coverage riders that are not in the typical homeowner's policy. Because of the increased liability risk for rental properties, your current insurance company may not even offer this coverage. Certain insurance companies specialize in this business. Either way, make sure that you have proper landlord's coverage for your rental property, or you could face the possibility of having your claim denied.

If you own multiple rental units, you may receive discounts if you have a single insurance policy that covers all locations. Rather than have separate policies for each rental property, you will also be able to get better coverage. For example, if you currently have three properties each with a $1 million policy, you could get a single policy with a $3 million limit at a more competitive cost. This would provide up to $3 million in coverage for each property. You could also benefit if you have an *aggregate deductible,* which is the portion of your loss that you essentially self-insure, because the losses at any of your three properties could be used towards meeting the aggregate deductible.

Umbrella coverage

Umbrella coverage can be a very cost-effective way to dramatically increase your liability exposure and is designed to supplement your other policies. Your primary policy may have liability limits of $500,000, but an umbrella policy can provide an additional $1 million in vital coverage at a reasonable cost. Depending on the value of your property and the value of the assets you are seeking to protect, buying an umbrella liability policy with higher limits makes sense.

Get your umbrella policy with the same company that handles your underlying liability insurance or you may find that there are conflicting strategies on how best to defend you in litigation.

Other insurance coverage

A variety of other insurance coverage options makes sense for certain rental property owners. For example, a policy that includes *loss-of-rents coverage* would provide income if your property is uninhabitable due to fire or other calamity and allow you to continue making your mortgage and other payments.

Paying attention to coinsurance clauses

Some insurance companies have a *coinsurance clause* that requires rental property owners to carry a minimum amount of coverage. If you carry less than the minimum amount of coverage, the insurance company will impose a coinsurance penalty that comes out of your recovery. Coinsurance penalties reduce the payment on the loss by the same percentage of the insurance shortfall.

If you carry only $1 million in coverage when you should have $2 million, you are only carrying 50 percent of the minimum required insured value. If the building suffers a loss, the insurance company will only pay 50 percent of the loss.

If you will have any maintenance or management employees assisting you with your rental activities, consider having *non-owned auto liability coverage.* This coverage protects you from liability for accidents and injuries caused by your employees while working and using their own vehicles.

A *fidelity bond* will provide reimbursement if you have a dishonest employee who steals your rents. An *endorsement for money and securities* can protect you from losses occasioned by the dishonest acts of non-employees.

Another important coverage is *building ordinance,* which protects you in the event your rental property is partially or fully destroyed. It covers the costs of demolition and cleanup, plus the increased costs to rebuild if the property needs to meet new or stricter building code requirements.

Don't assume that all potential losses are covered by your insurance coverage. Your best defense against losses is to properly manage your rentals and assertively eliminate, transfer, or control the inherent risks of owning and managing rental property.

Determining the right deductible

A *deductible* is the amount of money that you must pay out-of-pocket before your insurance coverage kicks in. Deductibles generally range from $250 to $500 or even $1,000. The higher the deductible, the lower your insurance premium will be.

Evaluate the possibility of having a higher deductible and using your savings to purchase other important coverage.

Letting your tenants know about renter's insurance

Renter's insurance is something your tenants get and pay for themselves; it covers losses to the tenant's personal property as a result of fire, theft, water damage, or other loss. Tenants often think they do not need renter's insurance because they have few valuables, but renter's insurance covers much more than just their personal possessions. It also provides protection against claims made by injured guests or visitors. The insurance offers supplemental living expenses if the rental unit becomes uninhabitable due to fire or smoke damage. And it protects the tenant in the event that the tenant causes damage to another tenant's property.

As a rental property owner, you benefit from renter's insurance because it covers any claims in the event that the tenant starts a fire or flood. The tenant's premiums go up instead of yours.

Be sure to have a clause in your rental agreement that clearly points out the requirement that every tenant must have his or her own renter's insurance policy. Depending on the policy limits, renter policies typically cost from $100 to $300 per year with deductible amounts of $250 or $500. As with car insurance, the insurance company only pays for losses over and above the deductible amount.

The importance of renter's insurance was reinforced early in my management career when there was a bad fire at one of the properties I managed. Apparently, a new tenant was getting help from the "six-pack movers" — friends that assist with the move in exchange for a six-pack of their favorite beverage. The fire started when the new tenant's friend negligently placed a box of paper goods right on top of the gas-stove pilot light. Luckily, no one was seriously injured, but 12 of 16 rental units were completely destroyed. None of the tenants had renter's insurance, and even the innocent neighbors lost everything they owned. Although legally you can point to the fact that each and every one of the tenants had initialed the rental agreement clause indicating they should have renter's insurance, facing tenants who have just lost everything because they didn't get around to buying renter's insurance is still difficult.

Handling potential claims

Immediately document all facts when you have an incident occur on your rental property, particularly if it involves injury. Use the Incident Report Form (like the one shown in Form 17-1) to record all the facts. Be sure to immediately contact your insurance company or your insurance agent. Follow up with a written letter to ensure they were notified and have the information on file.

The Tax Man Cometh: Knowing Which Taxes You're Responsible for Paying

Taxation laws regarding investment real estate are unique and far more complex than those regarding homeownership. If you're just starting out in property management and you're confused by tax laws, you're not alone. Because tax laws can work for or against real estate investors, you need to have a general understanding of the basic concepts.

Tax laws change frequently, so be sure to check with your tax advisor before taking any action. Use a certified public accountant (CPA) or tax specialist to prepare your tax returns if you have investment real estate.

Income taxes

Taxpayers generally have two types of income: ordinary income and capital gains. *Ordinary income* includes wages, bonuses and commissions, rents, dividends, and interest and is taxed at various rates up to 39.6 percent. *Capital gains* is income generated when possessions are sold for a profit, including real estate and stock. Capital gains are classified as *short-term* (12 months or less) or *long-term.* Short-term capital gains are taxed at the same rate as ordinary income. Long-term gains are taxed at lower rates than ordinary income with a maximum of 20 percent. The taxable income you receive from your rental property is subject to taxation as ordinary income. The positive cash flow is determined by deducting all operating expenses, debt service interest, capital improvement expenses, damages, theft, and depreciation from rental income.

One of the advantages to owning real estate is the ability to deduct all operating expenses from your rental income. These operating expenses include payroll, maintenance and repair costs, management fees, utilities, advertising costs, insurance, property taxes, and interest paid on mortgage debt.

You don't have to pay taxes on security deposits received until they become income. When received, the security deposits are a liability that must be paid back to the tenants at a later time. However, after your tenant vacates and you withhold a portion of the security deposit, it may become classified as income. Essentially, the security deposit is not taxable as long as you have an expense for the same amount as the deduction. For example, if you deduct $300 from a tenant's security deposit in order to paint the rental unit, and if you actually hire a painter for $300, then you don't owe any taxes on that $300 you retained. But if you deducted $300 and then did the work yourself for $100, you owe taxes on the $200 difference, which is classified as income.

Incident Report

Date ________ Time ________ Name of Reporting Person ____________________
Date of Incident ________ Time of Incident ________ Property ________________
Specific Location of Incident ____

Type of Incident: Accident ____ Crime ____ Fire ____ Police ____ Paramedic ____
Mechanical ____ Theft ____ Flood ____ Other ____________________________

Details of what happened: ____
____
____
____

Details of injury/damages: ____
____
____
____

Names, addresses, phone numbers of people involved: ______________________
____
____

Names, addresses, phone numbers of witnesses: __________________________
____
____

Specific conditions at time of incident: _________________________________
____
____
____

Name of insurance company ______________________ Policy number ____________
Name, address and phone number of insurance agent: _______________________
____
Date and time insurance company notified ______________ By phone ___ By mail ___

Request from/permission granted by insurance company to document incident: Yes or No
If yes, how: Photos ____ Video ____ Audio ____ Written statements ____________

Date and time police/paramedic notified: ________________________________
Time of police/paramedic arrival: ________________ Report number ____________

Follow-up required/taken: ____
____

Form 17-1: Incident Report Form.

Understanding passive and active activity

Rental property owners often start out with their real estate activities serving as a second income. They typically generate the majority of their income from professions and sources totally unrelated to real estate. The taxation rules that apply to these part-time real estate investors are different than the ones that apply to real estate professionals. Unless you qualify as a real estate professional, the IRS classifies all real estate activities as *passive* and sets limits on your ability to claim real estate loss deductions.

The IRS has defined a *real estate professional* as a person who performs at least 50 percent of his or her services in businesses related to real estate or spends at least 750 hours per year in these endeavors. These individuals are considered *active investors* and are allowed to claim all their real estate loss deductions in the year incurred. All others are considered *passive investors,* and they are subject to limitations on the deductibility of their real estate loss deductions. However, if you're a passive investor, you may still be able to use rental property losses to shelter ordinary income if you are "actively involved" in the management of your rental property. According to the IRS, you're *actively involved* if you oversee or approve the setting of rent, the approval of tenants, and decisions about capital improvements.

This doesn't mean, however, that you can't hire a property management company to handle the day-to-day activities while you oversee their efforts.

If you meet the IRS standard of "actively involved," you can take a rental property loss deduction up to $25,000 against other income in the current tax year, as long as your adjusted gross income does not exceed $100,000. If your adjusted gross income exceeds $100,000, you will be denied 50 cents of the loss allowance for every dollar over $100,000 so that the entire $25,000 loss allowance disappears at an adjusted gross income of $150,000. Any losses disallowed in one year can be saved and applied to reduce rental or other passive income in future years. If the losses cannot be used in this manner, you will be able to use them when you sell your property to effectively reduce the taxable gain. Thus, the losses will ultimately benefit you.

Taking advantage of depreciation

Depreciation is one expense that allows you to shelter positive cash flow from taxation. Depreciation is an accounting concept that allows you the right to claim as a deduction a certain portion of the value of a rental property just because you own it, with no relationship to whether it is actually wearing out or losing value. Depreciation lowers your income taxes in the current year by essentially providing a government interest-free loan until the property is sold.

Before 1993, depreciation could be accelerated in the early years of rental property ownership, but under current tax laws, recently acquired rental properties can only use *straight-line depreciation.* Straight-line depreciation reduces the value of the rental property by set equal amounts each year over its established economic life. The period of time during which depreciation is taken is called the *recovery period.* Currently, the IRS has established that residential rental property has a recovery period of 27.5 years, and owners are required to use straight-line depreciation and deduct a depreciation loss of 1/27.5 or about 3.64 percent each year. Depreciation is prorated for the first or last year of ownership.

Depreciation is only allowed for the value of the buildings; land is not depreciable. Often, you can use the property tax assessor's allocation between the value of your buildings and land to determine the appropriate basis for calculating depreciation.

Using tax-deferred exchanges to your benefit

A *tax-deferred exchange* is an important tool if you're looking to increase the size of your real estate holdings. You can defer taxation of capital gains by effectively exchanging one property for another. Therefore, you can keep exchanging upward in value, adding to your assets over your lifetime without ever having to pay any capital gains tax.

Section 1031 of the Internal Revenue Code allows exchanges, sometimes called *Starker exchanges,* that permit the postponement of capital-gains tax payment when another property of like-kind is purchased within a specified time period. The tax is deferred, not eliminated. The IRS defines *like-kind property* for real estate purposes as any property held for business, trade, or investment purposes. This broad definition allows real estate investors to use a Section 1031 exchange to defer taxes when they sell an apartment building and buy raw land, or vice versa.

There are several basic rules for the 1031 exchange:

- **The sale property and the purchase property must both be investment real estate located in the United States.**
- **A neutral third party, called a *facilitator, exchanger,* or *accommodator,* must be appointed prior to the closing of any escrow, an exchange agreement must be signed, and the neutral third party must hold the proceeds unless the properties close simultaneously.**
- **The potential purchase property must be identified within 45 days from the close of the sale property.**
- **The price of the purchase property must be equal to or higher than the amount of the sale property, with all mortgages equal to or more than the balance of the mortgage on the sale property.**
- **The closing of the purchase property must occur within 180 days of the close of the sale property.**

Recently, the IRS has issued new guidelines that will allow a reverse Section 1031 exchange. This allows real estate investors to purchase their new investment property first and then follow the 1031 guidelines and close on the sale property within the 180-day limitation while deferring any capital gains tax.

Property taxes

Local municipality and governmental agencies generally receive a major portion of their operating funds by taxing real estate within their jurisdictions. Typically, property taxes are an *ad valorem* tax (based on the property's value). In certain areas of the country, improvement districts have been established with special assessments *in addition to* the property tax obligations. These taxes are usually flat fees or based on square footage as opposed to the property's value.

Naturally, problems can arise in determining the value to place on a property. Real estate is valued, or *assessed,* for real estate taxation purposes by governmental tax assessors or appraisers. The public assessor or appraiser is responsible for determining a market value for each property in a jurisdiction. The *market value* of a property is the price the property would most likely sell for in a competitive market.

The assessor often uses the sales comparison or market approach to valuation, which uses the most recent sale of a given property and/or recent sales of comparable properties. However, there are three basic methods to estimating the fair market value of a property: the sales comparison or market approach, the cost approach, and the income approach. Appraisers and assessors will often use each method to serve as a check against the others and narrow the ranges within which the final estimate of value will fall.

The building and land are appraised separately, and most states have laws that require the property to be periodically reassessed or revalued. A tax or mill rate is then applied to the assessed value to determine the actual tax billed to the property owner. The higher the assessed value of your property, the higher your property tax bill will be. Property taxes are typically due in two semiannual installments, and unpaid taxes or special assessments become liens on the property.

You may feel helpless against the property tax bureaucracy in your area, but remember that tax assessors have been known to make clerical errors or fail to take all pertinent factors into account when placing a value on your rental property. If you feel that your property assessment is too high, contact you local tax assessor. The assessor may be willing to make an adjustment if you can back up your opinion with careful research and a good presentation. Or you may need to make a formal property tax protest. Tax protests are often first heard within the tax assessor's office or a local board of appeal. If a dispute still exists, appeals may be taken to court in many states.

If real estate values decline in your area, contact your local assessor and inquire about getting a reassessment. A lower assessment will lead to a direct reduction in your property tax bill and a corresponding increase in your cash flow.

Many municipalities have implemented business license or rental unit taxes for rental property owners. Sometimes these resources are used to finance code enforcement or mandatory inspections of some or all rental properties. But these special taxes may just generate revenue for the general fund. Be sure you have contacted your local government to ensure that you are meeting all of their specific requirements. The licensing or rental taxes are high enough, but the fines and penalties can be extreme.

Chapter 18

Financial Management and Recordkeeping

In This Chapter

- Setting up a filing system to keep track of your paperwork
- Hanging on to the records you need for the right amount of time
- Taking advantage of computer software to help you with your accounting

If you asked a group of rental property owners their least favorite part of the job, you'd probably hear "the paperwork" more than any other response. Most owners don't mind the hands-on aspects of managing their properties, like cleaning or painting the rental unit; many of them even enjoy it. And meeting rental prospects and showing the property is fun compared to recording rents, sending out late notices, and writing checks to pay the bills. But the financial management aspects of accounting for all the funds you receive and expend are critical elements of running your rental housing venture. In this chapter, I show you how to get a handle on it.

Organizing Your Files

If you have an aversion to keeping track of documents, then managing your own rental properties may not be for you. If you own rental property, you need to prepare many important written records and keep them ready for prompt retrieval. Every rental property owner must have a basic filing system with separate records kept for each rental property.

If you own one or even a few rental units, your filing system can be a simple accordion filing box with dividers, available at any office supply store. If you own more properties and outgrow the accordion filing box, moving up to a filing cabinet (preferable one that is lockable) makes sense.

From the moment you take your first steps towards purchasing an investment property, begin storing your paperwork in a property ownership file. Keep all the important documents of this transaction, including purchase offers and contracts, the closing statement, appraisals, loan documents, insurance policies, due diligence inspection and pest control reports, and correspondence. Also keep a photocopy of your deed in the property file, and place the original in a fireproof safe or bank safety deposit box.

Each of your rental properties should have its own file section with separate folders for income items as well as a separate folder for each of the property expense categories. Keep copies of all receipts in the expense folders, so that when tax time rolls around, you can easily locate the information you need.

I recommend keeping a master maintenance file for the records and receipts for all maintenance and capital improvements of each rental unit. This will give you a history of the physical condition of each rental unit throughout your ownership of it.

In addition to having a file for expenses and income, create a tenant file for each rental unit that contains all the important documents for each specific tenant, including his rental application, lease or rental agreement, and all other legal notices, tenant maintenance requests, and correspondence. Always keep the original of each document and provide the tenant with a photocopy.

You may opt to keep many of these files on your computer, but for owners of only a few rental units, a manual system will work just fine.

Use a system for recording all significant tenant complaints and maintenance requests. This will provide a valuable paper trail if a dispute ever arises regarding your conduct as an owner in properly maintaining the premises. Failing to have good records could very well result in a court dispute being determined solely on your word against your tenant's word — and the odds aren't good under such circumstances.

When your tenants vacate, attach a copy of their Security Deposit Itemization report and bind the entire tenant file together. Transfer it to a separate file for all former tenants, filed alphabetically by rental property.

Insurance is such an important issue that you should have a master insurance file that contains current policies for all types of insurance coverage on all your rental policies. This file should also have a calendar in which you can track the expiration or renewal dates for each policy and ensure that you have requested competitive bids well in advance of the policy expiration date. Keeping accurate records of any incident reports or claims made against your insurance coverage is critical as well.

Maintaining Property Records

Maintaining complete and accurate records of all transactions is extremely important in the world of property management. Courts typically take the stance that tenants are merely consumers, so the burden is primarily on the owner to provide any documents outlining the relationship or understanding between the parties. If the owner cannot provide the required records, the tenant will almost always prevail.

But maintaining proper records is also important, because you have to report your income and expenses for each rental property on Schedule E to determine whether you have a profit. The Internal Revenue Service requires rental property owners to substantiate all income and expenses by maintaining proper records, including detailed receipts of all transactions. You don't want to be in a situation where you cannot support the accuracy of your tax returns.

Document your income on income journals, and keep all bank deposit slips. Rental property expenses, even if you write a business check, must have a written receipt to fully document the expenditure. The IRS may not accept a check as proof of a deductible property expense unless you have a detailed receipt as well.

If you have multiple rental properties, you can develop and assign a one- or two-character code for each property and mark each receipt accordingly. (Indicate the unit number, if appropriate.) When you have information for multiple properties on a single receipt, make photocopies and store the receipts in the folders you've set up for your respective properties. This way, you can provide evidence of the expense for each property instead of having to wade through all your folders looking for the information you need.

If you are using your vehicle for your rental property activities, be sure to keep a detailed written log of all your mileage. Your mileage is a deductible business expense as long as it is directly related to your rental property and you have accurate records to document the mileage. This simple log should indicate the date, destination, purpose, and total number of miles traveled. You may be surprised at the number of miles you travel each year in your rental activities — and the deductible expense can be substantial.

Keep all records pertaining to your rental property for a minimum of three to five years. (The time period depends on the legal requirements of the state regulatory commission or department of real estate where you live and/or own property.) Records regarding the purchase and capital improvements made during your ownership need to be maintained for as long as you own the property, for taxation purposes. Certain rental property records such as those concerning injuries to minors should be maintained forever. Although even the IRS has a statute of limitations, except in the case of fraud, there is no statute of limitation for injuries to minors. For example, if a young child is hurt on your property, the statute of limitations does not begin until the child has reached 18 years of age. In these cases, the tenancy records and maintenance records could be subpoenaed and critical to defending your actions of 20 years ago.

Taking Care of Business: Rental Property Accounting

The Internal Revenue Service does not require you to keep a separate checking account for each rental property that you own, but you do need to keep your rental property activities separate from your personal transactions.

If you only have a few rentals, you may be able to keep track of your tenants' rent payments in your head. But don't rely on your memory. Always track each rental payment in writing. If your tenants pay by check, you can always let the cancelled check serve as the tenant's receipt, but the best policy is to provide a receipt whenever possible, regardless of the method of payment.

Record any other income you may receive — from laundry, vending, parking, or furniture rental, for example.

Be sure you accurately record the payment of a tenant's security deposit. These funds are typically not considered income; instead, they are a future liability that is owed back to the tenant if the tenant honors the terms of the lease or rental agreement. The security deposit may become income at a later date, if you apply any portion of it to cover delinquent rent, cleaning, repairs, or other charges.

Although rental property accounting is fairly straightforward, you may not have the time or inclination to do it yourself. If you aren't prepared to handle your own accounting and record keeping, hire an accountant or a property management company to handle it for you. There are some property management firms willing to perform only rental property accounting services for a fee.

Creating a budget and managing your cash flow

Every rental property should have a budget. A *budget* is a detailed estimate of the future income and expenses of a property for a certain time period, usually one year. A budget allows you to anticipate and track the expected income and expenses for your rental property. Many rental owners neglect to allocate and hold back enough money for projected expenses, so when it comes time to make a repair, for example, they don't have the money set aside to cover it. But if you set up a budget, you'll be better able to anticipate your expenses.

Although the budget for a single-family or rental condo is fairly simple, a proper budget for a newly acquired multi-unit apartment building can require some careful planning. That planning will include a thorough review of past expenses and the current condition of the property. Trends in expenses, such as utilities, can also be important when estimating the future cash flow of a rental property, so be sure you don't overlook them.

Many owners rely on cash flow from their rental properties not only to cover their expenses but also to supplement their personal income. But particularly if you're a small rental property owner, you need to have a built-in reserve fund set aside before you start taking out any rental income funds for personal reasons. Maintain a reserve balance large enough to pay your mortgage and all the basic property expenses for *at least* one month without relying on any rental income.

Set up a bank account where you set aside money for anticipated major capital improvements. For example, you may own a rental property that will need a new roof in the next five years. Rather than see your cash flow wiped out for several months when it comes time to pay for that new roof, you can begin setting aside small amounts of money into a capital reserve account over several years.

Don't forget to allocate funds to cover semi-annual and annual expenses such as your property taxes and potential income tax due on your rental property net income.

Doing your accounting manually

Most rental property owners begin their real estate investing with a single rental home or condo. At this level, the accounting is extremely simple and can be done manually with pencil and paper in a simple spiral notebook or using an accountant's columnar pad. But when you expand to multiple rental units, you need to look for better and more efficient systems that are geared to the specific needs of rental property accounting.

The classic rental property manual accounting system is the pegboard that allows for a *one-write system,* in which each transaction is entered once using stacked carbonized documents. A single entry records information needed for a consecutively numbered rental receipt, the tenant's individual ledger card, a bank deposit ticket, and the daily journal that provides a master record of all transactions. This popular rental accounting system is available from Peachtree Business Products (800-241-4623 or `www.property.pbp1.com`).

Using computers for financial management

If you only have a handful of rental units, you can easily handle the property accounting with a manual system. But when you own at least four rental units, consider using a computer and a spreadsheet or general accounting software program.

Many basic software spreadsheet programs (such as Microsoft Excel) can handle a few rental units. Somewhat better are the general business accounting packages, such as the entry-level Quicken, and the more advanced QuickBooks or Peachtree Accounting. These programs can handle and streamline all the basic accounting requirements of managing a handful of rental units.

However, as good as these programs are, they lack the specific rental-housing industry information and reporting that are invaluable to effective property management. So I strongly recommend purchasing a professional rental accounting software program if you have more than ten rental units. These programs typically offer the following:

- Complete accounting (general ledger, accounts receivable, accounts payable with check writing, budgeting, and financial reporting)
- Tenant and lease management, including many standard rental management forms
- Tenant service requests, maintenance scheduling, and reminder notes
- Additional services such as tenant screening, payroll, and utility billing

When evaluating different software packages, gather as much information as possible. Be sure to talk to actual users of the product, preferably people in your area who have comparable rental properties and similar accounting needs. Determine what features the program offers, how easy the program is to operate, the computer hardware requirements, the availability and cost of technical support, and the strength and reputation of the company backing the product. Be sure to get a demo or trial version of the software that you can use before you buy, just to make sure it's what you want.

Many property management accounting packages are available for a nominal investment, but as with just about everything else in this world, you get what you pay for. Although many of the less expensive systems may work in the short run, if something goes wrong, you could be left stranded without technical support or help. If a software firm only has a few systems in place, there is a much higher risk of program errors or incorrect results. The software may not even be updated or supported at all years down the road. Your financial investment and all the timesaving and other significant benefits of computerized accounting may be lost if the software package is not backed by a solid company.

Another advantage to using the computerized rental property accounting software packages is the ability to have your mortgage and other bills deducted electronically. Or you can work with these software packages to pay your bills online. If your tenants pay their rent electronically as well, you can decrease the time you spend handling rent collection and accounting.

Although many different types of programs are available and each has it own strengths and weaknesses, I have found two programs that I highly recommend:

- **TenantPro for Windows:** If you have between 10 and 200 rental units, I recommend TenantPro for Windows, a rental accounting software package from Property Automation Software Corporation based in Richardson, Texas (`www.tenantpro.com`). This is an excellent accounting package for rental owners who want to have the benefits of efficient accounting and record keeping. You can combine the rental property accounting software with optional modules for tenant screening and maintenance requests as well. Another great feature available is the Property Automation Software Corporation's module for utility metering and billing that simplifies charging tenants for their individual utility usage.
- **Yardi Professional:** For rental property owners or property management companies with significant portfolios of at least 100 or more rental units, I recommend the Yardi Professional software (`www.yardi.com`). My property management company uses a higher-end version of Yardi software, and we have been very impressed with the software's ability to provide our property managers with the online real-time daily and weekly reporting we need to effectively manage our properties. It also offers the detailed monthly accounting reports expected by our clients.

The future of rental property accounting is Web-based software, such as Yardi Voyager. This new breed of software actually stores property records on the software company's remote central server and permits you and your property manager access to real-time information via the Internet from anywhere in the world. These software solutions have all the basics features of prospect and tenant management, fully integrated accounts receivable and accounts payable, general ledger, and cash management, but they also allow ready access to information, elimination of duplicate entries, and spontaneous delivery of reporting. Although the initial users of these services will be only the largest real estate owners and property managers, they may soon be available for owners with small rental property portfolios, so keep an eye out for them in the future.

When you use a management company, you will typically receive several important accounting reports within a couple of weeks after the end of each accounting month. If you review these reports regularly, they can provide you with a good understanding of your rental investments and give you the opportunity to inquire about or suggest changes in the operations. But if you manage your own property and do your own accounting, it's important to actually review and analyze the financial reports in the same manner as you would if you had entrusted your investment to a property manager. You may think that you know everything you need to know about your rental property, and setting aside those monthly reports until tax time may seem harmless, but they are great tools to improve your management results if you use them properly.

You can customize the financial reporting offered by software programs to meet your needs. Monthly reports often contain income and expense information compared to the monthly budget as well as year-to-date numbers.

Part VI
Only for the Daring

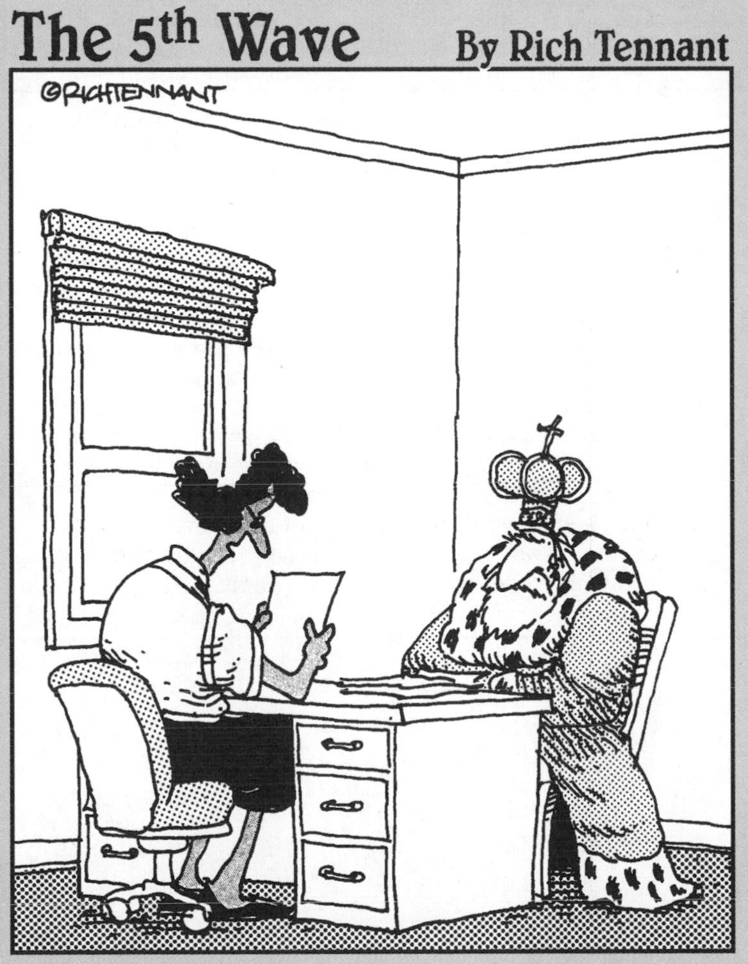

"Let's see – you might be just right for a little 2-turret, 1½-moat unit I'm renting on West 58th street."

In this part . . .

When you're looking to increase your cash flow (and who isn't?), and after you have a little landlording experience under your belt, you may want to try your hand at some less common endeavors, like lease options. And although government programs sometimes get a bad rap, they're often a great way to get a reliable source of rental income — and to set your property apart from the competition in a favorable way. Finally, you may want to think about appealing to niche markets — people with special needs that your property may be perfect for. In this part, I guide you through each of these areas so that you can figure out whether they're right for you and use them to your advantage — with few worries.

Chapter 19

Non-Rent Revenue and Lease Options

In This Chapter

- Getting creative with ways to increase your non-rent revenue
- Taking advantage of lease options as a way to increase your income

Your primary source of rental property income is most likely rent. Although you should always focus on ways to maximize rent, you may be able to take advantage of other opportunities to generate income. *Non-rent revenue* is income from sources other than basic rent, such as income from parking, storage, laundry machines, vending, or Internet access. Just as important, these services can give your rental property the competitive advantage to attract and retain your tenants long term.

You may also be able to generate additional cash by offering short-term lease options. A lease option agreement generally consists of a standard lease, plus a separate contract that gives the tenant the right to purchase the property at either a later fixed date or within a mutually agreed timeframe. Lease option agreements typically require an upfront payment and/or monthly payments to secure the purchase option, which is often credited toward the down payment or the purchase price.

Finding New Ways to Increase Your Cash Flow with Non-Rent Revenue

Savvy rental property owners are always looking for additional ways to increase the building income. And you can do this regardless of whether you have a rental home or condo, a small apartment property, or a large multifamily apartment building. Each property is different, so you need to evaluate what services or features you can actually put to work for you. The best way to do this is to look at your property from the perspective of your tenants and prospective tenants.

You can charge your tenants for these non-rent services and amenities separately from the rent or bundle them together as rent. The method you choose may depend on the common practices in your local rental market.

Laundry machines

Providing your tenants with laundry equipment is one of the best ways you can increase your non-rent revenue. But your ability to meet this need will probably depend on the size of your rental property.

If you own a single-family rental home, including a washer and dryer can allow you to charge an extra $50 to $75 in monthly rent. The plumbing and connections are probably already installed (or if they aren't, they can easily be added). But unless you want to see all your potential profits go down the drain, be sure that your tenant pays for the utilities, including the water and sewer charges.

The owners of rental properties with two to twelve rental units have the toughest time offering laundry equipment, because they often lack an appropriate location. If the washer and dryer cannot be installed directly in the rental units, look for a location to build a common area laundry facility. You may be able to convert a garage or build an enclosure in a carport space, but be sure the location is safe and secure, and always use a licensed and bonded general contractor and get the proper permits.

Larger rental properties are ideally suited for common area laundry facilities with coin-operated, or better yet, coinless smart card washers and dryers. Typically, one washer and dryer for every eight to ten rental units will be sufficient, but check first with other owners in your area to see what they're offering. If you purchase your own equipment, you'll have an initial cash investment and the burden of ongoing equipment maintenance, but you'll have added to your net income. You can also negotiate very competitive contracts with laundry service contractors who install, maintain, and collect the revenue from the machines. They often pay upfront bonuses, plus send you a monthly check for your share of the gross proceeds to cover your utility costs and generate a profit.

Some laundry service companies will lease or sell you laundry equipment with a service contract; then you handle your own collections.

Storage

If your rental property doesn't have proper storage, you may be faced with the challenge of tenants who regularly leave items on their patios, balconies, or even in the yard. If that's the case, your property can really begin to look unsightly in very little time. Instead of getting upset with your tenants, keep in mind that they don't have much choice: New rental units are becoming smaller and smaller, and they often don't include adequate storage. At the same time, many renters are acquiring more and more possessions and their need for storage is increasing.

If you're creative, you can turn this lemon into lemonade. Consider adding secure, weatherproof, lockable storage units. Ideally your storage units should be at ground level and at least 5-x-5 feet square with a height of 6 feet or more, have a heavy-duty locking mechanism, and be constructed out of solid material so that no one can see the contents. The money spent in obtaining quality storage units is a great investment, because the price per square foot of storage in many urban rental markets rivals or even exceeds the cost of the rental unit itself. Plus, if you offer storage facilities with your rental unit, you will have a competitive advantage that will help you keep your property occupied and allow you to charge a higher rent.

Parking

You may have a rental property where parking is abundant, but at many properties parking is a real problem and can be an excellent source of additional revenue. Carports and garages are in very high demand in many areas of the country and can generate significant income. Look at other properties in your area; you may be surprised to see what the going rates for parking are.

If your rental property doesn't have extra parking, look to see if you can add a parking area. Parking is very important to many tenants, and they will gladly pay for the convenience of a reserved space.

Even if you have limited parking, consider charging separately for rent and parking. Some tenants may not have vehicles, so rather than include a fee in their rent for a parking space that they won't use, you can keep their rent lower while generating additional income by renting parking spaces to tenants who need them.

If you charge for parking, be sure to implement detailed parking rules, put up proper signage in keeping with local code that allows you the ability to enforce your parking regulations through fines or towing, and have reserved parking stickers or permits.

Internet access

As the use of computers increases dramatically, there is a very significant demand for access to high-speed Internet access. Providers of high-speed Internet access often will offer to wire your rental property at no cost and even provide you with a share of the revenues. Currently, owners of small rental properties in urban areas can usually only offer their tenants Internet access through a local cable television company. However, soon even small urban rental properties will have additional services available.

The technology is improving all the time, and the costs to provide service are dropping. Currently, there are primarily four basic types of high-speed Internet connections available: cable modem, digital subscriber lines (DSL), fixed wireless, and satellite. Check with service providers in your area; certain technologies are better suited and more cost-effective for certain properties and locations.

Furnished rentals

The majority of rental properties are offered unfurnished, because most tenants already have their own furnishings. In urban areas, short-term renters may need furnished units, but this is a specific market that is usually addressed by one or more major apartment owners or hospitality companies. However, in some suburban or rural areas there is a demand for furnished rental units for short-term or long-term rentals.

Your target market and specific location will often have a bearing on whether you want to consider offering your rental units partially or fully furnished. Furnishing your rental is a major investment, but if your rental property is adjacent to a major employer that regularly relocates employees into the area, you can often generate significantly higher rents for a furnished rental unit.

Putting Lease Options to Work for You

A *lease option* is a real estate rental transaction combined with the potential of a real estate sale and financing technique. The typical lease option combines a standard lease with a separate contract giving the tenant the option to purchase the rental property during a limited period of time for a mutually agreed purchase price. You agree to sell the property during a limited period of time, but the tenant is not required to exercise the option.

Although each lease option is unique, here is an example of how a deal may be structured for a rental home with a current market rent of $1,000 per month and a current market value of $120,000. Real estate forecasts indicate that appreciation will be 4 percent, or approximately $5,000, in the next 12 months. The tenant signs a 12-month standard lease and agrees to pay $1,200 per month with $1,000 in rent and $200 as a nonrefundable option fee that will be applied to the down payment. At the same time, you and the tenant enter into an option-to-purchase agreement that offers the tenant the right to buy the rental property within 12 months of the lease for an amount of $125,000. This is the mutually agreed estimated fair market value of the rental property by the end of the option period. You receive an additional cash flow of $200 per month, and usually the tenant treats the property with care because he may very well be the new owner soon. If the tenant exercises the option, the tenant receives a credit toward the down payment of $200 per month for each month that he paid the option fee. On the other hand, you have used your standard lease form, so if the lease option documents are drafted properly, you still have the right to evict the tenant for nonpayment of rent or any other material lease default.

In most instances, the tenant won't be able to exercise the purchase option, because he will not have accumulated the money required for the down payment and his share of the closing costs. In the meantime, you'll have increased your monthly rental income by $200 and had a good tenant. Of course, at the end of the option, the tenant is well aware that he has paid an additional $2,400 in rent that would have been applied to the down payment or purchase price if he had exercised his purchase option. Depending on the circumstances, you can either renegotiate an extension of the purchase option with the tenant, or you can negotiate a new lease without the purchase option.

Lease options are a strategy to consider as a way to increase cash flow from your rental under the right circumstances. They can work very well or they can be a complete disaster if you don't have the right agreement in place. Both you and the tenant must have a thorough understanding of the unique benefits and challenges of lease options in order for them to work to the advantage of both of you. Table 19-1 lists some pros and cons of lease options for rental property owners.

The availability of lease options often fluctuates with the strength of the rental market. When you're having difficulty finding qualified tenants, a lease option may make good sense. If you have an abundance of qualified tenants, however, a lease option offers you fewer advantages.

One serious potential downside to lease options is the possibility that the property will greatly appreciate in value during the next year. This is why agreeing to an option price that is slightly *higher* than the current market rent is important. Check with a professional real estate appraiser in your area, but in most real estate markets, annual appreciation of 5 percent is very good.

Avoid long-term lease options, because the appreciation in real estate can be very unpredictable. Do not provide a set option purchase price for any longer than one or two years, or be sure to include a clause that the purchase price will increase by an amount equal to the increase in the average median home price in your area.

Have a real estate attorney with extensive experience in lease options review your lease option contract in advance. Lease options can have very serious business and even ethical problems if they aren't drafted properly. If it's not structured properly, a lease option could be considered a sale and could trigger the due-on-sale clause with your lender, causing you to lose the tax benefits of depreciation and deductible expenses. Your property could be reassessed for property taxes, you could be liable for failure to comply with seller disclosure laws, or you could be prevented from evicting the tenant even if he has defaulted on the lease. Keep the nonrefundable option fee reasonable, so if the value of the property declines or your tenant doesn't exercise his option for any reason, you can feel comfortable that you've treated the tenant fairly. Or you may want to renegotiate or consider offering an extension.

Table 19-1 The Pros and Cons of Lease Options

Pros	*Cons*
The lease-option tenant is usually better financially qualified.	The lease-option tenant may not be willing or able to buy the rental property at the end of the lease.
The lease-option tenant will pay a nonrefundable option fee upfront or with his rent that will be applied to the down payment or purchase price.	Lease options have tax ramifications and can trigger due-on-sale clauses in your financing or a reassessment of your property under certain circumstances.
There is strong tenant demand for lease options, and the tenant will typically stay longer and will often treat the property better.	The agreed option purchase price could be lower than actual fair market value of rental property if the property appreciates significantly during the option period.
A lease-option tenant may be willing to pay a top-dollar option price.	The lease-option tenant may not exercise the option but will insist on the return of the extra rent paid or demand a renegotiation of the option terms.
You continue to receive tax benefits of owning rental property.	A lease-option tenant who does not exercise the option after paying a large nonrefundable fee could get even by damaging your rental property.

Noted real estate attorney and nationally syndicated columnist Robert J. Bruss is an avid proponent of real estate investors using lease options to purchase as well as sell rental properties under the right conditions. For a nominal cost, he has an excellent special report available that outlines the pros, cons, and details of buying or selling with a lease option. You can order this report by calling 1-800-736-1736.

Chapter 20

Government Programs

In This Chapter

- Making sense of subsidized housing programs
- Figuring out whether working with Section 8 is right for you
- Getting rehabilitation loans to upgrade your rental property

Housing is generally the largest single expense for many families, and the U.S. is facing a very severe affordable housing crisis. According to the federal government's definition, housing is "affordable" as long as the rent and utility costs do not exceed 30 percent of household income. But people who may be receiving Supplemental Security Income (SSI) or who work in low-wage jobs often have trouble finding affordable housing.

Demand for new rental units is high in most areas of the country, yet the construction of new rental housing is at all-time lows. When the demand for rental housing exceeds the supply, a shortage of available rental units occurs, which leads to increased rents. In this situation, many tenants are forced to pay a very large share of their income in rent.

With such a shortage of decent, affordable rental housing units, low-income tenants have a very difficult time finding rental housing. To make matters worse, many rental property owners have a firm policy that they won't accept rental applicants who rely upon subsidies to assist with their rent payments. Rental property owners' most common complaints about subsidy programs are that the rent limitations are too low, there is a lack of cooperation from program administrators, and some rental property inspectors are unreasonable in their required repairs and extensive paperwork.

In this chapter, I review some of the benefits and concerns for rental property owners with rent subsidy programs. If you're not sure whether participating in rent subsidy programs is for you, read on.

Rental Subsidy Programs

A *rental subsidy* is a payment of some or all of the rent by a governmental or nonprofit agency for the use and occupancy of a rental unit for qualified individuals. These individuals may receive the subsidy as a result of insufficient income, disability, relocation assistance, or other similar programs. All aspects of the tenancy relationship with participants in rent subsidy programs are usually the same as they are with any other tenants.

Many types of rental subsidy programs are offered by local housing agencies, religious organizations, and charitable groups. The majority of the local rent subsidy programs only offer short-term assistance, whereas the national Section 8 program offers rent subsidies on an ongoing basis. Section 8 is a federal Department of Housing and Urban Development (HUD) program.

Be careful with local rental subsidy programs that only offer short-term financial assistance to your tenant. Some programs provide payment of the security deposit and assist with a few months' rent. But you need to be sure that the tenant meets your tenant-screening criteria, including sufficient income to meet the full rent and utility costs on an indefinite basis, so that when the short-term assistance runs out, the tenant can still pay the rent.

Section 8 and other rent subsidy programs have their limitations. But the need is significant, and many lower-income families and other needy tenants receive important assistance from them. Rent subsidy programs are targeted in their approach and allow you to retain control over selecting tenants and all other aspects of the rental relationship. These programs are much better than the "shotgun" alternative of rent control.

Section 8

The Section 8 program was established in 1974 by HUD as the federal government's major program for assisting very-low-income families, the elderly, and the disabled in renting decent, safe, and sanitary housing in the open market. Section 8 is the largest rental subsidy program, with over 3 million tenants participating, and is offered and administrated through the 3,000 local public housing authorities (PHAs) throughout the country. It helps twice as many families as are assisted by the next largest nationwide housing program, public housing. The program is available to qualified low-income tenants and requires the tenant to pay a percentage of his monthly income towards rent, with the balance paid by the local PHA.

The Section 8 program has two goals:

- To allow low-income households more choice in housing
- To reduce the concentration of low-income households living in particular neighborhoods

A wide variety of residential rental housing qualifies for Section 8 certification, including single-family homes, condos, duplexes, apartments, and mobile homes. HUD requirements state that the rental unit must have a bedroom for every two occupants. This is consistent with the HUD guidelines for occupancy standards.

The Section 8 program provides tenant-based rental subsidies or vouchers that can be used to rent privately owned rental housing chosen by the tenant. Tenants with household income of less than 50 percent of the median income for the area in which they live are eligible for Section 8 assistance. The Section 8 vouchers guarantee the tenant rental assistance for five years and can be renewed.

Traditionally, the Section 8 program had two forms of subsidy programs: project-based certificates and tenant-based vouchers. However, these two programs are being merged into the new Housing Choice Voucher Program that provides a rent subsidy paid by the PHA on behalf of the program participant directly to the rental property owner. Under this new program, the tenants cannot pay more than 40 percent of their household income in rent, and the Section 8 rent subsidy is based on the HUD Fair Market Rent available from local PHAs.

At least annually, the PHA surveys the local rental housing market and determines the median rents and utility allowance for each rental unit type based on the number of bedrooms. The amount of rent that owners can charge is limited to amounts set by the PHA that are up to a maximum of the HUD Fair Market Rent level for the particular county. Section 8 tenants may choose a rental unit with a higher rent than the PHA maximums and then pay the difference, or they may choose a lower cost rental unit and keep the difference for themselves.

In some areas of the country, the maximum allowable rents are reasonable. But in many areas, the maximum rents set by the local PHA precludes many of the rental units in the area. In these areas, Section 8 participants and rental property owners are effectively unable to work together to provide decent affordable housing. The PHAs have been allowed to adjust the maximum Section 8 rents up to 10 percent higher than the HUD Fair Market Rent, to allow tenants more alternatives.

The maximum rents vary based on whether the owner or the tenants pay the utilities. In general, you're better off having the tenants pay their own utilities, because the HUD utility allowances are typically insufficient and owner-paid utilities do not encourage conservation efforts by tenants.

You cannot charge higher rent for a Section 8 rental unit than you would if you were renting the same unit to a private, unassisted tenant.

If you participate in Section 8, you're required to enter into a one-year lease with the tenant using a standardized HUD-approved lease form or the owner's lease with a HUD addendum. You're locked into the one-year lease agreement except for nonpayment of rent or another serious breach of the lease. You must also sign a contract known as a Housing Assistance Payments (HAP) contract with the local public housing authority authorizing the payment of rent. The rent payment can even be deposited directly into your bank account.

Use your own standard rental application, lease, and all other forms and procedures. Attach the PHA lease and HAP contract to your paperwork. If your Section 8 tenant does not pay his share of the rent or you have another problem, immediately notify your contact person at the local PHA. Although there are limits to what the PHA can do, they *can* be helpful in resolving issues.

After they have qualified, tenants are given a Section 8 voucher or certificate and allowed up to 60 days to locate a rental unit. In certain tight rental markets, tenants are allowed up to 120 days to find a suitable rental unit. Inspections are made by the local PHAs to ensure that the rental unit meets the HUD Minimum Housing Quality Standards at the beginning of the tenancy, upon annual renewal, and upon request if the tenant believes the condition of the rental unit is unacceptable.

The greatest benefit to owners is that the PHA pays the majority of the tenant's monthly rent like clockwork, and the tenant's portion is low enough that they usually do not have any problem meeting their financial obligations. Also, if the tenant fails to pay their portion of the rent, you have the right to evict him and apply the security deposit to any unpaid rent or damage to the rental unit. Some PHAs may have a formal or even informal requirement to contact them to resolve any issues before beginning an eviction action.

Process the tenant move-out just like any other tenant. But be sure to notify the local PHA. The availability of Section 8 assistance is limited, with long waiting lists. This fact can be very helpful in motivating your tenants to be responsible, because the termination of their lease for nonpayment or another lease breach will often result in a loss of their rental assistance.

For most rental property owners, participating in the Section 8 program is very easy. Contact the PHA in your local city or county for more information. Be sure that your rental rates are within their maximum guidelines. If they are, your local PHA will refer eligible applicants to you and will prepare the necessary documents if you decide to rent to an eligible applicant. Make sure that you get a copy from HUD of the Section 8 rules and procedures before you determine whether the Section 8 rental program will work for you.

Here are some advantages to participating in the Section 8 program:

- There is less competition, because many rental property owners refuse to participate in the Section 8 housing program.
- A portion of the rent is guaranteed by the local PHA and backed by the federal government.
- You retain full control over the screening and selection process, with the PHA providing the names and addresses of the current and one prior landlord for verification and reference checking.
- You may collect a full security deposit up to the maximum allowed under state and local laws, plus rent may be adjusted annually subject to PHA maximum rents for comparable rental units in the area.
- There is a stable tenant profile with competitive rents and property that has been inspected regularly.

And here are some disadvantages to participating in the Section 8 program:

- There is a delay in initial occupancy due to additional paperwork.
- There is a delay in getting the first payment and you may have difficulty getting the rent payment to stop when the tenant leaves.
- You must meet HUD Minimum Housing Quality Standards through regular inspections by your local PHA and make all required repairs.
- Rents and utility costs cannot exceed HUD determination of fair market rents.

The Section 8 rental subsidy program can be a great resource for rental property owners in certain areas of the country. The key is to ensure that the PHA-determined maximum rental rates for your area are competitive and their inspection requirements are reasonable. If these criteria are reasonable, then Section 8 can provide you with additional rental prospects. Screen the tenants carefully and make sure that you work with the local PHA representative to avoid problems. Participating in Section 8 may provide you with stable, long-term tenants at market rents, where the majority of the rent is paid by a governmental agency and the tenants are highly motivated to pay their share of the rent and to abide by your rules and guidelines.

Rehabilitation Loans

A large percentage of the rental housing in the U.S. is old and in need of renovation and modernization. According to the U.S. Census Bureau, less than 10 percent of the apartments in the country have been built since 1990. So great opportunities exist for rental property owners to renovate rental units.

With the difficulty in providing new low-income rental housing, HUD encourages the rehabilitation of existing rental units through state and local government agencies, including the HOME program, community development block grants, and rural housing programs. Most programs are administrated by local PHAs. They allow owners of qualified rental units to obtain improvement grants or borrow money to upgrade and rehabilitate their rental housing properties. The grants cover weatherproofing and other health and safety issues, and the low- or even no-interest loans allow owners to make capital improvements.

As with most governmental programs, you can expect to fill out numerous forms and wait for processing, inspections, and approvals when you apply for a rehabilitation loan. However, besides offering below-market interest rates, these loans are often *assumable,* which means a purchaser is allowed to take over the below-market interest rate loan as part of his financing upon acquisition.

Some programs offer owners of larger rental properties rehabilitation funds if they provide housing for specific targeted groups. For example, people with physical and mental disabilities find it difficult to locate private affordable rental housing, so if you rent to people with mental or physical disabilities, you may qualify for rehabilitation funds.

There is a growing demand for special housing for the aging population, as well as for people struggling with AIDS and substance abuse. Due to the lack of construction of new rental housing, the government is developing programs to encourage the renovation and conversion of existing rental units, particularly single-family houses, targeted for these particular groups.

Contact your local PHA for more information on funding programs and qualification standards or HUD at `www.hud.gov`.

Chapter 21

Working in Niche Markets: Students, Seniors, and More

In This Chapter

- Reexamining your thoughts on pets
- Appealing to people with special rental requirements
- Offering smoke-free rental units

Sometimes thinking outside the box and looking for angles that other rental property owners overlook or are not willing to pursue makes sense. You may own property in a soft rental market or maybe you just want to find a market niche where your rental units can outperform other rental properties.

This chapter explores several of the niche rental markets that you can use to your benefit — everything from students to senior citizens to tenants with pets. These niche markets may or may not be right for you. But be sure to consider whether you could dip into one or more of these niche markets and increase your cash flow in the process.

Taking Another Look at Your Pet Policy

In today's rental market, one of the most effective strategies to keep your rental units occupied with stable, paying tenants is to allow pets. Although many owners immediately reject this idea, the reality is that the rental options are extremely limited for many tenants with pets — which means that if you're one of the few who accepts pets, you'll immediately increase the demand for your rental unit.

Even "no pet" properties must accommodate renters who have companion or service animals if they are prescribed by a medical doctor under the Americans with Disabilities Act (ADA).

Allowing pets under certain conditions can result in much higher rental income and fewer vacancies. For example, accepting pets can be successful if you:

- **Have a rental property that is suitable for pets.** Some rental properties are particularly well suited for tenants who have pets. An older rental property, or one with certain features such as a fenced yard, hard-surface flooring (as opposed to carpeting), and vertical blinds (as opposed to curtains) would be a good candidate for tenants with pets.
- **Verify through references and an interview that your tenant is a responsible pet owner.** Be sure to verify all references and ask specific questions about the pet. Conducting an actual "interview" with the pet to determine its demeanor is a good idea. Be sure to properly complete the pet or animal agreement addendum to your lease and have the tenant agree to your terms. Restrict any animal with dangerous or potentially dangerous tendencies, and take a photo of the pet for your tenant file.
- **Implement and enforce stringent pet policies and rules.** For your pet policy to run smoothly, you need detailed rules, including a limit on the number of animals. You also need to have clear policies about pet and tenant behavior. For example, you'll want to forbid tenants from flushing cat litter down the toilet (otherwise you'll end up with clogged pipes). Be sure to put limits on what you'll consider as an acceptable pet; consider making exotic animals off-limits.
- **Require an extra deposit for tenants with pets.** Because so few rental properties accept tenants with pets, those that do are able to charge higher rental rates and collect much larger security deposits from tenants with pets. Most responsible pet owners won't balk at a reasonable monthly rental rate premium or an increased security deposit of several hundred dollars. Avoid using the labels *pet rent* or *pet deposit;* instead, try to keep the language generic. A "pet deposit" could limit your use of those funds to damage that you can prove was caused by the pet. Your goal is to ensure that the rental rate and larger security deposit provide adequate compensation and protection against any or *all* damage to the rental unit resulting in increased costs of cleaning or repair.

If you're still concerned about taking pets, you can take advantage of private firms that sell tenants or owners pet deposit warranties against pet damage in rental property. The warranties can supplement or replace the usual pet damage deposit. These warranties cover soiled, chewed, and destroyed carpets, linoleum, woodwork, drapes, and doors in rental units with a cat or dog that is at least 1 year old. The typical cost is a couple hundred dollars per year, plus a refundable deposit. If you're interested in finding out more about these kinds of warranties, check out one such service, LeaseWithPets.com, online at `www.leasewithpets.com`.

The Humane Society of the United States is among the many pet advocacy and rescue organizations that are becoming increasingly involved in addressing the issue of pets in rental housing. The Humane Society offers advice and tips for both tenants and owners at its Web site, `www.rentwithpets.org`.

Renting to Students: It Doesn't Have to Be Animal House

A large number of rental properties are located near colleges and universities, and yours may be one of them. But many rental property owners have the same strong feelings against renting to students as they do about accepting pets. The major problem, however, is that (except for the ADA exemption) you can legally have a "no pet" policy, but you can't unlawfully discriminate against students if they meet your tenant screening criteria.

If you have rental properties that attract prospective student tenants, be sure to adopt policies that will allow you to take advantage of this large target market while minimizing the downside.

One of the most common problems that comes with renting to students is the fact that students have special needs regarding the length of their lease. Many schools are in session for only four or five months in the fall and spring and two or three months in the summer. If you only offer a 12-month lease, you may end up with student tenants who default on their lease agreements and leave right after the end of the semester.

One strategy is to offer 3-month and 9-month leases at a premium rental rate over the 12-month leases available at competitive rental properties. Students attending the fall and spring sessions will be delighted with the 9-month term, and summer students will go for the 3-month term.

The other primary concern with renting to students is their behavior. Make sure that you implement strict policies and rules concerning noise and, ideally, have an onsite manager to enforce them. Be sure to consistently require a larger security deposit and/or cosigner or guarantor of the lease at rental properties where you rent to students. Also, (as discussed in Chapter 10) you should insist on receiving the full rent each month in a single check.

Catering to Senior Citizens

The need for rental housing for active seniors is increasing as America's rapidly expanding population of older adults chooses to maintain and prolong their independent living status. The U.S. Census estimates that the number of seniors will be increasing from the present 35 million to a projected 70 million by the year 2050, so many rental property owners are finding the demand for senior housing a great investment opportunity.

The Housing for Older Persons Act of 1995 was amended to make it easier for rental property owners to qualify for the special fair-housing law exemption. This exemption bars familial status discrimination claims for those housing developments that qualify as housing for persons age 55 or older. In other words, qualified rental properties for seniors can exclude families with children without violating the Fair Housing Act.

Rental housing for seniors no longer is required to offer "significant facilities and services" designed for the elderly, but they must show that one person who is 55 years of age or older lives in at least 80 percent of the occupied rental units. Federal law also requires that rental property owners follow policies and procedures that demonstrate intent to be housing for persons age 55 or older. This typically means that a sign should be posted and all literature provided to the public must include a statement indicating that housing for older persons is offered.

Before designating your multi-family rental property as housing for older persons, be sure to check with an attorney about discrimination laws in your area. Many state and local fair-housing laws may still be modeled after the former federal fair housing law and require owners to provide "significant facilities and services."

Seniors are typically excellent long-term tenants; however, be sure to do some advance research to determine whether your multi-family rental property is ideally suited for seniors. Evaluate your rental units to consider the proximity to local transportation, shopping, medical facilities, special senior centers or activities, and places of worship.

If your rental property has services and facilities for seniors, you'll attract a senior target market. Be sure to advise local agencies catering to seniors about the availability of your rental units.

Designating Your Rental Units Smoke-Free

One of the most controversial issues in rental housing management today concerns the ability of a rental property owner to restrict the use of the rental unit to nonsmoking status. The growing trend in America is to restrict smoking in almost all public areas; the elimination of smoking on airplanes is even becoming widely accepted internationally. Although the hotel industry has successfully implemented policies offering both smoking and nonsmoking rooms for years, rental property owners are just beginning to address this issue.

I've found that there is a strong demand for rental properties and rental units where smoking is partially or completely restricted. One frequent complaint I receive from tenants who write to my *Rental Roundtable* newspaper column is secondhand smoke from a neighbor. Unfortunately, in some rental properties, tobacco smoke can drift from one rental unit directly into another. The smoke can enter from hallways, stairs, balconies, and patios, usually through windows and doors or even from the building's common ventilation system.

The majority of Americans are nonsmokers. Smoking is considered a controllable behavior, not a disease, so people who smoke are not considered a "protected class" under federal and state fair-housing or antidiscrimination laws. Although tenants who smoke need places to live, so do nonsmoking tenants who want to avoid drifting secondhand smoke.

Currently, there are no federal or state laws that prohibit you from adopting a policy that requires all or part of a building to be smoke-free, including individual rental units. However, because the rights of individuals who smoke and those opposed to secondhand smoke are constantly changing, be sure to check local and state laws in your area before making a decision to implement a smoke-free rental program.

Although you can prohibit the behavior or act of smoking in rental units or on the premises, you cannot refuse to rent to a person just because the person is a smoker. Not renting to a smoker is a form of discrimination and a violation of fair-housing laws.

There are several good business reasons to consider offering smoke-free rental units. Most rental owners have seen the additional damage caused by smokers, including damage from burns, the need to thoroughly clean the carpets, drapes, and all surfaces, plus even repaint the entire unit to remove the smoke that has permeated it. Reduced insurance premiums are also possible if your rental unit is smoke-free.

There are even groups that promote the concept of rental properties that do not allow smoking on the premises. For example, in southern California, the Smokefree Apartment House Registry (`www.smokefreeapartments.org`) offers a free service to rental property owners where they can list available rental properties with a total or partial smokefree policy. I believe that this concept will be very popular throughout many areas of the country in the next few years.

Although you can simply put a "No smoking allowed" clause in the lease or rental agreement, before you do so, I recommend surveying your current tenants. You may find that prohibiting smoking in common areas, rental units, balconies, and patios is a popular idea — or you may be met with more resistance than you anticipated. Knowing where your tenants stand on this issue should be an important part of your decision.

As with any major policy change, be sure to implement a conversion to a smoke-free rental property upon tenant turnover or only after giving proper legal notice. And if you want to implement a smoke-free policy at a larger rental property, start by prohibiting smoking in all common areas, like the rental office, laundry room, and recreational facilities. Then you can expand the smokefree policy to individual rental units if the program is positively received by your tenants.

Part VII

The Part of Tens

The 5th Wave
By Rich Tennant
GLEN REMEMBERED HOW THE LANDLORD TOLD HIM TO USE THE PLUNGER TO UNCLOG THINGS. ONE DAY, THE ELECTRICITY STOPPED FLOWING...
©RICHTENNANT

In this part . . .

This wouldn't be a *For Dummies* book without the Part of Tens. Here you'll find short bursts of information on everything from why you should buy rental property in the first place, to how to rent a vacancy when you do, to increasing your cash flow. So if you're looking for a lot of information but you don't have much time, you've come to the right part.

Chapter 22

Ten Reasons to Become a Rental Property Owner

In This Chapter

- Understanding the benefits to owning rental property
- Figuring out whether owning rental property is right for you

Owning rental property isn't for everyone. So if you're just starting to think about investing in real estate through rental property, in this chapter I offer ten great reasons to take the plunge.

You Can Diversify Your Investments

If you already have significant assets in mutual funds, bonds, or the stock market, you can diversify your investments by buying rental property. Owning your own home is a first step towards diversification, but owning investment real estate is a prudent strategy to protect your assets from volatility in certain areas of the economy.

You Don't Need Much Money to Start

Many people think that real estate is an investment only for the wealthy. In fact, a lack of money is often cited as the number one factor that keeps people from investing in real estate. But real estate is a tangible asset that you can typically purchase for a down payment of 20 percent or less, with the balance provided by others. Real estate loans are readily available at very competitive terms throughout the U.S. Some sellers are willing to assist the buyer by financing a portion of the purchase price. Plus, many first-time homebuyer programs offer up to 100 percent financing. So if you don't already own your own home, you can take advantage of a first-time buyer program, build up equity in your home, and then refinance your home to generate additional capital, which you can use as the down payment to buy rental property.

It Can Be a Second Income

Many of the greatest rags-to-riches stories are based on real estate investors who started from scratch. The majority of residential rental real estate in America is owned by working middle-class individuals of all backgrounds and ages who sought viable opportunities to augment their current income or career. Real estate investing can truly begin as a part-time job and offer a second income.

You Gain Tax Advantages

Real estate is one of the most favored investments from a taxation standpoint. The IRS code has many unique taxation advantages for real estate. You can benefit from deductibility of expenses, depreciation write-offs, tax-deferred exchanges, and favorable capital gains tax rates. Owning and operating rental property is a business, and the tax laws allow deductions against your rental income. That means you can deduct all operating expenses, including the cost of payroll, property management, advertising, maintenance and repairs, utilities, insurance, and property taxes.

Your rental property can be depreciated, giving you another tax break. Current federal tax laws allow you to depreciate your residential income property improvements over a 27.5 year lifespan. The depreciation loss can reduce your taxable income or give you a taxable loss on the property, even if you have a positive cash flow. For example, if your annual cash flow is $5,000 and your depreciation is $4,000, you only pay taxes on $1,000 of income. This depreciation will be recaptured and taxed at a 25 percent tax rate when you sell the property.

After you have depleted your depreciation on income-producing real estate, you can also take advantage of the IRS code 1031 (also known as a "Starker" tax-deferred exchange) to postpone taxation on any gain by rolling over your equity into a new and often larger rental property. This is a tremendous tax benefit, but remember that tax-deferred exchanges have some very detailed rules that must be followed exactly or you will become ineligible for the exchange and required to pay taxes.

As with all taxation matters, be sure you understand the basic concepts of real estate taxation issues, but rely on a tax specialist, accountant, or attorney for advice on details, procedures, and tax laws. Tax codes change from year to year, so discussing your personal tax situation with your accountant or tax preparer is always a good idea.

Real Estate Holds Its Value

Real estate has proven to be one of the most popular investments available, because income-producing rental properties have endured and held their value through many economic cycles over the decades. Throughout history, the tangible nature of real estate has been extremely important to both people and the economy.

Remember: Real estate is cyclical. Many businesses have their ups and downs, and real estate is no exception. However, real estate usually rebounds and grows in value after a slump in appreciation. Historically, many solid real estate investments have depreciated for a period of time, but then they have grown again in value. Real estate appreciates because its quantity is limited. Over the long run, real estate has been an established performer and offers a solid foundation for your financial future.

You Get Leverage

Real estate *leverage* is the use of mortgage financing to purchase an investment property with only a small cash outlay, with the expectation that appreciation and inflation will create a disproportionately high return on the original cash investment upon sale. The key to successfully using leverage is having a mortgage interest rate *lower* than the return on your real estate investment. Here's an oversimplified example: A buyer purchases a $100,000 rental home for $20,000 cash down and an $80,000 loan at a 9 percent interest rate. If the property appreciates and sells in three years for a net of $120,000, the owner will have earned $20,000 or 100 percent return on their money. This is called *positive leverage.* Conversely, high interest rates and flat real estate values with no increases in cash flow will result in *negative leverage,* and undercapitalized investors may lose their property.

It Beats Inflation

Inflation is the loss of buying power as prices rise. Most investments, such as money market accounts, bonds, stocks, and mutual funds, provide certain rates of return but have trouble keeping up with the rate of inflation. Thus, investors in these assets often find that they are actually losing purchasing power over time. However, real estate has some unique advantages that make it a formidable tool in the battle against inflation. When rental property has been purchased with fixed rate financing, the price and financing cost of the property is fixed. Other operating costs such as property taxes and utilities are bound to increase; however, rental property owners typically are able to increase the amount of rent charged to offset the increased operating costs.

Of course, temporary softness or downturns in the rental market may delay rent increases in the short run, but historically real estate cash flows have been able to maintain the owner's purchasing power in the long run.

You Can Shelter Your Income

Currently, the taxation laws that affect real estate offer tax advantages to those individuals who are actively involved in the management of their rental properties. If you qualify as an active investor and do not exceed the adjusted gross income limits, you may be able to qualify for substantial deductions for rental property losses to reduce your taxable earned income from other sources, which is known as *sheltering other income.* Using a property management firm will not preclude you from taking advantage of the tax write-offs as long as you are involved in setting the rents and the policies for your rental property.

Qualified real estate professionals are allowed to claim all real estate loss deductions in the year incurred; however, the requirements to achieve the status of a real estate professional are strict, so you should consult your tax advisor.

You Get a Positive Cash Flow

Rental property owners know that the right investment property will generate sufficient rental income to cover the mortgage and all operating expenses of the property. And after the tax advantages of depreciation, real estate generally provides positive cash flow. This may not always be true in the first few years of ownership, but positive cash flow is a real benefit for many investors. Of course, after the mortgage has been paid, the positive cash flow can be very significant.

It Can Help You Retire

Real estate investment is one of the best methods to fulfill the dream of retiring wealthy. This worthy goal requires a diversified investment strategy with assets that can be purchased with leverage, generate cash flow, appreciate consistently over time, and maintain their purchasing power in an inflationary environment. Like most investments, the earlier you begin your real estate investment career, the better your results. Buying and holding the right rental properties for 20 to 30 years is an ideal way to hedge inflation, take advantage of unique tax benefits, and build wealth for retirement.

Chapter 23

Ten Ways to Rent Your Vacancy

In This Chapter

- Staying ahead of the competition
- Keeping the interests of your prospective tenants in mind

Every day that a rental unit sits vacant is a loss of revenue that you can never fully recover. Even if you get a higher rent, the lost rent due to vacancy is usually gone for good. In this chapter, I give you ten specific tips or tools to help you rent your vacancy right away.

Maintain Curb Appeal

When you're leasing rental units, the rental prospect's first impression is the exterior curb appeal of the property when he drives up. If your rental property doesn't look clean and attractive on the outside, the tenant will often never even wait to see the inside! Your chances of leasing your rental unit at a competitive market rent to a stable and financially solid rental prospect is just about nil when your property doesn't have good curb appeal. You can't always dramatically improve the architectural look of your rental property, but you can usually control the curb appeal of the grounds and overall appearance from the street. Familiarity is the enemy of rental property owners; when you're familiar with your property, you may have trouble looking at it with an independent and critical eye. Drive up to your property and continually ask yourself what catches your eye and looks tacky or poorly maintained. You may really have to focus, but you will find several items that need immediate attention. Take care of them now.

Keep the Unit in Rent-Ready Condition

Although you may eventually be able to find a tenant who will accept your rental unit before it is in rent-ready condition, you can almost guarantee that the unit will be returned to you in even worse condition when that tenant vacates. Of course, the tenant will then argue with you if you try to make any deductions from his security deposit, and the courts will probably side with the tenant because the unit wasn't clean originally. Spare yourself the agony, and set your goal to have a rent-ready unit that is clean and free of defects.

You need to distinguish your rental unit from the others out there. So although your property may have certain factors or issues that are negatives beyond your control, the professionally maintained, clean, bright, and airy appearance of your rental unit is a noticeable difference that will appeal to the best rental prospects.

Establish a Competitive Rent

If you don't have vacancies on a regular basis and you're in a rental market where rents are fluctuating, setting the rental rate at the right amount can be a real challenge. Be sure to do your homework and carefully review the local rental market for rental properties that are truly comparable. If you set your rent too low, you will have multiple qualified applicants and can select the best one, but you will not maximize your rental income. If the rent is too high, you will suffer lost rental income that is tough or impossible to ever recover, even if you ultimately succeed in getting an above-market rent. The key is to set your rent at or slightly below market rent for your area.

Offer Prospects a Rental Rate Guarantee

Most prospective tenants are concerned about the rent. Although they may feel comfortable with your current rent, virtually all rental prospects are concerned about your ability to unilaterally raise their rent unless you offer a lease. Of course, a long-term lease is not in your best interest because you not only cannot increase the rent, you may have trouble evicting a problem tenant.

If you know that you have no intention of raising the rent of your new tenant in the near future, offer the prospect a rental rate guarantee for a set period of time. This will allay the prospect's fears of being hit with an unreasonable rent increase soon after they move-in, while at the same time not locking you into a long-term lease that requires expensive and aggravating court action with proof that the tenant broke the lease.

Stay Ahead of the Technology Curve

Every day, access to technology becomes more important, so pre-wiring your rental property for high-speed Internet access can be a great way to distinguish your property from the competition. Currently, there are four basic types of high-speed Internet connections available: cable, digital subscriber lines (DSL), fixed wireless, and satellite. Each type has its advantages and not all may be available in your area.

Owners of larger rental properties typically find that the Internet service provider (ISP) will cover the installation costs plus offer to share in the revenues. If you own single-family or small rental properties, you may have more trouble getting service in many areas, but you may be able to get free installation with a tenant commitment to subscribe to the service for a minimum time period.

Offer Referral Fees

Often, your current tenants or the neighbors near your rental property can be the best source for finding your next tenant. They may work or go to school with someone who is looking for a new rental. Or maybe they have social, recreational, or religious activities with people who need a new place to live. So let them know that you have a vacancy coming up, and that you want to reward them for taking the time to refer a rental prospect to you. Referral fees can be an extremely cost-effective source of qualified renters. Another benefit is that most people will not personally refer a potential tenant whom they don't respect and trust. Referral feels allow tenants to make some money and have a hand in picking their own neighbors!

Accept Pets

Although many rental property owners have very firm policies against accepting pets, they are eliminating nearly 50 percent of the potential renters, according to the Humane Society of the United States. With the requirement to accept certain pets for tenants qualified under the Americans with Disabilities Act, many owners already find their ability to enforce "no pet" policies diminished.

So, if you can't beat them, why not join them? If you establish sound pet policies, collect a larger security deposit, and meet both the tenant and pet, you will often find that you have an excellent, stable tenant for many years to come.

Offer Move-In Gifts or Upgrades

The word *free* is one of my favorite words — and one of the most powerful sales tools ever! If you want to rent your vacancy today, seriously consider offering your prospect a move-in gift or an upgrade to the rental unit. Remember that every day your rental unit is sitting vacant, you are losing money that you will never see again, so you may as well sweeten the pot!

You have a choice: You can offer a move-in gift that immediately belongs to the tenant, or you can offer an upgrade to the rental unit that stays when they leave. For example, countertop microwave ovens make great move-in gifts whereas a built-in microwave range hood or ceiling fan is an excellent unit upgrade. If you're planning to replace the carpet, consider giving your incoming tenants the option to choose among their favorite neutral carpet colors.

Contact Corporate Relocation Services

In many areas of the U.S., there is a high demand for rental units for corporate employees who are relocating into the area. In particular, corporate relocation services have an extremely difficult time finding rental properties for families of executives who need single-family homes with yards and plenty of storage. Corporate relocation services are often willing to pay significantly above-market rents for rental units or homes on short-term leases of 6 to 12 months. If the rent is enough, it can be worth the additional turnover. Remember that their only alternative may be to place their clients in extended-stay lodging — and that can quickly become very expensive and cannot match the benefits of most rental properties.

Some corporate relocation professionals will want to lease your property for multiple years with the provision that they can move in different occupants. Make sure that you have very firm house rules and a reasonable limit on the frequency of tenant turnover. Plus, require a detailed inspection upon each move.

Accept Section 8

As I discuss in Chapter 20, the HUD Section 8 program is administrated by 3,000 local public housing authorities located throughout the country. Some of those agencies are not easy to work with; some have maximum allowable rents that are well below market value. However, if this is not a problem in your area, you may find some tangible benefits in participating in the Section 8 program. The most important benefit if you have a vacancy may be the fact that there is a severe shortage of rental units available for Section 8 tenants in many areas. Plus, the government typically pays the majority of the rent promptly each month, so you at least have that guarantee.

Chapter 24

Ten Ways to Increase Cash Flow

In This Chapter

- Finding ways to bring in more cash
- Figuring out how to reduce your expenses

Maximizing your cash flow is one of the most important goals of owning rental property, because cash flow essentially represents profit. Cash flow can be *positive,* which means you receive income from your rental property, or *negative,* which means you must put in cash to meet your expenses. Even if your cash flow is currently positive, you may be able to improve or increase your cash flow.

Raise the Rent

Raising the rent is one of the easiest ways to increase your cash flow. Most rental property owners fail to keep their rents up to market levels because they are worried that they will lose their good tenants. Some owners are just too nice, or they become personally involved with their tenants and can't operate their rentals like a business. Minimizing turnover is one of the most important concepts of rental property management, but it should not be at the expense of lost rental income because your rental rates are significantly below market. ***Remember:*** Most tenants realize that the costs of operating and properly maintaining rental properties are rising, and they will readily accept a reasonable cost-of-living increase at least once a year. Keep the increases low and you can increase your cash flow without significant tenant turnover.

Decrease Your Operating Expenses

Reducing your operating expenses will lead to a direct increase in your cash flow or profit. Of course, you can only reduce your expenses so much. If you become too zealous at saving money, you may find that you're compromising the physical integrity of your rental property — and that will only hurt you in the long run. So each year, prepare a simple budget for the upcoming year and look at every single one of your current expenses. Some items, like a business license or property inspection fees, are beyond your control. Other expenses, like utility rates, will definitely go up, and you may think the costs are out of your hands — but you have some control over usage. For example, a conversion to water-saving toilets and showerheads could drastically reduce your water consumption and sewer usage and result in a much lower expense.

Make Your Tenant Pay for Utility Costs

A current trend in many parts of the country is to shift the burden for utility costs to the tenant by installing sub-meters or using the Residential Utility Billing System (RUBS) method. *RUBS* is an accounting system that uses a formula to allocate the water and sewer costs back to individual tenants based on the size or number of occupants of the rental unit. A more accurate and much better system is one in which the utility company physically installs small in-line water meters for each rental unit (called *sub-meters*) and individually bills the tenant for his own water usage. Sub-metering has two primary benefits: Tenants have a direct incentive to conserve water, and you're only responsible for the water used in the property's common areas.

Many rental properties were converted to individual electric meters in the 1970s; however, almost all rental properties in the country were still master-metered for water until very recently. A *master-metered* building has one or more water meters, but the meter records the usage both in common areas and in individual rental units on a single meter and the owner typically pays the bill for the entire property. Of course, the tenant indirectly pays for the water and sewer costs through his rent, but he has no incentive to conserve because the services are included in the rent.

Appeal Your Property Taxes

The general real estate tax on rental properties is made up of the taxes levied by your local municipality and various governmental agencies. These taxes are levied to support the services offered by the government and are called *ad valorem taxes.* They vary in accordance with the value of the property. Real estate is valued, or assessed, for real estate taxation purposes by governmental tax assessors. Your building and land are appraised separately, and most states have laws that require the property to be periodically reassessed or revalued. A tax rate is then applied to the assessed value to determine the actual tax billed to the property owner. The higher the assessed value of your property, the higher your property tax bill.

If you believe that your property's assessed value as calculated by the tax assessor is too high, contact your local assessor and ask for a reassessment. Tax appeals or protests are often first heard within the tax assessor's office or a local board of appeal. If a dispute still exists, ultimately appeals may be taken to court in many states. If you're able to get a lower assessment, this will lead to a direct reduction in your property tax bill.

Reduce Your Turnover

Turnover is one of the most costly problems for owners of small rental properties. And no matter what you do, your tenants will move eventually. So turnover is inevitable. But if you can keep your tenants for longer periods of time, you can greatly reduce your operating expenses while maintaining steady rental income. If you take the time to properly screen and select your tenants and look for someone who intends to stay for a long time, you're usually rewarded. Treating the tenants respectfully and responding promptly to their reasonable requests often leads to longer tenancies as well.

Refinance Your Rental Property

Most rental property owners acquire their investment properties using financing, in which they pay a cash down payment along with a loan. Refinancing is simply taking out another loan to replace the one you currently have on your rental property — and generally on more favorable terms. The interest you pay each month on your property loan is generally one of the largest single expense items you have. If the interest rates available on new loans for similar rental properties decrease below your current loan rate, you may be able to refinance. One of the primary goals and benefits of refinancing without changing the term of your loan is to obtain a lower interest rate and lower monthly payments. The lower the monthly payments, the higher your cash flow.

Give Your Tenants a Lease Option

A *lease option* is an agreement that allows the tenant the right to purchase the leased property at a predetermined price for a certain period of time. Lease options offer many benefits for both the owner and the tenant. The tenant is able to become a property owner even if he is short on money for a down payment. And lease options generate more money for the landlord. See Chapter 19 for more information.

Upgrade Your Rental Property

Next to just raising the rents, one of the quickest ways to increase your cash flow is to upgrade or renovate your rental units. Rental properties can become stale and dated and not very competitive when their curb appeal falters compared to the newer rental units in your area. Installing new carpeting and painting the walls a lighter, brighter color can really make a difference. A new microwave range vent unit or a ceiling fan and contemporary window coverings will increase the demand for your rental properties. Spending some more money now can help you increase your cash flow through higher rents in the future.

Pre-Lease to Minimize Downtime between Tenants

Seek permission to inspect the rental unit as soon as the tenant gives notice that she will be leaving. Then you can prepare a list of the work you need to do in the unit to bring it to a rent-ready condition and schedule all of the work for the two to three days right after the tenant vacates. In the meantime, you can advertise the rental unit and, upon giving the current occupant proper notice, show it to interested prospects while the current tenant is still in possession. This way, you can get your property pre-leased and the new tenant moved in within a week of the former tenant's departure, decreasing your loss of rent and increasing your cash flow.

Use the Tax Advantages of Depreciation

Depreciation (covered in more detail in Chapter 17) is an accounting concept that offers the advantage of deferring taxes to rental property owners. It allows you to recover in tax deductions the basis of your rental property over a certain number of years. Keep in mind that depreciation is only an accounting rule and may have very little relationship to the actual physical deterioration of the rental property or whether the property has gained or lost value in the marketplace.

The IRS rules state that whether a property is brand-new or 60 years old, it has an economic life of 27.5 years from the date of purchase.

When you have fully utilized the allowed depreciation for a particular building, consider a tax-deferred exchange for a new property. The newly acquired property often has a higher depreciable tax basis, which provides larger depreciation deductions and lower income taxes. This results in higher after-tax cash flow.

Appendix

Resources

Media

Bob Bruss Real Estate Newsletter: Bob Bruss is a California attorney and a nationally recognized real estate expert who provides solid advice for real estate investors on a wide array of real estate issues. You can get a free sample issue of his highly informative newsletter and a list of available special reports by calling 800-736-1736 or visiting `www.bobbruss.com`.

Professional Apartment Management: A monthly newsletter from Brownstone Publishers, *Professional Apartment Management* is full of feature articles and money-making and money-saving ideas. Each issue has several comprehensive articles with excellent tips and forms from an impressive Board of Advisors. This publication is highly useful for both the small and large rental property owner. The *Fair Housing Coach* newsletter published by Brownstone Publishers is also a great resource. Call 800-643-8095 and ask for a free trial issue and subscription information. Or visit `www.brownstone.com` for information on the many publications Brownstone offers.

Property Managers' Hotline: Quinlan Publishing is a leading publisher of legal and informational newsletters for property management and real estate professionals, including *Property Managers' Hotline.* Another great reference is Quinlan's *Landlord Tenant Law Bulletin.* For information on obtaining a free trial issue, call 617-542-0048 or visit Quinlan online at `www.landlord-tenant-online.com`.

Real Estate Today! with Robert Griswold: A weekly live radio show with guests and open phones to answer listener questions on all aspects of real estate, including tenant/landlord and property management issues; the buying, selling and financing of all types of real estate; and community association issues. Listen online to a live or archived show through Yahoo! Broadcast.com. Visit the *Real Estate Today!* Web site at `www.retodayradio.com` for a time in your area and a listing of upcoming and past guests. Call in with your real estate question or submit a question online.

Rental Forum: An Inman News Features nationally syndicated tenant/landlord question-and-answer column for all 50 states, written by Robert Griswold with attorneys Ted Smith and Steve Kellman. Visit www.inman.com for more information.

Rental Roundtable: A syndicated tenant/landlord question-and-answer column exclusively for California, written by Robert Griswold with tenant/landlord legal attorneys Ted Smith and Steve Kellman. The column appears regularly in the *San Diego Union-Tribune* Sunday Home section, the *Los Angeles Times* Sunday Real Estate section, and the *San Francisco Chronicle* Sunday Real Estate section. Visit www.rentalroundtable.com for more information.

Professional and Trade Organizations

Institute of Real Estate Management (IREM): IREM has been *the* source for education and professional recognition for real estate managers and management organizations for over 60 years. As the leading resource in real estate management in the U.S., IREM provides training, information, research, and practical advice for real estate management professionals at all career levels. IREM's services support its members' commitment to safeguarding and maximizing the value of the real estate entrusted to them. Call 312-329-6000 or visit www.irem.org for more information.

National Apartment Association (NAA): The NAA is a federation of more than 155 state and local associations throughout the United States and Canada. Together, they represent more than 28,000 members and 4.2 million apartment homes. NAA membership includes multifamily owners, managers, leasing consultants, builders, service technicians, and suppliers. NAA provides a wealth of information through advocacy, research, technology, education, strategic partnerships, and an ever-growing membership base. Contact NAA at 703-518-6141 or online at www.naahq.org to get in touch with the local affiliated association in your area.

National Association of Housing and Redevelopment Officials (NAHRO): NAHRO is the leading housing and community development advocate for the provision of adequate and affordable housing and strong, viable communities for all Americans — particularly those with low and moderate incomes. Its members administer HUD programs such as Public Housing, Section 8, CDBG and HOME. For more information, call 877-866-2476 or visit NAHRO online at www.nahro.org.

Computer and Manual Accounting Systems

Peachtree Business Products: Peachtree is a great resource offering a wide variety of property management items, including manual rental accounting systems and supplies. Phone: 800-241-4623; Web site: www.property.pbp1.com.

Property Automation Software Corporation: Tenant Pro 5.0, the flagship product of Property Automation Software, has become one of the fastest-selling property management software programs in the U.S. and Canada. The easy-to-use software combines a complete accounting package with a comprehensive database, providing owners and managers with instant information on tenants, units, vendors, and properties. Tenant Pro now has more than 14,000 users throughout the United States and Canada. It's great for owners or managers with a small- to medium-size rental property portfolio. A free CD trial version is available. Phone: 800-964-2792; Web site: www.tenantpro.com.

Yardi Systems, Inc.: Since 1982, Yardi has been the industry leader in the design, development, and support of software solutions for the real estate industry. The Yardi software product line includes the Yardi Professional, Yardi Advantage, and Yardi Voyager. Yardi Professional is a feature-rich system designed to meet the needs of small- to mid-sized residential management companies and includes full accounting with property, owner, vendor, applicant, and tenant databases. The system easily handles management of single- and multi-family residential units. As your business grows, affordable housing, commercial, maintenance, and other feature sets can be added easily. Phone: 800-866-1144; Web site: www.yardi.com.

Legal Information

Nolo is the nation's leading provider of self-help legal information, software, and Web-based tools. Since its founding in 1971, Nolo has been making the law more accessible to the public. I highly recommend its highly specific national tenant/landlord law book, *Every Landlord's Legal Guide,* plus many of their other excellent sources of information. Phone: 800-728-3555; Web site: www.nolo.com.

Rental Housing Suppliers

Maintenance Warehouse, a subsidiary of Home Depot, is the largest supplier of repair and replacement products for the rental housing industry. You can request its free annual catalog, which features thousands of items, online. The catalog is easy to use, provides 3-D drawings, and features three-tier pricing that's guaranteed for the life of the catalog. Phone: 877-694-4932; Web site: www.mwh.com.

Credit Reporting Agencies

Equifax, P.O. Box 740256, Atlanta, GA 30374-0256; phone: 800-997-2493; Web site: www.equifax.com.

Experian, P.O. Box 9600, Allen, TX 75013; phone: 800-311-4769; Web site: www.experian.com.

Trans Union, P.O. Box 2000, Chester, PA 19022; phone: 800-888-4213; Web site: www.tuc.com.

Index

• A •

abandoned unit, 242–243
abbreviations in ads, 86–87
accepting
  application, 125
  cash, 178–179, 200
  check, 180, 181
access control systems, 274–275
accounting. *See* financial management
Accredited Management Organization (AMO), 19
acoustic ceiling, 43
actual cash value, 286
ad valorem tax, 293, 334
address
  including in ad, 87
  visibility of, 46
adults, verifying identity of, 145
advertising
  brochure, 96
  broker referral, 95–96
  community bulletin board, 93–94
  curb appeal, 73–74
  direct mailing, 94–95
  fair-housing laws and, 74–76, 95
  features, emphasizing, 71
  flyer, 88–91
  Internet, 92–93
  leasing agency, 95
  local employers, 94, 332
  methods, comparing, 72
  newspaper classifieds, 81–88
  overview of, 70–71, 76
  property signs, 78–80
  rental publications, 91–92
  rifle vs. shotgun approach, 71–72
  television and radio, 97
  toll-free phone number, 81
  word of mouth, 76–78
affirmative defense, 223
affordable housing, definition of, 311
age discrimination, 161
aggregate deductible, 286
agreement. *See also* contract; lease agreement
  with property management company, 23–24
  with security firm, 276
  short-term lease option, 305, 308–310, 335
A.M. Best Company, 285
amenities in unit
  marketing plan and, 70, 71
  rental inquiry call and, 112
  tenants and, 35, 36–37
Americans with Disabilities Act, 75, 165, 250
animal. *See* pet
animal agreement, 176–177, 179
answering machine, 101–102
answering phone, 108–110
apartment association, 152
Apartment Guide, 91, 92
appliances
  carbon monoxide and, 278–279
  inspecting, 41–42
  providing manuals or instructions for, 187
  upgrading or replacing, 37
  warranties on, 267–268
application. *See also* verifying information
  completing after showing unit, 124–125
  notification of decision on, 155–157
  occupancy guidelines, reviewing, 145, 148
  Rental Application and Application Fee Receipt form, 126, 127
  rental history, checking, 148–149
  updating information on, 31
arbitration services, 221
area code, 81
asbestos, 36, 43, 133–135
assignment of interest in rental unit, 227
attorney, using, 224, 226, 228

• B •

bank account, 19, 21, 52, 298, 299
bankruptcy of tenant, 226
bathroom, cleaning, 43
Bob Bruss Real Estate Newsletter, 337
bond, 19, 21
broad-form coverage, 285
brochure, 96
broker referral, 95–96
Bruss, Robert J., 310, 337
budget, 298–299
building codes, 37
building ordinance coverage, 287
Burglary Prevention Council, 270
business accounting packages, 300
buying property
  documents to have, 25–29
  due diligence period, 25–26
  tenants, working with, 29–32
  unoccupied, 32
  upgrading property, 32

• C •

call forwarding, 100–101
caller ID, 101
cancelling management agreement, 23
capital gains, 289, 292
capital reserve account, 299
carbon monoxide, 278–279
career and property management, 14–15
carpet, 44, 187
cash, policy on, 178–179, 200
cash flow, 8–9, 49, 328, 333–336
cash investment, 8, 325
caulking, 42
ceiling, 43
cell phone, 102
certificate of mailing, 239
Certified Property Manager (CPM), 19
check
  accepting, 181, 199–200
  certifying or cashing, 180
  returned, handling, 204–205
checking account, 298
children
  fair-housing laws and, 162–163
  injuries to, 297–298
  unsupervised, 220
classified ad. *See* newspaper classified ad
cleaning service, 43
cleanliness of unit, 39, 43–44, 170
coinsurance clause, 287
collecting judgment, 225
collecting rent
  early-payment discount, 205
  incentive for on time payment, 207
  late fee, 203–204
  late payment, 202–203, 218
  legal notice, serving, 206
  location for, 198–199
  method of payment, 199–201
  multiple checks, 201
  partial payment, 205–206
  policy and procedures for, 195–196, 201–202
  preventing problems, 195
  returned check, 204–205
  schedule for, 196–198
commercial rental property, sale of, 27
commitment to succeed, 10
common areas
  laundry facility, 306
  smoking in, 321–322
  upgrading or renovating, 37–38, 207
  utility bills for, 174
community bulletin board, 93–94
community-interest development, 38
companion animal, 75, 165–166
comparable property, 50
comparison chart, 106–108
compensation
  of employee, 248
  of manager, 251
  of property management company, 21–22
competition
  features offered by, 37
  market analysis of, 50–51
  for tenants, 68

complaints
about manager, 252, 253
about unit, 296
comprehensive insurance policy, 284
condo rental unit, 49
confidentiality, 151, 273
conservation issues, 42
constructive eviction, 224–225
contested eviction, 224
contract. *See also* agreement
emergency repairs, 19–20
obtaining copy of when taking over property, 28
property management company, 23–24
contractor
behavior of, 263
delegating work to, 11
selecting, 14, 254–256
turnover work, 46
converting lease or agreement, 30–31
convincing prospect, 123
corporate relocation service, 332
corrective maintenance, 261
cosigner, 154–155, 156
cosmetic maintenance, 262
cost. *See also* fees
of ad, 82, 83
of flyer, 88–89
of owning and operating property, 49
of renovation or upgrade, 36
credentials of property management company, 19
credit history
denial based on, 156–157, 159
Fair Credit Reporting Act, 156, 157, 249–250
reviewing, 150–153
credit reporting agencies Web sites, 152, 340
crime on property. *See also* safety issues
accepting cash and, 178–179, 200
illegal activity, 150
individual walk-through and, 118–119
lock, changing, 190–191, 274
responding to, 273
vandalism, 79, 94
Crime- and Drug-Free Housing Addendum, 271
Crime-Free Multi-Housing Program, 270
criminal history, checking, 153–154, 250
curb appeal, 73–74, 261, 262, 329
Cure or Quit notice, 223
custodial maintenance, 261–262

• D •

damage vs. ordinary wear and tear, 237–238, 241
date, setting for move-in, 169–170
deadbeat tenant, professional, 140
death of tenant, 228–229
deductible for insurance, 286, 287–288
deferred maintenance, 262
deposit. *See also* security deposit
holding, 125–127, 128
pet and, 318
priority waiting list, 129
depreciation, 8, 291–292, 326, 336
desktop publishing software, 89
digital camera, 89, 93
digital pager, 102
direct mailing, 94–95
directions, giving, 119
disability
reasonable accommodation to, 163–164
reasonable modification to property, 75, 164, 267
disclosures, mandatory
asbestos, 133–135
lead-based paint, 130–133
radon, 135–136
sexual offenders, 136–137
discrimination
advertising and, 74–76
application process, 125
children, 162–163
companion or service animal, 165–166
complaints, avoiding, 158–160
laws regarding, 161
protected class, 174
reasonable accommodations, 163–164
rent collection and, 204, 206
screening process and, 140, 141, 142, 154, 157
sexual harassment, 166
steering, 162
waiting list and, 129

disparate impact, 158–159
display ad, 83
distance, managing property from, 15–16
distressed property, 22
distributing flyer, 90–91
documents. *See also* documents for taking over property; written documentation
  for Section 8, 314
  for tenant, reviewing and signing, 175–177
documents for taking over property
  filing, 296
  licenses and permits, 27
  personal property list, 26
  rent roll, 26
  security deposit list, 26–27
  seller's insurance policy, 28–29
  service agreement, 28
  tenant files, 26
  utility billing, 27–28
domestic disputes, 228
door lock, 45, 190, 274, 275
down payment, 8, 325
due diligence period, 25–26

• E •

early-payment discount, 205
educational resources, 11
electromagnetic fields (EMFs), 279
electronic payment, 200–201
e-mail, 103, 261
emergency repairs, 19–20, 259–260
employee
  complaint about, 252–253
  duties, schedule, and compensation, 248
  firing, 253–254
  hiring, 247–248
  independent contractor vs., 254
  screening, 249–250
employee leasing company, 252
employer
  advertising with, 94
  relocation services of, 332
  responsibilities as, 250–251
employment, verifying, 149–150
employment-screening firms, 250
encapsulation of asbestos, 134
endorsement for money and securities, 287
energy-efficiency issues, 42
environmental issues. *See also* safety issues
  asbestos, 36, 43, 133–135
  carbon monoxide, 278–279
  disclosure forms, 176
  electromagnetic fields (EMFs), 279
  fire safety, 277–278
  lead-based paint, 36, 130–133
  radon, 135–136
Environmental Protection Agency (EPA), 131, 133, 136
Equal Housing Opportunity logo, 76
estoppel agreement, 27
eviction action
  abandoned unit and, 243
  alternatives to, 221
  bankruptcy and, 226
  collecting judgment, 225
  legal notice, serving, 222–225
  mediation or arbitration services, 221
  partial rent payment and, 206
  record of, 113
  small claims court, 222
  voluntary move-out, 221
exterior
  curb appeal, 73–74, 261, 262, 329
  improving, 37–38
  lighting, 275–276
exterminator, 42

• F •

Fair Credit Reporting Act, 156, 157, 249–250
fair-housing laws
  advertising and, 74–76, 95
  Americans with Disabilities Act, 165
  avoiding complaint based on, 158–160
  children, 162–163
  companion or service animal, 165–166
  discrimination, 161
  exemptions to, 160
  Housing for Older Persons Act and, 320
  reasonable accommodations, 163–164
  reasonable modifications, 75, 164, 267
  risk scoring service and, 157

sexual harassment, 166
smoking and, 321
steering, 162
familial status discrimination, 158–159
features in rental unit
marketing plan and, 70, 71
rental inquiry call and, 112
tenants and, 35, 36–37
Federal Emergency Management Agency, 280
fees
credit report, 153
late payment of rent, 203–204
lockout and lost key, 190
pet, 318
property management company, 21–22
referral, 77–78, 96, 331
returned check, 205
sign on nearby property, 80
fidelity bond, 19, 21, 287
filing system. *See also* written documentation
organizing, 295–296
protecting, 273
setting up, 191–192, 297–298
financial management
accounting systems, 339
budget and cash flow, 298–299
cash flow, 8–9, 49, 328, 333–336
computer system, 300–302
maintaining records, 297–298
manual system for, 299
operating expenses, 289, 333–334
fire extinguisher, 45, 278
fire safety, 277–278
fireplace, 42, 278–279
firing employee, 253–254
first impression
curb appeal, 73–74, 261, 262, 329
directions to property, 87
of exterior, 37–38
phone call, 109
signs, 80
of unit, 35, 38–39
welcome package, 192
floor covering, 44, 187
flyer
cost of, 88–89
creating, 89–90
distributing, 90–91
For Rent magazine, 91, 92
Form 1099 (IRS), 46, 256
forms
Addendum to Lease or Rental Agreement, 62–64
Animal Agreement, 176–177, 179
Comparison Chart, 106–108
Crime- and Drug-Free Housing Addendum, 271
Deposit Assignment and Release Agreement, 229
Disclosure of Information on Lead-Based Paint and/or Lead-Based Paint Hazards, 132
Guarantee of Lease or Rental Agreement, 154–155, 156
Holding Deposit Agreement and Receipt, 128
Incident Report, 288, 290
Lease Agreement, 56–62
Lease or Rental Agreement Violation Letter, 219
Maintenance Request, 263, 264
Move-In/Move-Out Inspection Checklist, 30, 180–187, 231, 236
Move-Out Information Letter, 233–235
Notice of Denial to Rent, 157, 159
Notice of Intent to Enter Rental Unit, 263, 265
Notice of Intent to Vacate Rental Unit, 232, 233
Policies and Rules, 172–173
Property Knowledge Sheet, 105–106, 107
Rental Application and Application Fee Receipt, 126, 127
Rental Application Verification Form, 146–148
Rental Rate Guarantee Certificate, 64–65
Security Deposit Itemization, 238–241
Smoke Detector Agreement, 176, 178
Statement of Rental Policy, 141–142, 143–144
Telephone Prospect Card, 104–105
Tenant Information Letter, 188–189, 231

friable, 134
furnished units, 308

• G •

good funds, 180
government programs
  rehabilitation loans, 315–316
  rental subsidy, 312
  Section 8, 312–315, 332
grace period for paying rent, 198
ground-fault interrupter (GFI) circuit, 45
grounds
  curb appeal, 73–74, 261, 262, 329
  renovating, 38
guarantor, 154–155, 156
guard service, 276–277

• H •

handyman, choosing, 14
hazard reduction laws, 130
hazardous materials, 36
health risk, documenting, 186
hiring employees, 247–248
"hold harmless" clause, 23
holding deposit, 125–127, 128
holdover tenant, 226
home ownership, leaving apartment for, 216
homeowners' association, 38
hook, including in ad, 84–85
house rules, 171–175, 214
Housing Choice Voucher Program, 313
Housing for Older Persons Act of 1995, 320
HUD. *See* U.S. Department of Housing and Urban Development (HUD)
Humane Society of the United States, 318

• I •

identity of adults, verifying, 145
implied warranty of habitability, 257
Incident Report Form, 288, 290
income
  from property, estimating, 49
  verifying, 149–150, 151
income taxes, 8, 289
increasing
  cash flow, 333–336
  rent, 31–32, 36, 207–209, 214–215, 333
  security deposit, 54
independent contractor, 254
inspecting rental unit
  annually, 258
  at move-out, 236
  prior to buying, 30
  prior to move-in, 38–40, 180–188
  safety inspection, 45–46
Institute of Real Estate Management (IREM), 11, 19, 338
insurance
  claim, handling, 288
  of contractor, checking, 46, 255
  deductible, 286, 287–288
  file for, 296
  of property management company, 19, 21
  renter's type, 288
  right coverage, determining, 283–284
  of security firm, 276
  of seller, obtaining copy of, 28–29
  taking over property, 28
  types of coverage, 284–287
interest, paying on security deposit, 53–54
Internal Revenue Service. *See* IRS
Internet
  access to, providing, 307–308, 330–331
  advertising on, 92–93
  credit information on, 153, 157
interviewing
  landlord, 148–149
  pet, 318
  property management company, 20–21
  prospective tenant, 110–111
investments, diversifying, 325
inviting prospect to lease, 124
invoices, paying, 12
IRS
  Form 1099, 46, 256
  Section 1031 exchange, 292–293, 326

• K •

keys
  access control systems and, 274–275
  giving to tenant, 176, 190–191
kitchen, cleaning, 43

• L •

landlord
  apathy, perception of, 212
  basic skills for, 9
  rental history, checking, 148–149
landlord's policy, 286
landscaping, 38, 73–74
"last month's rent," collecting, 53
laundry machines, 306
lawn care staff, choosing, 14
lawsuit, insurance coverage and, 283–284
lead-based paint, 36, 130–133
lease agreement
  addendum to, 63–64
  breaking, 226–227
  converting, 30–31
  disclaimers in, 272
  renewing, 215–216
  rental agreement vs., 48, 54–55
  reviewing with tenant, 175
  short-term lease option, 305, 308–310, 335
  standard agreement example, 56–63
lease option, 305, 308–310, 335
LeaseWithPets.com, 318
leasing agency, 95
leasing rental unit, fee for, 22
legal issues. *See also* eviction action; fair-housing laws
  abandoned unit, 242–243
  Americans with Disabilities Act, 75, 165, 250
  asbestos, 133–135
  attorney, using, 224, 226, 228
  confidentiality of credit report, 151
  disclosures, 129–130
  due date of rent, 197, 199
  as employer, 250–252
  employment screening, 249–250
  Fair Credit Reporting Act, 156, 157, 249–250
  grace period, 198
  late fee, 203–204
  lead-based paint disclosure, 130–133
  maintenance, 257
  moving notice, 232
  Nolo, 339
  notice for nonpayment of rent, 206
  occupancy standards, 145, 148
  onsite manager, 248
  records retention, 297–298
  rent-control laws, 209
  repair-and-deduct remedy, 266
  safety and security, 272
  security deposit, 51–52, 53–54, 232, 235, 239
  sexual harassment, 166, 253
  sexual offenders, 136–137
  tenant/landlord laws, 55, 56
letter of introduction, 29
letter of recommendation, 235
leverage, 8, 327
liability, security deposit funds as, 52
liability insurance, 284, 287
license
  contractor, checking, 46, 255
  obtaining copy of when taking over property, 27
  property management company, verifying, 19
lighting, 275–276
like-kind property, 292
linoleum, 44
local neighborhood newspaper, 82
lock
  changing between tenants, 190–191, 274
  on door, 45, 190, 274, 275
  on window, 45, 190, 275
lockout call, 190
loss leader, 19
loss-of-rents coverage, 286
lung cancer and asbestos, 134

• M •

mail, returned, 239
mailing rent check, 199
maintenance
  corrective type, 261
  cosmetic type, 262
  custodial type, 261–262
  deferred type, 262
  emergency repairs, 19–20, 259–260
  eviction action and, 224
  file for, 296

maintenance *(continued)*
legal issues, 257
plan for, 258–259
preparing unit for occupancy, 41–42
preventive type, 260
purchasing parts and supplies, 267–268
repair and deduct remedy, 266
request, responding to, 262–265
request, tracking, 296
retaining tenant and, 73, 212–213
saving on costs of, 14
by tenant, 266–267
Maintenance Warehouse, 340
management company. *See* property management company
manager. *See* property manager
managing property
basic skills for, 9
challenges of, 12
delegating activities, 11–12
from distance, 15–16
experience and, 11
learning from professionals, 13
self-evaluation of skills, 9–10
self-management pros and cons, 14–15
time management skills, 12
market level of rent, determining, 47, 50–51, 330
market value of property, 293
marketing plan
description of, 67–68
Internet access, providing, 330–331
pets, allowing, 317–318, 331
senior citizens, 319–320
smoke-free units, providing, 320–322
students, 319
target market, determining, 68–69, 94–95
WIFM approach, 69–70, 71
master-metered building, 334
mediation services, 221
meeting with tenants, 29
Megan's Law, 136–137
mileage deduction, 297
military newspaper, 88
model rental unit, 120–121
month-to-month rental agreement
addendum to, 62–64
lease compared to, 48, 54–55
rental rate guarantee and, 64–65
standard agreement example, 56–62
Move-In/Move-Out Inspection Checklist, 30, 180–187, 231, 236
move-in procedure
collecting money, 177–180
date, setting, 169–170
documents, reviewing and signing, 175–177
file, setting up, 191–192
gift, 331–332
informational letter, 188–189
inspection prior to, 180–188
meeting prior to, 171
overview of, 169
prorating rent, 197–198
rules, reviewing, 171–175
welcome package, 192–193
Move-Out Information Letter, 233–235
move-out procedure
abandoned unit, 242–243
damage and, 237–238, 241
disputes over deposit, 242
encouraging compliance with, 231
inspection, 236
Move-Out Information Letter, 233–235
notification of intent to vacate, 232–233
Security Deposit Itemization Form, 238–241

• N •

National Apartment Association (NAA), 11, 46, 74, 338
National Association of Housing and Redevelopment Officials, 338
National Lead Information Clearinghouse, 131
natural disasters, 279–280
negative leverage, 327
newspaper classified ad
abbreviations, 86–87
address, including, 87
choosing newspaper, 82–83
days to run, 87–88
hook, including, 84–85
rules for, 81–82
size of, 83–84
writing, 84–87

niche marketing
Internet access, 330–331
pets, allowing, 317-318, 331
senior citizens, 319–320
smoke-free units, 320–322
students, 319
"no" index in rules, 173–174
noisy tenant, 220
Nolo, 339
non-owned auto liability coverage, 287
non-rent revenue
description of, 305–306
furnished units, 308
Internet access, 307–308
laundry machines, 306
parking, 307
storage, 306–307
nonrefundable deposits, 53
Notice of Intent to Enter Rental Unit, 263, 265
Notice to Quit, 223
notifying
applicant of decision, 155–157
tenant of crime, 273
tenant of rent increase, 208

• O •

objections
handling during call, 114–115
resolving during showing, 122–123
occupancy guidelines
disparate impact of, 158–159
reviewing with tenant, 145, 148
occupancy rate, 51
occupied unit, showing, 121–122
one-write system, 299
online advertising, 92–93
onsite manager. *See* property manager
open house, 100, 116, 117–118
operating expenses, 289, 333–334
opportunity cost, 14–15
option-to-purchase agreement, 305, 308–310, 335
oral vs. written rental agreement, 55, 176
ordinary wear and tear. *See* wear and tear, ordinary
organizing files, 295–296
ownership, notifying government of change in, 27

padding for carpet, 44
painting vacant unit, 42–43
parking, 307
Pay Rent or Quit notice, 222
Peachtree Business Products, 299, 339
periodic rental agreement
addendum to, 62–64
lease compared to, 48, 54–55
rental rate guarantee and, 64–65
standard agreement example, 56–62
permit, obtaining copy of, 27
personal digital assistant, 102
personal property
abandoned, 243
list of, 26
personal references, checking, 154
personality for management, 9–10, 12
pest control, 42
pet
animal agreement, 176–177, 179
companion animal, 75, 165–166
defining and limiting, 180
fees for, 53
niche marketing and, 317–318, 331
photo of, keeping, 177
phone call. *See also* telephone
comparison chart, 106–108
converting to showing of unit, 115–117
name, using, 110
objections, handling, 114–115
preparing for, 103–104
pre-qualifying during, 112–114
proper business use of, 104
Property Knowledge Sheet, 105–106, 107
providing and obtaining information during, 110–111
rental inquiry type, 104
selling property during, 111–112
sense of urgency, creating, 116
telephone prospect card, 104–105
photocopying ID of adult tenant, 145

photographing unit, 187
plumbing problems, 193
policy implementation, 31
pool, 42
positive leverage, 8, 327
posters, 251
pre-leasing, 336
preparing unit for occupancy
  carpet or floor covering, 44
  cleaning, 41
  contractor for, 46
  final cleaning, 43–44, 170
  maintenance, 41–42
  painting, 42–43
  plan for, 40–41
  safety inspection, 45–46
pre-qualifying prospective tenant
  during call, 112–114
  during rental showing, 122
preventive maintenance, 260
priority waiting list, developing, 127, 129
problems with tenant. *See also* eviction action
  additional occupant, 218–220
  assignment or sublease, 227
  bankruptcy, 226
  broken lease, 226–227
  departing roommate, 227–228, 229
  domestic disputes, 228
  illegal holdover, 226
  late payment of rent, 218
  noise, 220
  response to, 217–218
  unsupervised children, 220
professional and trade organizations, 338
Professional Apartment Management newsletter, 337
professional deadbeat tenant, 140
property, managing. *See* managing property
property, taking over
  documents to have, 26–29
  due diligence period, 25–26
  tenants, working with, 29–32
  unoccupied, 32
  upgrading, 32
Property Automation Software Corporation, 339
property knowledge sheet, 105–106, 107
property management company
  accounting reports from, 301–302
  advantages of, 16, 18
  agreement with, 23–24
  compensation of, 21–22
  disadvantages of, 17
  insurance of, 19, 21
  interviewing, 20–21
  references, checking, 18
  selecting, 18–21
  services of, 17–18
  size of, 22
  tax laws and, 24
property manager
  advantages of, 248
  compensation of, 251
  duties, schedule, and compensation, 248
  evaluating and selecting, 249–250
  independent contractor vs. employee status, 254
  working with, 11, 12, 252–253
Property Managers' Hotline, 337
property taxes, 293–294, 334–335
prorating rent, 197–198
protected class, 174
public housing authority (PHA), 312–316
purchase option, 305, 308–310
purchasing property. *See* taking over property

qualified rental traffic, 79

• R •

radio, advertising on, 97
radon, 135–136
raising
  rent, 31–32, 36, 207–209, 214–215, 333
  security deposit, 54

real estate
inflation and, 327–328
investing in, 325
purchasing, 8–9
sheltering other income, 328
success record of, 2, 7
tax laws, 24, 326
value of, 327
real estate agent
referral from, 95–96
services of, 19
real estate professional, IRS definition of, 291
Real Estate Today! With Robert Griswold (radio show), 337
reasonable accommodations, 163–164
"reasonable care" provision, 23
recovery period, 292
references, checking
contractor, 46
property management company, 18
tenant, 154
referral fee, 77–78, 96, 331
referrals, 72, 76–78, 95–96
refinancing, 335
rehabilitation loans, 315–316
renewing lease agreement, 215–216
renovating
cash flow and, 336
exterior and common areas, 37–38
vacant unit, 36–37
rent. *See also* collecting rent
guarantee certificate, 64–65, 330
increasing, 31–32, 36, 207–209, 214–215, 333
lease vs. rental agreement, 54–55
mailing, 12
market analysis of, 47, 50–51, 330
return on investment and, 49
security deposit and, 235
setting, 48
sign, including on, 80
tracking, 298
unpaid portion exceeding security deposit, 241
rent roll, 26
rental accounting software program, 300–301
rental agreement. *See also* lease agreement; month-to-month rental agreement
oral vs. written, 55
reviewing with tenant, 175
rental history, checking, 148–149
rental property. *See also* vacant unit
advantages of owning, 8–9, 325–328, 336
key to success with, 68
preparing, 35
taking over, 25–32
rental publications, 91–92
rental subsidy program, 312–315
rental traffic, 71, 79
rent-control laws, 209
renter's insurance, 288
repair-and-deduct remedy, 266
repairs, markups on, 20
replacement cost, 286
reserve balance, 299
Residential Lead-Based Paint Hazard Reduction Act, 130–131
residential rental property, sale of, 27
Residential Utility Billing System, 334
resources
accounting systems, 339
credit reporting agencies, 340
educational, 11
Maintenance Warehouse, 340
media, 337–338
professional and trade organizations, 338
retaining tenant
communication and, 212
house rules and, 214
importance of, 211
lease, renewing, 215–216
maintenance and, 212–213
maintenance, curb appeal, and, 73
privacy and, 213–214
rent and, 214–215
satisfaction and, 212
retention of records, 297–298
retirement, 328
return on investment and rent, 49
rifle approach to advertising, 71–72
roof, 45
rules and regulations, 171–175, 214

• S •

safety inspection, 45–46
safety issues. *See also* crime on property; environmental issues
  carbon monoxide, 278–279
  electromagnetic fields (EMFs), 279
  fire safety, 277–278
  keys, access control, and, 274–275
  lighting, 275–276
  natural disasters, 279–280
  responding to, 270–272
  security firms, 276–277
Schedule E, 24
scheduling
  move-in date, 169–170
  rent due date, 196–198
  walk-through, 118–119
screening employee, 249–250
screening tenant. *See also* verifying information
  application and, 124
  criteria, establishing, 140–144
  importance of, 140, 181
  process of, 123
  system for, 139
screens, 45
second job, property management as, 14–15
Section 8 program, 312–315, 332
security deposit
  acquiring property and, 26–27
  collecting, 177
  damage and, 237–238, 241
  disputes over, 242
  importance of, 48
  increasing, 54
  inspection checklist and, 180–181
  interest, paying on, 53–54
  itemization form, 238–241
  keeping funds separate, 52
  laws regarding, 51–52, 53–54
  Move-Out Information Letter and, 233–235
  move-out inspection and, 236
  nonrefundable fees, 53
  purpose of, 51, 52
  recording, 298
  refunding, 231–232, 235, 239
  setting amount of, 52–53
  tax issues, 289
security issues. *See* safety issues; crime on property
security service, 276–277
selecting
  contractor, 14, 254–256
  employees, 247–248
  insurance company, 285
  lawn care staff, 14
  newspaper to advertise in, 82–83
  property management company, 18–21
  tenant. *See* screening tenant
  vendor, 254–256, 267
self-help eviction, 224–225
self-management of property, 14–15
seniors
  housing for, 159, 160
  renting to, 319–320
sense of urgency, creating, 116, 118
service agreement, obtaining copy of, 28
setting rent
  market analysis, 47, 50–51, 330
  methods for, 48
  return on investment and, 49
setting security deposit, 52–53
sexual harassment, 166, 253
sexual offenders, 136–137
sheet vinyl, 44
sheltering other income, 328
short-term lease option agreement, 305, 308–310, 335
shotgun approach to advertising, 71–72
showing of unit
  application, completing after, 124–125
  converting phone call to, 115–117
  convincing prospect, 123
  deposit, holding, 125–127
  greeting prospective tenant, 119–120, 121
  individual appointment, 118–119
  inviting prospect to lease, 124
  objections, resolving, 122–123
  occupied, 121–122
  open house, 117–118
  pre-qualifying during, 122
  unsupervised, 116–117
  vacant, 120–121

signs advertising vacancy, 72, 78–80
single-family rental unit, 49
small claims court, 222, 235, 239
smart card, 274–275
smell of unit, 43–44
smoke detector, 45, 177, 278
smoke detector agreement, 176, 178
Smokefree Apartment House Registry, 321
smoke-free units, 320–322
software programs, 300–301
special form coverage, 285
spreadsheet program, 300
Starker exchange, 292–293, 326
statement of rental policy, 141–142, 143–144
steering, 162
storage units, 306–307
straight-line depreciation, 292
students, renting to, 319
sublease, 227
sub-meter, 334

• T •

taking over property
  documents to have, 25–29
  due diligence period, 25–26
  tenants, working with, 29–32
  unoccupied, 32
  upgrading property, 32
target market, determining, 68–69, 94–95
tax advantages, 8, 326, 336
tax issues
  capital gains, 289, 292
  depreciation, 8, 291–292, 326, 336
  income taxes, 8, 289
  lease option agreement, 310
  management company, 24
  passive vs. active activities, 291
  property taxes, 293–294, 334–335
tax-deferred exchange, 292–293
tear sheet, 88
technology
  cell phone, 102
  digital pager, 102
  overview of, 99–100
  personal digital assistant, 102
  telephone, 100–102
  using, 103
telephone. *See also* phone call
  answering, 108–110
  call forwarding, 100–101
  caller ID, 101
  importance of, 100
  voice mail, 101–102
telephone prospect card, 104–105
television, advertising on, 97
Tenant Information Letter, 188–189, 231
tenant screening service, 153, 157
tenant turnover, 22, 208, 335
tenant/landlord laws, 55, 56
TenantPro for Windows, 301, 339
tenants. *See also* move-in procedure; move-out procedure; problems with tenant; retaining tenant; screening tenant
  competition for, 68
  condition of rental unit and, 35
  converting lease or agreement, 30–31
  death of, 228–229
  features preferred by, 35, 36–37, 70, 71
  files, obtaining copies of, 26
  inspecting unit, 30
  late payment by, 202
  meeting with, 29
  move, reasons for, 55
  occupied unit, showing, 121–122
  professional deadbeat type, 140
  raising rent, 31–32
  showing unit to, 38–40
  warning signs during phone call, 113
Tenants' Maintenance Request Form, 263, 264
Tenant's Notice of Intent to Vacate Rental Unit, 232, 233
terminating lease, 55
time management skills, 12
toll-free phone number, 81
tracking
  maintenance requests, 263, 296
  rent and security deposits, 298
  rental calls, 104–105, 106

• U •

umbrella coverage, 286
Unconditional Quit notice, 223
uncontested eviction, 224

unoccupied property, buying, 32
updating information on application, 31
upgrading
  appliances, 37
  to attract tenants, 85, 336
  before close of escrow, 32
  cosmetic maintenance and, 262
  exterior and common areas, 37–38
  increasing rent and, 207–208
  before lease renewal, 215
  at move-in, 331–332
  rental unit, 36–37, 207–208
U.S. Department of Housing and Urban Development (HUD), 75, 76, 133, 312, 316
U.S. Occupational Safety and Health Administration, 134
utilities, turning off, 188, 259
utility billing
  application and, 149
  changing name on, 174
  obtaining copy of, 27–28, 122
  tenant and, 334

• V •

vacant unit. *See also* advertising; showing of unit
  carpet or floor covering, 44
  cleanliness of, 39, 41
  contractor for turnover work, 46
  deterring vandalism of, 79, 94
  final cleaning, 43–44, 170
  inspection checklist for, 38–40
  maintenance issues, 41–42
  painting, 42–43
  plan to handle, 36, 40–41
  renovation and upgrade to, 36–37
  safety inspection, 45–46
  showing, 120–121
  tips for renting, 329–332
vandalism, 79, 94
vendor, selecting, 254–256, 267
verifying information
  application, 144
  companion animal, 165
  credit history, 150–153
  criminal history, 153–154
  employment and income, 149–150, 151
  identity of adults, 145
  personal references, 154
  reasonable modifications, 164
  rental history, 148–149
  taking over property, 29
  utility bill payment history, 149
videotaping unit, 187, 242
vignette, 121
voice mail, 101–102
voluntary move-out, 221

• W •

waiting list, developing, 127, 129
warranty
  appliances, 267–268
  pet damage, 318
wear and tear, ordinary, 145, 231–232, 235, 237–238
Web sites
  accounting systems, 339
  advertising, 92
  A.M. Best Company, 285
  Americans with Disabilities Act, 165
  Burglary Prevention Council, 270
  credit reporting agencies, 152, 340
  educational resources, 11
  Environmental Protection Agency (EPA), 131, 136
  Equifax, 340
  Experian, 340
  Federal Emergency Management Agency, 280
  government employment posters, 251
  Humane Society of the United States, 318
  LeaseWithPets.com, 318
  Maintenance Warehouse, 340
  media, 337–338
  Nolo, 339
  Peachtree Business Products, 299
  professional and trade organizations, 338
  showing property on, 93
  Smokefree Apartment House Registry, 321
  TenantPro for Windows, 301
  Trans Union, 340
  U.S. Department of Housing and Urban Development, 75, 76, 316
  Yardi Professional, 301
Web-based e-mail, 103

welcome package, 192–193
white space, 83
WIFM (what's in it for me) concept, 69–70, 71
window lock, 45, 190, 275
window treatments, 42
word-of-mouth advertising, 76–78
workers' compensation, 251–252
workplace violence, 252–253
writing classified ad, 84–87
written documentation. *See also* documents; filing system
  of damages, 241
  of denial of application, 157, 159
  of employee performance, 253
  of income, requiring, 150
  income and expenses, 297–298
  of intent to vacate, 232
  of problems with tenant, 218, 219
written vs. oral rental agreement, 55, 176

Yardi Professional, 301, 339

Notes

BUSINESS, CAREERS & PERSONAL FINANCE

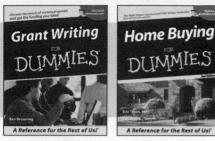

0-7645-5307-0

0-7645-5331-3 *†

Also available:

- Accounting For Dummies †
  0-7645-5314-3
- Business Plans Kit For Dummies †
  0-7645-5365-8
- Cover Letters For Dummies
  0-7645-5224-4
- Frugal Living For Dummies
  0-7645-5403-4
- Leadership For Dummies
  0-7645-5176-0
- Managing For Dummies
  0-7645-1771-6
- Marketing For Dummies
  0-7645-5600-2
- Personal Finance For Dummies *
  0-7645-2590-5
- Project Management For Dummies
  0-7645-5283-X
- Resumes For Dummies †
  0-7645-5471-9
- Selling For Dummies
  0-7645-5363-1
- Small Business Kit For Dummies *†
  0-7645-5093-4

HOME & BUSINESS COMPUTER BASICS

0-7645-4074-2

0-7645-3758-X

Also available:

- ACT! 6 For Dummies
  0-7645-2645-6
- iLife '04 All-in-One Desk Reference For Dummies
  0-7645-7347-0
- iPAQ For Dummies
  0-7645-6769-1
- Mac OS X Panther Timesaving Techniques For Dummies
  0-7645-5812-9
- Macs For Dummies
  0-7645-5656-8
- Microsoft Money 2004 For Dummies
  0-7645-4195-1
- Office 2003 All-in-One Desk Reference For Dummies
  0-7645-3883-7
- Outlook 2003 For Dummies
  0-7645-3759-8
- PCs For Dummies
  0-7645-4074-2
- TiVo For Dummies
  0-7645-6923-6
- Upgrading and Fixing PCs For Dummies
  0-7645-1665-5
- Windows XP Timesaving Techniques For Dummies
  0-7645-3748-2

FOOD, HOME, GARDEN, HOBBIES, MUSIC & PETS

0-7645-5295-3

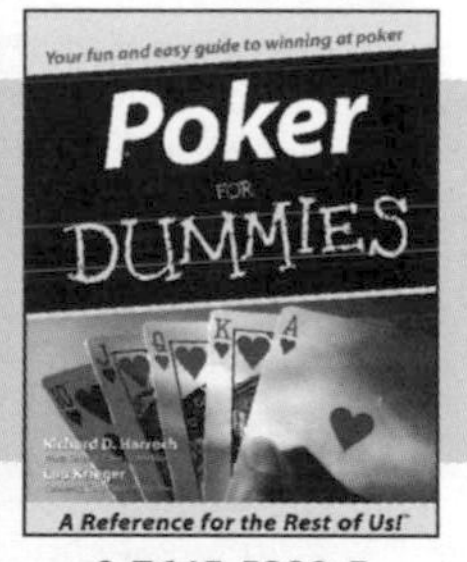

0-7645-5232-5

Also available:

- Bass Guitar For Dummies
  0-7645-2487-9
- Diabetes Cookbook For Dummies
  0-7645-5230-9
- Gardening For Dummies *
  0-7645-5130-2
- Guitar For Dummies
  0-7645-5106-X
- Holiday Decorating For Dummies
  0-7645-2570-0
- Home Improvement All-in-One For Dummies
  0-7645-5680-0
- Knitting For Dummies
  0-7645-5395-X
- Piano For Dummies
  0-7645-5105-1
- Puppies For Dummies
  0-7645-5255-4
- Scrapbooking For Dummies
  0-7645-7208-3
- Senior Dogs For Dummies
  0-7645-5818-8
- Singing For Dummies
  0-7645-2475-5
- 30-Minute Meals For Dummies
  0-7645-2589-1

INTERNET & DIGITAL MEDIA

0-7645-1664-7

0-7645-6924-4

Also available:

- 2005 Online Shopping Directory For Dummies
  0-7645-7495-7
- CD & DVD Recording For Dummies
  0-7645-5956-7
- eBay For Dummies
  0-7645-5654-1
- Fighting Spam For Dummies
  0-7645-5965-6
- Genealogy Online For Dummies
  0-7645-5964-8
- Google For Dummies
  0-7645-4420-9
- Home Recording For Musicians For Dummies
  0-7645-1634-5
- The Internet For Dummies
  0-7645-4173-0
- iPod & iTunes For Dummies
  0-7645-7772-7
- Preventing Identity Theft For Dummies
  0-7645-7336-5
- Pro Tools All-in-One Desk Reference For Dummies
  0-7645-5714-9
- Roxio Easy Media Creator For Dummies
  0-7645-7131-1

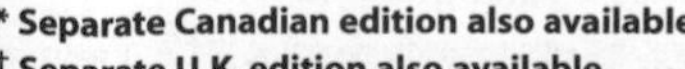

*** Separate Canadian edition also available**
† Separate U.K. edition also available

Available wherever books are sold. For more information or to order direct: U.S. customers visit www.dummies.com or call 1-877-762-2974. U.K. customers visit www.wileyeurope.com or call 0800 243407. Canadian customers visit www.wiley.ca or call 1-800-567-4797.

SPORTS, FITNESS, PARENTING, RELIGION & SPIRITUALITY

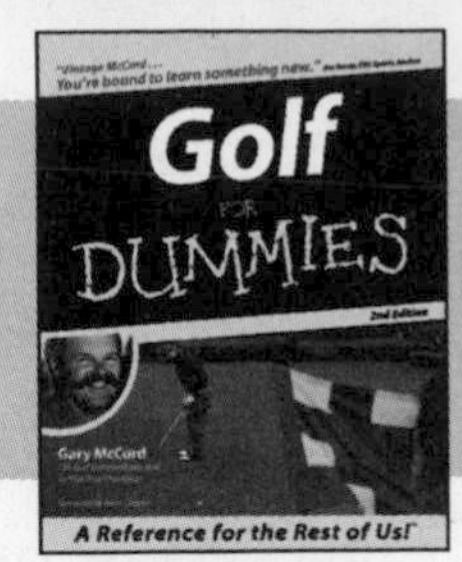

0-7645-5146-9

0-7645-5418-2

Also available:

- Adoption For Dummies 0-7645-5488-3
- Basketball For Dummies 0-7645-5248-1
- The Bible For Dummies 0-7645-5296-1
- Buddhism For Dummies 0-7645-5359-3
- Catholicism For Dummies 0-7645-5391-7
- Hockey For Dummies 0-7645-5228-7
- Judaism For Dummies 0-7645-5299-6
- Martial Arts For Dummies 0-7645-5358-5
- Pilates For Dummies 0-7645-5397-6
- Religion For Dummies 0-7645-5264-3
- Teaching Kids to Read For Dummies 0-7645-4043-2
- Weight Training For Dummies 0-7645-5168-X
- Yoga For Dummies 0-7645-5117-5

TRAVEL

0-7645-5438-7

0-7645-5453-0

Also available:

- Alaska For Dummies 0-7645-1761-9
- Arizona For Dummies 0-7645-6938-4
- Cancún and the Yucatán For Dummies 0-7645-2437-2
- Cruise Vacations For Dummies 0-7645-6941-4
- Europe For Dummies 0-7645-5456-5
- Ireland For Dummies 0-7645-5455-7
- Las Vegas For Dummies 0-7645-5448-4
- London For Dummies 0-7645-4277-X
- New York City For Dummies 0-7645-6945-7
- Paris For Dummies 0-7645-5494-8
- RV Vacations For Dummies 0-7645-5443-3
- Walt Disney World & Orlando For Dummies 0-7645-6943-0

GRAPHICS, DESIGN & WEB DEVELOPMENT

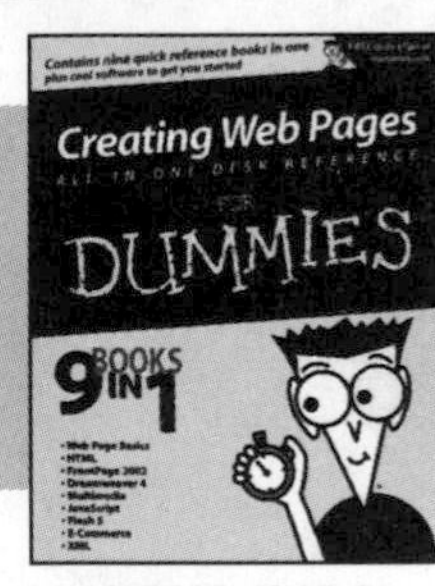

0-7645-4345-8

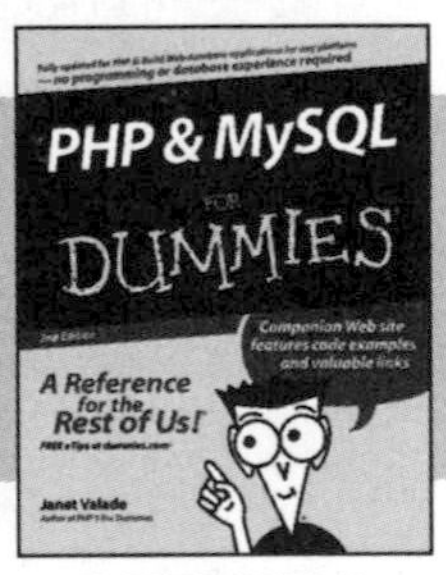

0-7645-5589-8

Also available:

- Adobe Acrobat 6 PDF For Dummies 0-7645-3760-1
- Building a Web Site For Dummies 0-7645-7144-3
- Dreamweaver MX 2004 For Dummies 0-7645-4342-3
- FrontPage 2003 For Dummies 0-7645-3882-9
- HTML 4 For Dummies 0-7645-1995-6
- Illustrator cs For Dummies 0-7645-4084-X
- Macromedia Flash MX 2004 For Dummies 0-7645-4358-X
- Photoshop 7 All-in-One Desk Reference For Dummies 0-7645-1667-1
- Photoshop cs Timesaving Techniques For Dummies 0-7645-6782-9
- PHP 5 For Dummies 0-7645-4166-8
- PowerPoint 2003 For Dummies 0-7645-3908-6
- QuarkXPress 6 For Dummies 0-7645-2593-X

NETWORKING, SECURITY, PROGRAMMING & DATABASES

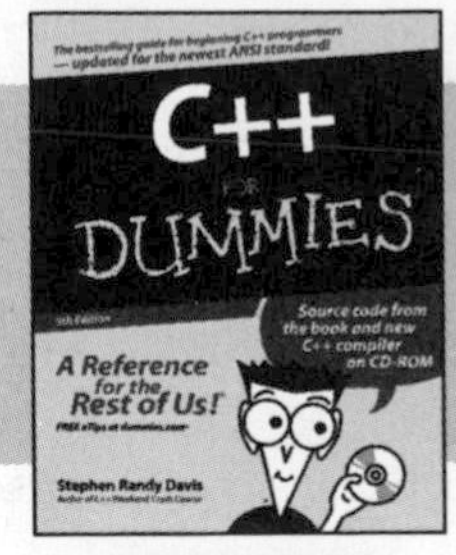

0-7645-6852-3

0-7645-5784-X

Also available:

- A+ Certification For Dummies 0-7645-4187-0
- Access 2003 All-in-One Desk Reference For Dummies 0-7645-3988-4
- Beginning Programming For Dummies 0-7645-4997-9
- C For Dummies 0-7645-7068-4
- Firewalls For Dummies 0-7645-4048-3
- Home Networking For Dummies 0-7645-42796
- Network Security For Dummies 0-7645-1679-5
- Networking For Dummies 0-7645-1677-9
- TCP/IP For Dummies 0-7645-1760-0
- VBA For Dummies 0-7645-3989-2
- Wireless All In-One Desk Reference For Dummies 0-7645-7496-5
- Wireless Home Networking For Dummies 0-7645-3910-8